GARTH ENNIS
WRITER

STEVE DILLON
ARTIST

MATT HOLLINGSWORTH
COLORIST

CLEM ROBINS
LETTERER

GLENN FABRY
COVERS

PREACHER CREATED BY GARTH ENNIS AND STEVE DILLON

Gone to TEXAS
PREACHER

PREACHER: GONE TO TEXAS Published by DC Comics. Cover, introduction and compilation copyright © 1996 DC Comics. All Rights Reserved.
Originally published in single magazine form as PREACHER 1-7. Copyright © 1995 Garth Ennis and Steve Dillon. All Rights Reserved.
All characters, their distinctive likenesses and related elements featured in this publication are trademarks of Garth Ennis and Steve Dillon.
Vertigo is a trademark of DC Comics. The stories, characters and incidents featured in this publication are entirely fictional.
DC Comics does not read or accept unsolicited submissions of ideas, stories or artwork.

DC Comics, 1700 Broadway, New York, NY 10019
A Warner Bros. Entertainment Company
Printed in Canada. Ninth Printing.
ISBN: 1-56389-261-8
ISBN 13: 978-1-56389-261-5
Cover painting by Glenn Fabry.
Publication design by Eddie Ortiz.
Cover design by Brainchild Studios/NYC.

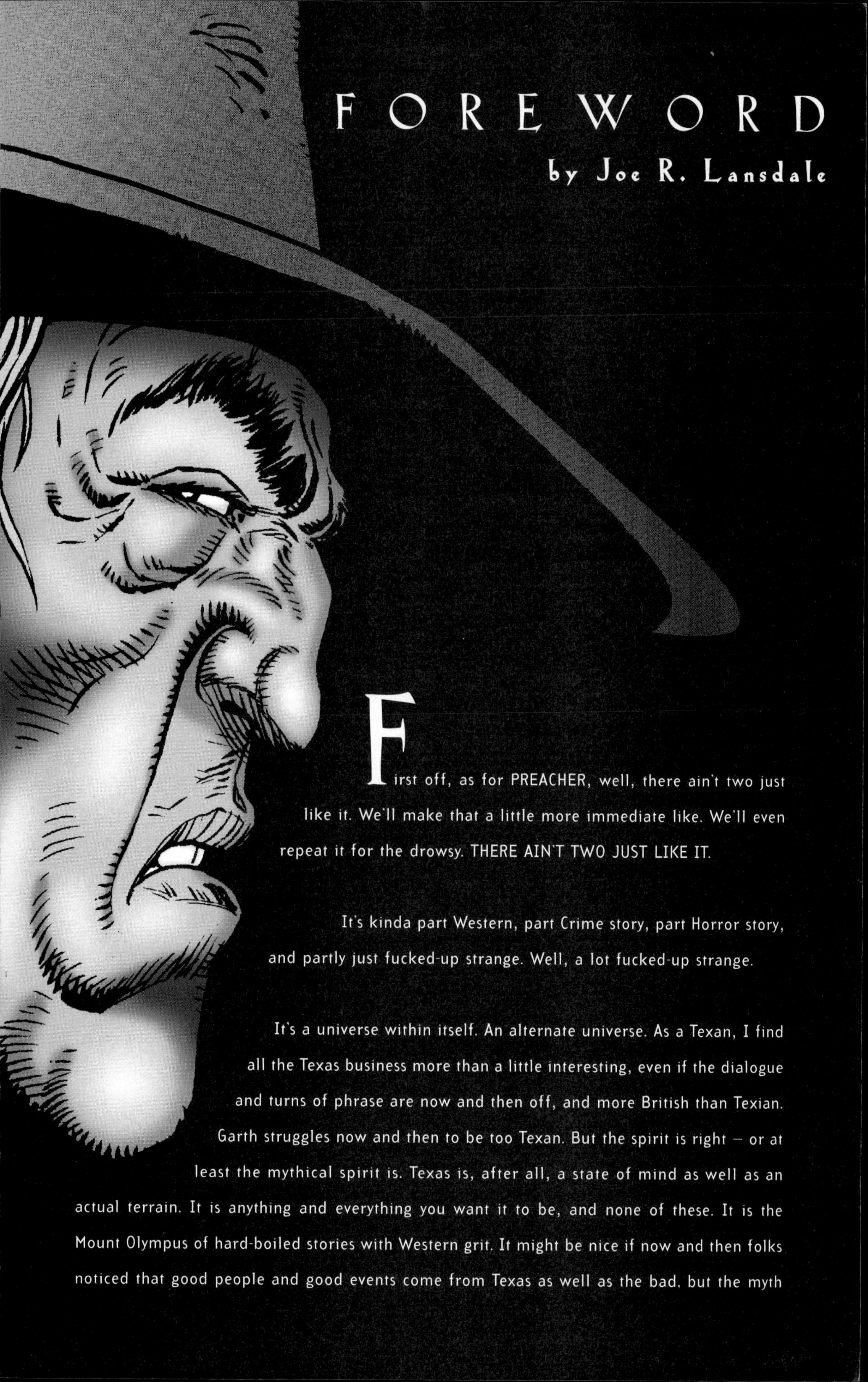

FOREWORD

by Joe R. Lansdale

First off, as for PREACHER, well, there ain't two just like it. We'll make that a little more immediate like. We'll even repeat it for the drowsy. THERE AIN'T TWO JUST LIKE IT.

It's kinda part Western, part Crime story, part Horror story, and partly just fucked-up strange. Well, a lot fucked-up strange.

It's a universe within itself. An alternate universe. As a Texan, I find all the Texas business more than a little interesting, even if the dialogue and turns of phrase are now and then off, and more British than Texian. Garth struggles now and then to be too Texan. But the spirit is right — or at least the mythical spirit is. Texas is, after all, a state of mind as well as an actual terrain. It is anything and everything you want it to be, and none of these. It is the Mount Olympus of hard-boiled stories with Western grit. It might be nice if now and then folks noticed that good people and good events come from Texas as well as the bad, but the myth this rebel universe prevails, and if it must prevail, it's nice to know that there are writers like Garth Ennis playing with that myth in a smart and savvy way.

Got to tell you, stories like this, people read them and say, "This is a hoot." A way to wind down from the more serious stuff. They see the raw language and the action and the brutality, the splatter, and they see little else. Most of the time they are right. But PREACHER...

Let me clue you. This is just as serious as any of Vertigo's highly-praised "intellectual" stuff, and better than a lot of it. Don't confuse "intelligent" with "intellectual." Pretention can confuse a soul if they're not paying attention. This stuff, well, pretentious it ain't, but smart it is.

And it's fun. Well, is "fun" the word I'm looking for here? Maybe, maybe not. Fascinating. That's the word.

And we all know it's a comic book. That it isn't real. It's our chance to look at the dark side without having to be a part of it. It's like watching an alligator eat a pig. Ugly, but still mesmerizing. Especially since we're not the pig. I wonder what the pig's point of view is, looking up from its unique position to see curious faces looking down on its last moments. But that's another consideration.

Another thing about PREACHER, and I'm damn sure not giving anyone who has read it a news flash: It's scary as a psychopathic greased gerbil

with a miner's hat and a flashlight and your bare asshole in sight. Actually, it's scarier than that. This stuff really bothered me, and at times I thought it might be a little too much. But I found myself waiting for the next issue with anticipation. I can't say that about most comics. In fact, I start a lot of comics that I don't finish, and considering it takes so little time to read a comic, I guess that's a serious statement of some kind.

This stuff is unique. It's intriguing. It touches on a base level. Makes things crawl around in the viscera (Where is that gerbil with the flashlight anyway?) and the brain. It stays true to its intent as well. It doesn't suddenly go from being this dark and terrible tale to being warm and squishy with a catch in its throat. You get yourself a rattlesnake, it'll bite today, and it'll bite tomorrow. And unless it's toothless, it'll bite two years from now. A rattlesnake is always a rattlesnake, and Garth's tale is always just what it started out to be—grim and grey with flashes of blackness.

And while we're praising the writing, the mood, let's talk about the artwork, which ain't slouchy either. It puts the paint on the conception, brightens it up and makes it burn. Or maybe, in this case, darkens it up and makes it smolder. Steve Dillon's art is perfect for the story. It puts tainted saliva on the fangs of Garth Ennis's prose. It puts the shadow behind the curtain and makes the blood on the floor crawl.

These first seven comics, collected here together, are to my way of thinking a milestone for Vertigo. This is unique stuff, a hole in the dike of sameness. And the water rushing through that hole, spider-webbing the concrete of the dam, cracking it, blasting it apart, is a nasty black water leaking directly from the brains of Messrs. Ennis and Dillon. This is not to imply that Garth Ennis or Steve Dillon are bad folks. I don't know them. But I will say this: They know fucked-up when they see it, and like Flannery O'Connor, they're willing to put their fingers on it and make it squirm for your observation.

I'm not sure it's a learning experience, but it's a thinking experience, and most important, as I said early on, it's unique, and I hope its uniqueness does not encourage a hundred writers to go out and try to repeat it. What they will come up with is just meanness for meanness' sake. It won't have the edge, the special feel of PREACHER. They'll just be imitations. Because there is only one Garth Ennis, and only one Steve Dillon, and only one PREACHER, a tale out of Ireland, dragged through Texas with a bloody hard-on, wrapped in barbed wire and rose thorns. And it's out to get you.

Joe R. Lansdale

Nacogdoches, Texas

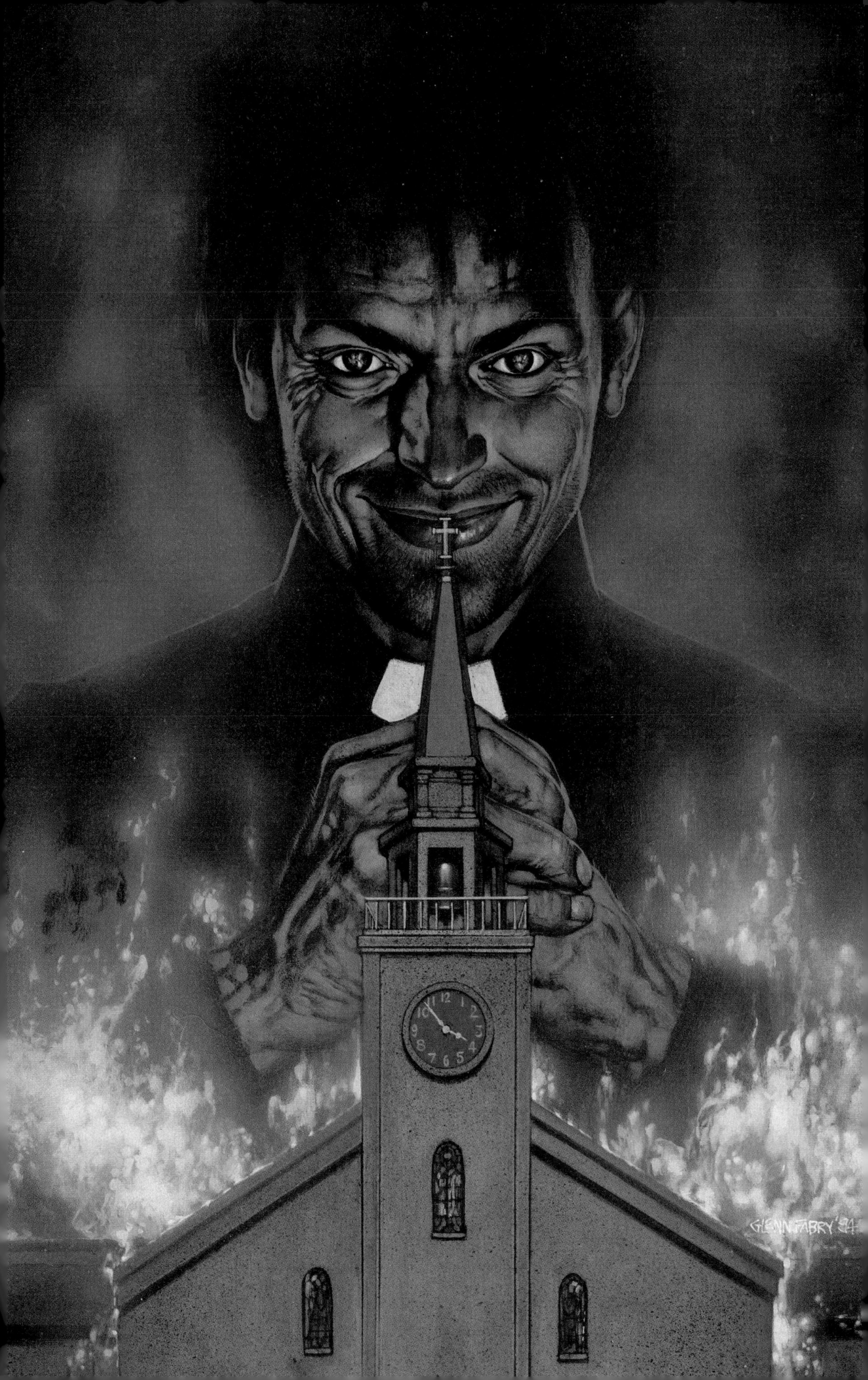
GLENN FABRY '94

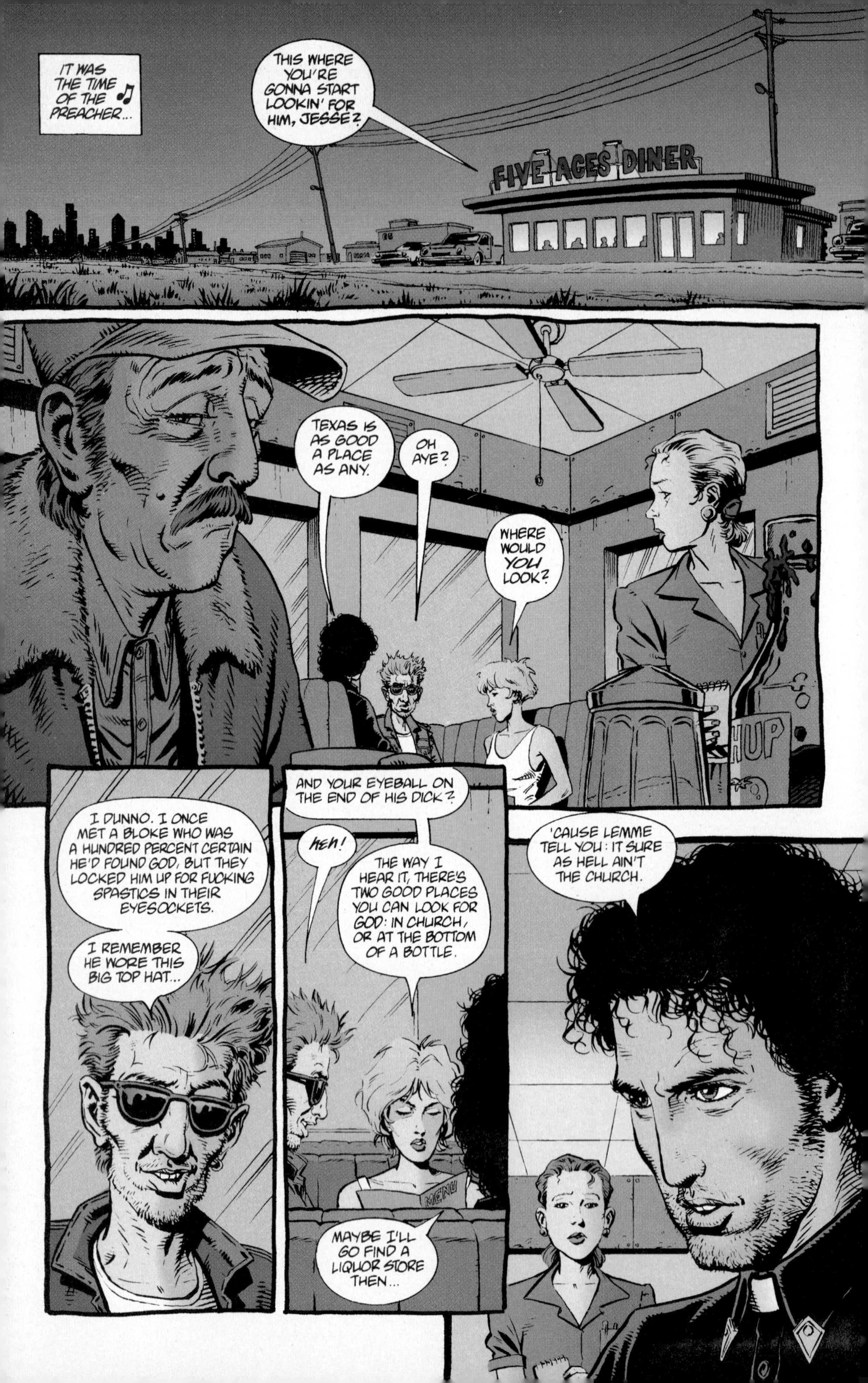
IT WAS THE TIME OF THE PREACHER...
THIS WHERE YOU'RE GONNA START LOOKIN' FOR HIM, JESSE?
FIVE ACES DINER
TEXAS IS AS GOOD A PLACE AS ANY.
OH AYE?
WHERE WOULD YOU LOOK?
SHUP
I DUNNO. I ONCE MET A BLOKE WHO WAS A HUNDRED PERCENT CERTAIN HE'D FOUND GOD, BUT THEY LOCKED HIM UP FOR FUCKING SPASTICS IN THEIR EYESOCKETS.
I REMEMBER HE WORE THIS BIG TOP HAT...
AND YOUR EYEBALL ON THE END OF HIS DICK?
KEH!
THE WAY I HEAR IT, THERE'S TWO GOOD PLACES YOU CAN LOOK FOR GOD: IN CHURCH, OR AT THE BOTTOM OF A BOTTLE.
MENU
MAYBE I'LL GO FIND A LIQUOR STORE THEN...
'CAUSE LEMME TELL YOU: IT SURE AS HELL AIN'T THE CHURCH.

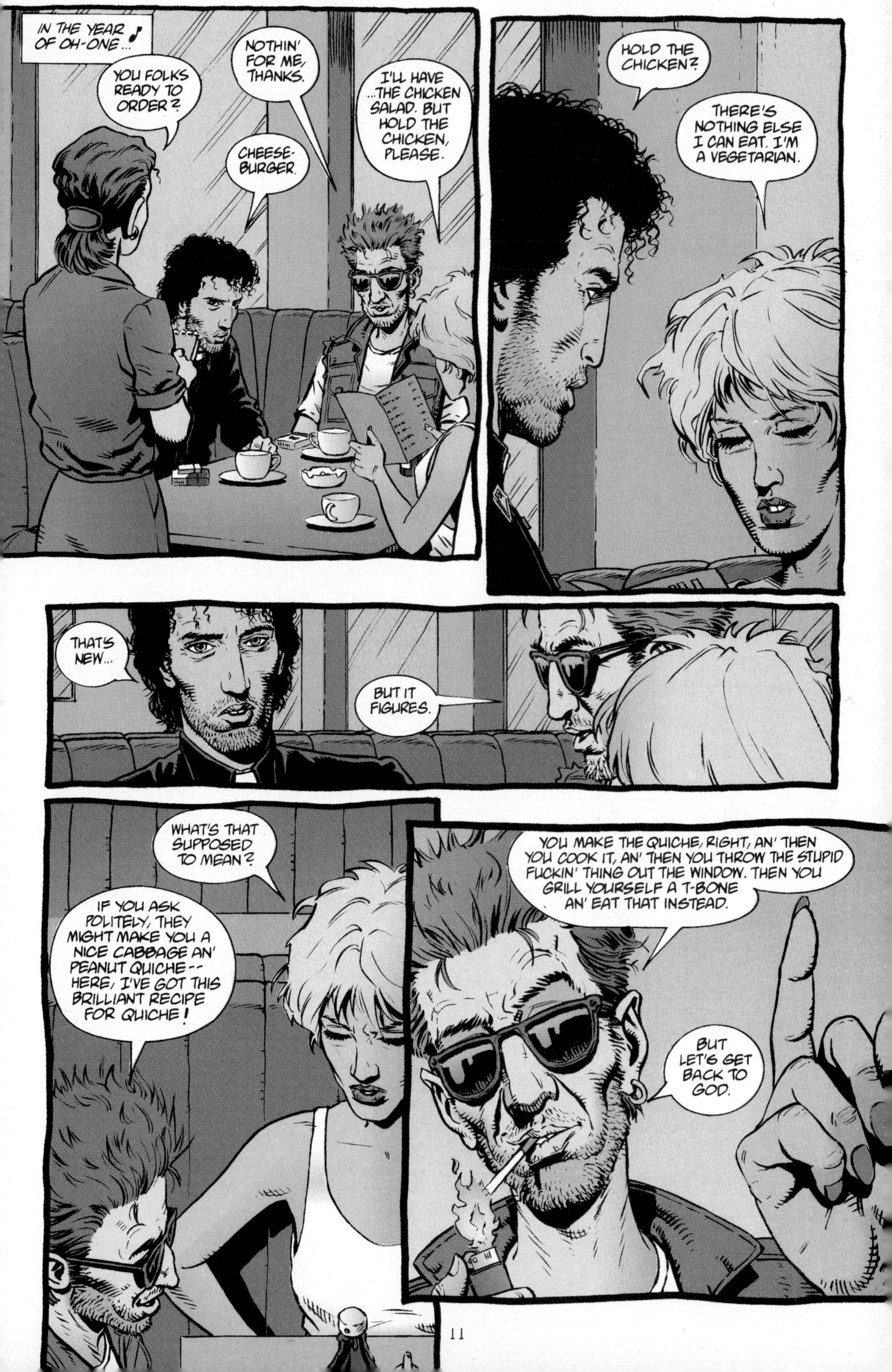
IN THE YEAR OF OH-ONE...
YOU FOLKS READY TO ORDER?
NOTHIN' FOR ME, THANKS.
CHEESE-BURGER.
I'LL HAVE ...THE CHICKEN SALAD. BUT HOLD THE CHICKEN, PLEASE.
HOLD THE CHICKEN?
THERE'S NOTHING ELSE I CAN EAT. I'M A VEGETARIAN.
THAT'S NEW...
BUT IT FIGURES.
WHAT'S THAT SUPPOSED TO MEAN?
IF YOU ASK POLITELY, THEY MIGHT MAKE YOU A NICE CABBAGE AN' PEANUT QUICHE-- HERE, I'VE GOT THIS BRILLIANT RECIPE FOR QUICHE!
YOU MAKE THE QUICHE, RIGHT, AN' THEN YOU COOK IT, AN' THEN YOU THROW THE STUPID FUCKIN' THING OUT THE WINDOW. THEN YOU GRILL YOURSELF A T-BONE AN' EAT THAT INSTEAD.
BUT LET'S GET BACK TO GOD.

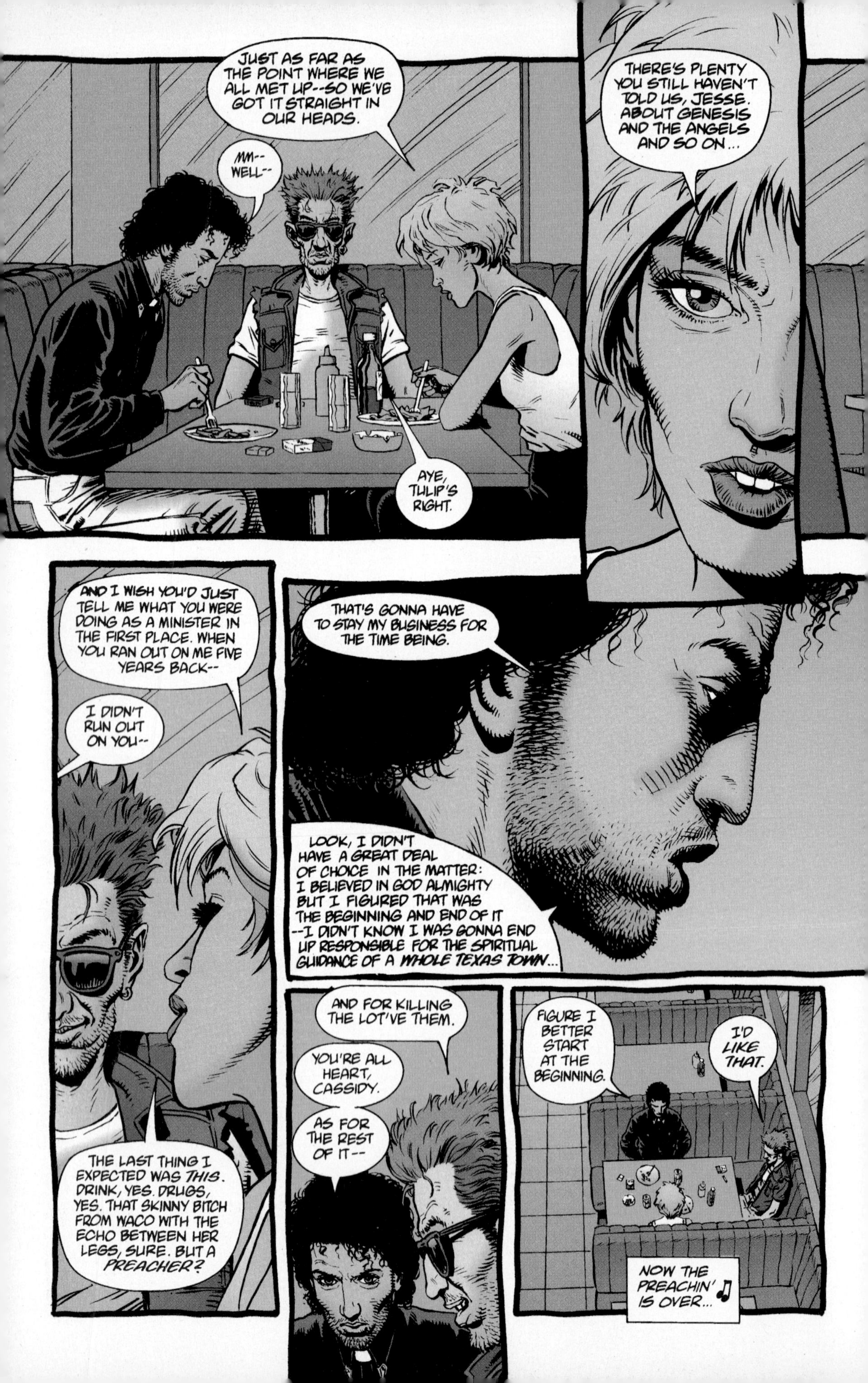
JUST AS FAR AS THE POINT WHERE WE ALL MET UP--SO WE'VE GOT IT STRAIGHT IN OUR HEADS.
MM-- WELL--
AYE, TULIP'S RIGHT.
THERE'S PLENTY YOU STILL HAVEN'T TOLD US, JESSE. ABOUT GENESIS AND THE ANGELS AND SO ON...
AND I WISH YOU'D JUST TELL ME WHAT YOU WERE DOING AS A MINISTER IN THE FIRST PLACE. WHEN YOU RAN OUT ON ME FIVE YEARS BACK--
I DIDN'T RUN OUT ON YOU--
THE LAST THING I EXPECTED WAS THIS. DRINK, YES. DRUGS, YES. THAT SKINNY BITCH FROM WACO WITH THE ECHO BETWEEN HER LEGS, SURE. BUT A PREACHER?
THAT'S GONNA HAVE TO STAY MY BUSINESS FOR THE TIME BEING.
LOOK, I DIDN'T HAVE A GREAT DEAL OF CHOICE IN THE MATTER: I BELIEVED IN GOD ALMIGHTY BUT I FIGURED THAT WAS THE BEGINNING AND END OF IT --I DIDN'T KNOW I WAS GONNA END UP RESPONSIBLE FOR THE SPIRITUAL GUIDANCE OF A WHOLE TEXAS TOWN...
AND FOR KILLING THE LOT'VE THEM.
YOU'RE ALL HEART, CASSIDY.
AS FOR THE REST OF IT--
FIGURE I BETTER START AT THE BEGINNING.
I'D LIKE THAT.
NOW THE PREACHIN' IS OVER... ♫

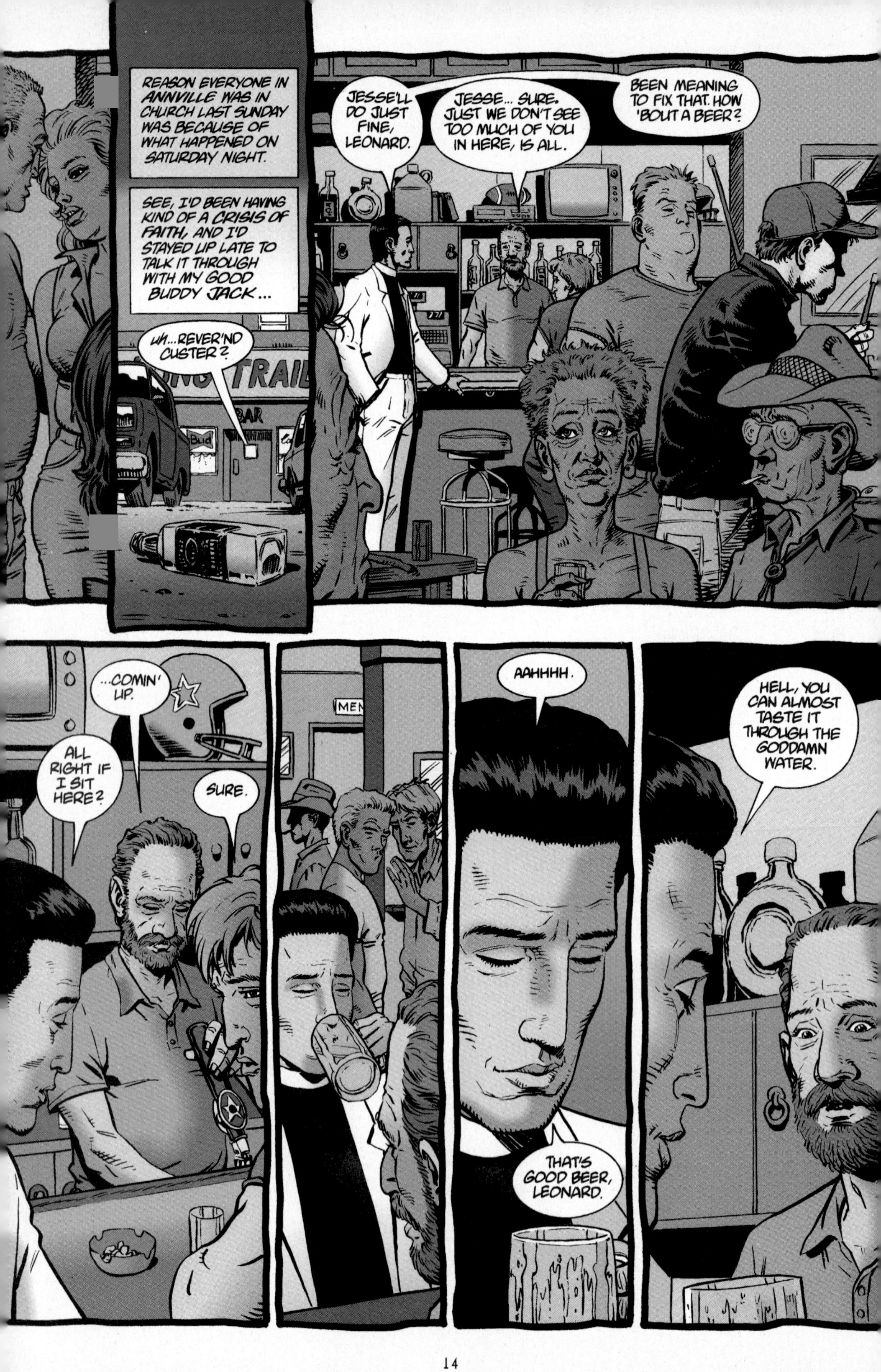
REASON EVERYONE IN ANNVILLE WAS IN CHURCH LAST SUNDAY WAS BECAUSE OF WHAT HAPPENED ON SATURDAY NIGHT.
SEE, I'D BEEN HAVING KIND OF A CRISIS OF FAITH, AND I'D STAYED UP LATE TO TALK IT THROUGH WITH MY GOOD BUDDY JACK...
UH...REVER'ND CUSTER?
TRAIL
BAR
Bud
JESSE'LL DO JUST FINE, LEONARD.
JESSE... SURE. JUST WE DON'T SEE TOO MUCH OF YOU IN HERE, IS ALL.
BEEN MEANING TO FIX THAT. HOW 'BOUT A BEER?
...COMIN' UP.
ALL RIGHT IF I SIT HERE?
SURE.
MEN
AAHHHH.
THAT'S GOOD BEER, LEONARD.
HELL, YOU CAN ALMOST TASTE IT THROUGH THE GODDAMN WATER.

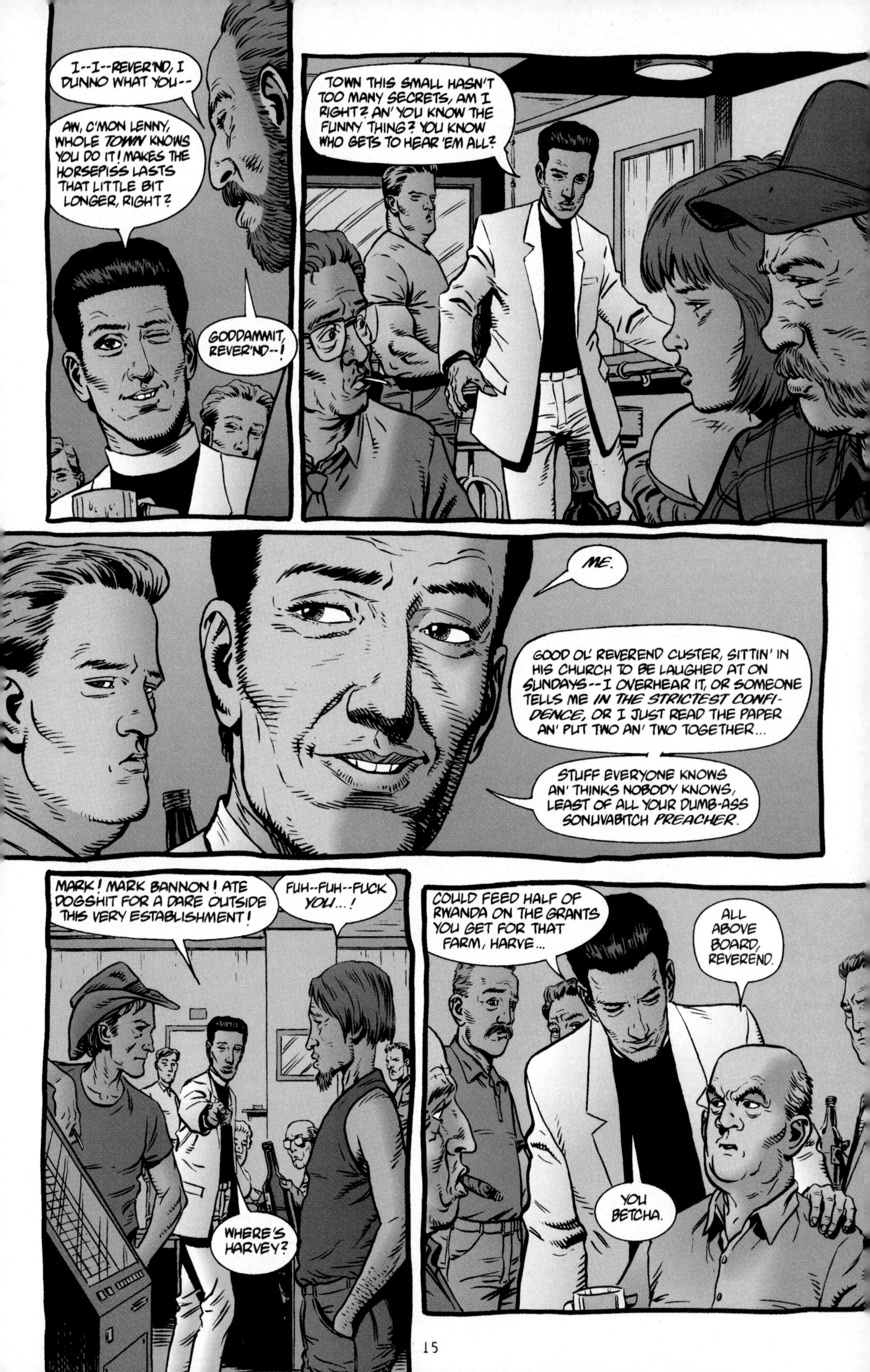
I--I--REVER'ND, I DUNNO WHAT YOU--
AW, C'MON LENNY, WHOLE TOWN KNOWS YOU DO IT! MAKES THE HORSEPISS LASTS THAT LITTLE BIT LONGER, RIGHT?
GODDAMMIT, REVER'ND--!
TOWN THIS SMALL HASN'T TOO MANY SECRETS, AM I RIGHT? AN' YOU KNOW THE FUNNY THING? YOU KNOW WHO GETS TO HEAR 'EM ALL?
ME.
GOOD OL' REVEREND CUSTER, SITTIN' IN HIS CHURCH TO BE LAUGHED AT ON SUNDAYS--I OVERHEAR IT, OR SOMEONE TELLS ME IN THE STRICTEST CONFIDENCE, OR I JUST READ THE PAPER AN' PUT TWO AN' TWO TOGETHER...
STUFF EVERYONE KNOWS AN' THINKS NOBODY KNOWS, LEAST OF ALL YOUR DUMB-ASS SONUVABITCH PREACHER.
MARK! MARK BANNON! ATE DOGSHIT FOR A DARE OUTSIDE THIS VERY ESTABLISHMENT!
FUH--FUH--FUCK YOU...!
WHERE'S HARVEY?
COULD FEED HALF OF RWANDA ON THE GRANTS YOU GET FOR THAT FARM, HARVE...
ALL ABOVE BOARD, REVEREND.
YOU BETCHA.

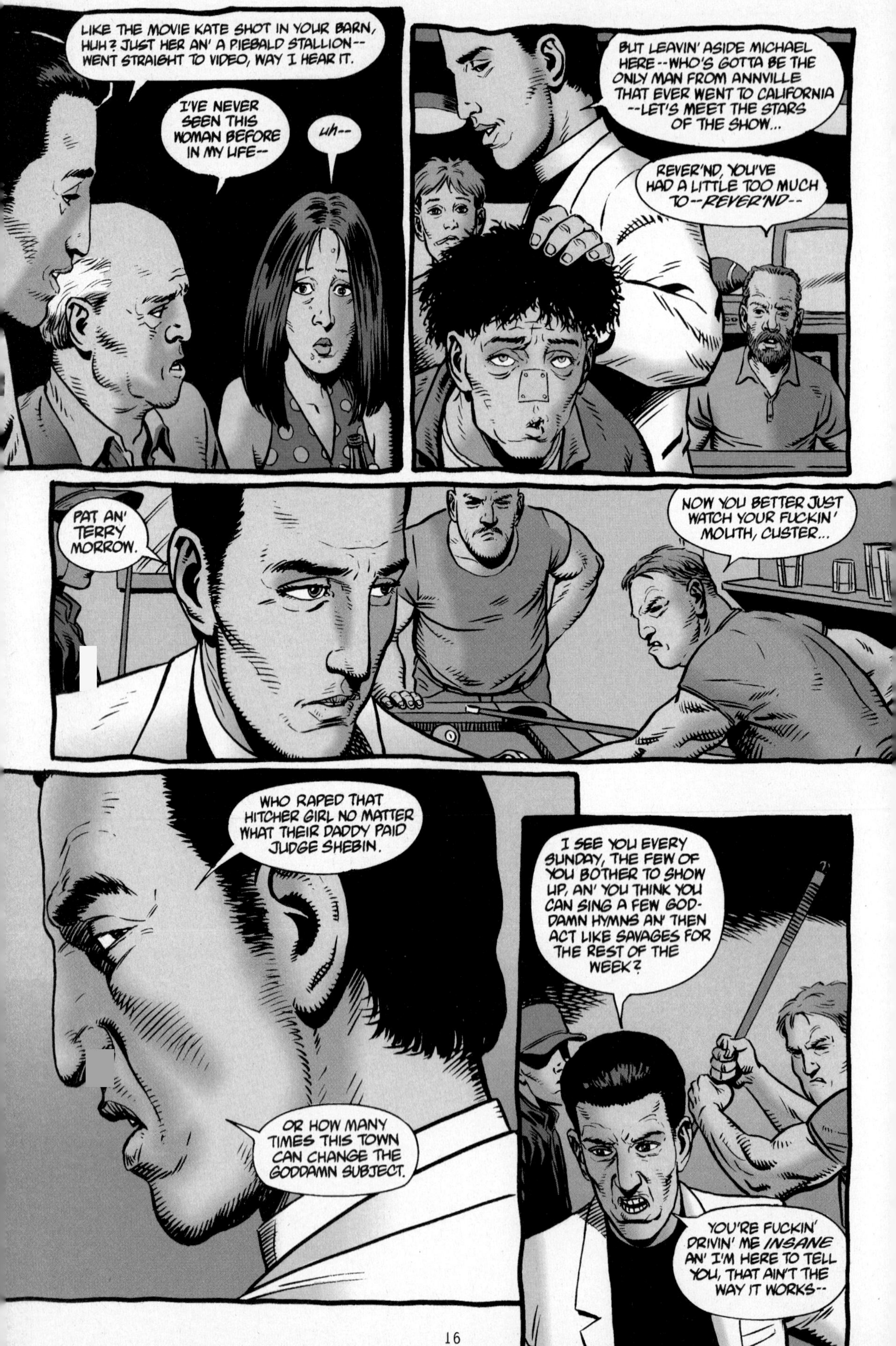
LIKE THE MOVIE KATE SHOT IN YOUR BARN, HUH? JUST HER AN' A PIEBALD STALLION-- WENT STRAIGHT TO VIDEO, WAY I HEAR IT.
I'VE NEVER SEEN THIS WOMAN BEFORE IN MY LIFE--
uh--
BUT LEAVIN' ASIDE MICHAEL HERE--WHO'S GOTTA BE THE ONLY MAN FROM ANNVILLE THAT EVER WENT TO CALIFORNIA --LET'S MEET THE STARS OF THE SHOW...
REVER'ND, YOU'VE HAD A LITTLE TOO MUCH TO--REVER'ND--
PAT AN' TERRY MORROW.
NOW YOU BETTER JUST WATCH YOUR FUCKIN' MOUTH, CUSTER...
WHO RAPED THAT HITCHER GIRL NO MATTER WHAT THEIR DADDY PAID JUDGE SHEBIN.
OR HOW MANY TIMES THIS TOWN CAN CHANGE THE GODDAMN SUBJECT.
I SEE YOU EVERY SUNDAY, THE FEW OF YOU BOTHER TO SHOW UP, AN' YOU THINK YOU CAN SING A FEW GOD-DAMN HYMNS AN' THEN ACT LIKE SAVAGES FOR THE REST OF THE WEEK?
YOU'RE FUCKIN' DRIVIN' ME INSANE AN' I'M HERE TO TELL YOU, THAT AIN'T THE WAY IT WORKS--

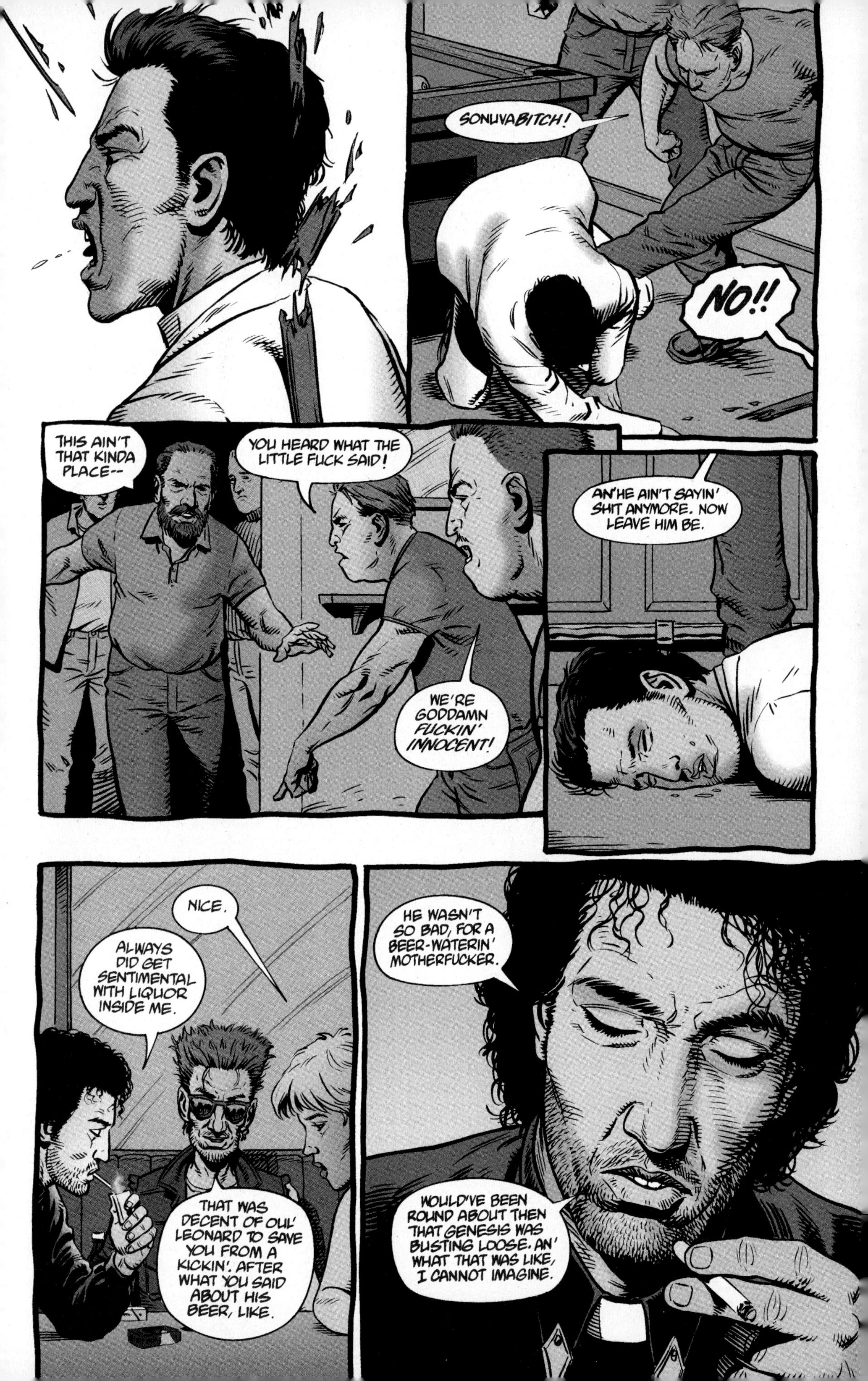
SONUVABITCH!
NO!!
THIS AIN'T THAT KINDA PLACE--
YOU HEARD WHAT THE LITTLE FUCK SAID!
WE'RE GODDAMN FUCKIN' INNOCENT!
AN'HE AIN'T SAYIN' SHIT ANYMORE. NOW LEAVE HIM BE.
NICE.
ALWAYS DID GET SENTIMENTAL WITH LIQUOR INSIDE ME.
THAT WAS DECENT OF OUL' LEONARD TO SAVE YOU FROM A KICKIN'. AFTER WHAT YOU SAID ABOUT HIS BEER, LIKE.
HE WASN'T SO BAD, FOR A BEER-WATERIN' MOTHERFUCKER.
WOULD'VE BEEN ROUND ABOUT THEN THAT GENESIS WAS BUSTING LOOSE. AN' WHAT THAT WAS LIKE, I CANNOT IMAGINE.

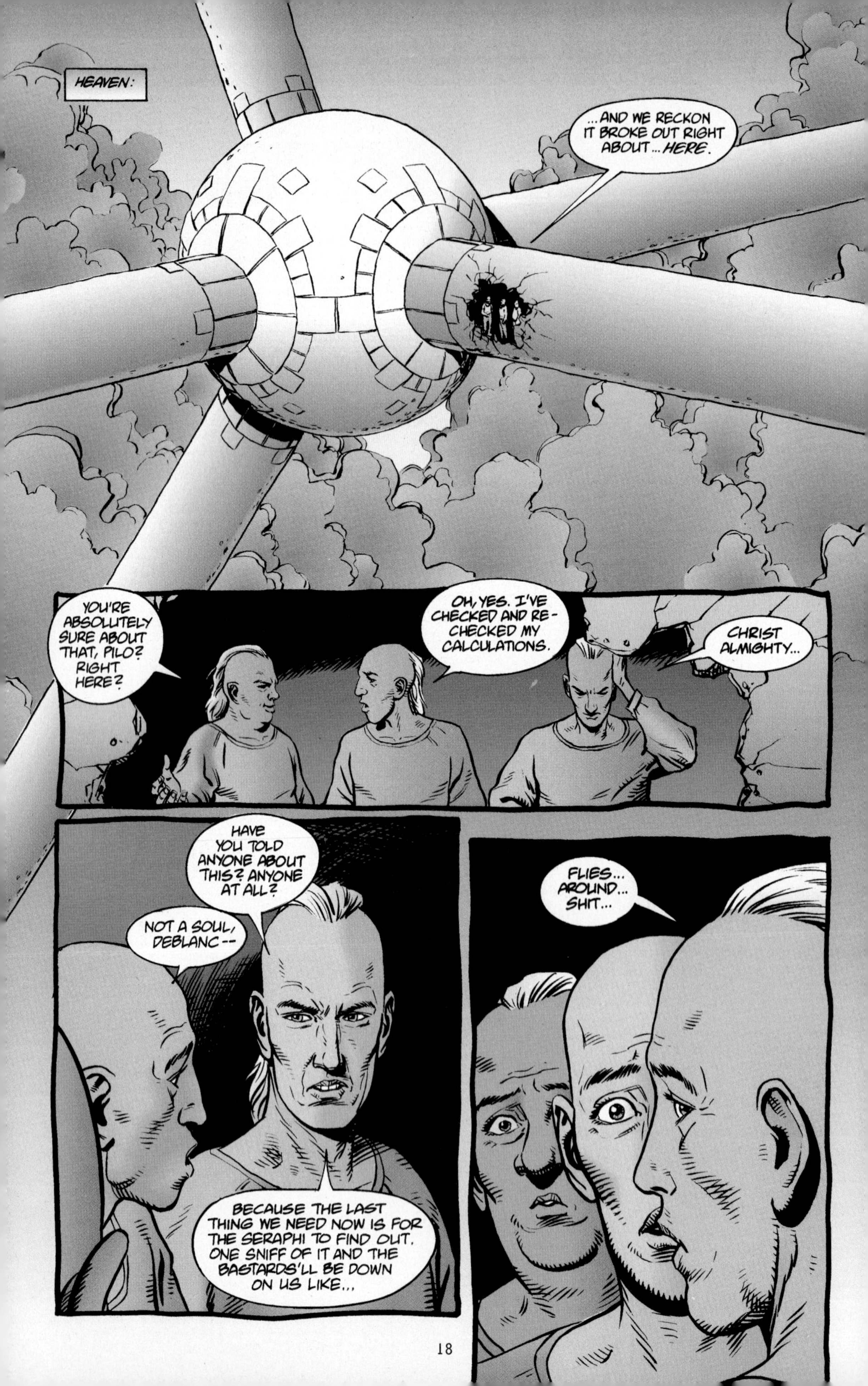
HEAVEN:
...AND WE RECKON IT BROKE OUT RIGHT ABOUT... HERE.
YOU'RE ABSOLUTELY SURE ABOUT THAT, PILO? RIGHT HERE?
OH, YES. I'VE CHECKED AND RE-CHECKED MY CALCULATIONS.
CHRIST ALMIGHTY...
HAVE YOU TOLD ANYONE ABOUT THIS? ANYONE AT ALL?
NOT A SOUL, DEBLANC--
BECAUSE THE LAST THING WE NEED NOW IS FOR THE SERAPHI TO FIND OUT. ONE SNIFF OF IT AND THE BASTARDS'LL BE DOWN ON US LIKE...
FLIES... AROUND... SHIT...

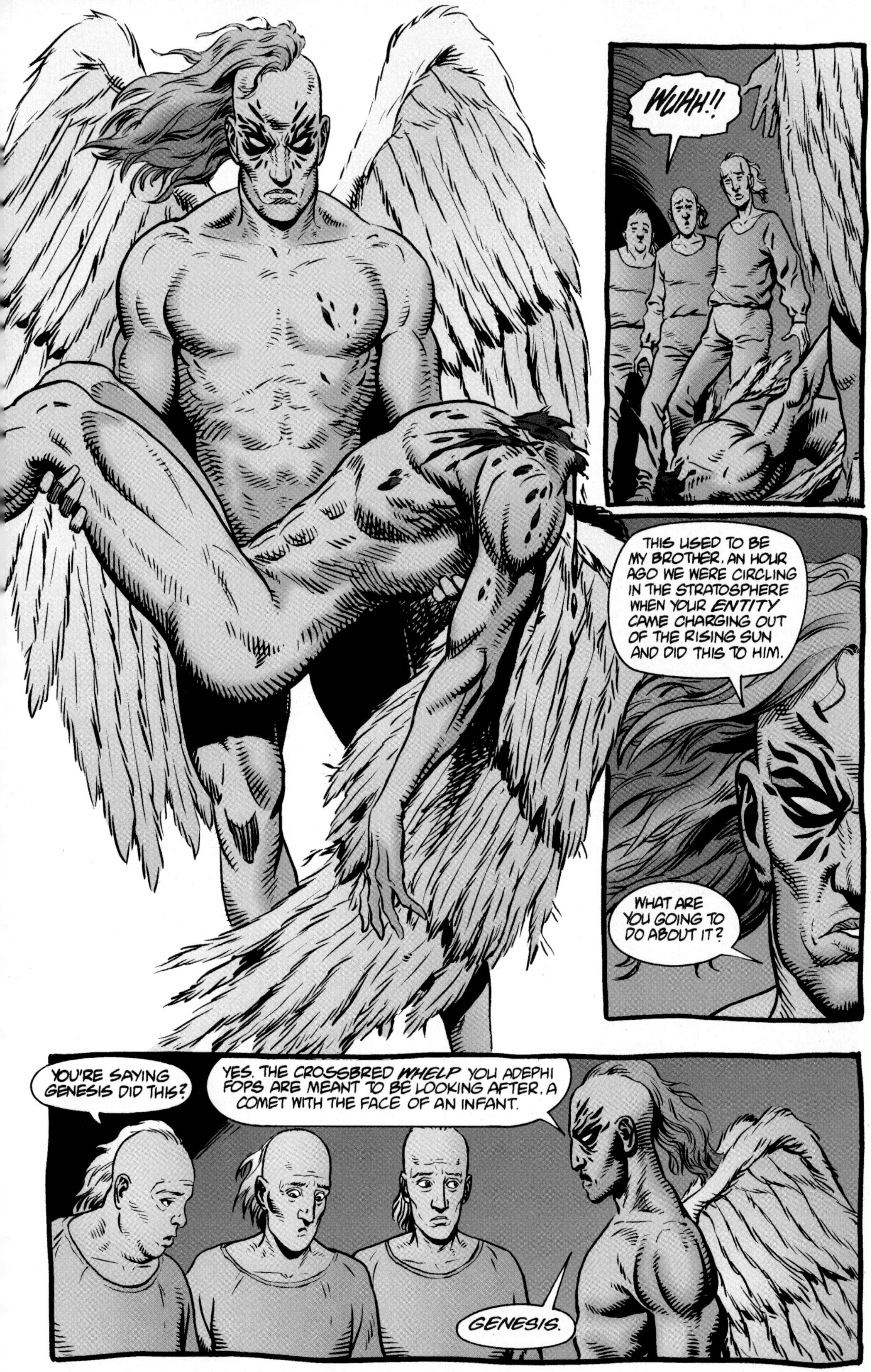
WUHH!!
THIS USED TO BE MY BROTHER. AN HOUR AGO WE WERE CIRCLING IN THE STRATOSPHERE WHEN YOUR ENTITY CAME CHARGING OUT OF THE RISING SUN AND DID THIS TO HIM.
WHAT ARE YOU GOING TO DO ABOUT IT?
YOU'RE SAYING GENESIS DID THIS?
YES. THE CROSSBRED WHELP YOU ADEPHI FOPS ARE MEANT TO BE LOOKING AFTER. A COMET WITH THE FACE OF AN INFANT.
GENESIS.

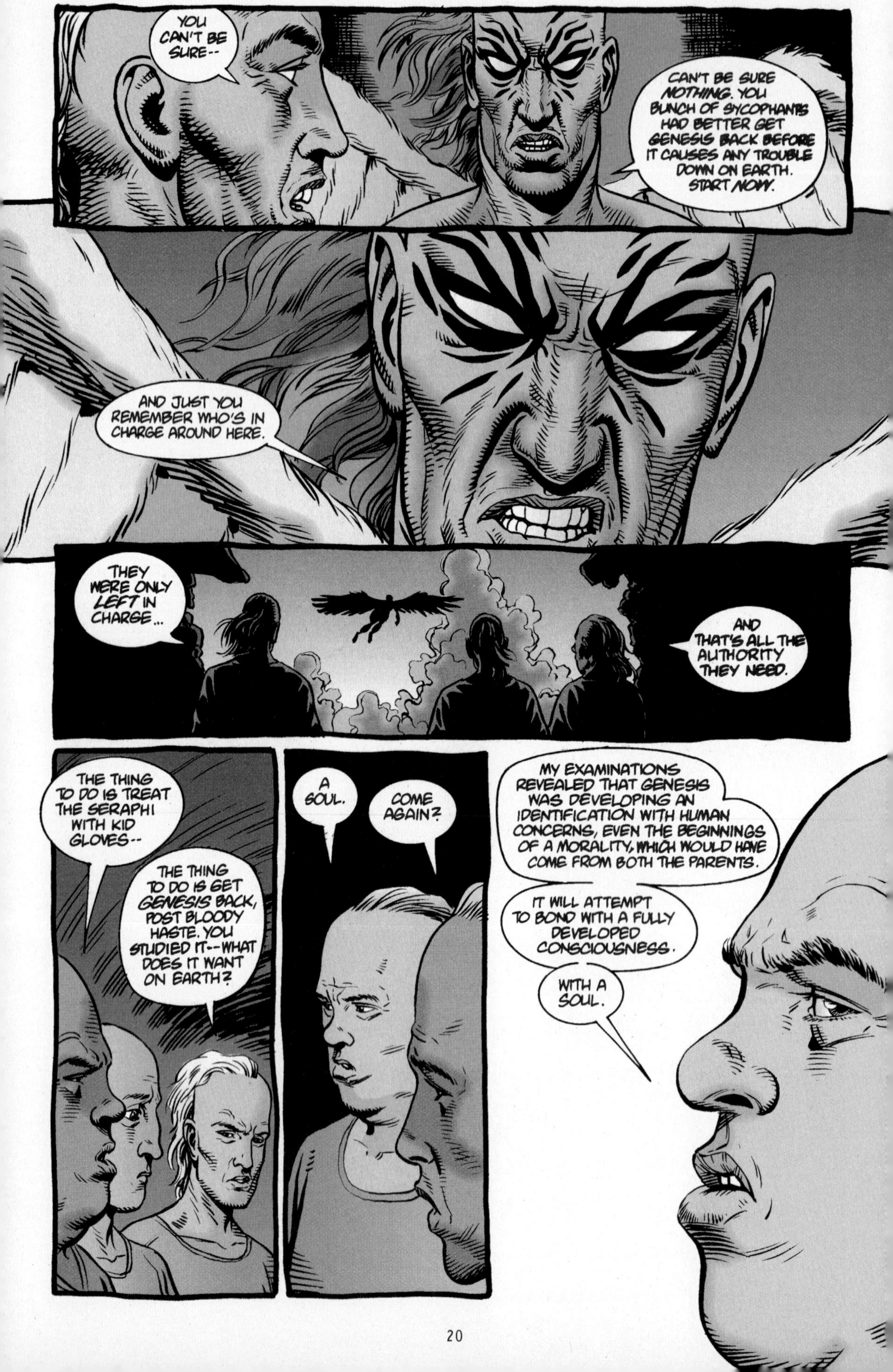
YOU CAN'T BE SURE--
CAN'T BE SURE NOTHING. YOU BUNCH OF SYCOPHANTS HAD BETTER GET GENESIS BACK BEFORE IT CAUSES ANY TROUBLE DOWN ON EARTH. START NOW.
AND JUST YOU REMEMBER WHO'S IN CHARGE AROUND HERE.
THEY WERE ONLY LEFT IN CHARGE...
AND THAT'S ALL THE AUTHORITY THEY NEED.
THE THING TO DO IS TREAT THE SERAPHI WITH KID GLOVES--
THE THING TO DO IS GET GENESIS BACK, POST BLOODY HASTE. YOU STUDIED IT--WHAT DOES IT WANT ON EARTH?
A SOUL.
COME AGAIN?
MY EXAMINATIONS REVEALED THAT GENESIS WAS DEVELOPING AN IDENTIFICATION WITH HUMAN CONCERNS, EVEN THE BEGINNINGS OF A MORALITY, WHICH WOULD HAVE COME FROM BOTH THE PARENTS.
IT WILL ATTEMPT TO BOND WITH A FULLY DEVELOPED CONSCIOUSNESS.
WITH A SOUL.

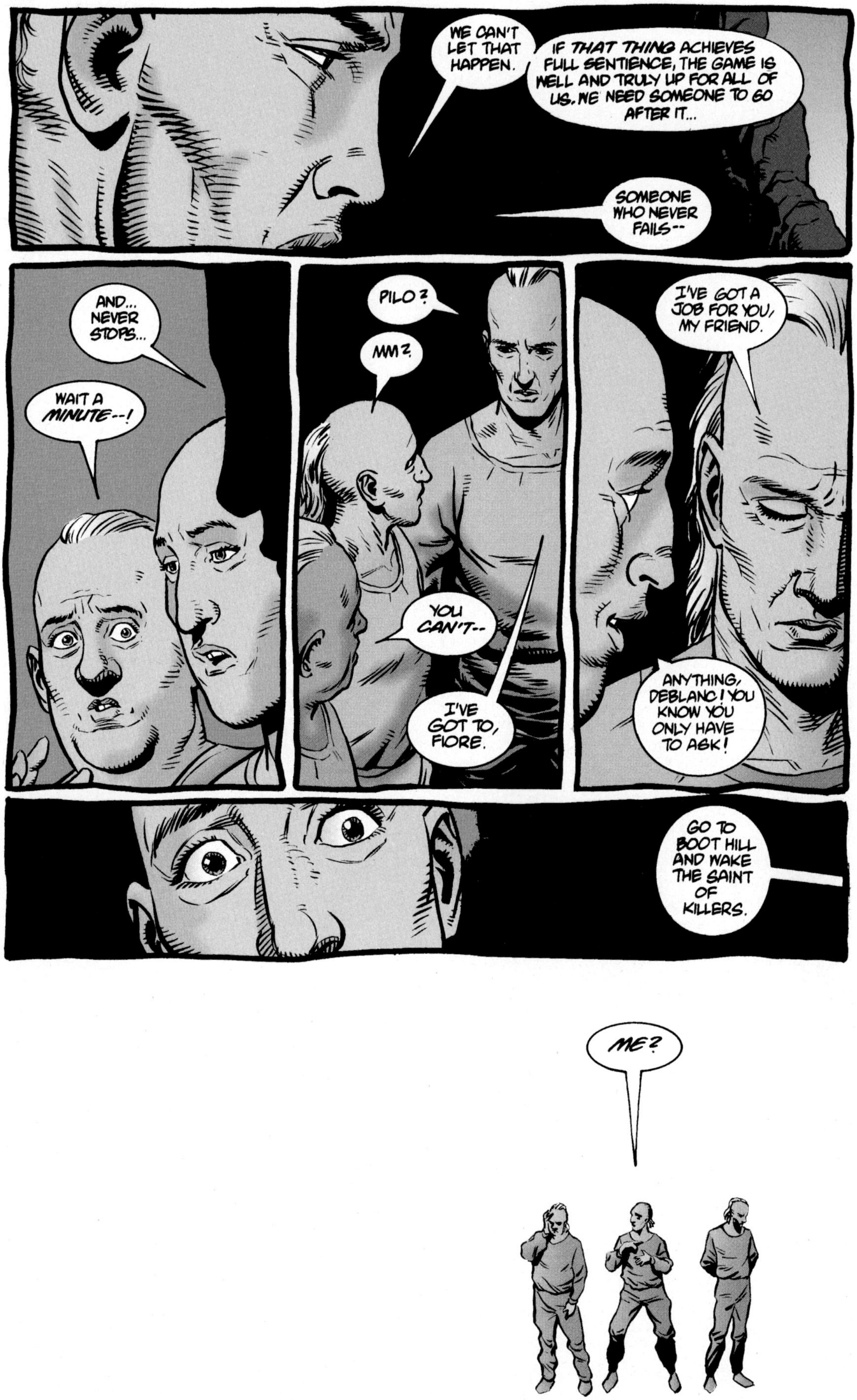
WE CAN'T LET THAT HAPPEN.
IF THAT THING ACHIEVES FULL SENTIENCE, THE GAME IS WELL AND TRULY UP FOR ALL OF US. WE NEED SOMEONE TO GO AFTER IT...
SOMEONE WHO NEVER FAILS--
AND... NEVER STOPS...
WAIT A MINUTE--!
PILO?
MM?
YOU CAN'T--
I'VE GOT TO, FIORE.
I'VE GOT A JOB FOR YOU, MY FRIEND.
ANYTHING, DEBLANC! YOU KNOW YOU ONLY HAVE TO ASK!
GO TO BOOT HILL AND WAKE THE SAINT OF KILLERS.
ME?

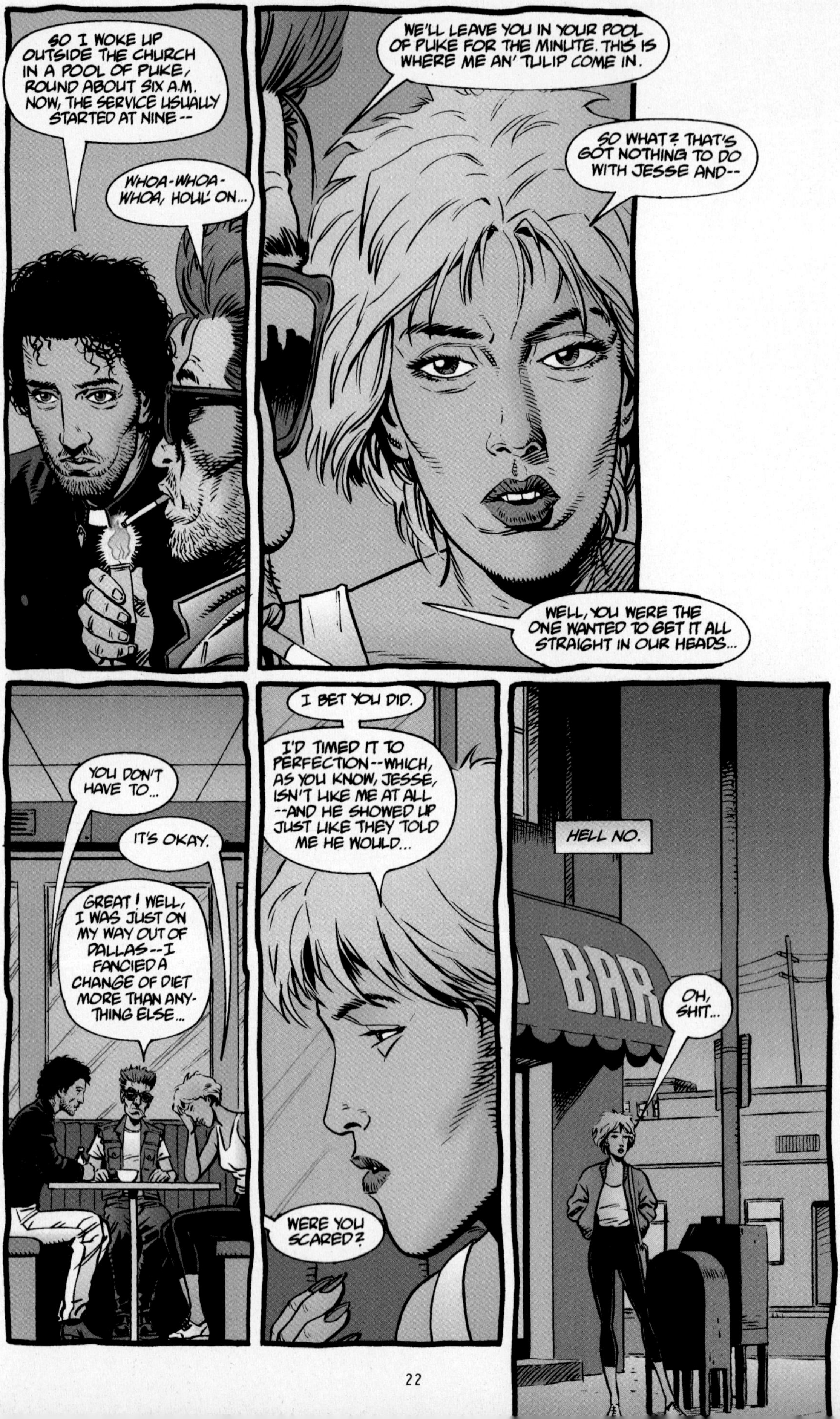
SO I WOKE UP OUTSIDE THE CHURCH IN A POOL OF PUKE, ROUND ABOUT SIX A.M. NOW, THE SERVICE USUALLY STARTED AT NINE --
WHOA-WHOA-WHOA, HOUL' ON...
WE'LL LEAVE YOU IN YOUR POOL OF PUKE FOR THE MINUTE. THIS IS WHERE ME AN' TULIP COME IN.
SO WHAT? THAT'S GOT NOTHING TO DO WITH JESSE AND--
WELL, YOU WERE THE ONE WANTED TO GET IT ALL STRAIGHT IN OUR HEADS...
YOU DON'T HAVE TO...
IT'S OKAY.
GREAT! WELL, I WAS JUST ON MY WAY OUT OF DALLAS--I FANCIED A CHANGE OF DIET MORE THAN ANYTHING ELSE...
I BET YOU DID.
I'D TIMED IT TO PERFECTION--WHICH, AS YOU KNOW, JESSE, ISN'T LIKE ME AT ALL --AND HE SHOWED UP JUST LIKE THEY TOLD ME HE WOULD...
WERE YOU SCARED?
HELL NO.
BAR
OH, SHIT...

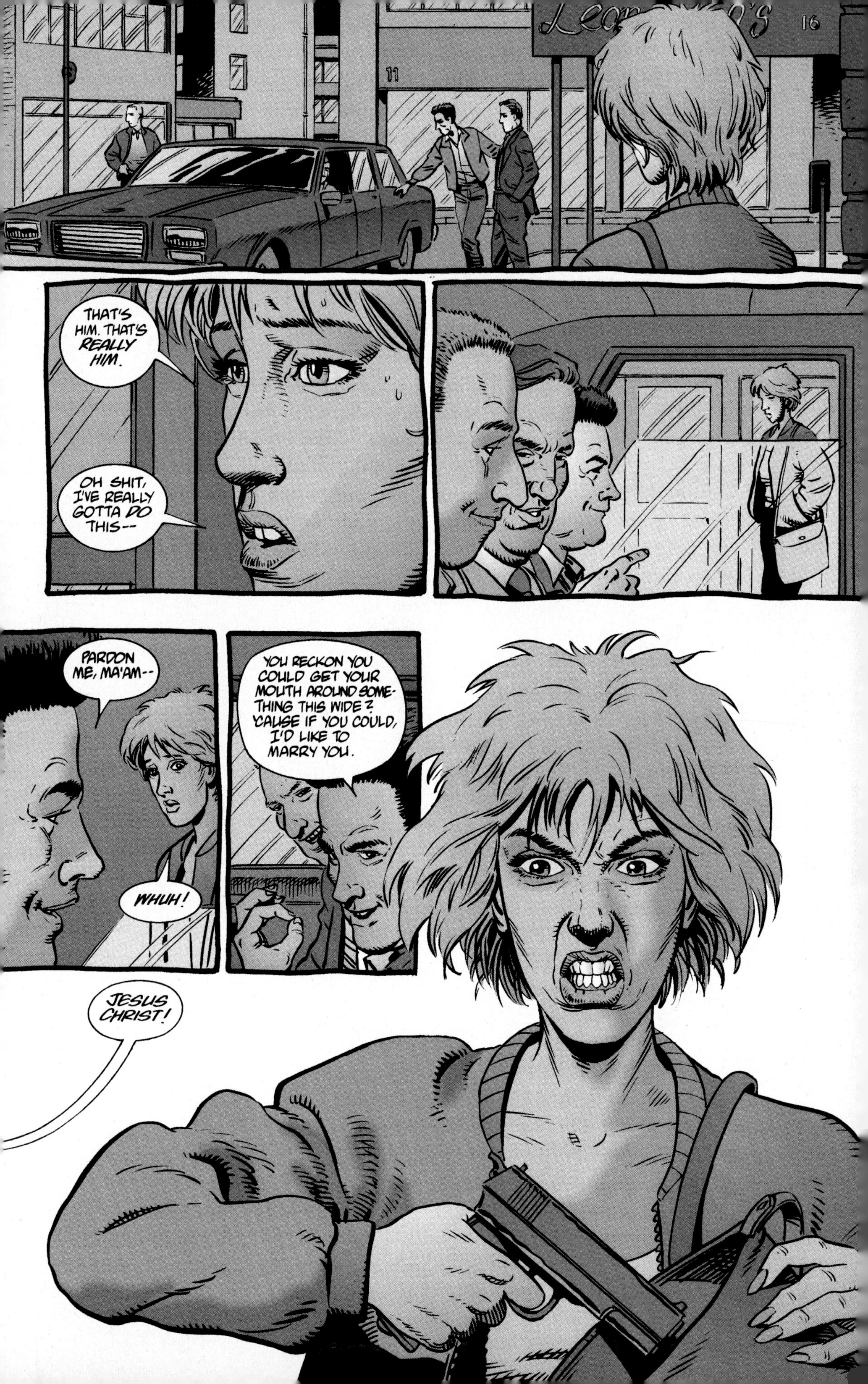
16
11
THAT'S HIM. THAT'S REALLY HIM.
OH SHIT, I'VE REALLY GOTTA DO THIS--
PARDON ME, MA'AM--
WHUH!
YOU RECKON YOU COULD GET YOUR MOUTH AROUND SOMETHING THIS WIDE? 'CAUSE IF YOU COULD, I'D LIKE TO MARRY YOU.
JESUS CHRIST!

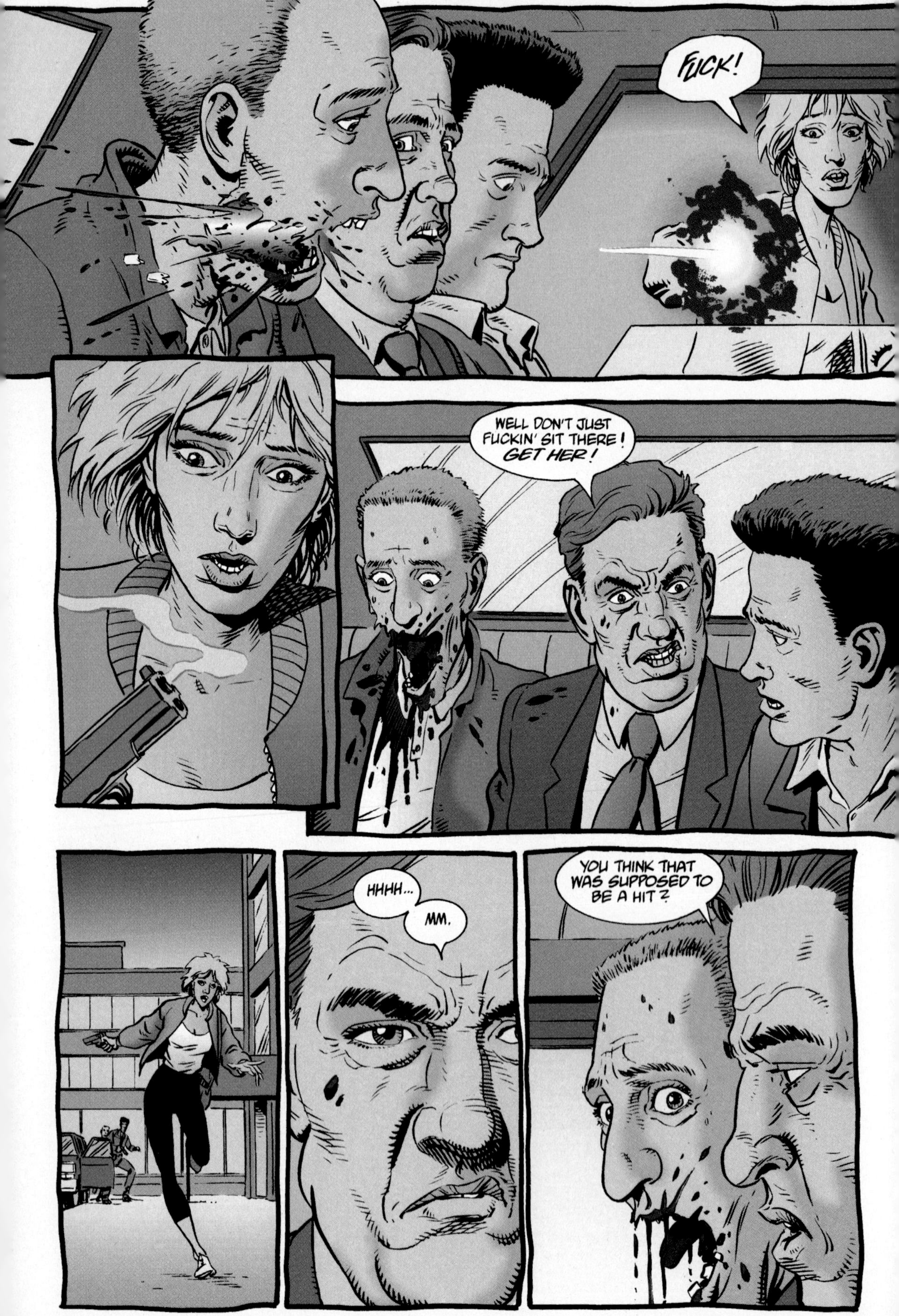
FUCK!
WELL DON'T JUST FUCKIN' SIT THERE! GET HER!
HHHH...
MM.
YOU THINK THAT WAS SUPPOSED TO BE A HIT?

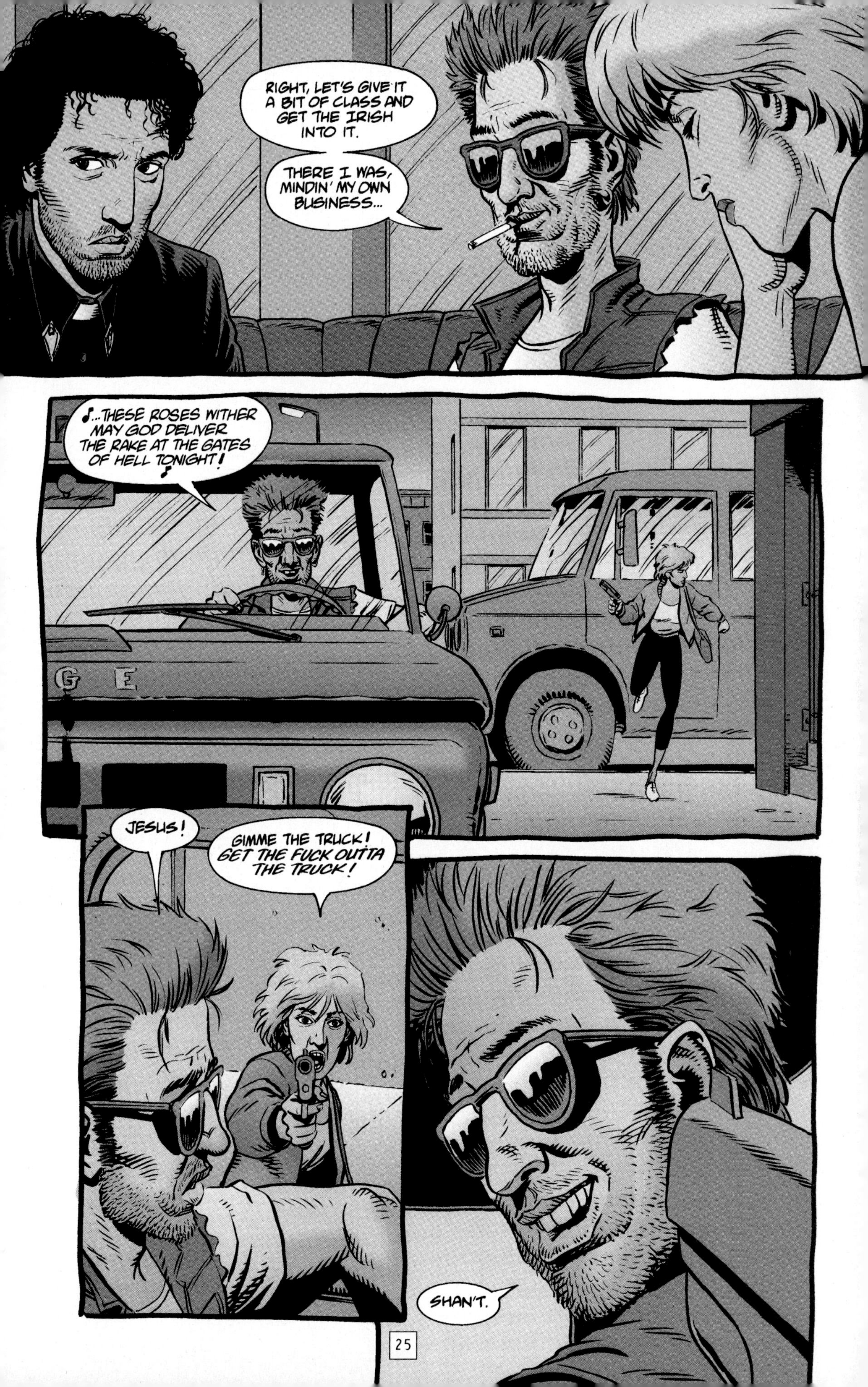
RIGHT, LET'S GIVE IT A BIT OF CLASS AND GET THE IRISH INTO IT.
THERE I WAS, MINDIN' MY OWN BUSINESS...
♪...THESE ROSES WITHER MAY GOD DELIVER THE RAKE AT THE GATES OF HELL TONIGHT! ♪
JESUS!
GIMME THE TRUCK! GET THE FUCK OUTTA THE TRUCK!
SHAN'T.

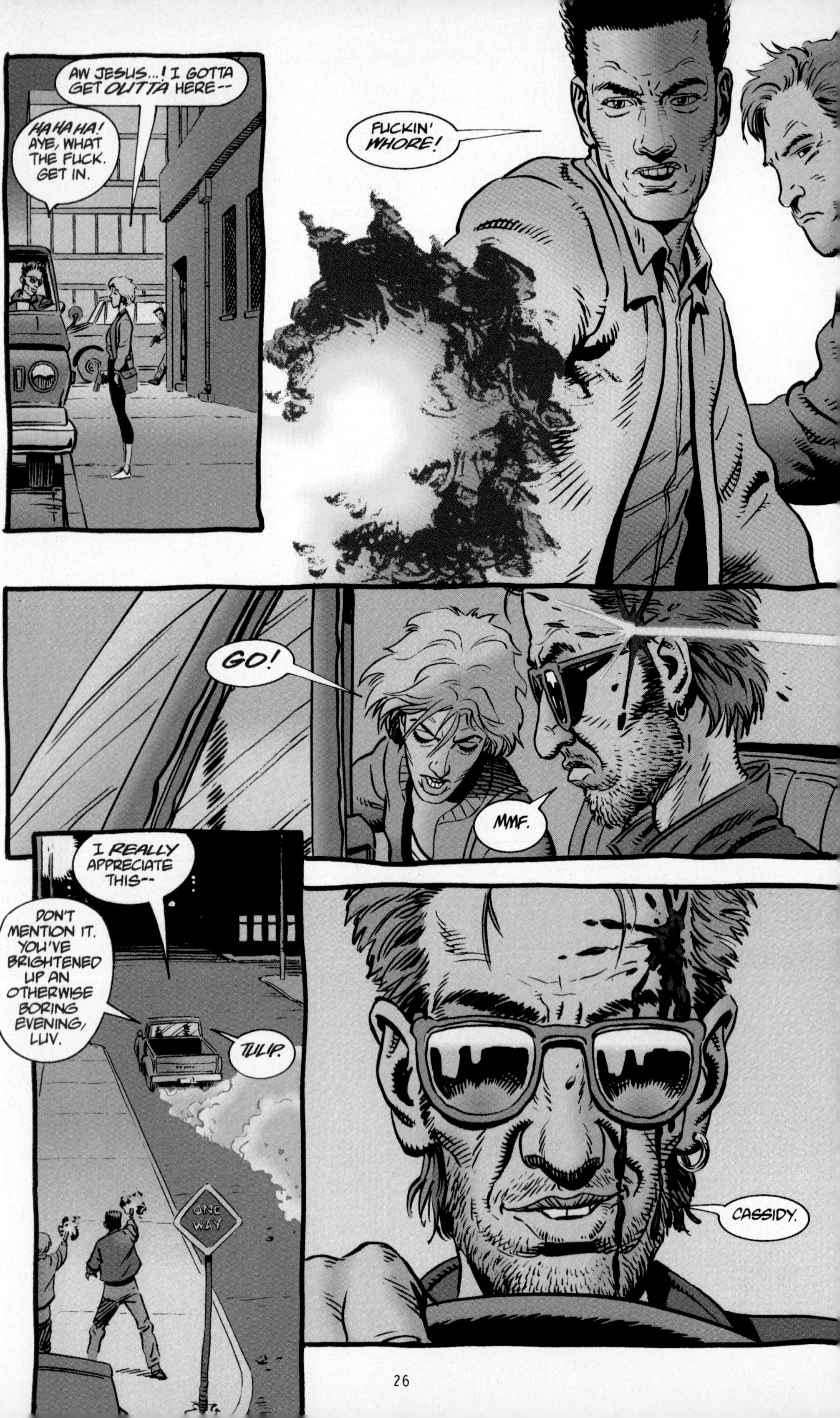
AW JESUS...! I GOTTA GET OUTTA HERE--
HAHAHA! AYE, WHAT THE FUCK. GET IN.
FUCKIN' WHORE!
GO!
MMF.
I REALLY APPRECIATE THIS--
DON'T MENTION IT. YOU'VE BRIGHTENED UP AN OTHERWISE BORING EVENING, LUV.
TULIP.
CASSIDY.
ONE WAY

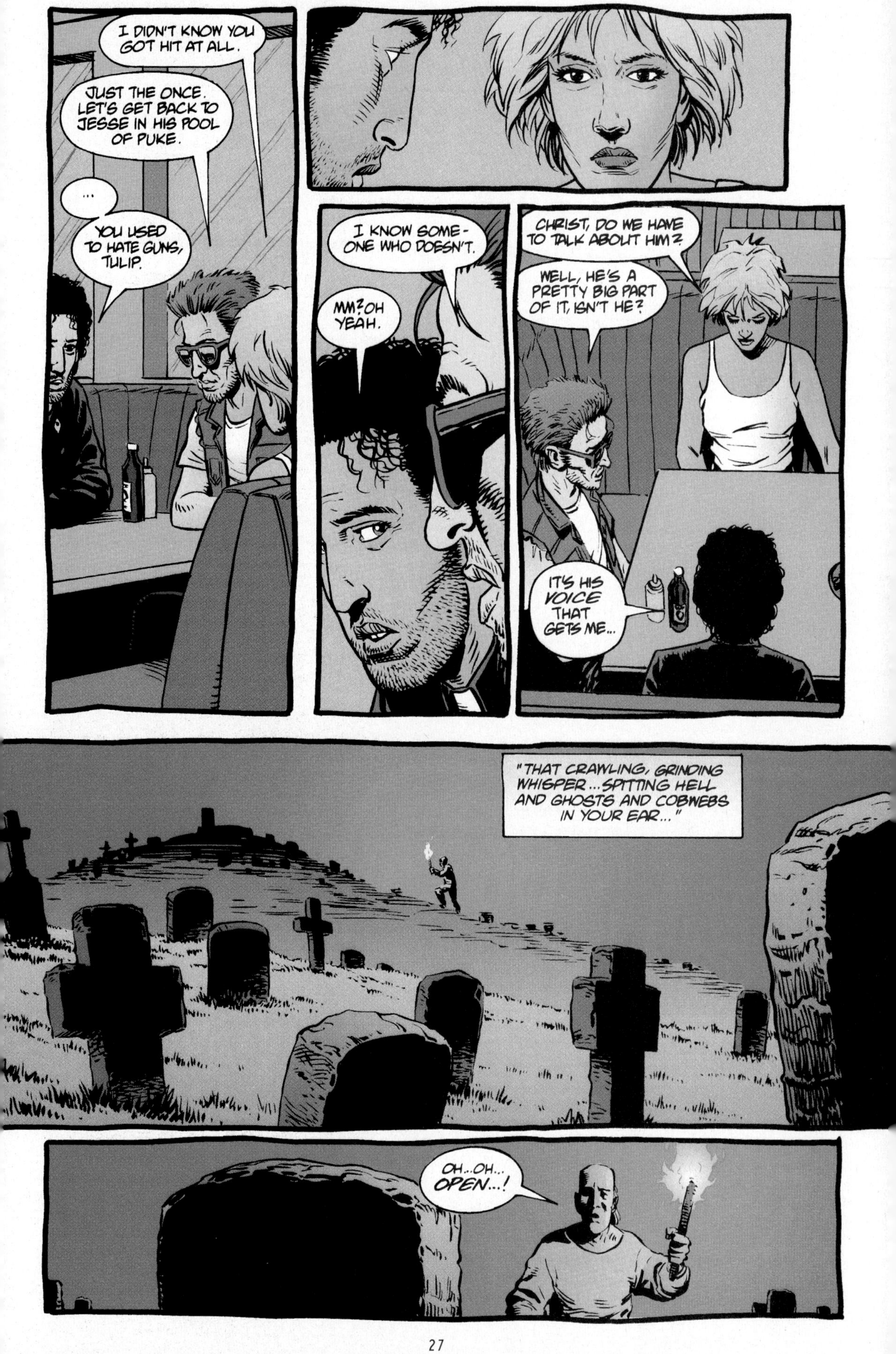
I DIDN'T KNOW YOU GOT HIT AT ALL.
JUST THE ONCE. LET'S GET BACK TO JESSE IN HIS POOL OF PUKE.
...
YOU USED TO HATE GUNS, TULIP.
I KNOW SOME-ONE WHO DOESN'T.
MM? OH YEAH.
CHRIST, DO WE HAVE TO TALK ABOUT HIM?
WELL, HE'S A PRETTY BIG PART OF IT, ISN'T HE?
IT'S HIS VOICE THAT GETS ME...
"THAT CRAWLING, GRINDING WHISPER ... SPITTING HELL AND GHOSTS AND COBWEBS IN YOUR EAR..."
OH...OH... OPEN...!

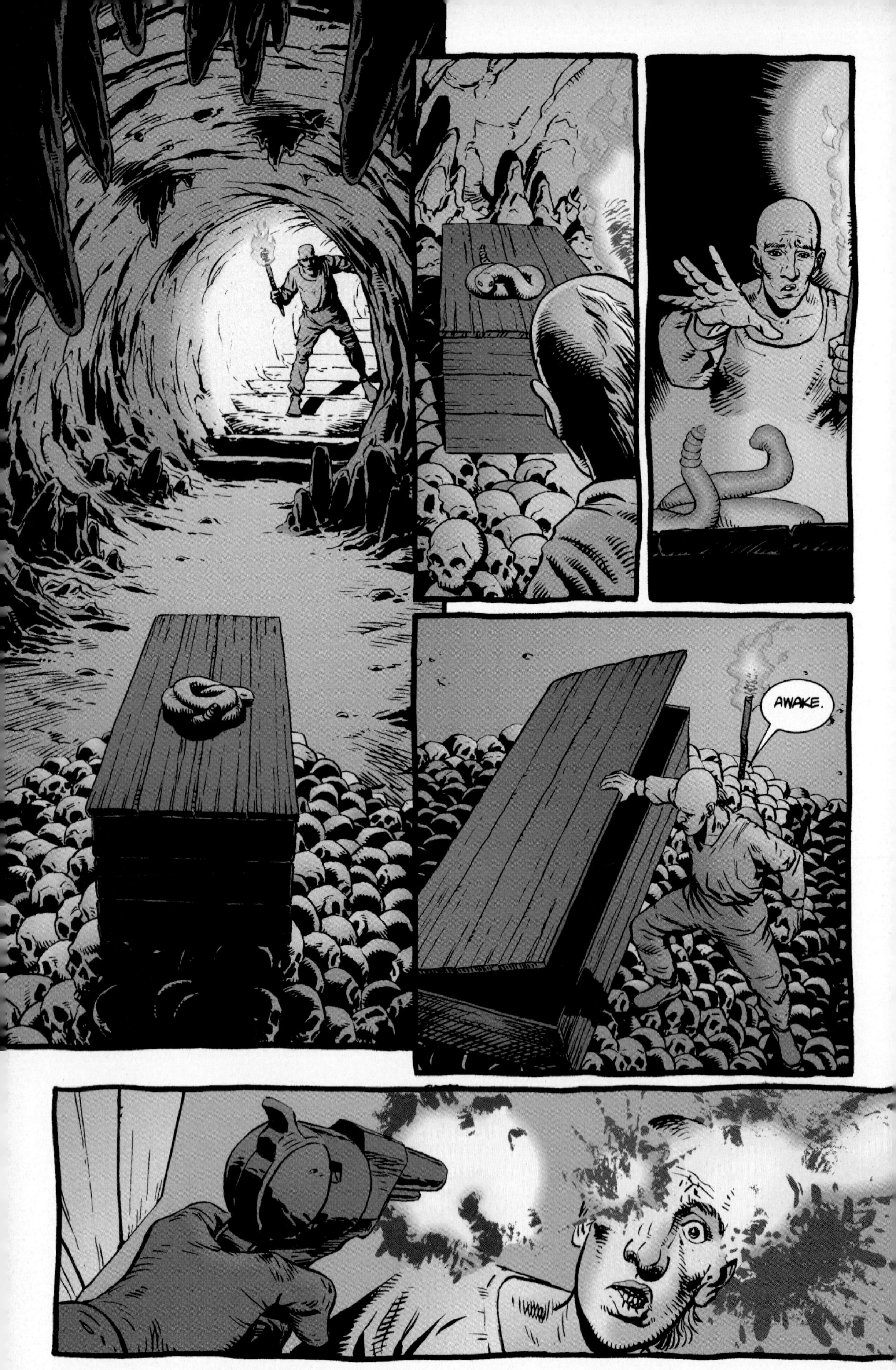
AWAKE.

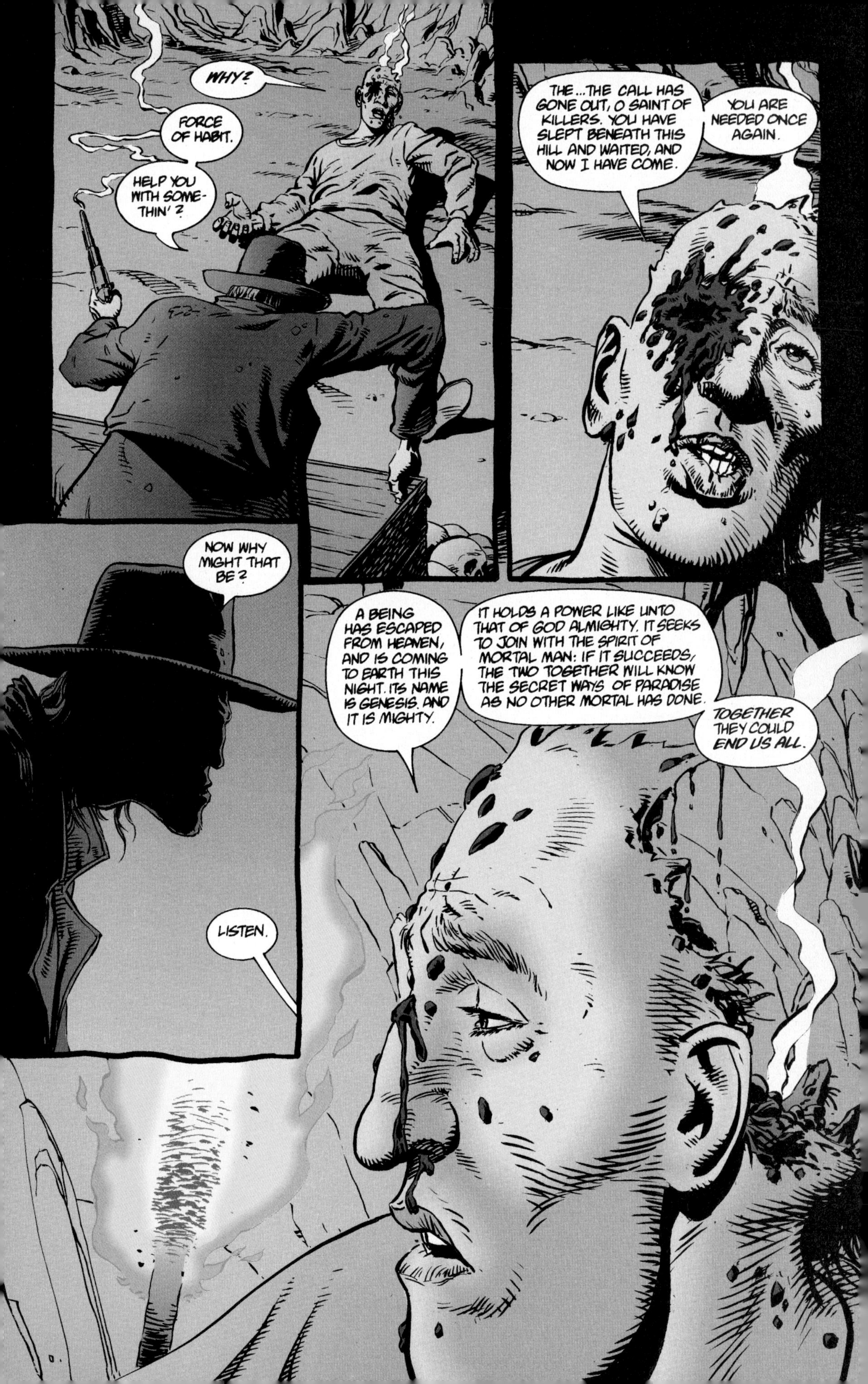
WHY?
FORCE OF HABIT.
HELP YOU WITH SOME-THIN'?
THE...THE CALL HAS GONE OUT, O SAINT OF KILLERS. YOU HAVE SLEPT BENEATH THIS HILL AND WAITED, AND NOW I HAVE COME.
YOU ARE NEEDED ONCE AGAIN.
NOW WHY MIGHT THAT BE?
LISTEN.
A BEING HAS ESCAPED FROM HEAVEN, AND IS COMING TO EARTH THIS NIGHT. ITS NAME IS GENESIS, AND IT IS MIGHTY.
IT HOLDS A POWER LIKE UNTO THAT OF GOD ALMIGHTY. IT SEEKS TO JOIN WITH THE SPIRIT OF MORTAL MAN: IF IT SUCCEEDS, THE TWO TOGETHER WILL KNOW THE SECRET WAYS OF PARADISE AS NO OTHER MORTAL HAS DONE.
TOGETHER THEY COULD END US ALL.

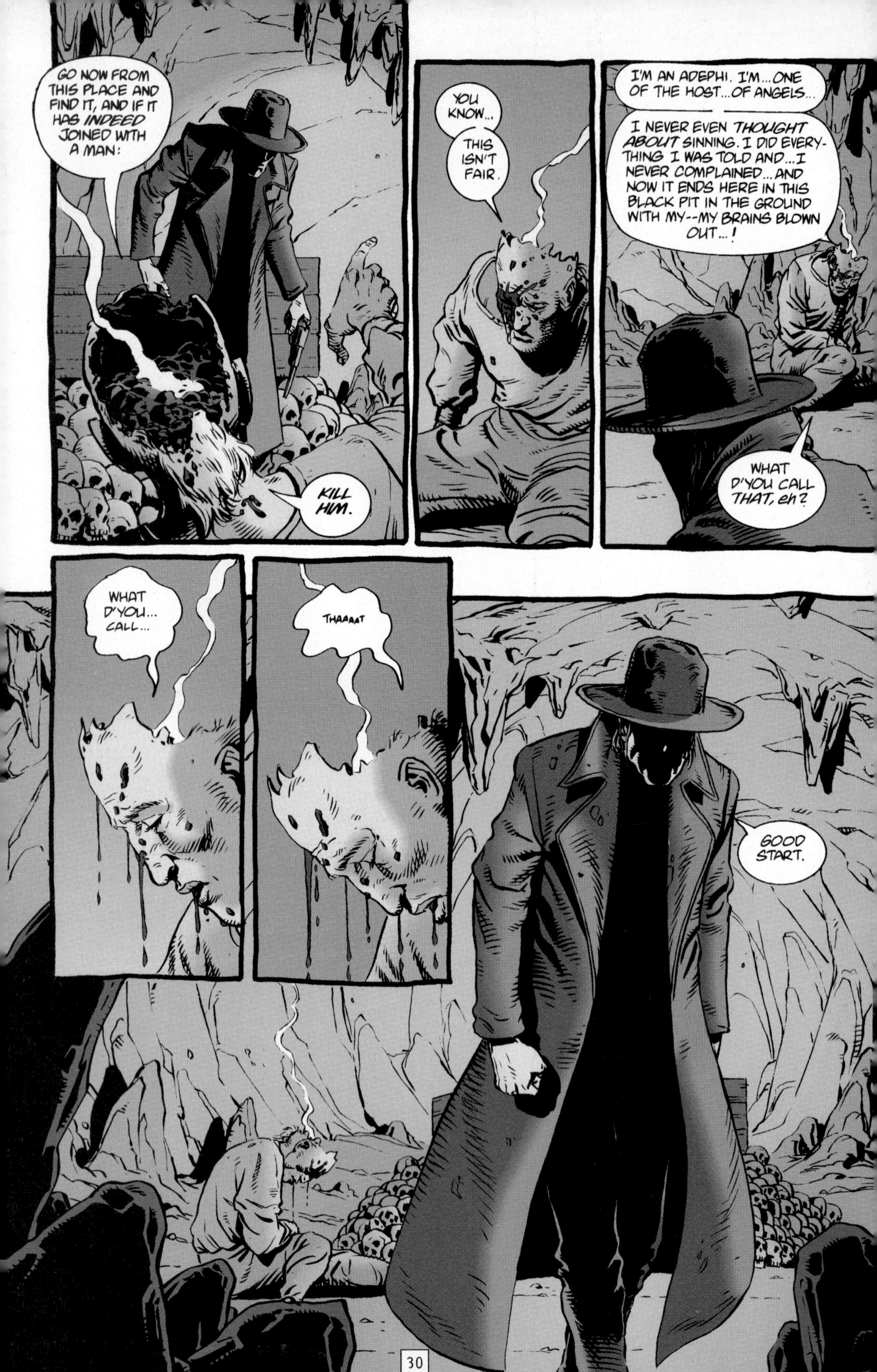
GO NOW FROM THIS PLACE AND FIND IT, AND IF IT HAS *INDEED* JOINED WITH A MAN:
KILL HIM.
YOU KNOW...
THIS ISN'T FAIR.
I'M AN ADEPHI. I'M...ONE OF THE HOST...OF ANGELS...
I NEVER EVEN *THOUGHT ABOUT* SINNING. I DID EVERYTHING I WAS TOLD AND...I NEVER COMPLAINED...AND NOW IT ENDS HERE IN THIS BLACK PIT IN THE GROUND WITH MY--MY BRAINS BLOWN OUT...!
WHAT D'YOU CALL *THAT, eh?*
WHAT D'YOU... CALL...
THAAAAT
GOOD START.

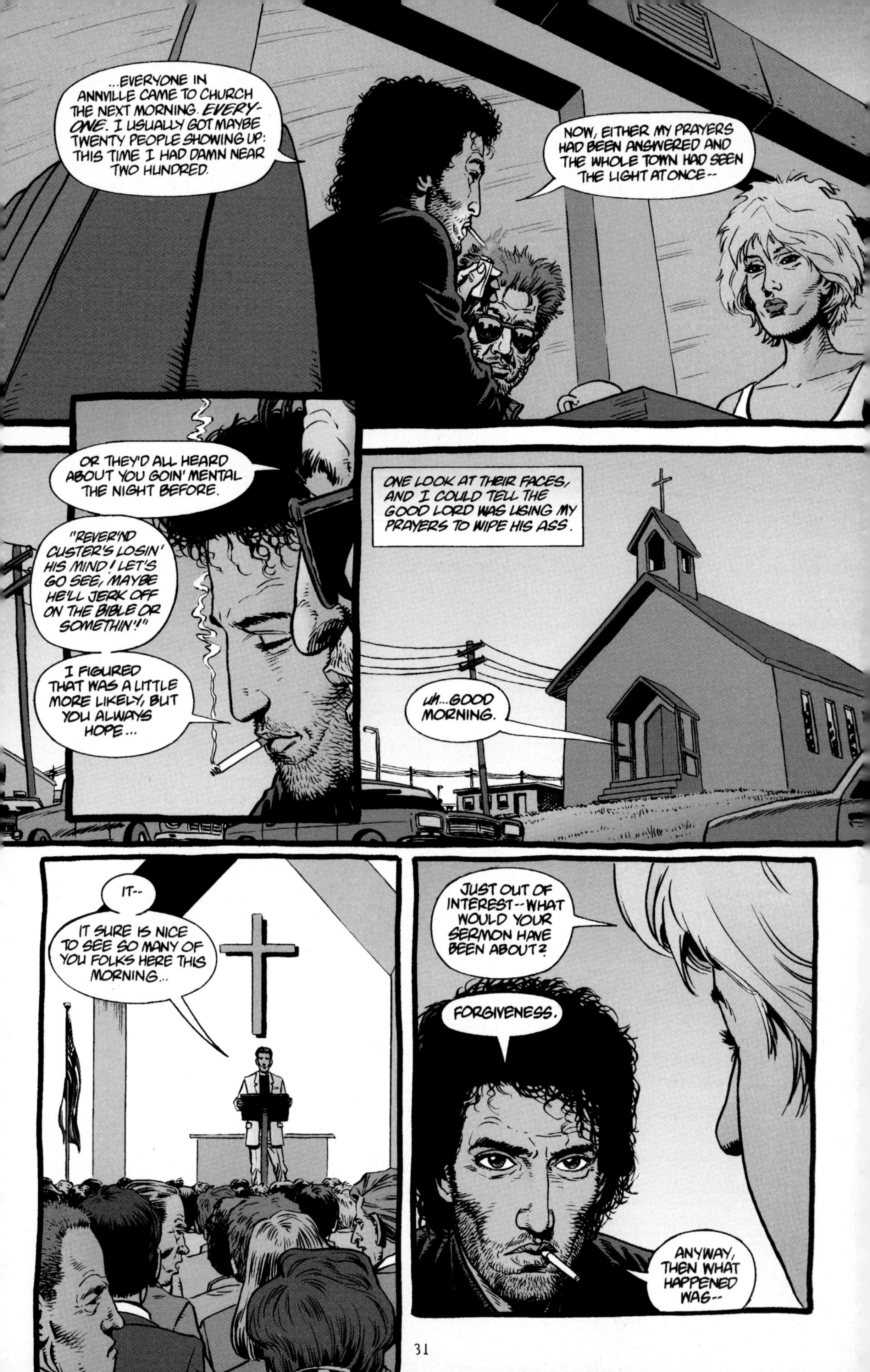
...EVERYONE IN ANNVILLE CAME TO CHURCH THE NEXT MORNING. EVERY-ONE. I USUALLY GOT MAYBE TWENTY PEOPLE SHOWING UP: THIS TIME I HAD DAMN NEAR TWO HUNDRED.
NOW, EITHER MY PRAYERS HAD BEEN ANSWERED AND THE WHOLE TOWN HAD SEEN THE LIGHT AT ONCE--
OR THEY'D ALL HEARD ABOUT YOU GOIN' MENTAL THE NIGHT BEFORE.
"REVER'ND CUSTER'S LOSIN' HIS MIND! LET'S GO SEE, MAYBE HE'LL JERK OFF ON THE BIBLE OR SOMETHIN'!"
I FIGURED THAT WAS A LITTLE MORE LIKELY, BUT YOU ALWAYS HOPE...
ONE LOOK AT THEIR FACES, AND I COULD TELL THE GOOD LORD WAS USING MY PRAYERS TO WIPE HIS ASS.
UH...GOOD MORNING.
IT--
IT SURE IS NICE TO SEE SO MANY OF YOU FOLKS HERE THIS MORNING...
JUST OUT OF INTEREST--WHAT WOULD YOUR SERMON HAVE BEEN ABOUT?
FORGIVENESS.
ANYWAY, THEN WHAT HAPPENED WAS--

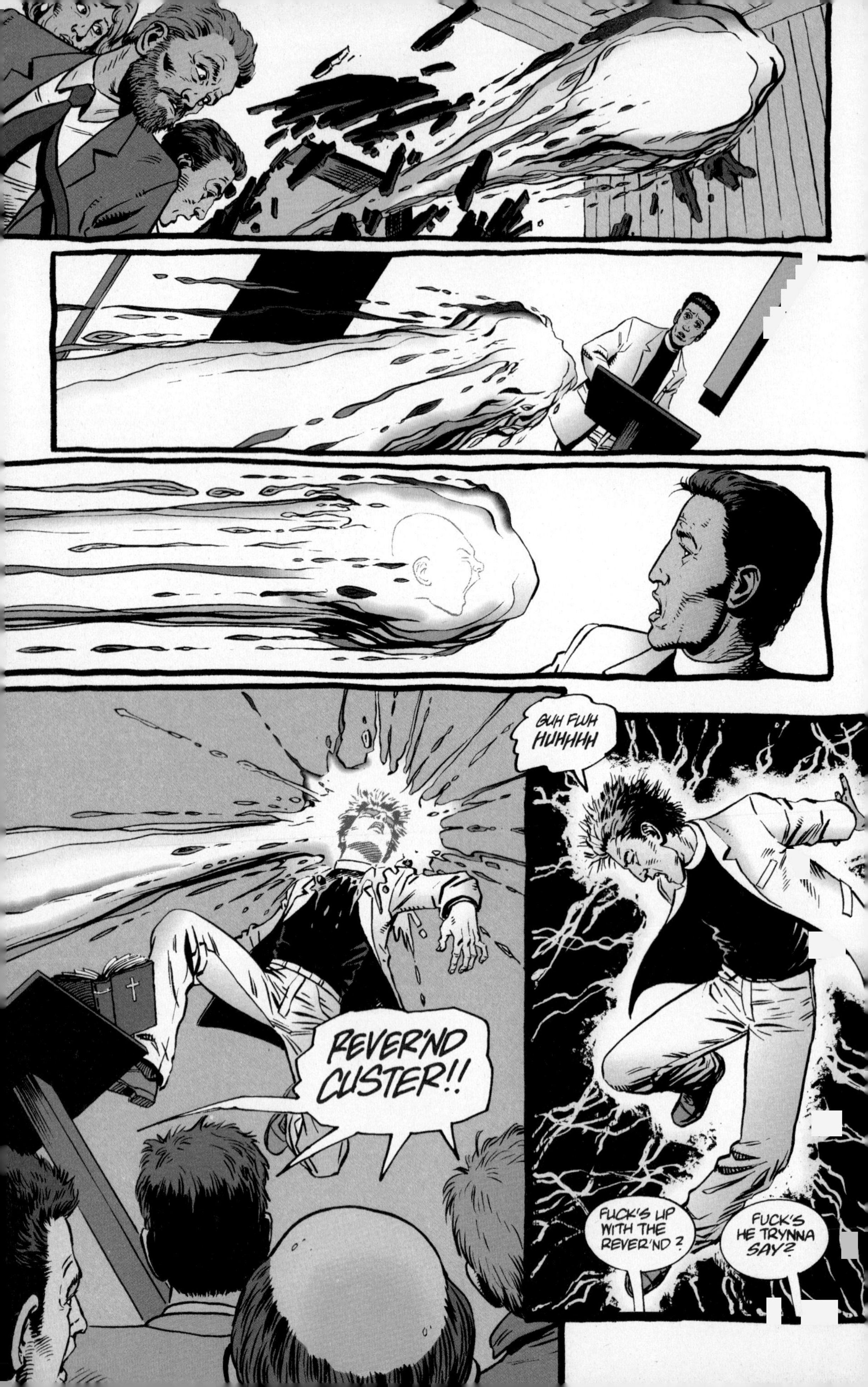
GUH FUH HUHHHH
REVER'ND CUSTER!!
FUCK'S UP WITH THE REVER'ND?
FUCK'S HE TRYNNA SAY?

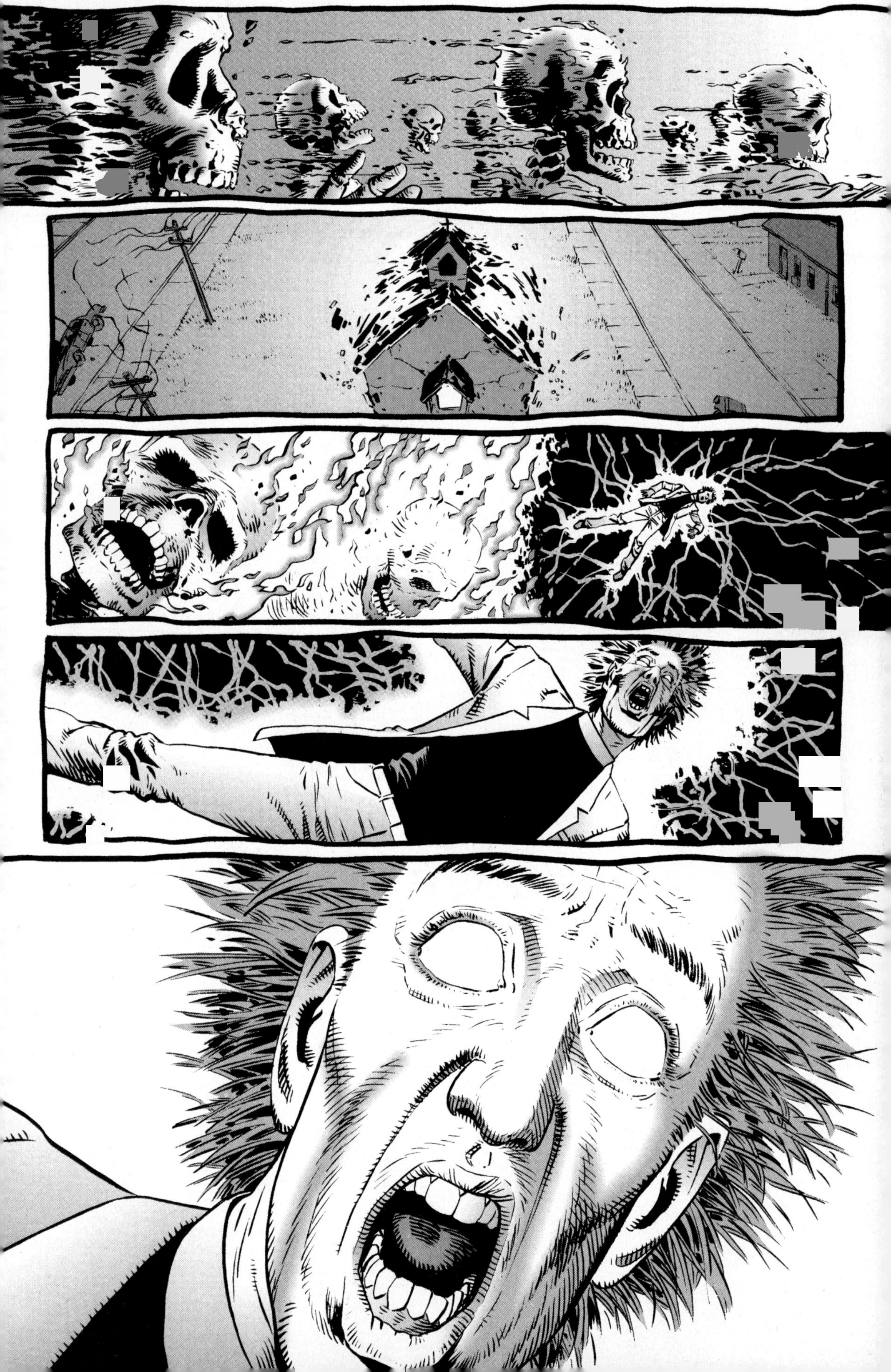

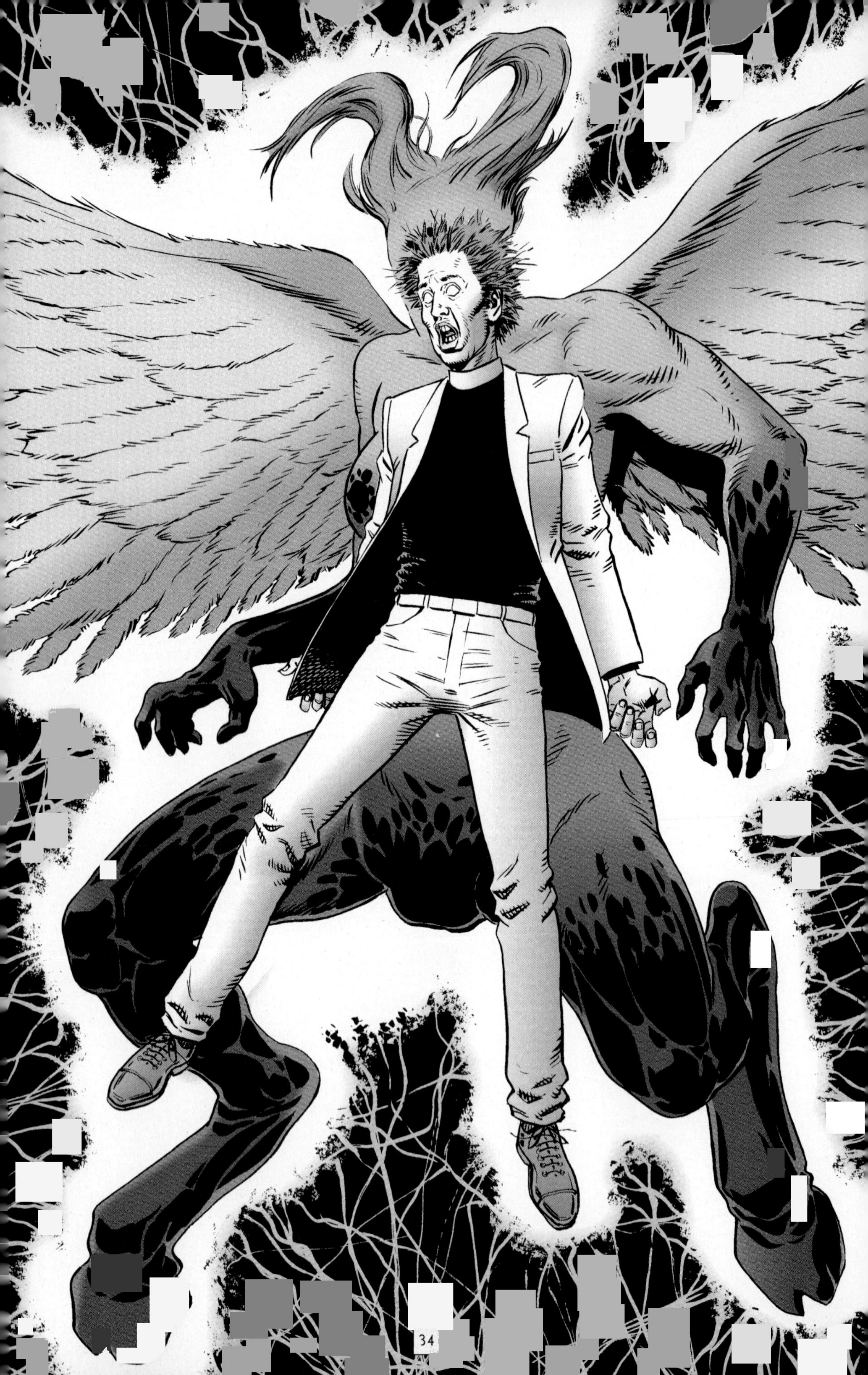

MY GOD...!

CASSIDY HAD PULLED OVER JUST BEFORE DAWN. THEN HE GOT IN THE BACK, COVERED HIMSELF IN A TARPAULIN, AND MADE ME *SWEAR* NOT TO TAKE IT OFF OF HIM.

THAT'S WHERE WE WERE WHEN I SAW THE FIRE...

HOLD ON. HIM DOING THIS DIDN'T MAKE YOU SUSPICIOUS?

OH, SO THE SECOND I SAW HIM SLEEPING LIKE THAT I SHOULD'VE FIGURED OUT WHAT HE IS? IT'S NOT EXACTLY A NORMAL--

RIGHT, *RIGHT*...

HEY! HEY!

THERE'S A *MUSHROOM CLOUD* DOWN THE ROAD--

I DON'T GIVE A FUCK! *STOP!*

YOU DIDN'T SAY NOT TO DRIVE THE TRUCK. ALL YOU SAID--

I THOUGHT IT WAS A BIT BLEEDIN' OBVIOUS!

I'M TELLIN' YOU, TULIP, *RIGHT FRIGGIN' NOW:* YOU PULL OVER AN' STOP THIS TRUCK *OR ELSE!*

I NOTICE YOU HAVEN'T STOPPED.

WELCOME TO ANNVILLE
PLEASE DRIVE CAREFULLY

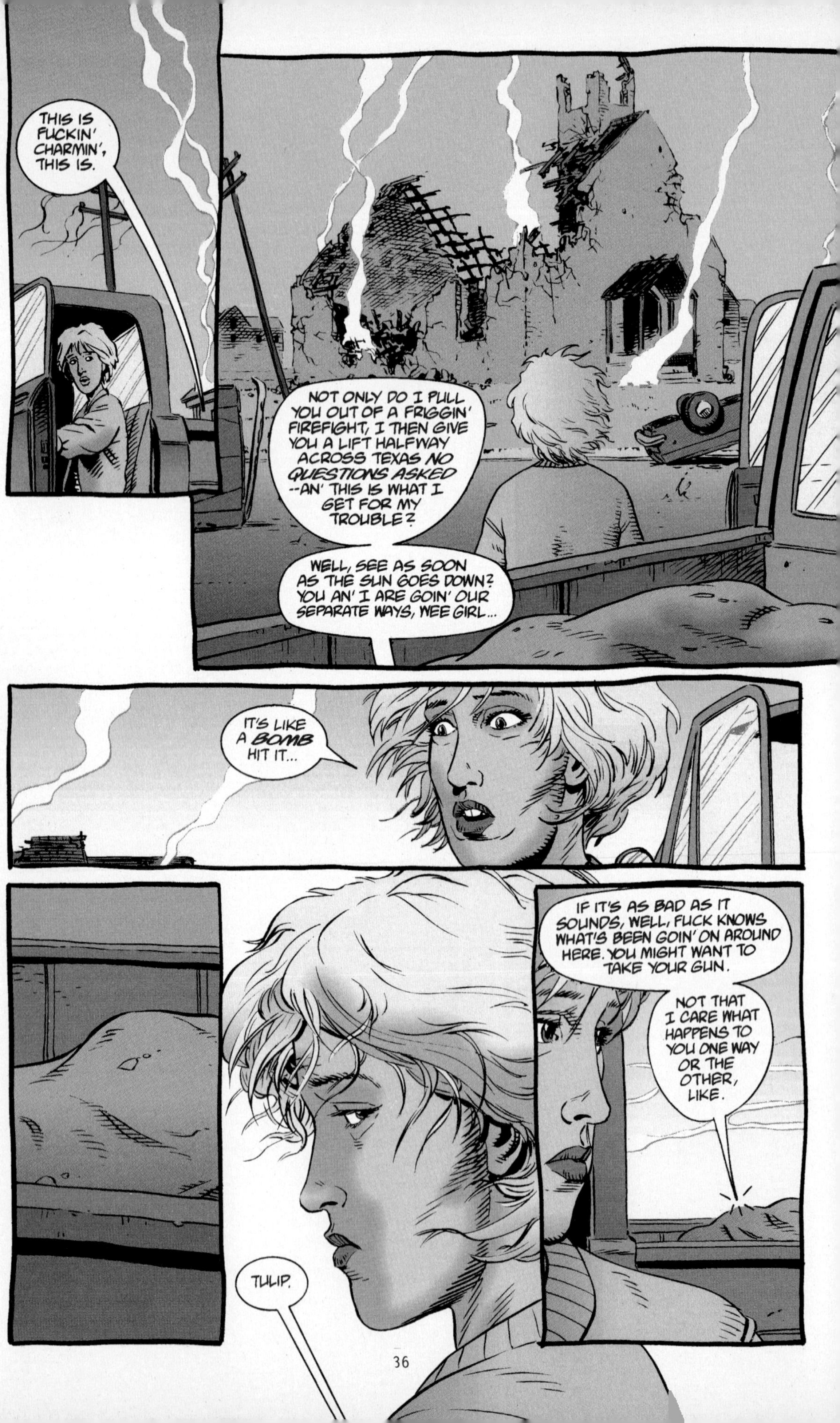
THIS IS FUCKIN' CHARMIN', THIS IS.
NOT ONLY DO I PULL YOU OUT OF A FRIGGIN' FIREFIGHT, I THEN GIVE YOU A LIFT HALFWAY ACROSS TEXAS NO QUESTIONS ASKED --AN' THIS IS WHAT I GET FOR MY TROUBLE?
WELL, SEE AS SOON AS THE SUN GOES DOWN? YOU AN' I ARE GOIN' OUR SEPARATE WAYS, WEE GIRL...
IT'S LIKE A BOMB HIT IT...
TULIP.
IF IT'S AS BAD AS IT SOUNDS, WELL, FUCK KNOWS WHAT'S BEEN GOIN' ON AROUND HERE. YOU MIGHT WANT TO TAKE YOUR GUN.
NOT THAT I CARE WHAT HAPPENS TO YOU ONE WAY OR THE OTHER, LIKE.

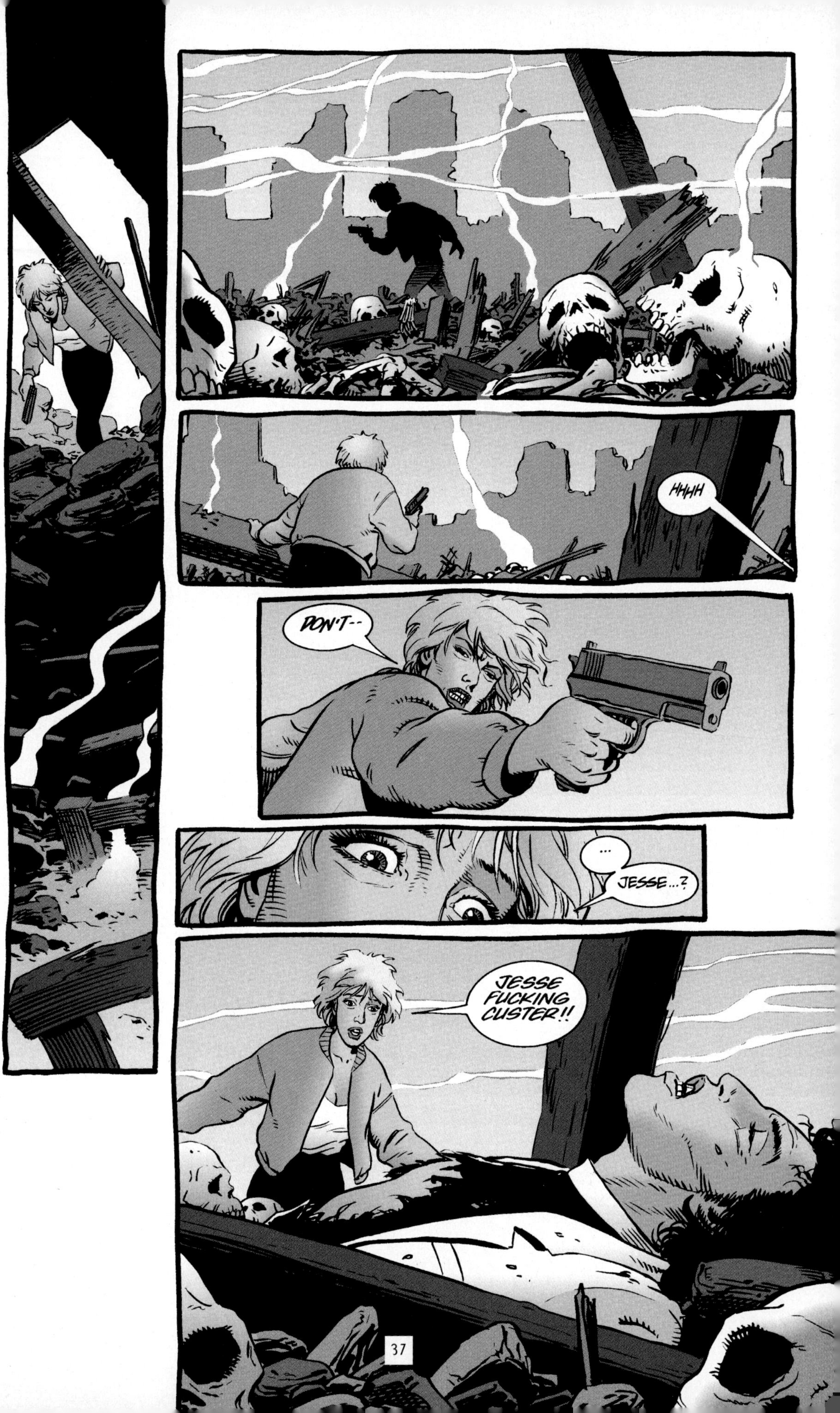
HHHH
DON'T--
...
JESSE...?
JESSE FUCKING CUSTER!!

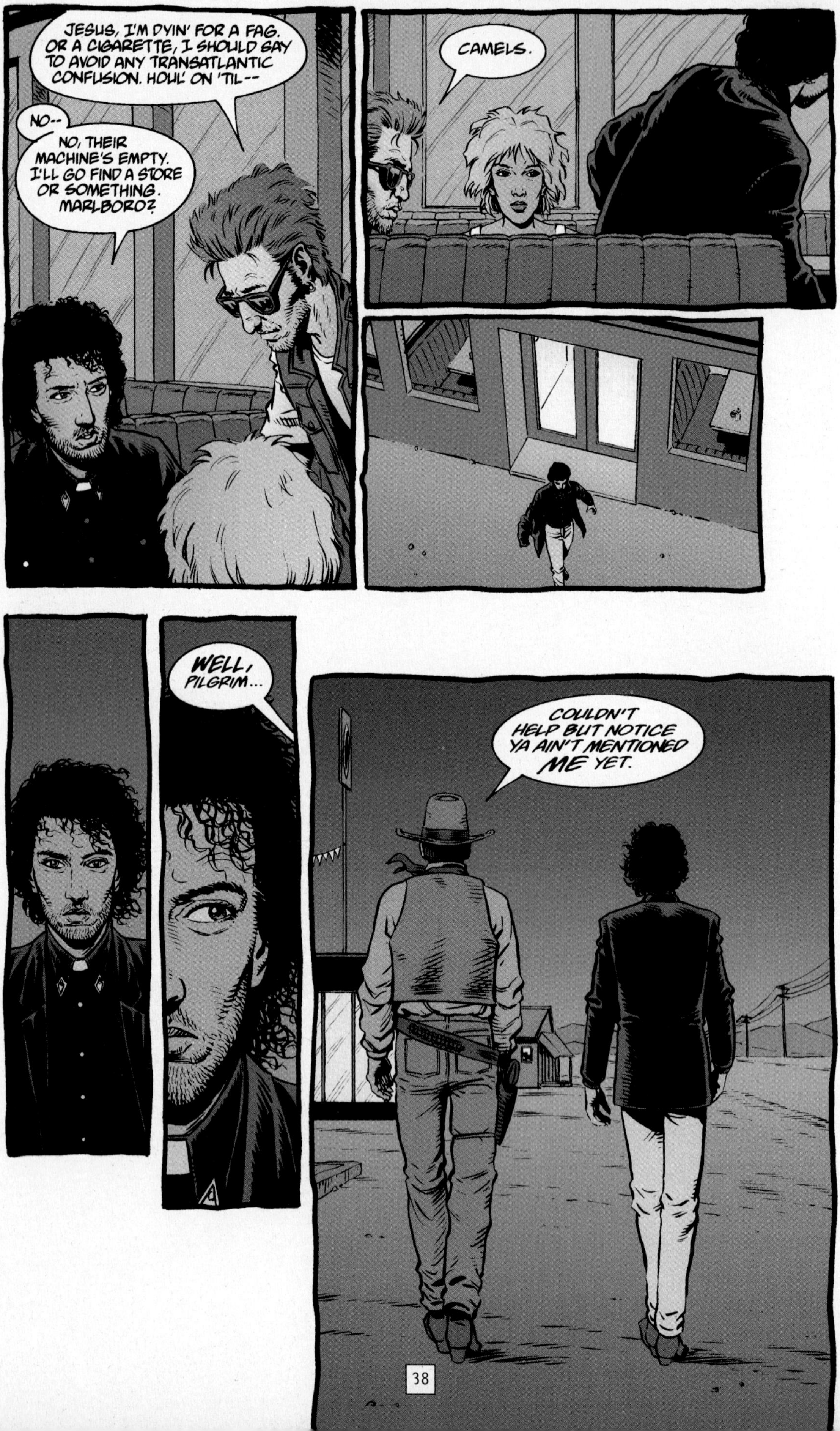
JESUS, I'M DYIN' FOR A FAG. OR A CIGARETTE, I SHOULD SAY TO AVOID ANY TRANSATLANTIC CONFUSION. HOUL' ON 'TIL--
NO--
NO, THEIR MACHINE'S EMPTY. I'LL GO FIND A STORE OR SOMETHING. MARLBORO?
CAMELS.
WELL, PILGRIM...
COULDN'T HELP BUT NOTICE YA AIN'T MENTIONED ME YET.

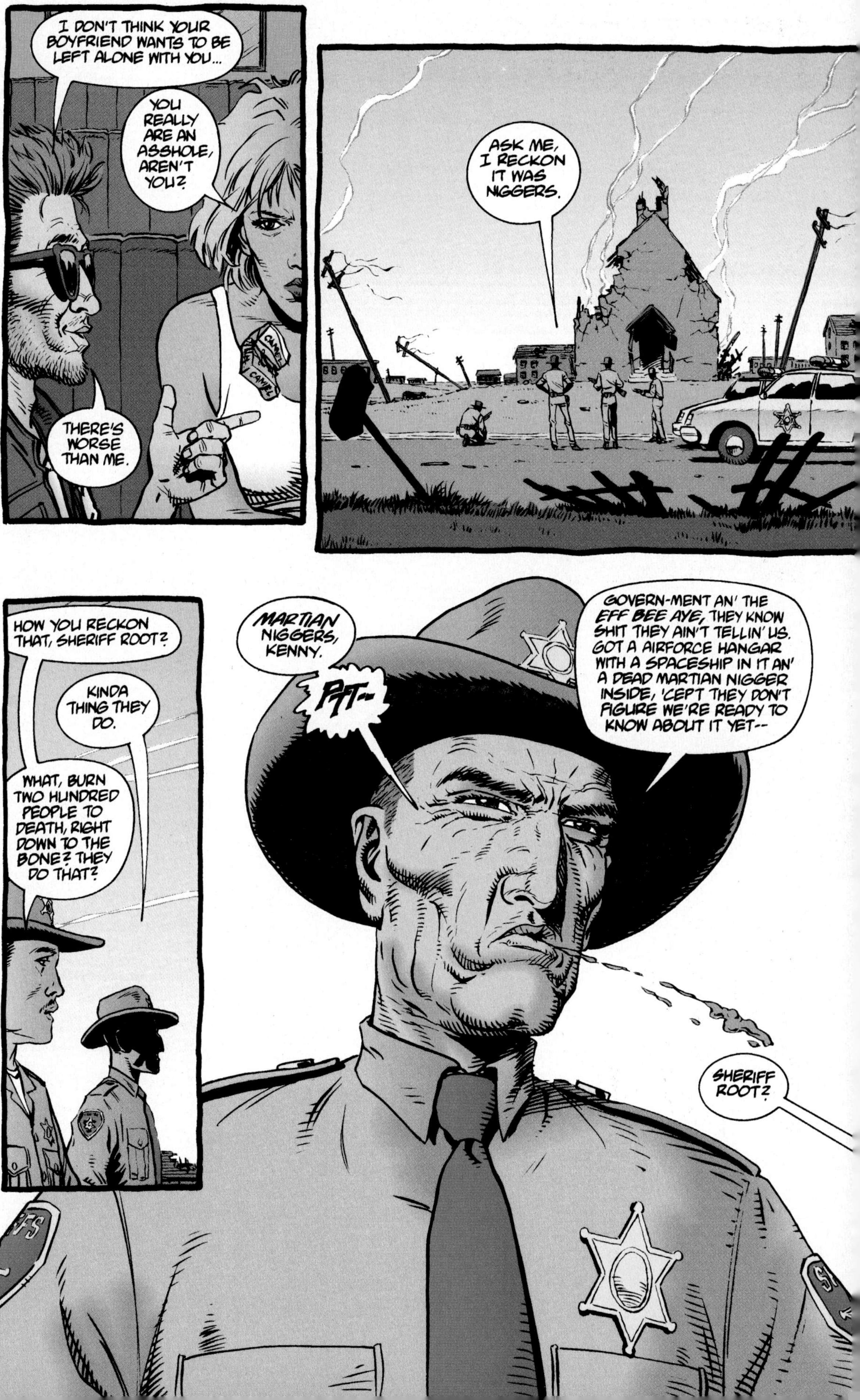
I DON'T THINK YOUR BOYFRIEND WANTS TO BE LEFT ALONE WITH YOU...
YOU REALLY ARE AN ASSHOLE, AREN'T YOU?
THERE'S WORSE THAN ME.
ASK ME, I RECKON IT WAS NIGGERS.
HOW YOU RECKON THAT, SHERIFF ROOT?
KINDA THING THEY DO.
WHAT, BURN TWO HUNDRED PEOPLE TO DEATH, RIGHT DOWN TO THE BONE? THEY DO THAT?
MARTIAN NIGGERS, KENNY.
PFFT--
GOVERN-MENT AN' THE EFF BEE AYE, THEY KNOW SHIT THEY AIN'T TELLIN' US. GOT A AIRFORCE HANGAR WITH A SPACESHIP IN IT AN' A DEAD MARTIAN NIGGER INSIDE, 'CEPT THEY DON'T FIGURE WE'RE READY TO KNOW ABOUT IT YET--
SHERIFF ROOT?

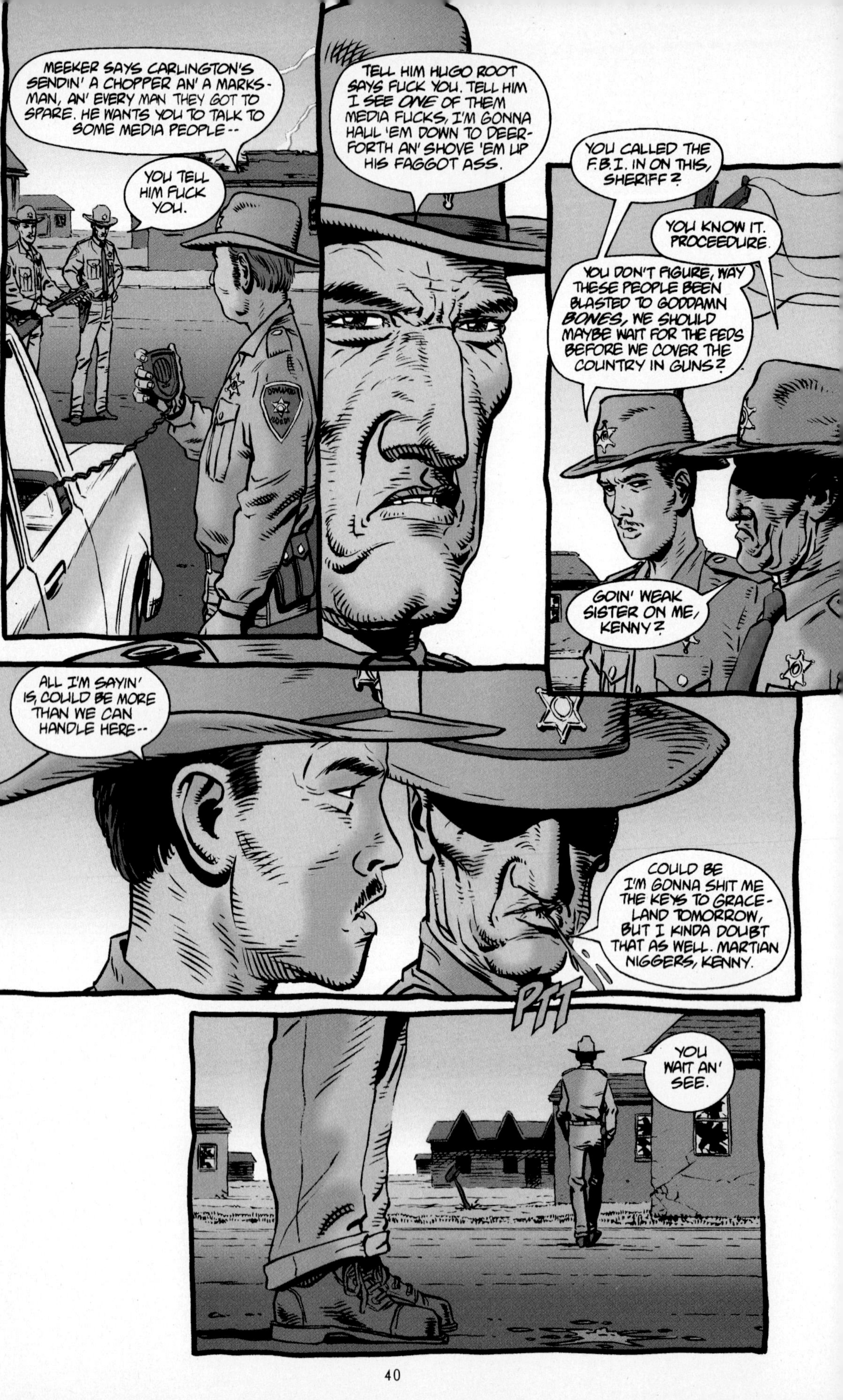
MEEKER SAYS CARLINGTON'S SENDIN' A CHOPPER AN' A MARKS-MAN, AN' EVERY MAN THEY GOT TO SPARE. HE WANTS YOU TO TALK TO SOME MEDIA PEOPLE--
YOU TELL HIM FUCK YOU.
TELL HIM HUGO ROOT SAYS FUCK YOU. TELL HIM I SEE ONE OF THEM MEDIA FUCKS, I'M GONNA HAUL 'EM DOWN TO DEER-FORTH AN' SHOVE 'EM UP HIS FAGGOT ASS.
YOU CALLED THE F.B.I. IN ON THIS, SHERIFF?
YOU KNOW IT. PROCEEDURE.
YOU DON'T FIGURE, WAY THESE PEOPLE BEEN BLASTED TO GODDAMN BONES, WE SHOULD MAYBE WAIT FOR THE FEDS BEFORE WE COVER THE COUNTRY IN GUNS?
GOIN' WEAK SISTER ON ME, KENNY?
ALL I'M SAYIN' IS, COULD BE MORE THAN WE CAN HANDLE HERE--
COULD BE I'M GONNA SHIT ME THE KEYS TO GRACE-LAND TOMORROW, BUT I KINDA DOUBT THAT AS WELL. MARTIAN NIGGERS, KENNY.
PTT
YOU WAIT AN' SEE.

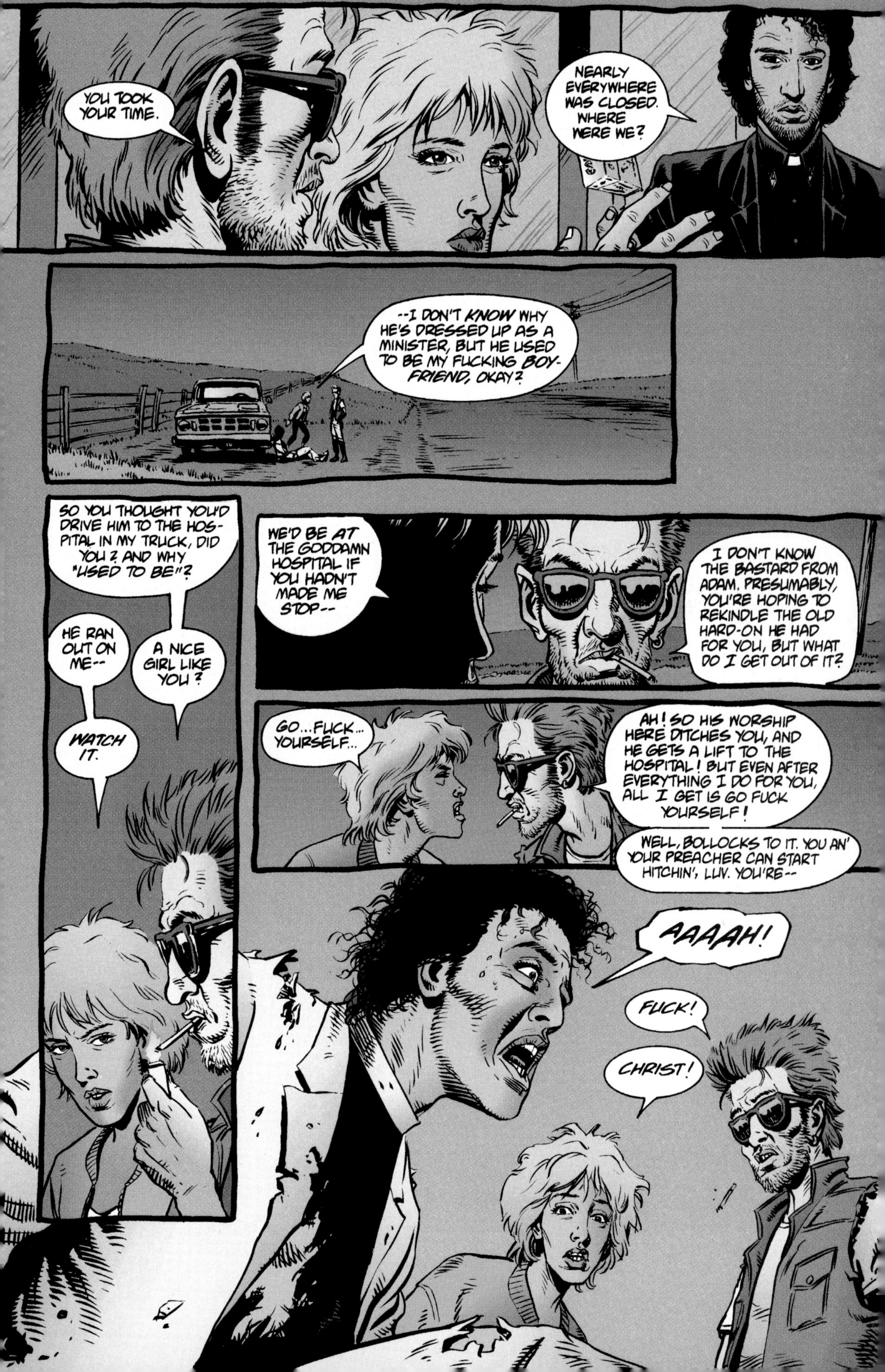
YOU TOOK YOUR TIME.
NEARLY EVERYWHERE WAS CLOSED. WHERE WERE WE?
--I DON'T KNOW WHY HE'S DRESSED UP AS A MINISTER, BUT HE USED TO BE MY FUCKING BOY-FRIEND, OKAY?
SO YOU THOUGHT YOU'D DRIVE HIM TO THE HOS-PITAL IN MY TRUCK, DID YOU? AND WHY "USED TO BE"?
HE RAN OUT ON ME--
A NICE GIRL LIKE YOU?
WATCH IT.
WE'D BE AT THE GODDAMN HOSPITAL IF YOU HADN'T MADE ME STOP--
I DON'T KNOW THE BASTARD FROM ADAM. PRESUMABLY, YOU'RE HOPING TO REKINDLE THE OLD HARD-ON HE HAD FOR YOU, BUT WHAT DO I GET OUT OF IT?
GO...FUCK... YOURSELF...
AH! SO HIS WORSHIP HERE DITCHES YOU, AND HE GETS A LIFT TO THE HOSPITAL! BUT EVEN AFTER EVERYTHING I DO FOR YOU, ALL I GET IS GO FUCK YOURSELF!
WELL, BOLLOCKS TO IT. YOU AN' YOUR PREACHER CAN START HITCHIN', LUV. YOU'RE--
AAAAH!
FUCK!
CHRIST!

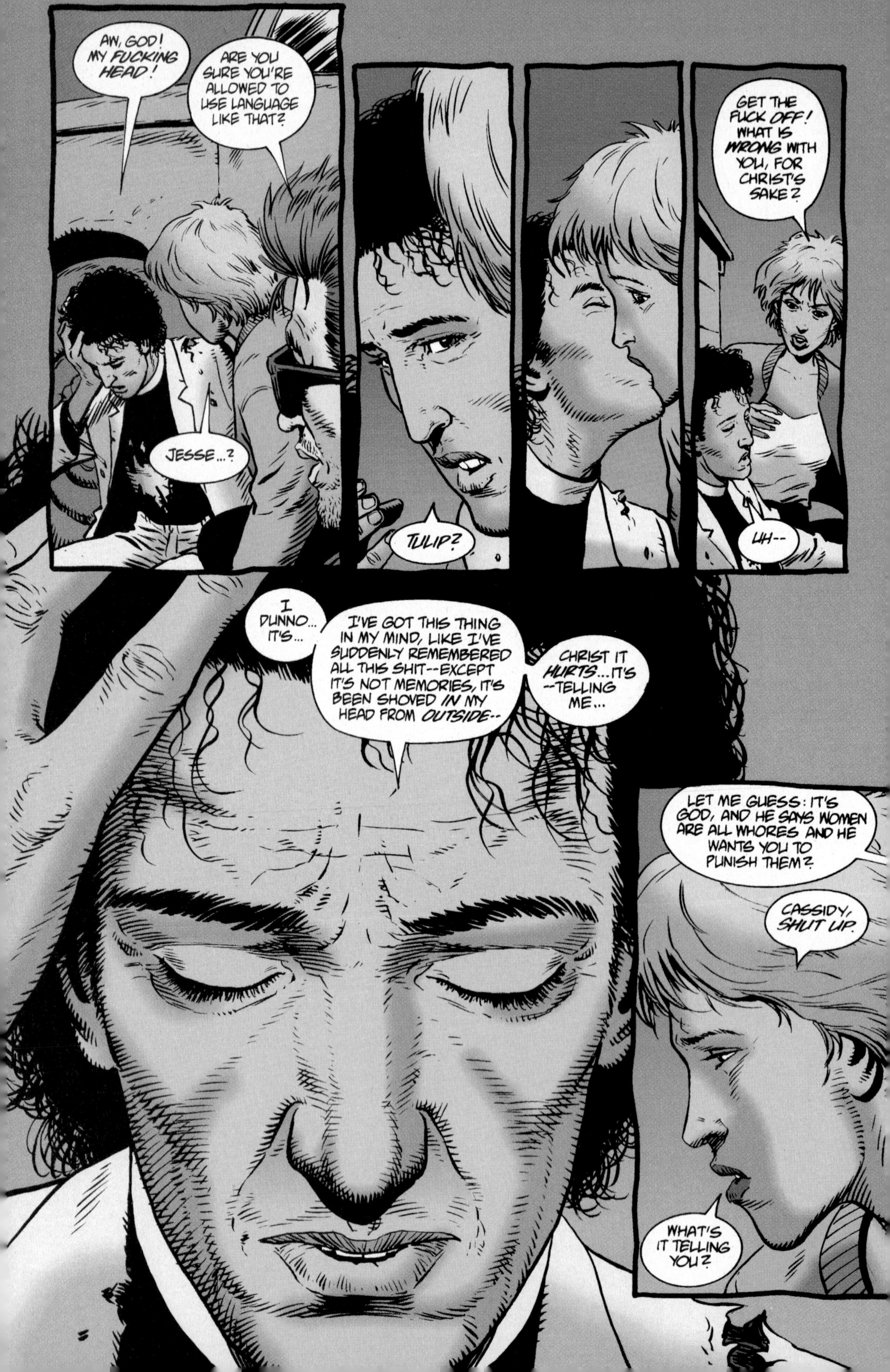
AW, GOD! MY FUCKING HEAD!
ARE YOU SURE YOU'RE ALLOWED TO USE LANGUAGE LIKE THAT?
JESSE...?
TULIP?
GET THE FUCK OFF! WHAT IS WRONG WITH YOU, FOR CHRIST'S SAKE?
UH--
I DUNNO... IT'S...
I'VE GOT THIS THING IN MY MIND, LIKE I'VE SUDDENLY REMEMBERED ALL THIS SHIT--EXCEPT IT'S NOT MEMORIES, IT'S BEEN SHOVED IN MY HEAD FROM OUTSIDE--
CHRIST IT HURTS...IT'S --TELLING ME...
LET ME GUESS: IT'S GOD, AND HE SAYS WOMEN ARE ALL WHORES AND HE WANTS YOU TO PUNISH THEM?
CASSIDY, SHUT UP.
WHAT'S IT TELLING YOU?

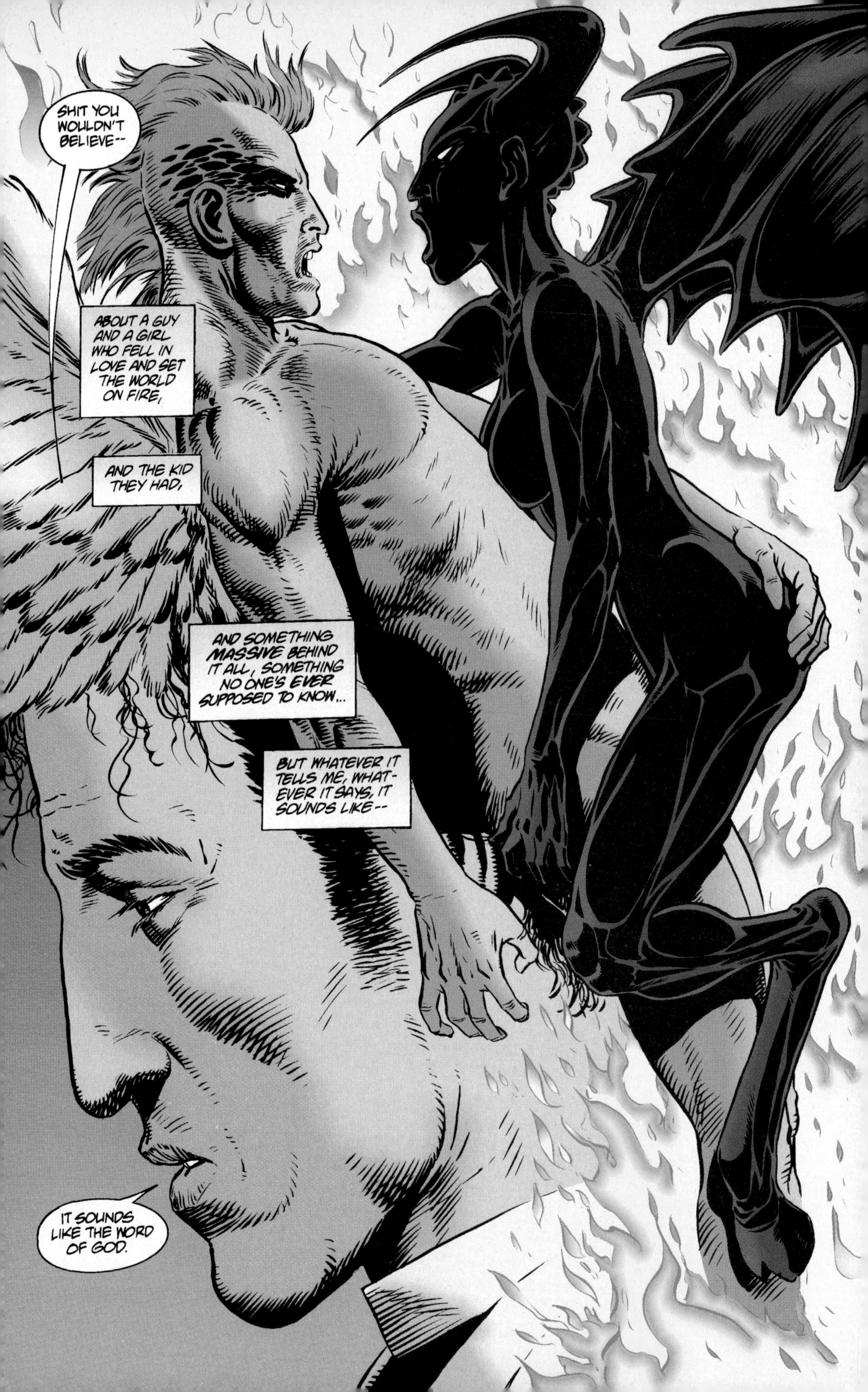
SHIT YOU WOULDN'T BELIEVE--
ABOUT A GUY AND A GIRL WHO FELL IN LOVE AND SET THE WORLD ON FIRE,
AND THE KID THEY HAD,
AND SOMETHING MASSIVE BEHIND IT ALL, SOMETHING NO ONE'S EVER SUPPOSED TO KNOW...
BUT WHATEVER IT TELLS ME, WHATEVER IT SAYS, IT SOUNDS LIKE--
IT SOUNDS LIKE THE WORD OF GOD.

TOLD YOU! HIS FUCKIN' HEAD'S CUT!

HE ALWAYS USED TO BE KIND OF, WELL, ECLECTIC--

BOLLICKS! ALL YOU HAVE TO DO TO BE ECLECTIC IN THIS COUNTRY IS OWN A CHILI PEPPERS ALBUM. WHAT *HE* IS, IS OFF HIS FUCKIN' ROCKER...

DO YOU MEAN LIKE WHEN YOU WERE CURIOUS ENOUGH TO DRIVE MY TRUCK INTO A SODDIN' DEATHZONE?

FOR JESUS' SAKE, TULIP, THIS BLOKE'S RIGHT AT THE EYE OF A FORCE TEN SHIT-STORM! CURIOSITY WON'T JUST *KILL* THE CAT, IT'LL BITE ITS HEAD OFF AND STUMP-FUCK THE REMAINS 'TIL THE SUN COMES UP!

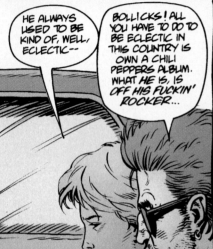

NO, I'M CURIOUS ABOUT THIS--

WELL, I'M NOT HANGIN' AROUND HERE TO BE--HERE, HOL' ON...I CAN SMELL COPS...

MM? WHAT D'YOU MEAN

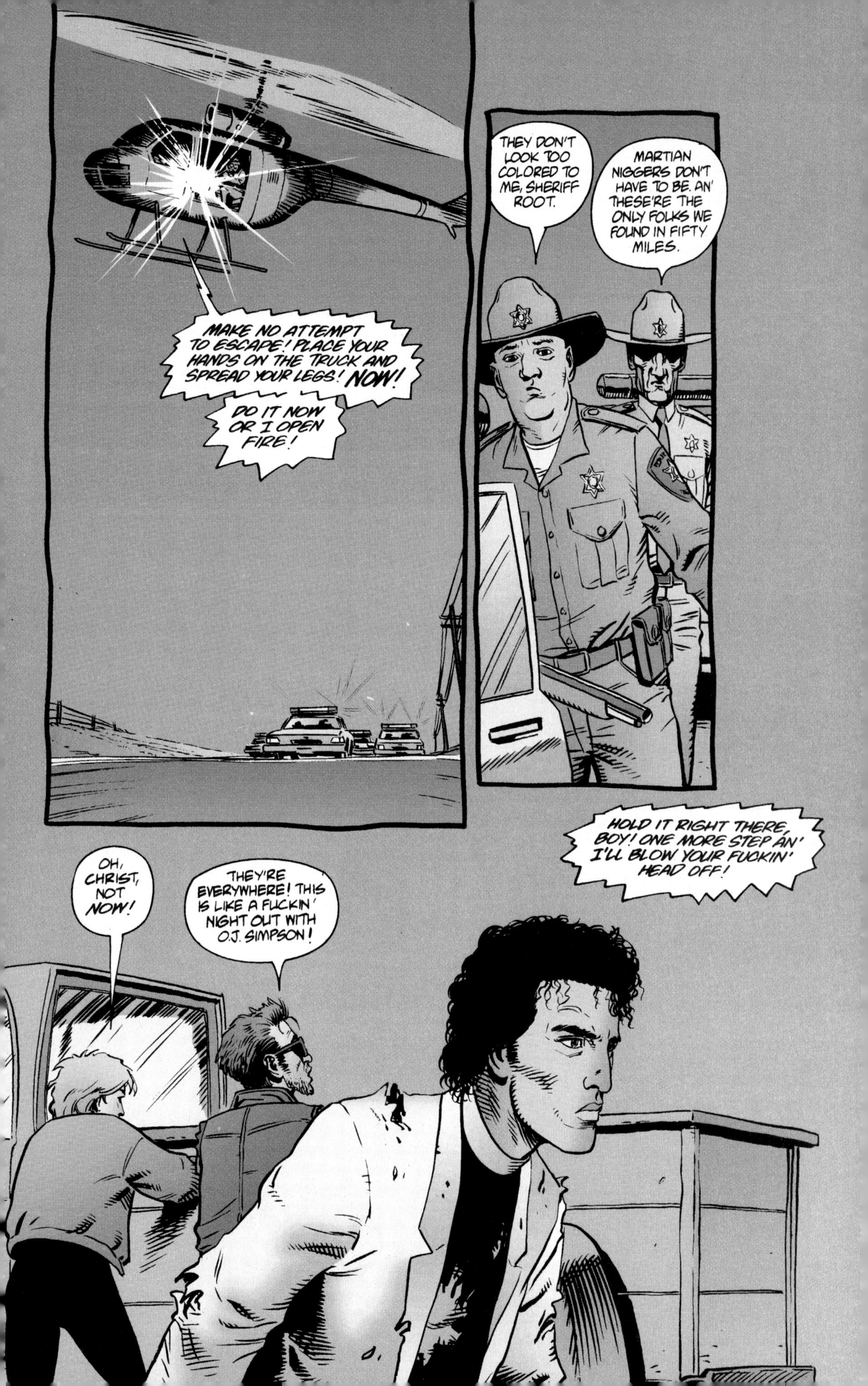
MAKE NO ATTEMPT TO ESCAPE! PLACE YOUR HANDS ON THE TRUCK AND SPREAD YOUR LEGS! NOW!
DO IT NOW OR I OPEN FIRE!
THEY DON'T LOOK TOO COLORED TO ME, SHERIFF ROOT.
MARTIAN NIGGERS DON'T HAVE TO BE. AN' THESE'RE THE ONLY FOLKS WE FOUND IN FIFTY MILES.
HOLD IT RIGHT THERE, BOY! ONE MORE STEP AN' I'LL BLOW YOUR FUCKIN' HEAD OFF!
OH, CHRIST, NOT NOW!
THEY'RE EVERYWHERE! THIS IS LIKE A FUCKIN' NIGHT OUT WITH O.J. SIMPSON!

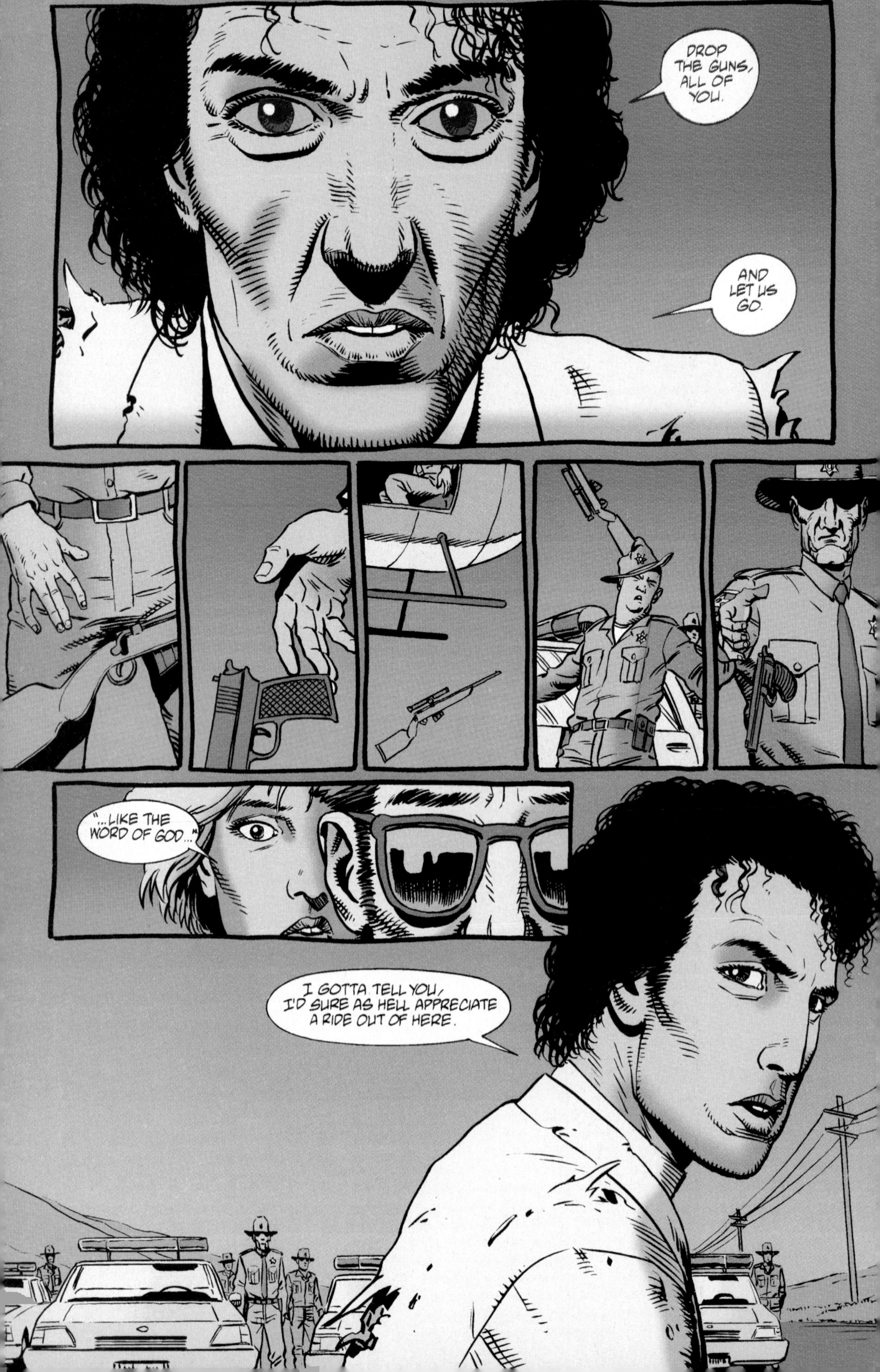
DROP THE GUNS, ALL OF YOU.
AND LET US GO.
"...LIKE THE WORD OF GOD..."
I GOTTA TELL YOU, I'D SURE AS HELL APPRECIATE A RIDE OUT OF HERE.

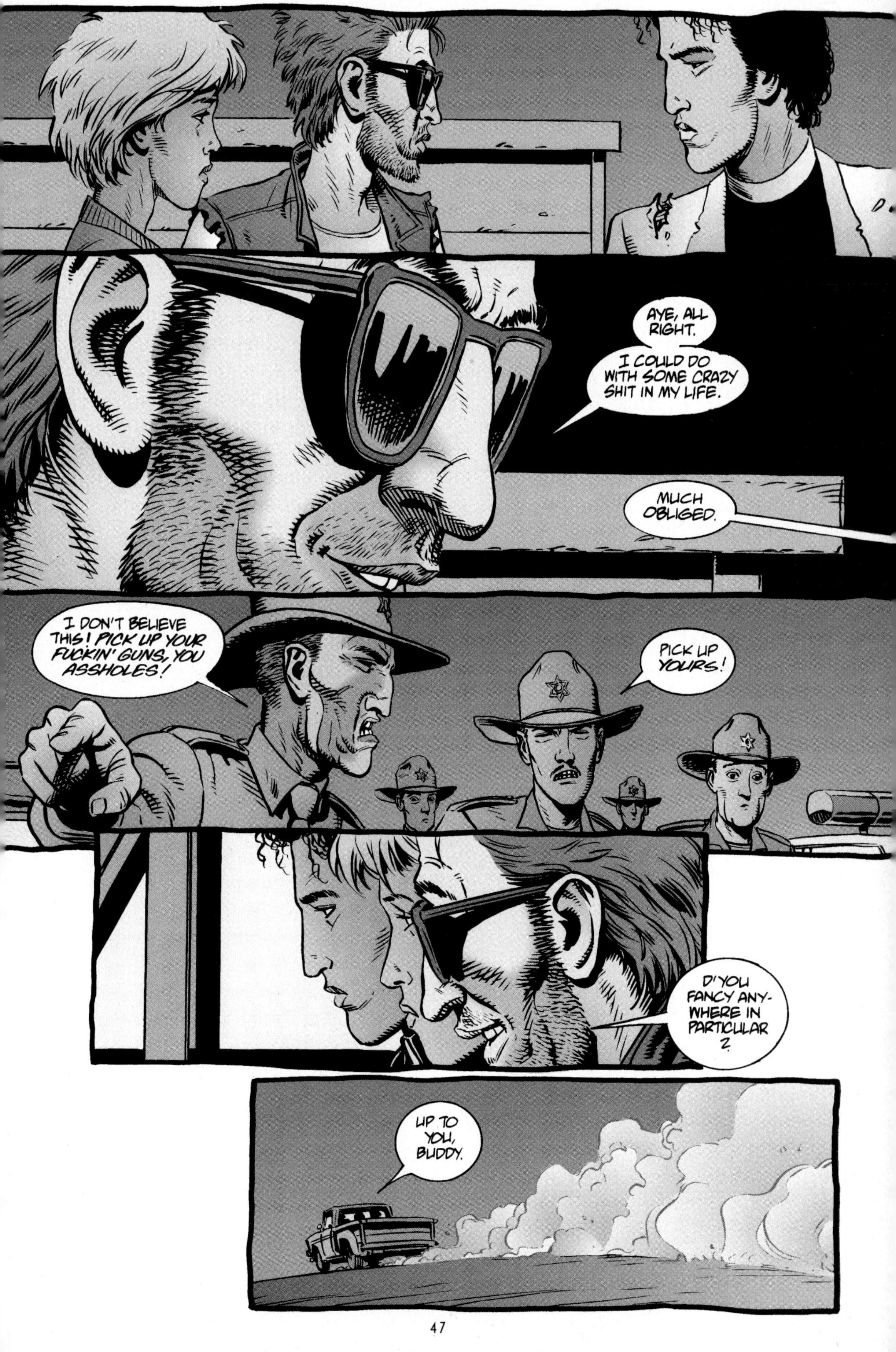
AYE, ALL RIGHT.
I COULD DO WITH SOME CRAZY SHIT IN MY LIFE.
MUCH OBLIGED.
I DON'T BELIEVE THIS! PICK UP YOUR FUCKIN' GUNS, YOU ASSHOLES!
PICK UP YOURS!
D'YOU FANCY ANY-WHERE IN PARTICULAR ?
UP TO YOU, BUDDY.

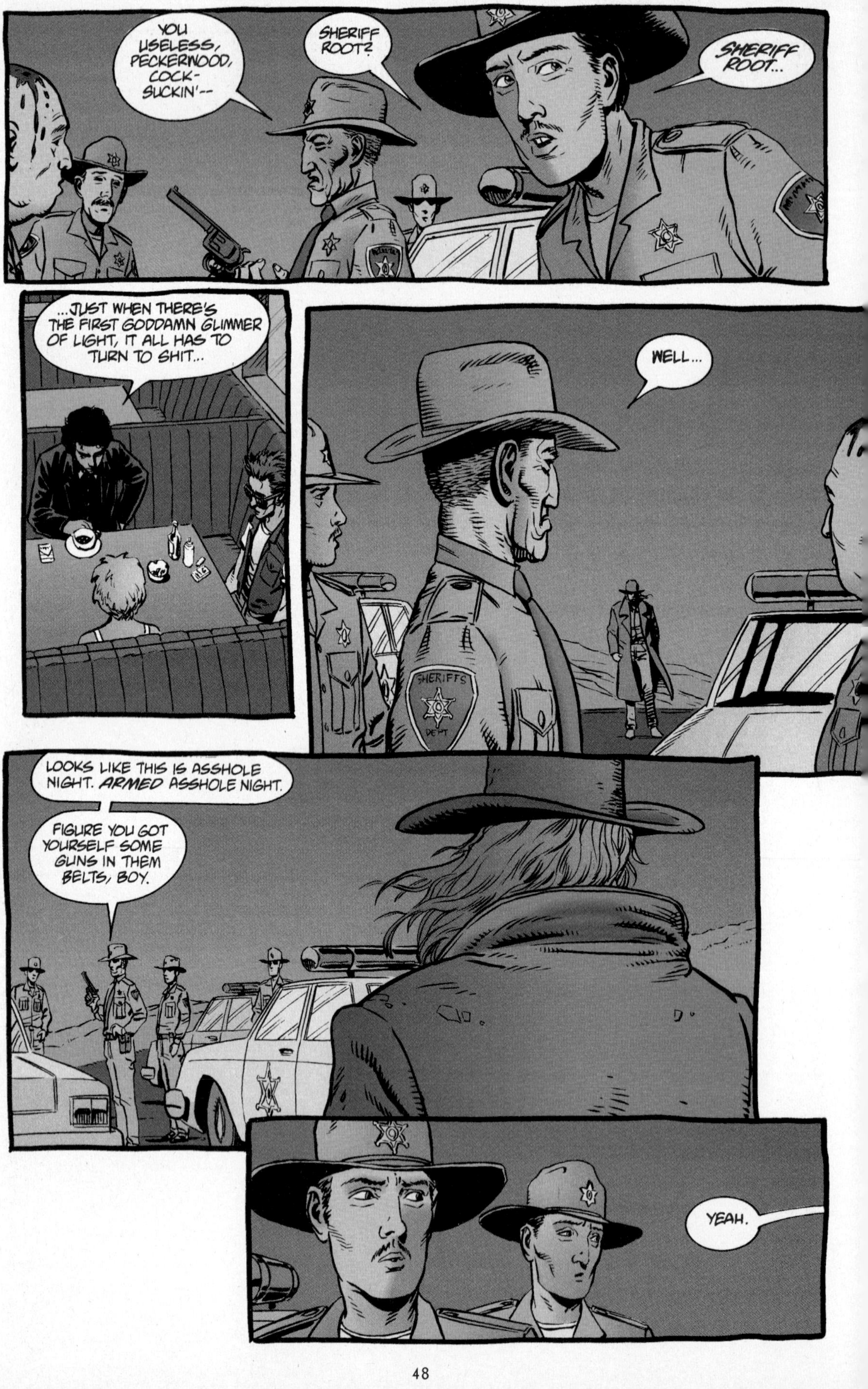
YOU USELESS, PECKERWOOD, COCK-SUCKIN'--
SHERIFF ROOT?
SHERIFF ROOT...
...JUST WHEN THERE'S THE FIRST GODDAMN GLIMMER OF LIGHT, IT ALL HAS TO TURN TO SHIT...
WELL...
SHERIFFS DEPT
LOOKS LIKE THIS IS ASSHOLE NIGHT. ARMED ASSHOLE NIGHT.
FIGURE YOU GOT YOURSELF SOME GUNS IN THEM BELTS, BOY.
YEAH.

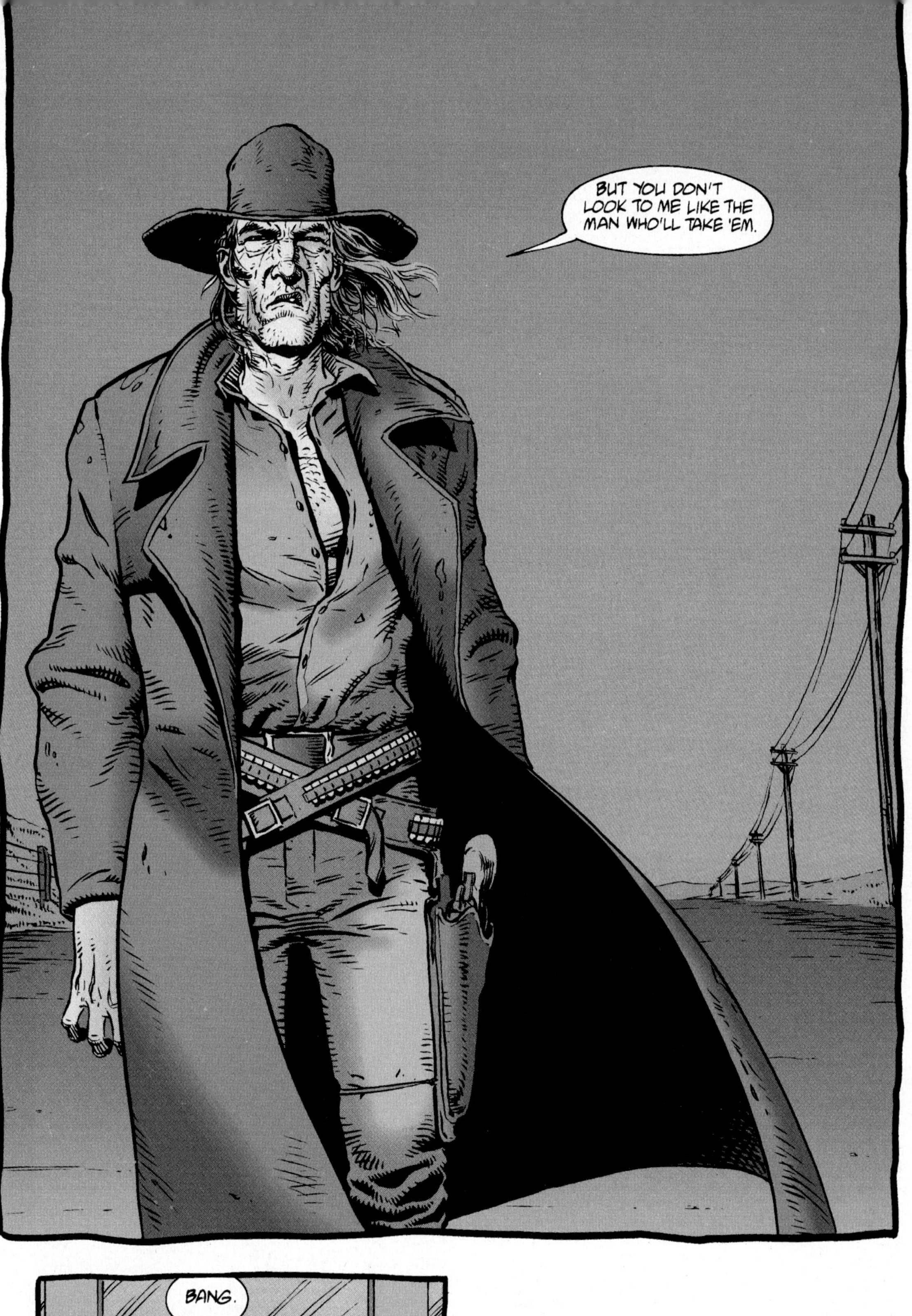
BUT YOU DON'T LOOK TO ME LIKE THE MAN WHO'LL TAKE 'EM.

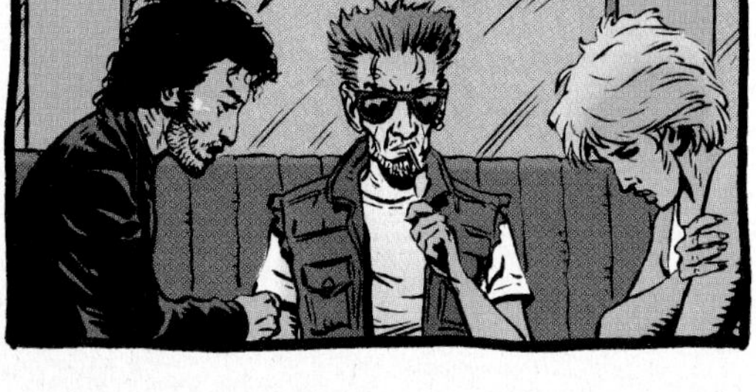
BANG.

NEXT: JUST A FEW COPS

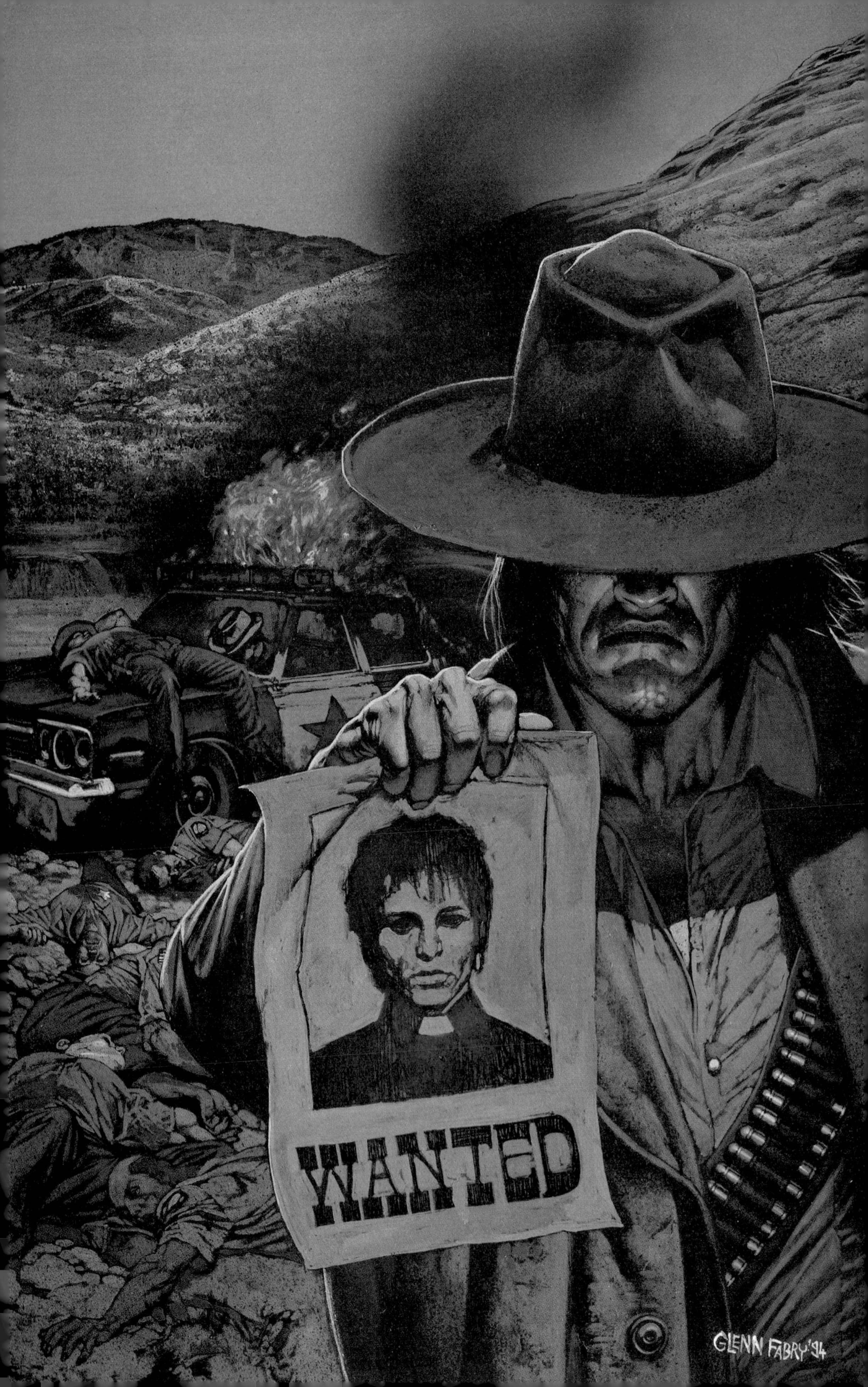
WANTED
GLENN FABRY '94

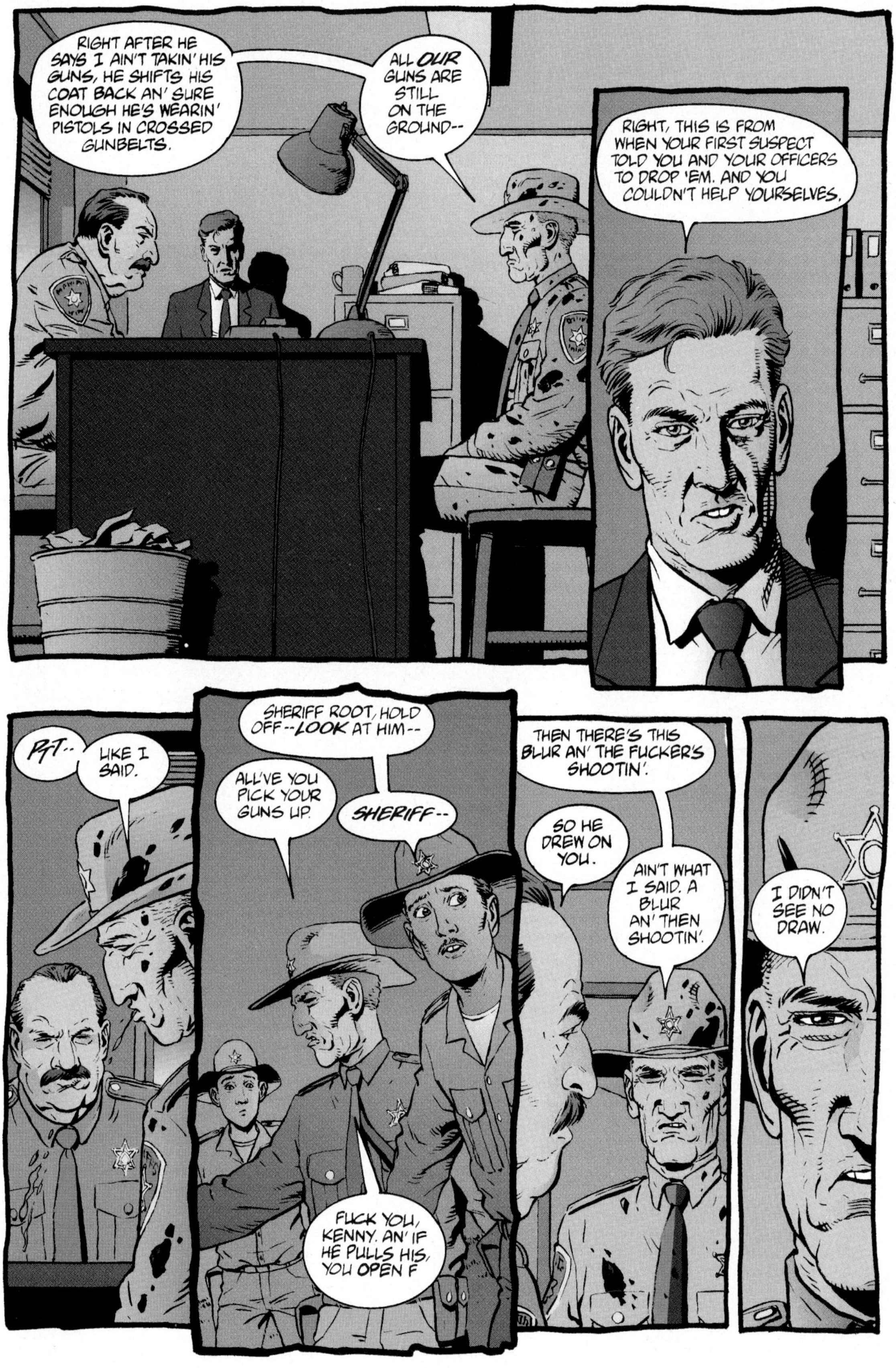
RIGHT AFTER HE SAYS I AIN'T TAKIN' HIS GUNS, HE SHIFTS HIS COAT BACK AN' SURE ENOUGH HE'S WEARIN' PISTOLS IN CROSSED GUNBELTS.
ALL OUR GUNS ARE STILL ON THE GROUND--
RIGHT, THIS IS FROM WHEN YOUR FIRST SUSPECT TOLD YOU AND YOUR OFFICERS TO DROP 'EM. AND YOU COULDN'T HELP YOURSELVES.
PTT..
LIKE I SAID.
SHERIFF ROOT, HOLD OFF--LOOK AT HIM--
ALL'VE YOU PICK YOUR GUNS UP.
SHERIFF--
FUCK YOU, KENNY. AN' IF HE PULLS HIS, YOU OPEN F
THEN THERE'S THIS BLUR AN' THE FUCKER'S SHOOTIN'.
SO HE DREW ON YOU.
AIN'T WHAT I SAID. A BLUR AN' THEN SHOOTIN'.
I DIDN'T SEE NO DRAW.

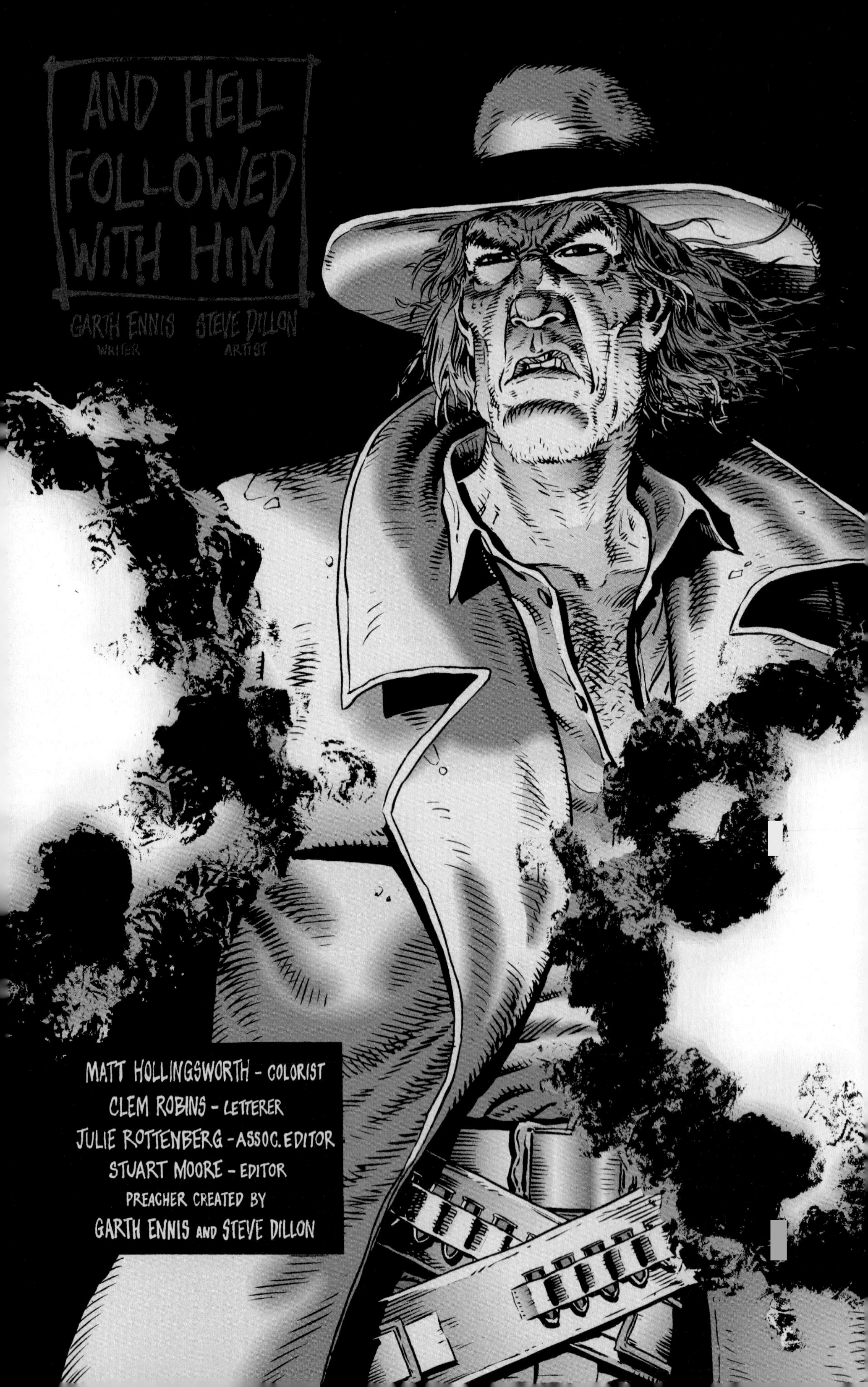
AND HELL FOLLOWED WITH HIM
GARTH ENNIS WRITER
STEVE DILLON ARTIST
MATT HOLLINGSWORTH - COLORIST
CLEM ROBINS - LETTERER
JULIE ROTTENBERG - ASSOC. EDITOR
STUART MOORE - EDITOR
PREACHER CREATED BY
GARTH ENNIS AND STEVE DILLON

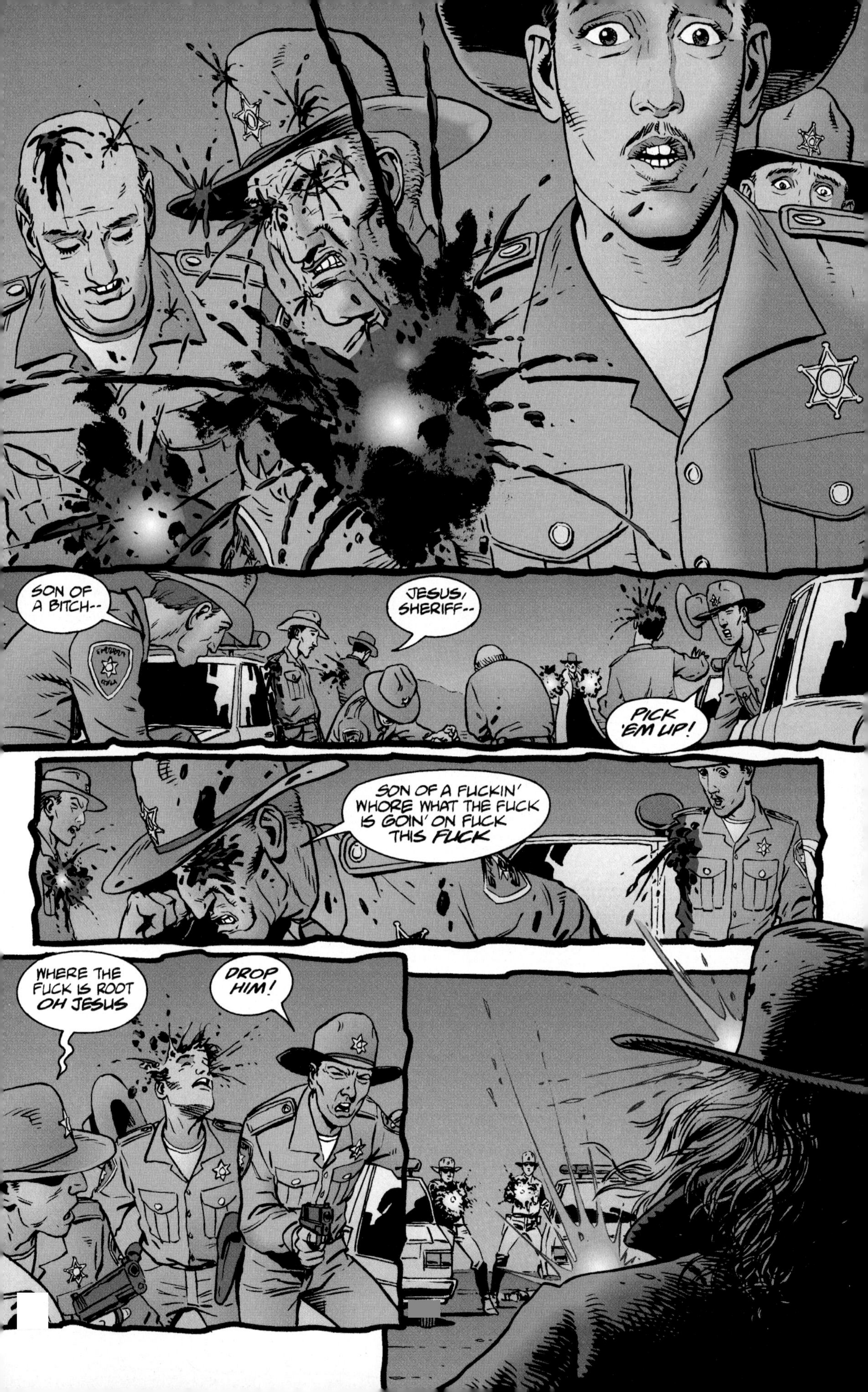
SON OF A BITCH--
JESUS, SHERIFF--
PICK 'EM UP!
SON OF A FUCKIN' WHORE WHAT THE FUCK IS GOIN' ON FUCK THIS FUCK
WHERE THE FUCK IS ROOT OH JESUS
DROP HIM!

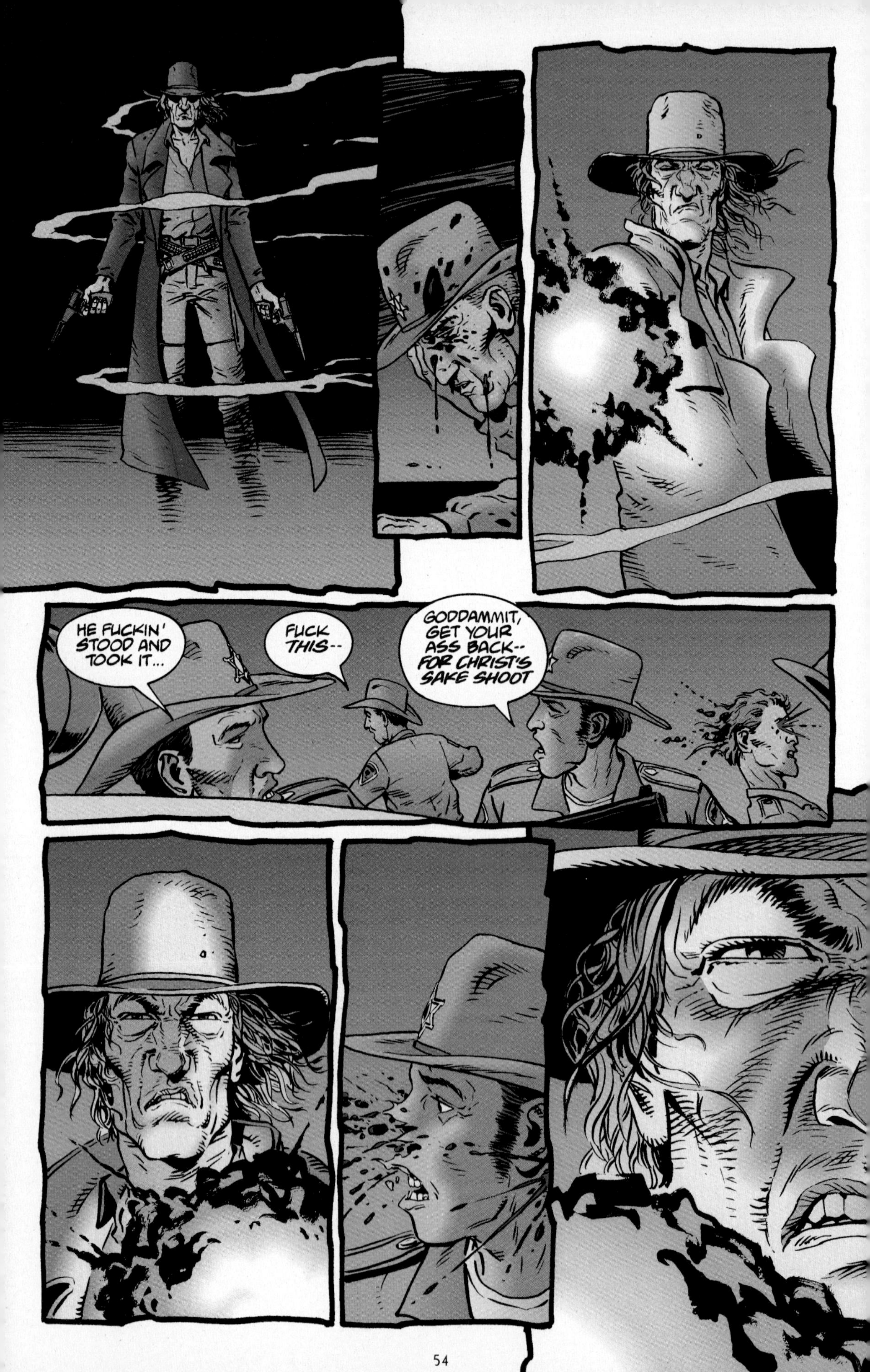
HE FUCKIN' STOOD AND TOOK IT...
FUCK THIS--
GODDAMMIT, GET YOUR ASS BACK-- FOR CHRIST'S SAKE SHOOT

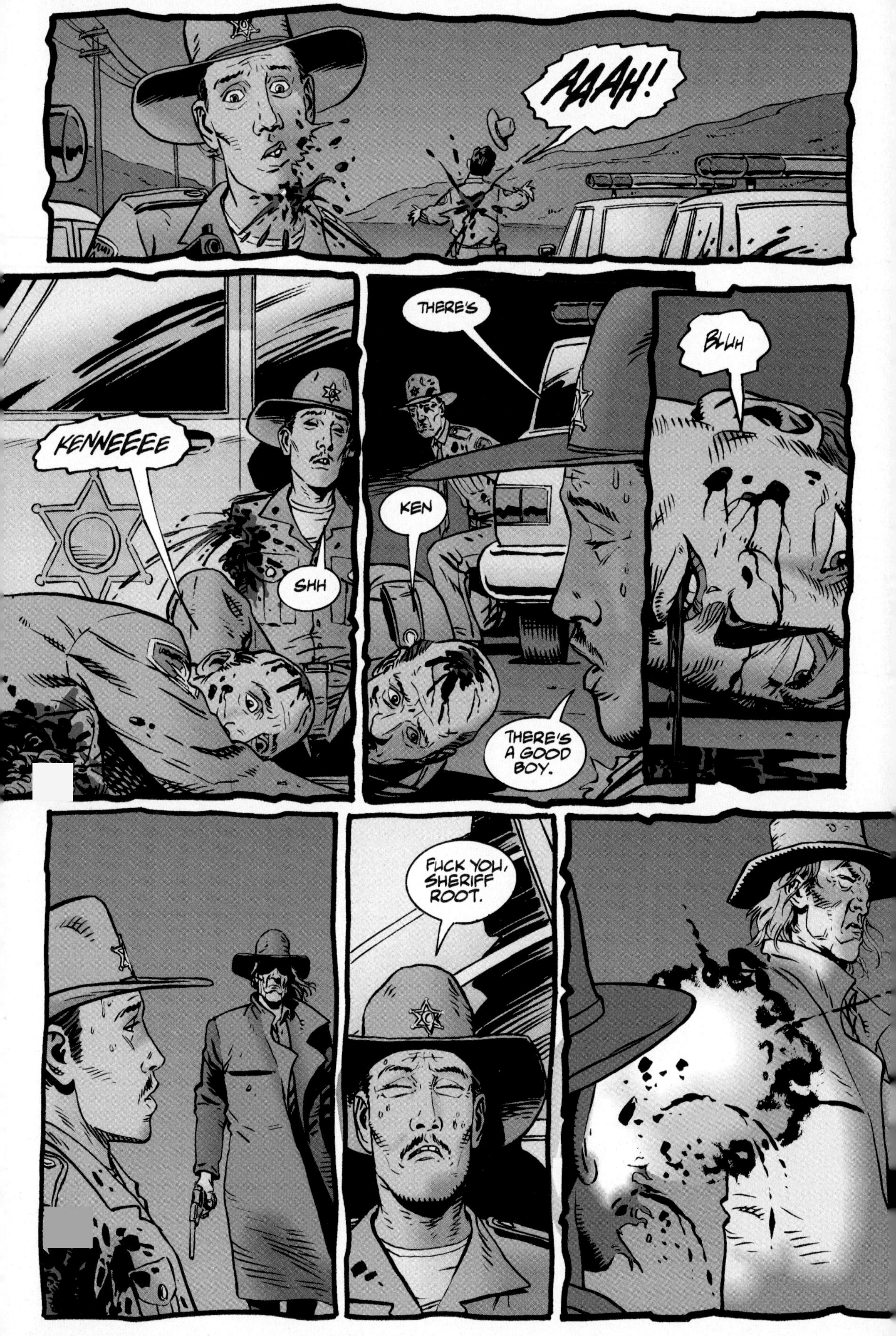
AAAH!
KENNEEEE
SHH
THERE'S
KEN
THERE'S A GOOD BOY.
BLUH
FUCK YOU, SHERIFF ROOT.

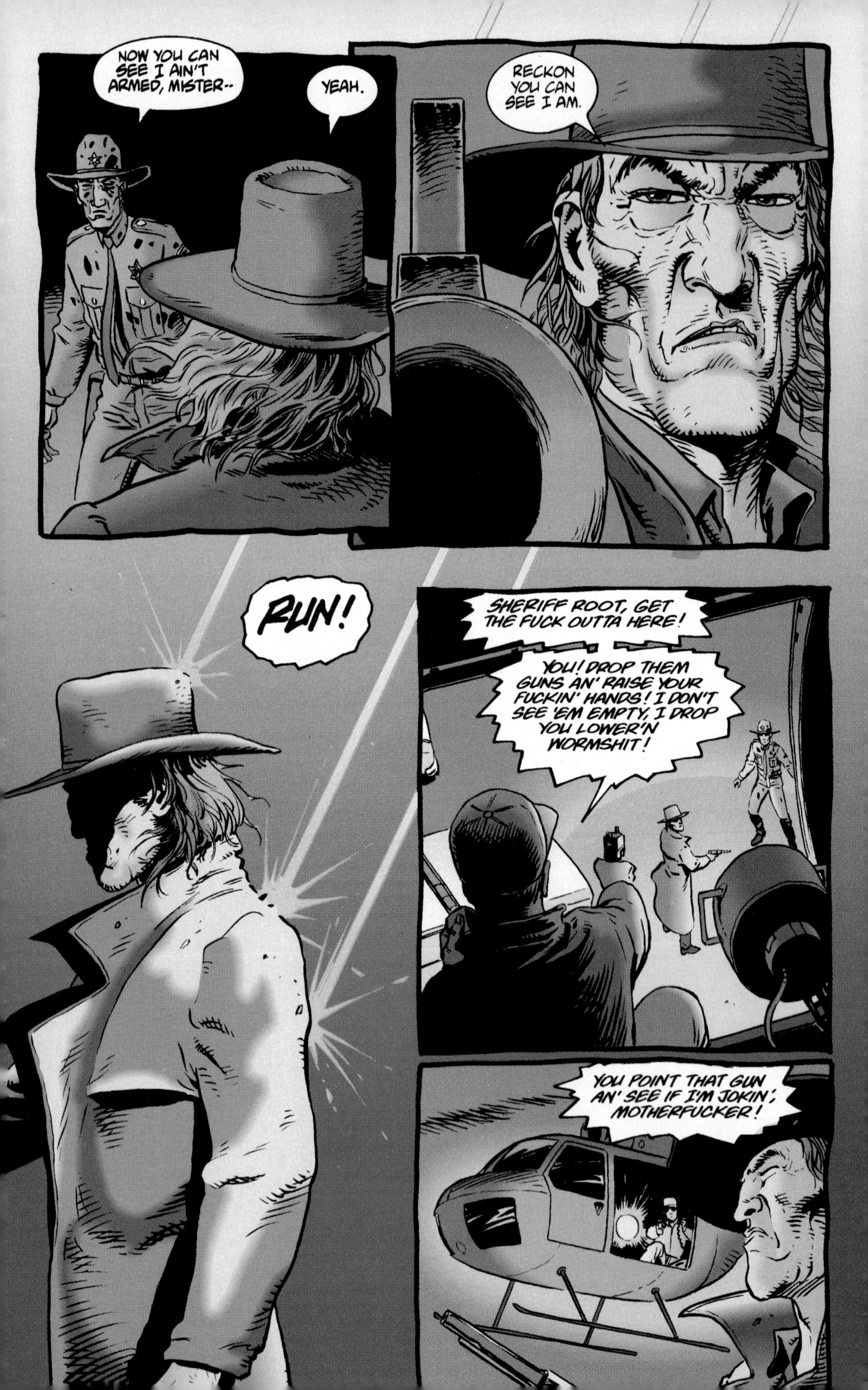

NOW YOU CAN SEE I AIN'T ARMED, MISTER--
YEAH.
RECKON YOU CAN SEE I AM.
RUN!
SHERIFF ROOT, GET THE FUCK OUTTA HERE!
YOU! DROP THEM GUNS AN' RAISE YOUR FUCKIN' HANDS! I DON'T SEE 'EM EMPTY, I DROP YOU LOWER'N WORMSHIT!
YOU POINT THAT GUN AN' SEE IF I'M JOKIN', MOTHERFUCKER!

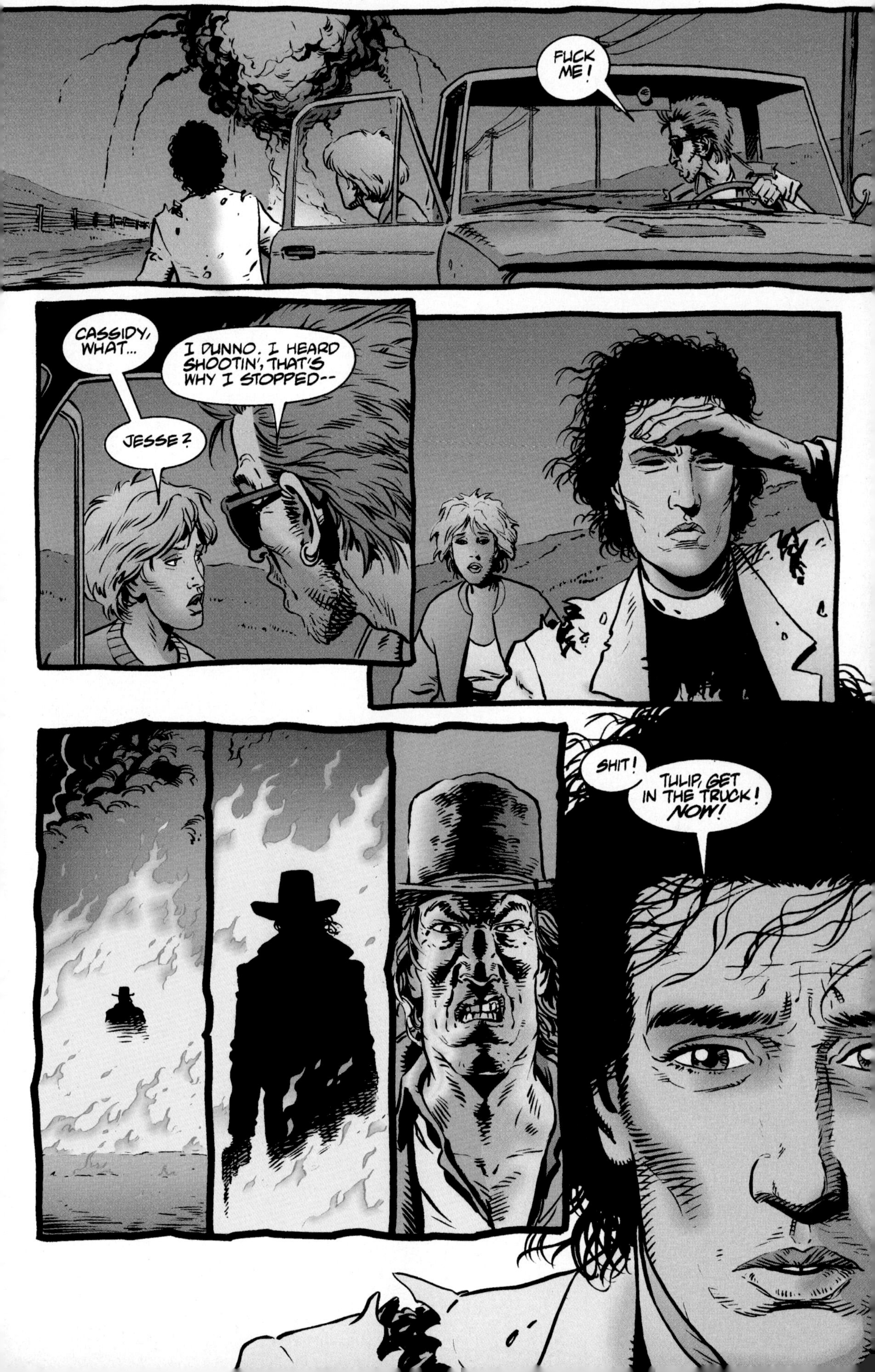
FUCK ME!
CASSIDY, WHAT...
I DUNNO. I HEARD SHOOTIN', THAT'S WHY I STOPPED--
JESSE?
SHIT!
TULIP, GET IN THE TRUCK! NOW!

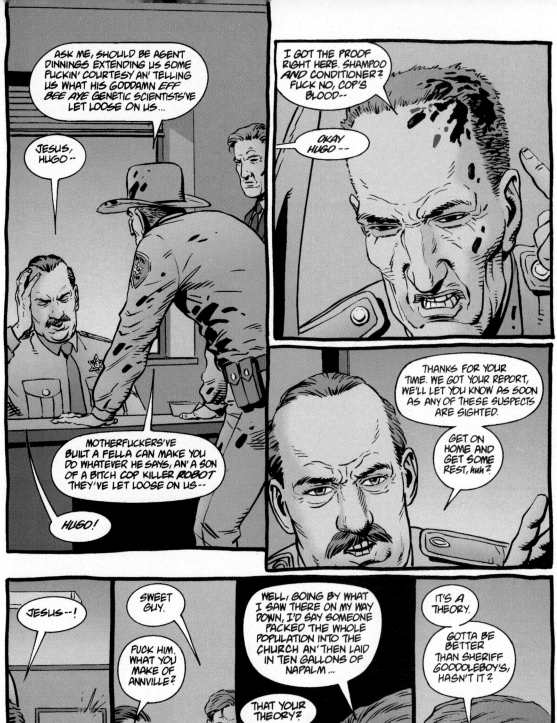

ASK ME, SHOULD BE AGENT DINNINGS EXTENDING US SOME FUCKIN' COURTESY AN' TELLING US WHAT HIS GODDAMN *EFF BEE AYE* GENETIC SCIENTISTS'VE LET LOOSE ON US...

JESUS, HUGO--

I GOT THE PROOF RIGHT HERE. SHAMPOO *AND* CONDITIONER? FUCK NO, COP'S BLOOD--

OKAY HUGO --

MOTHERFUCKERS'VE BUILT A FELLA CAN MAKE YOU DO WHATEVER HE SAYS, AN' A SON OF A BITCH COP KILLER *ROBOT* THEY'VE LET LOOSE ON US--

HUGO!

THANKS FOR YOUR TIME. WE GOT YOUR REPORT, WE'LL LET YOU KNOW AS SOON AS ANY OF THESE SUSPECTS ARE SIGHTED.

GET ON HOME AND GET SOME REST, huh?

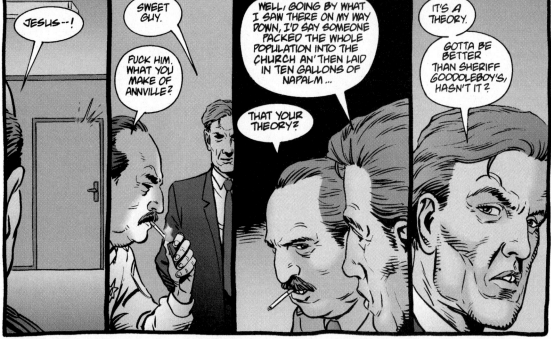

JESUS--!

SWEET GUY.

FUCK HIM. WHAT YOU MAKE OF ANNVILLE?

WELL, GOING BY WHAT I SAW THERE ON MY WAY DOWN, I'D SAY SOMEONE PACKED THE WHOLE POPULATION INTO THE CHURCH AN' THEN LAID IN TEN GALLONS OF NAPALM ...

THAT YOUR THEORY?

IT'S A THEORY.

GOTTA BE BETTER THAN SHERIFF GOODOLEBOY'S, HASN'T IT?

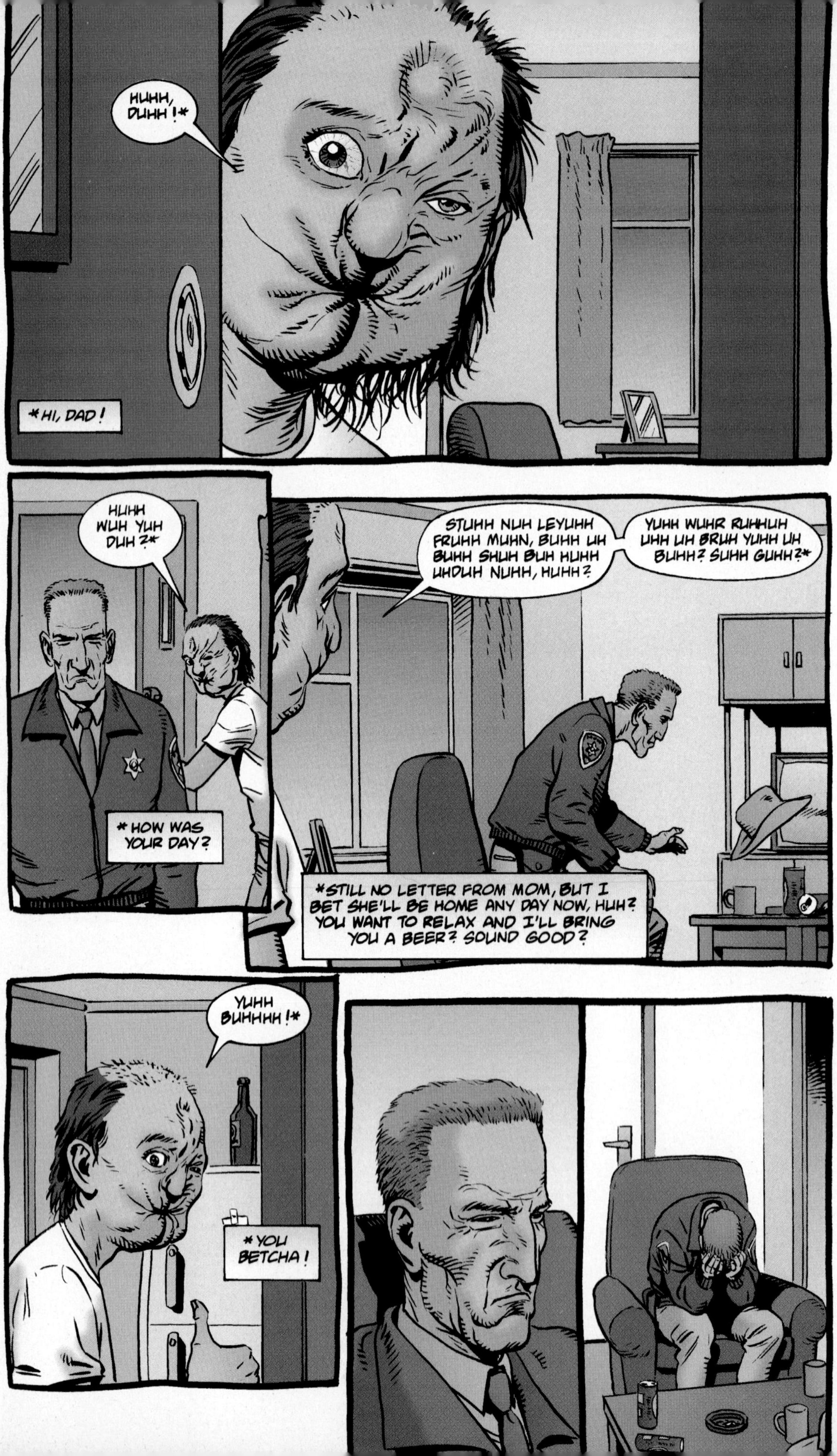

HUHH, DUHH!*
*HI, DAD!
HUHH WUH YUH DUH?*
*HOW WAS YOUR DAY?
STUHH NUH LEYUHH FRUHH MUHN, BUHH UH BUHH SHUH BUH HUHH UHDUH NUHH, HUHH?
YUHH WUHR RUHHUH UHH UH BRUH YUHH UH BUHH? SUHH GUHH?*
*STILL NO LETTER FROM MOM, BUT I BET SHE'LL BE HOME ANY DAY NOW, HUH? YOU WANT TO RELAX AND I'LL BRING YOU A BEER? SOUND GOOD?
YUHH BUHHHH!*
*YOU BETCHA!

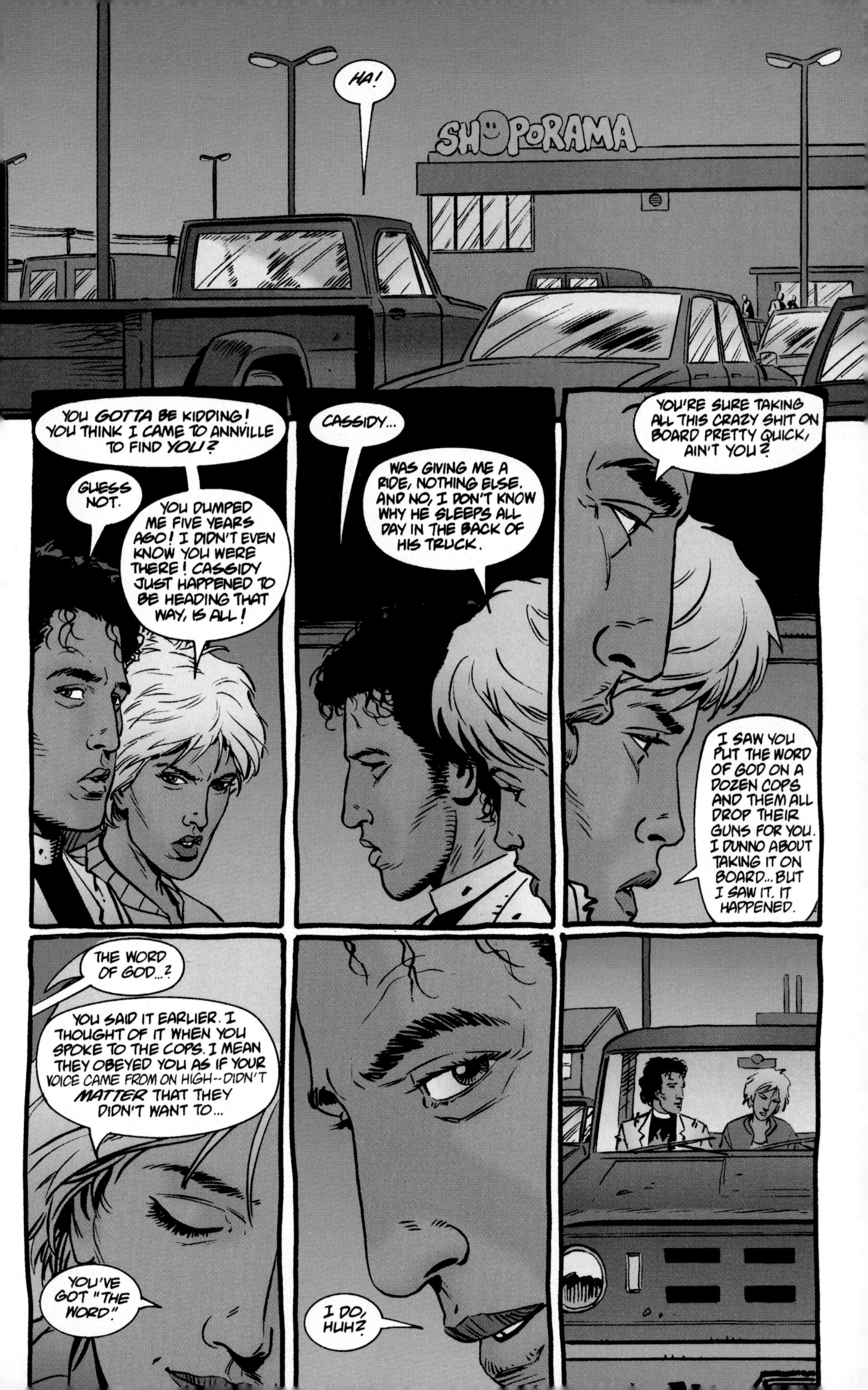
HA!
SHOPORAMA
YOU GOTTA BE KIDDING! YOU THINK I CAME TO ANNVILLE TO FIND YOU?
GUESS NOT.
YOU DUMPED ME FIVE YEARS AGO! I DIDN'T EVEN KNOW YOU WERE THERE! CASSIDY JUST HAPPENED TO BE HEADING THAT WAY, IS ALL!
CASSIDY...
WAS GIVING ME A RIDE, NOTHING ELSE. AND NO, I DON'T KNOW WHY HE SLEEPS ALL DAY IN THE BACK OF HIS TRUCK.
YOU'RE SURE TAKING ALL THIS CRAZY SHIT ON BOARD PRETTY QUICK, AIN'T YOU?
I SAW YOU PUT THE WORD OF GOD ON A DOZEN COPS AND THEM ALL DROP THEIR GUNS FOR YOU. I DUNNO ABOUT TAKING IT ON BOARD... BUT I SAW IT. IT HAPPENED.
THE WORD OF GOD...?
YOU SAID IT EARLIER. I THOUGHT OF IT WHEN YOU SPOKE TO THE COPS. I MEAN THEY OBEYED YOU AS IF YOUR VOICE CAME FROM ON HIGH--DIDN'T MATTER THAT THEY DIDN'T WANT TO...
YOU'VE GOT "THE WORD."
I DO, HUH?

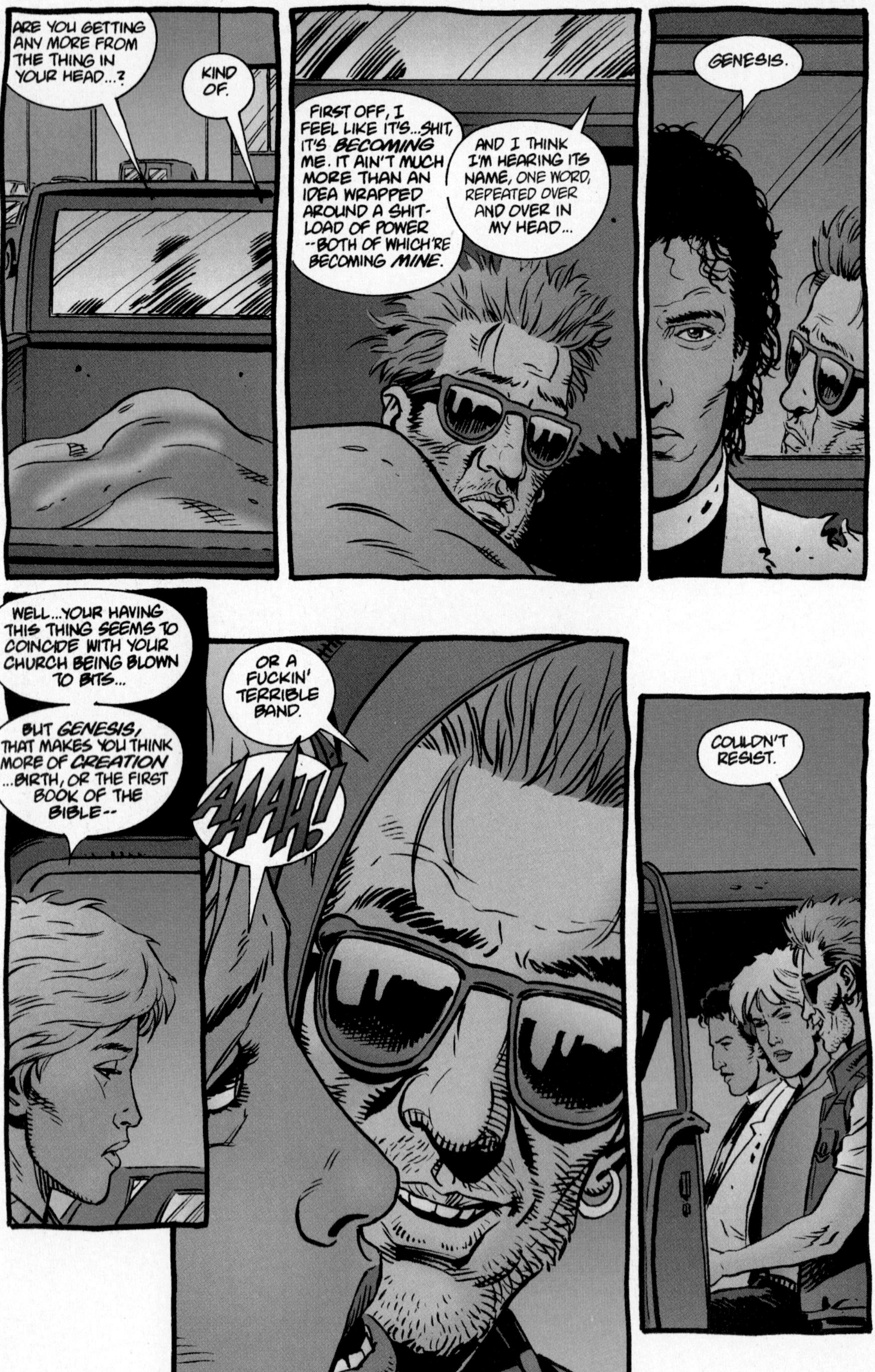
ARE YOU GETTING ANY MORE FROM THE THING IN YOUR HEAD...?
KIND OF.
FIRST OFF, I FEEL LIKE IT'S...SHIT, IT'S BECOMING ME. IT AIN'T MUCH MORE THAN AN IDEA WRAPPED AROUND A SHIT-LOAD OF POWER --BOTH OF WHICH'RE BECOMING MINE.
AND I THINK I'M HEARING ITS NAME, ONE WORD, REPEATED OVER AND OVER IN MY HEAD...
GENESIS.
WELL...YOUR HAVING THIS THING SEEMS TO COINCIDE WITH YOUR CHURCH BEING BLOWN TO BITS...
BUT GENESIS, THAT MAKES YOU THINK MORE OF CREATION ...BIRTH, OR THE FIRST BOOK OF THE BIBLE--
OR A FUCKIN' TERRIBLE BAND.
AAAH!
COULDN'T RESIST.

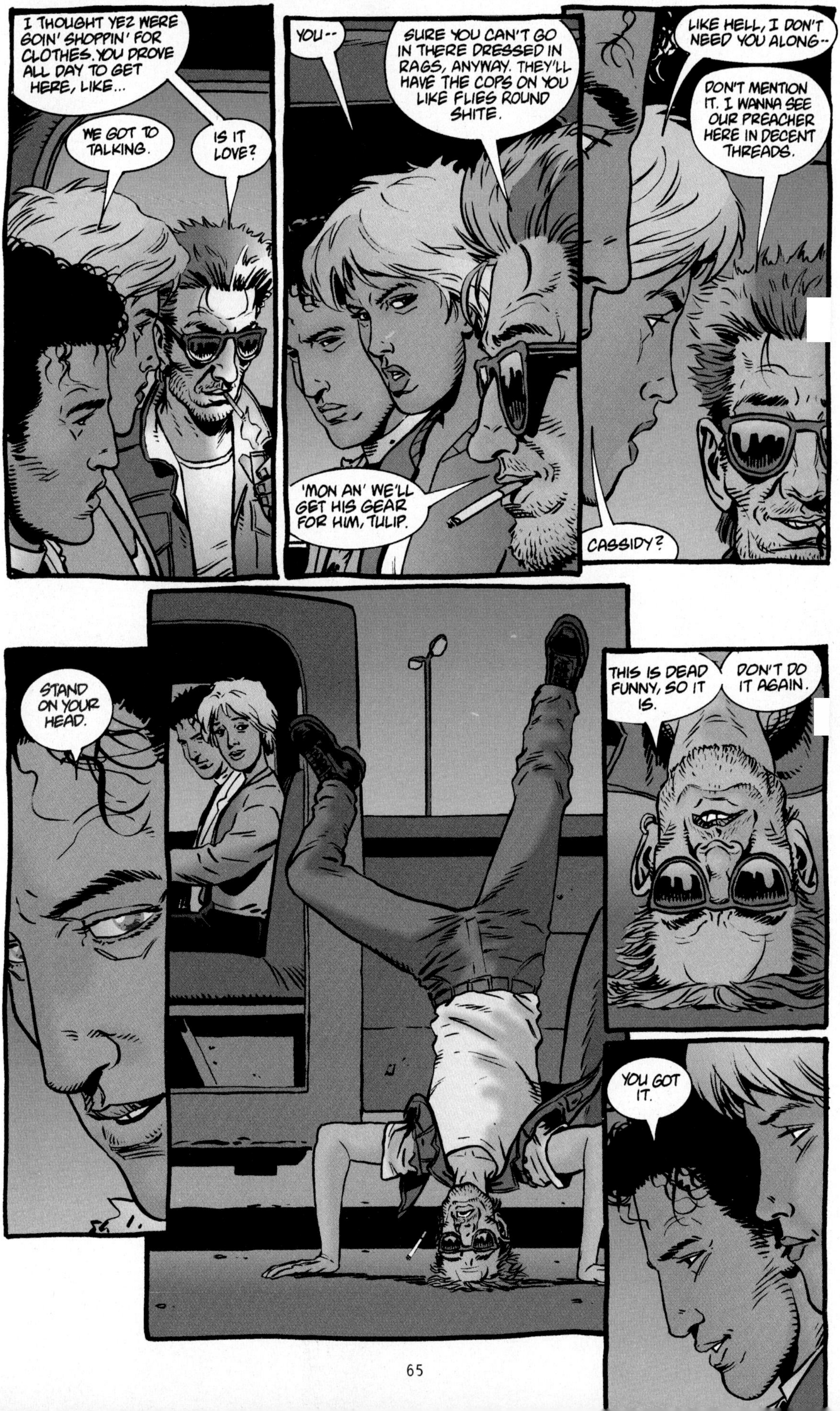
I THOUGHT YEZ WERE GOIN' SHOPPIN' FOR CLOTHES. YOU DROVE ALL DAY TO GET HERE, LIKE...
WE GOT TO TALKING.
IS IT LOVE?
YOU--
SURE YOU CAN'T GO IN THERE DRESSED IN RAGS, ANYWAY. THEY'LL HAVE THE COPS ON YOU LIKE FLIES ROUND SHITE.
'MON AN' WE'LL GET HIS GEAR FOR HIM, TULIP.
LIKE HELL, I DON'T NEED YOU ALONG--
DON'T MENTION IT. I WANNA SEE OUR PREACHER HERE IN DECENT THREADS.
CASSIDY?
STAND ON YOUR HEAD.
THIS IS DEAD FUNNY, SO IT IS.
DON'T DO IT AGAIN.
YOU GOT IT.

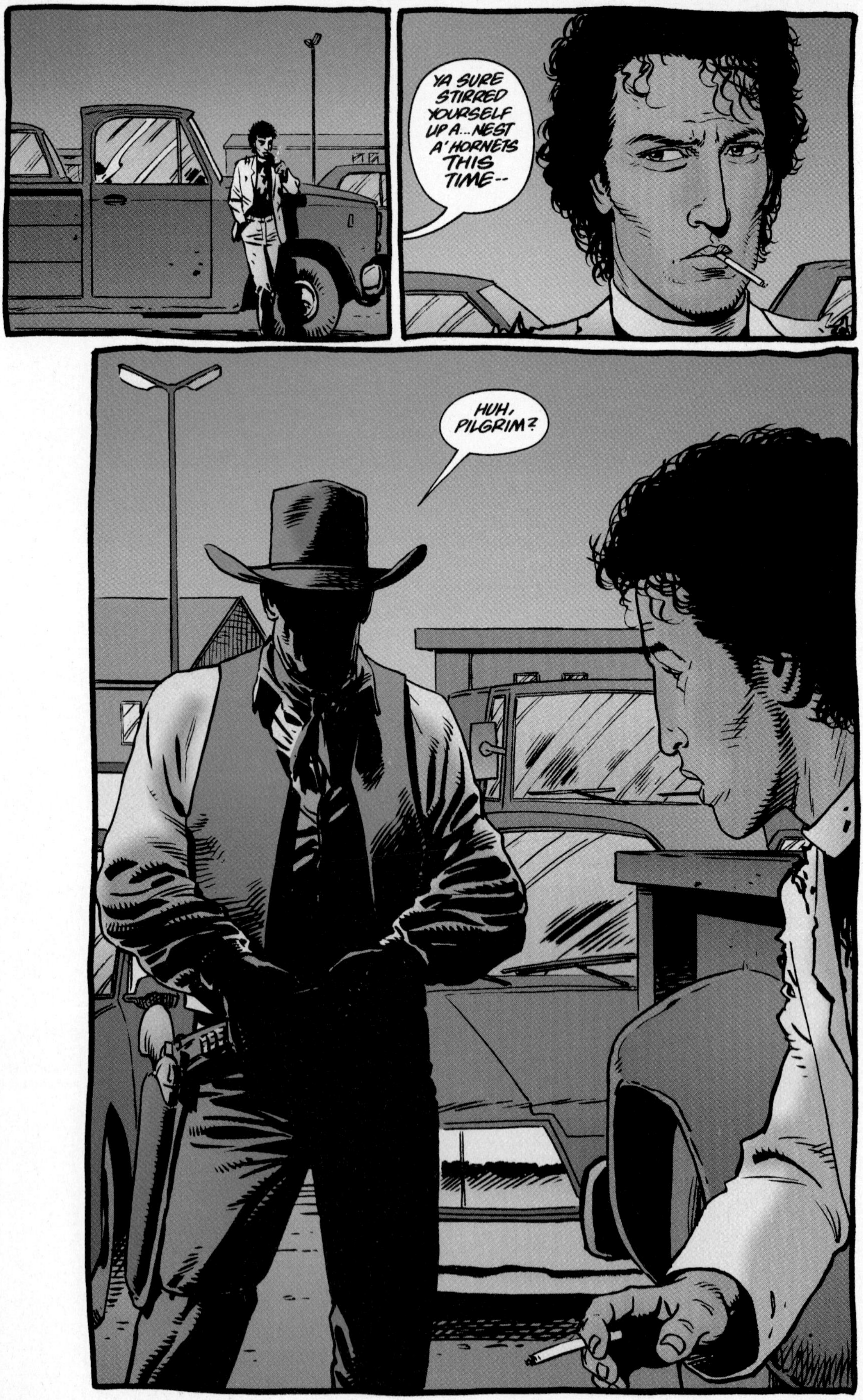
YA SURE STIRRED YOURSELF UP A...NEST A' HORNETS THIS TIME--
HUH, PILGRIM?

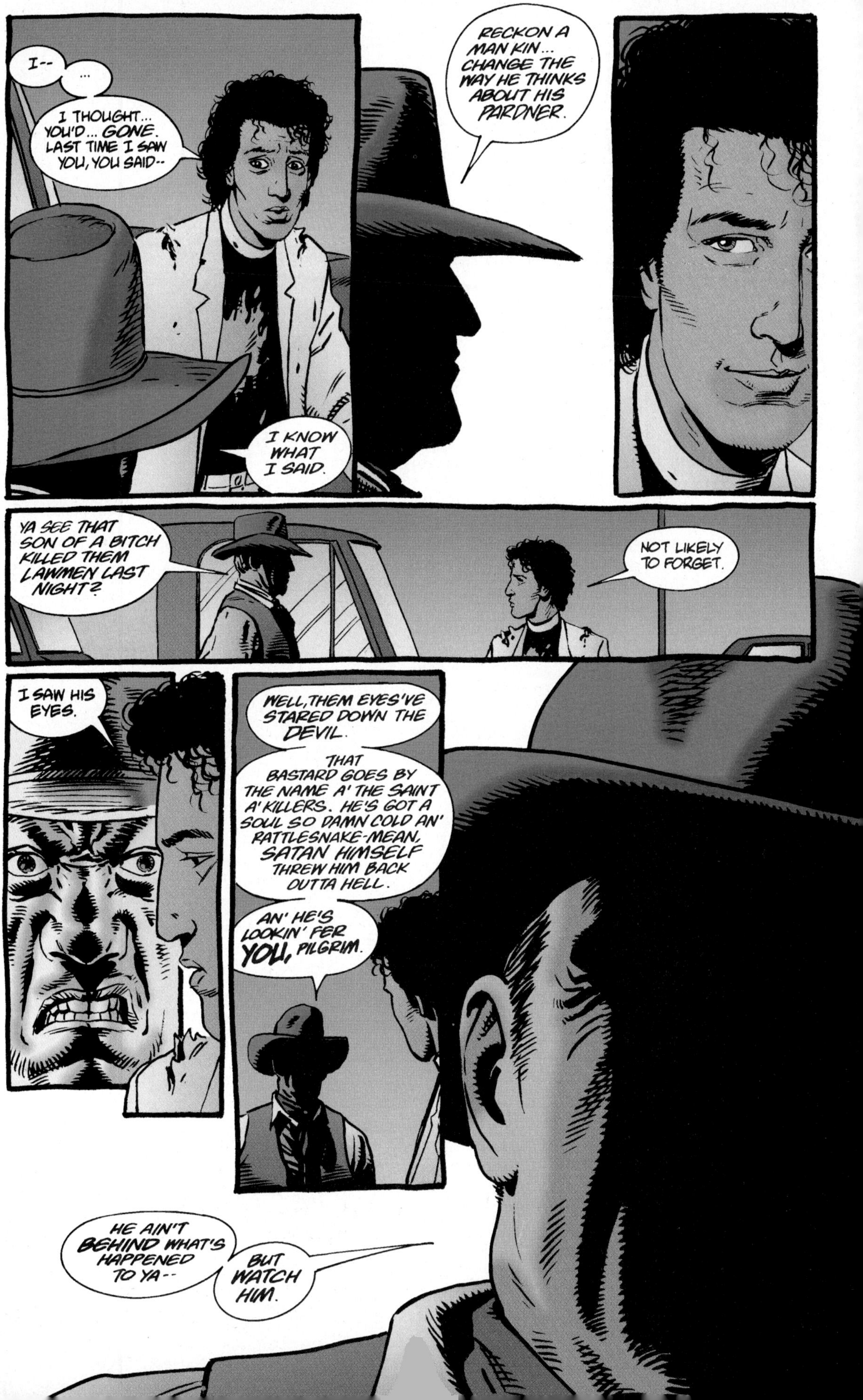
I--
...
I THOUGHT... YOU'D... GONE. LAST TIME I SAW YOU, YOU SAID--
I KNOW WHAT I SAID.
RECKON A MAN KIN... CHANGE THE WAY HE THINKS ABOUT HIS PARDNER.
YA SEE THAT SON OF A BITCH KILLED THEM LAWMEN LAST NIGHT?
NOT LIKELY TO FORGET.
I SAW HIS EYES.
WELL, THEM EYES'VE STARED DOWN THE DEVIL.
THAT BASTARD GOES BY THE NAME A' THE SAINT A' KILLERS. HE'S GOT A SOUL SO DAMN COLD AN' RATTLESNAKE-MEAN, SATAN HIMSELF THREW HIM BACK OUTTA HELL.
AN' HE'S LOOKIN' FER YOU, PILGRIM.
HE AIN'T BEHIND WHAT'S HAPPENED TO YA--
BUT WATCH HIM.

WHITE JEANS AN' A BLACK SHIRT?

IT'S WHAT HE LIKES.

YOU WOULD KNOW, I SUPPOSE.

WE WERE TOGETHER A YEAR AND A HALF. I CAN'T HELP IT, CAN I?

I'M NOT CRITICIZIN'.

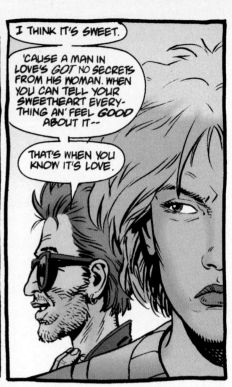

I THINK IT'S SWEET.

'CAUSE A MAN IN LOVE'S GOT NO SECRETS FROM HIS WOMAN. WHEN YOU CAN TELL YOUR SWEETHEART EVERYTHING AN' FEEL GOOD ABOUT IT--

THAT'S WHEN YOU KNOW IT'S LOVE.

I FUCKING HATE YOU, CASSIDY. I REALLY FUCKING HATE YOU--

STILL, AS I OFTEN SAY: SOMETIMES IT'S HARD TO BE A WOMAN, Y'KNOW? THE WAY YOU GIVE ALL YOUR LOVE TO ...JUST ONE MAN...

♪MM-HMM-HMM-HMM, MM-HMM-HMM...HMM-MM-HMM-HMMM, HMM-HM-MMM...

IS THERE A LEATHER GOODS STORE IN THE MALL?

UH... YEAH...

HOW ABOUT SOMEWHERE I CAN BUY MATCHES AN' GASOLINE?

'CAUSE AFTER ALL HE'S--JUST A MAN.

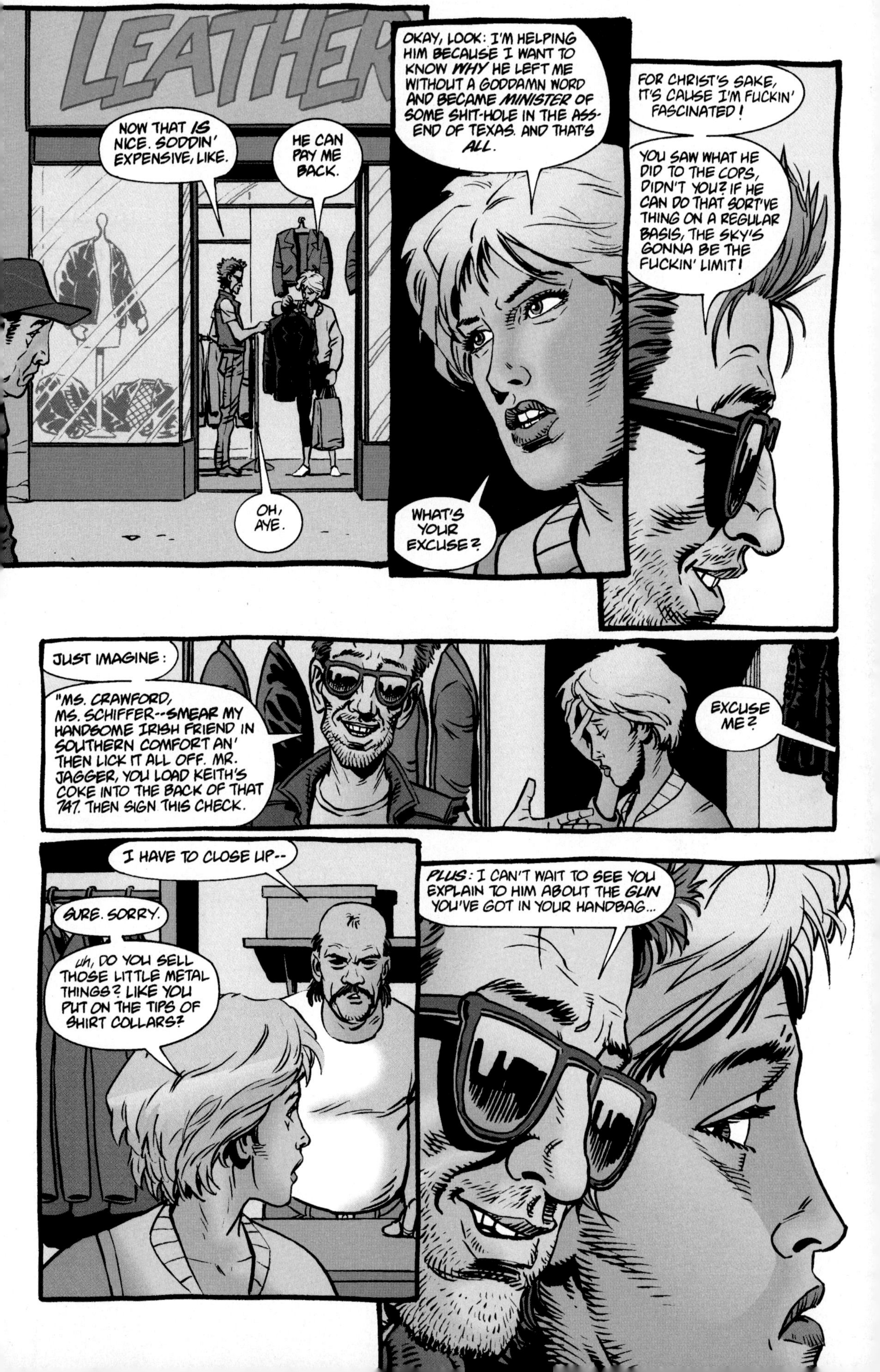
LEATHER
NOW THAT *IS* NICE. SODDIN' EXPENSIVE, LIKE.
HE CAN PAY ME BACK.
OH, AYE.
OKAY, LOOK: I'M HELPING HIM BECAUSE I WANT TO KNOW *WHY* HE LEFT ME WITHOUT A GODDAMN WORD AND BECAME *MINISTER* OF SOME SHIT-HOLE IN THE ASS-END OF TEXAS. AND THAT'S *ALL*.
WHAT'S YOUR EXCUSE?
FOR CHRIST'S SAKE, IT'S CAUSE I'M FUCKIN' FASCINATED!
YOU SAW WHAT HE DID TO THE COPS, DIDN'T YOU? IF HE CAN DO THAT SORT'VE THING ON A REGULAR BASIS, THE SKY'S GONNA BE THE FUCKIN' LIMIT!
JUST IMAGINE:
"MS. CRAWFORD, MS. SCHIFFER--SMEAR MY HANDSOME IRISH FRIEND IN SOUTHERN COMFORT AN' THEN LICK IT ALL OFF. MR. JAGGER, YOU LOAD KEITH'S COKE INTO THE BACK OF THAT 747. THEN SIGN THIS CHECK.
EXCUSE ME?
I HAVE TO CLOSE UP--
SURE. SORRY.
uh, DO YOU SELL THOSE LITTLE METAL THINGS? LIKE YOU PUT ON THE TIPS OF SHIRT COLLARS?
PLUS: I CAN'T WAIT TO SEE YOU EXPLAIN TO HIM ABOUT THE *GUN* YOU'VE GOT IN YOUR HANDBAG...

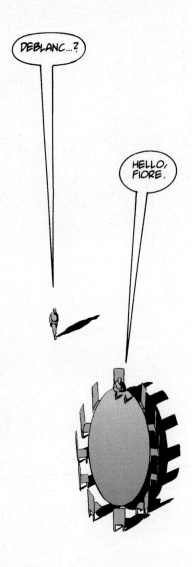

DEBLANC...?

HELLO, FIORE.

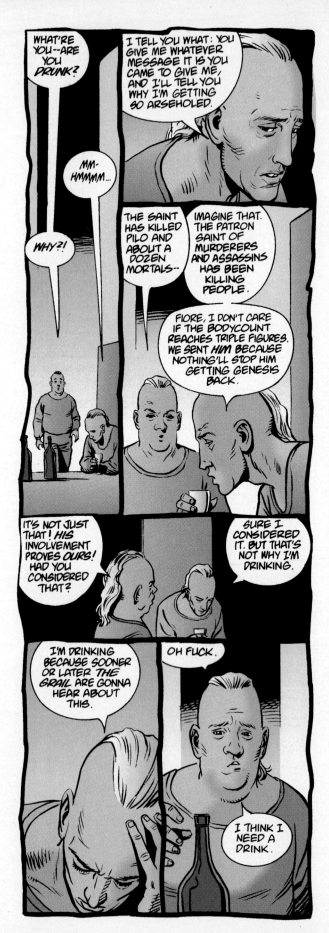

WHAT'RE YOU--ARE YOU *DRUNK?*

I TELL YOU WHAT: YOU GIVE ME WHATEVER MESSAGE IT IS YOU CAME TO GIVE ME, AND I'LL TELL YOU WHY I'M GETTING SO ARSEHOLED.

MM--HMMMM...

WHY?!

THE SAINT HAS KILLED PILO AND ABOUT A DOZEN MORTALS--

IMAGINE THAT. THE PATRON SAINT OF MURDERERS AND ASSASSINS HAS BEEN KILLING PEOPLE.

FIORE, I DON'T CARE IF THE BODYCOUNT REACHES TRIPLE FIGURES. WE SENT *HIM* BECAUSE NOTHING'LL STOP HIM GETTING GENESIS BACK.

IT'S NOT JUST THAT! *HIS* INVOLVEMENT PROVES *OURS!* HAD YOU CONSIDERED THAT?

SURE I CONSIDERED IT. BUT THAT'S NOT WHY I'M DRINKING.

I'M DRINKING BECAUSE SOONER OR LATER *THE GRAIL* ARE GONNA HEAR ABOUT THIS.

OH FUCK.

I THINK I NEED A DRINK.

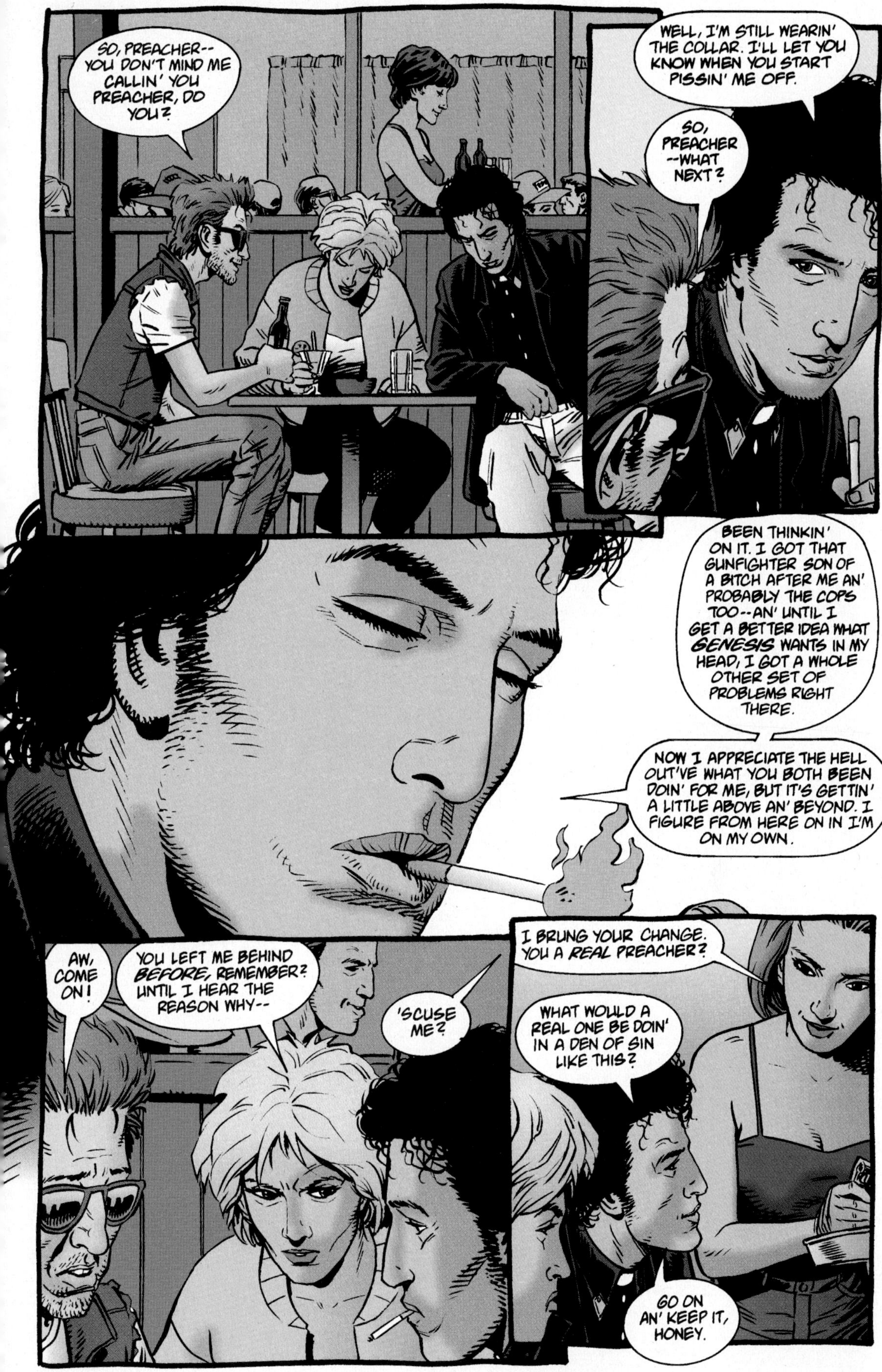
SO, PREACHER-- YOU DON'T MIND ME CALLIN' YOU PREACHER, DO YOU?
WELL, I'M STILL WEARIN' THE COLLAR. I'LL LET YOU KNOW WHEN YOU START PISSIN' ME OFF.
SO, PREACHER --WHAT NEXT?
BEEN THINKIN' ON IT. I GOT THAT GUNFIGHTER SON OF A BITCH AFTER ME AN' PROBABLY THE COPS TOO--AN' UNTIL I GET A BETTER IDEA WHAT GENESIS WANTS IN MY HEAD, I GOT A WHOLE OTHER SET OF PROBLEMS RIGHT THERE.
NOW I APPRECIATE THE HELL OUT'VE WHAT YOU BOTH BEEN DOIN' FOR ME, BUT IT'S GETTIN' A LITTLE ABOVE AN' BEYOND. I FIGURE FROM HERE ON IN I'M ON MY OWN.
AW, COME ON!
YOU LEFT ME BEHIND BEFORE, REMEMBER? UNTIL I HEAR THE REASON WHY--
'SCUSE ME?
I BRUNG YOUR CHANGE. YOU A REAL PREACHER?
WHAT WOULD A REAL ONE BE DOIN' IN A DEN OF SIN LIKE THIS?
GO ON AN' KEEP IT, HONEY.

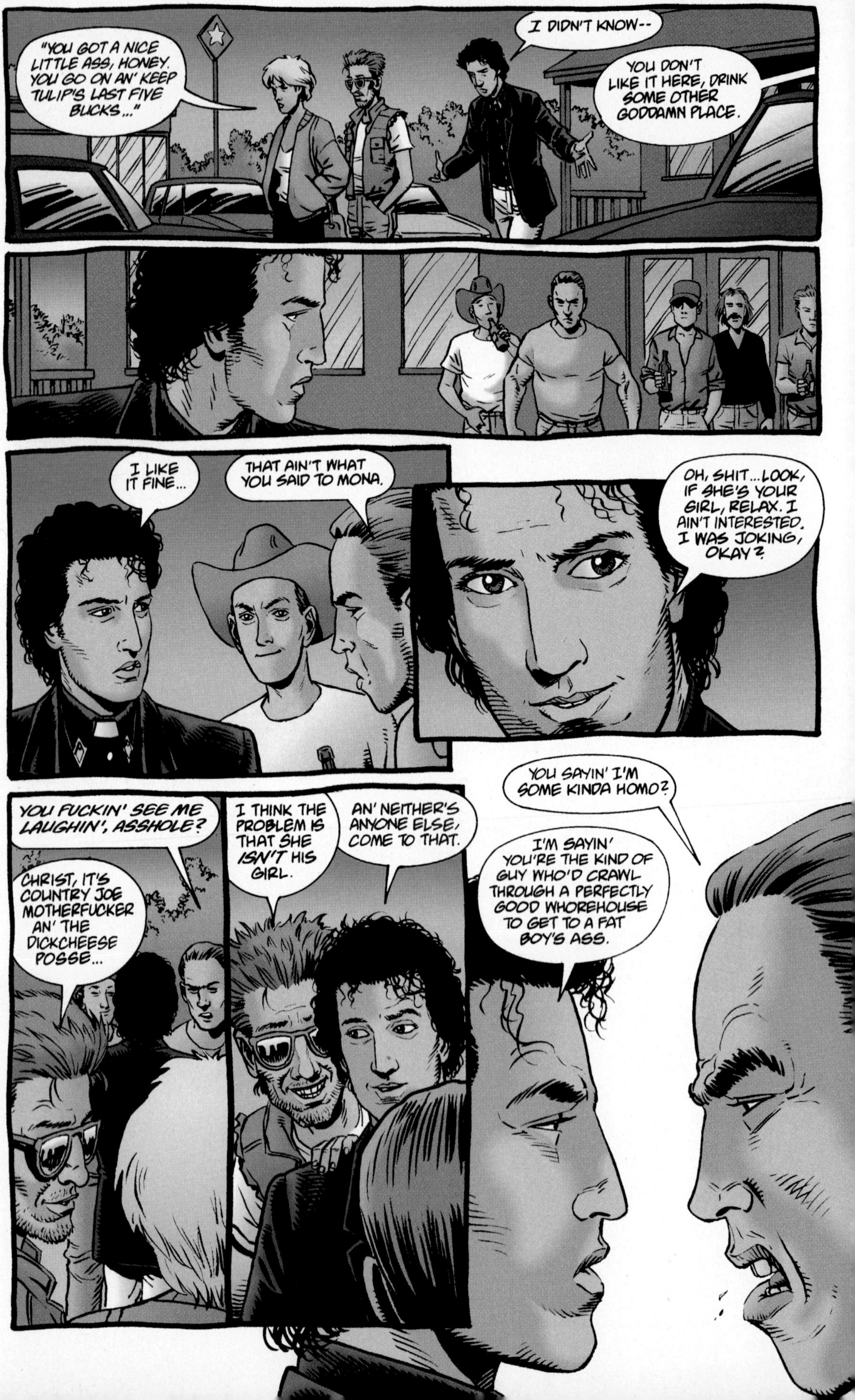
"YOU GOT A NICE LITTLE ASS, HONEY. YOU GO ON AN' KEEP TULIP'S LAST FIVE BUCKS..."
I DIDN'T KNOW--
YOU DON'T LIKE IT HERE, DRINK SOME OTHER GODDAMN PLACE.
I LIKE IT FINE...
THAT AIN'T WHAT YOU SAID TO MONA.
OH, SHIT...LOOK, IF SHE'S YOUR GIRL, RELAX. I AIN'T INTERESTED. I WAS JOKING, OKAY?
YOU FUCKIN' SEE ME LAUGHIN', ASSHOLE?
CHRIST, IT'S COUNTRY JOE MOTHERFUCKER AN' THE DICKCHEESE POSSE...
I THINK THE PROBLEM IS THAT SHE ISN'T HIS GIRL.
AN' NEITHER'S ANYONE ELSE, COME TO THAT.
YOU SAYIN' I'M SOME KINDA HOMO?
I'M SAYIN' YOU'RE THE KIND OF GUY WHO'D CRAWL THROUGH A PERFECTLY GOOD WHOREHOUSE TO GET TO A FAT BOY'S ASS.

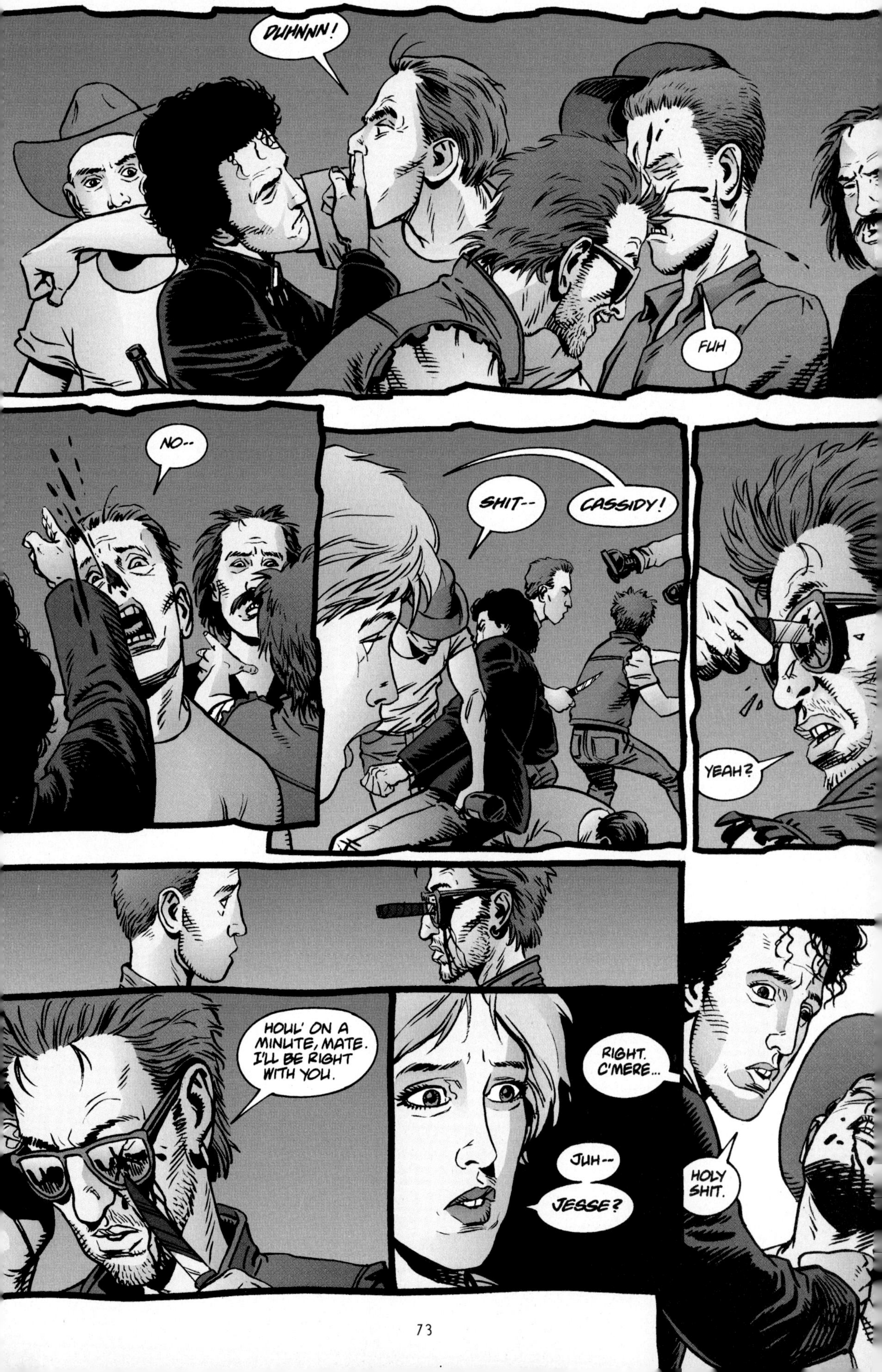
DUHNNN!
FUH
NO--
SHIT--
CASSIDY!
YEAH?
HOUL' ON A MINUTE, MATE. I'LL BE RIGHT WITH YOU.
JUH--
JESSE?
RIGHT. C'MERE...
HOLY SHIT.

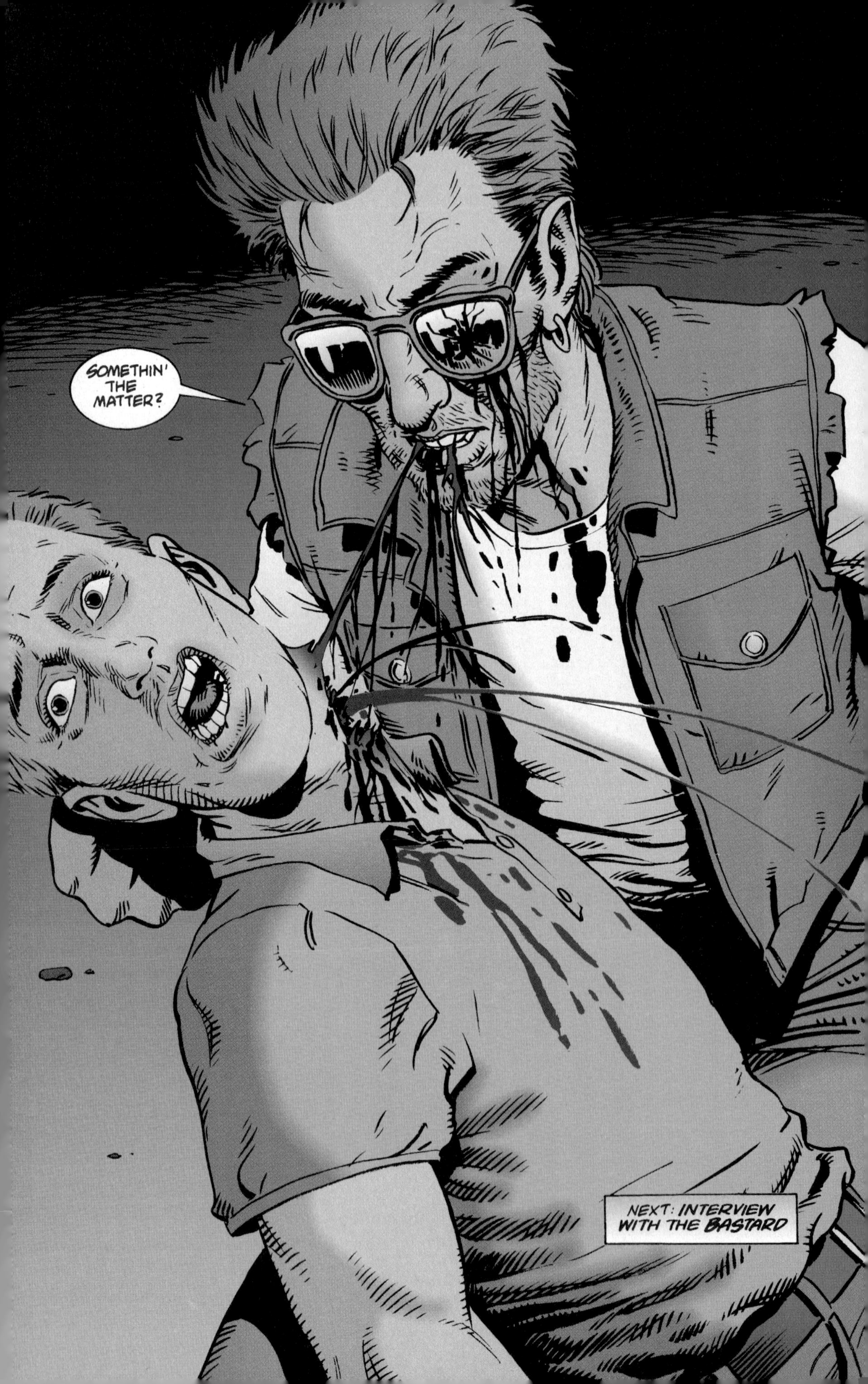
SOMETHIN' THE MATTER?
NEXT: INTERVIEW WITH THE BASTARD

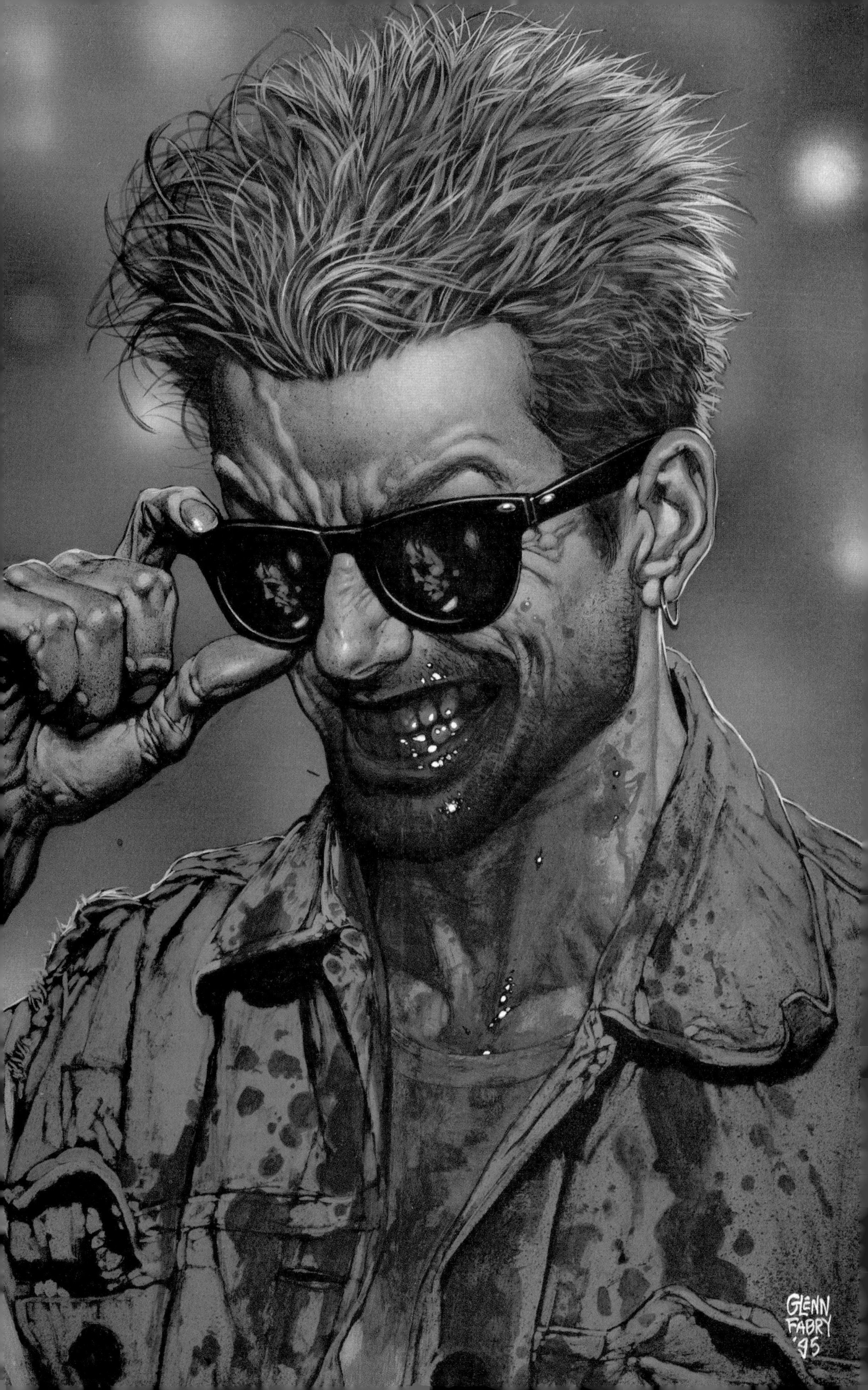
GLENN FABRY '95

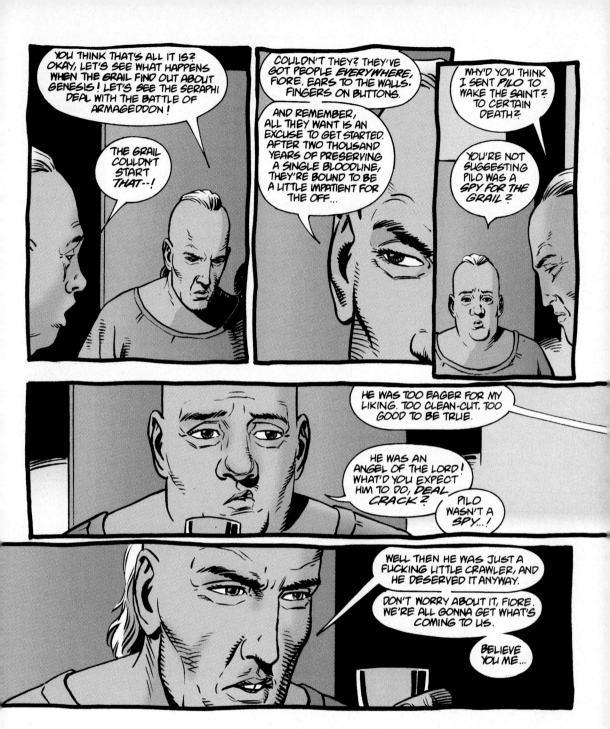

YOU THINK THAT'S ALL IT IS? OKAY, LET'S SEE WHAT HAPPENS WHEN THE GRAIL FIND OUT ABOUT GENESIS! LET'S SEE THE SERAPHI DEAL WITH THE BATTLE OF ARMAGEDDON!

THE GRAIL COULDN'T START *THAT*--!

COULDN'T THEY? THEY'VE GOT PEOPLE *EVERYWHERE*, FIORE. EARS TO THE WALLS. FINGERS ON BUTTONS.

AND REMEMBER, ALL THEY WANT IS AN EXCUSE TO GET STARTED. AFTER TWO THOUSAND YEARS OF PRESERVING A SINGLE BLOODLINE, THEY'RE BOUND TO BE A LITTLE IMPATIENT FOR THE OFF...

WHY'D YOU THINK I SENT *PILO* TO WAKE THE SAINT? TO CERTAIN DEATH?

YOU'RE NOT SUGGESTING PILO WAS A *SPY* FOR THE *GRAIL*?

HE WAS TOO EAGER FOR MY LIKING. TOO CLEAN-CUT. TOO GOOD TO BE TRUE.

HE WAS AN ANGEL OF THE LORD! WHAT'D YOU EXPECT HIM TO DO, DEAL CRACK?

PILO WASN'T A SPY...!

WELL THEN HE WAS JUST A FUCKING LITTLE CRAWLER, AND HE DESERVED IT ANYWAY.

DON'T WORRY ABOUT IT, FIORE. WE'RE ALL GONNA GET WHAT'S COMING TO US.

BELIEVE YOU ME...

THE KINGDOM OF HEAVEN IS *FUCKED*.

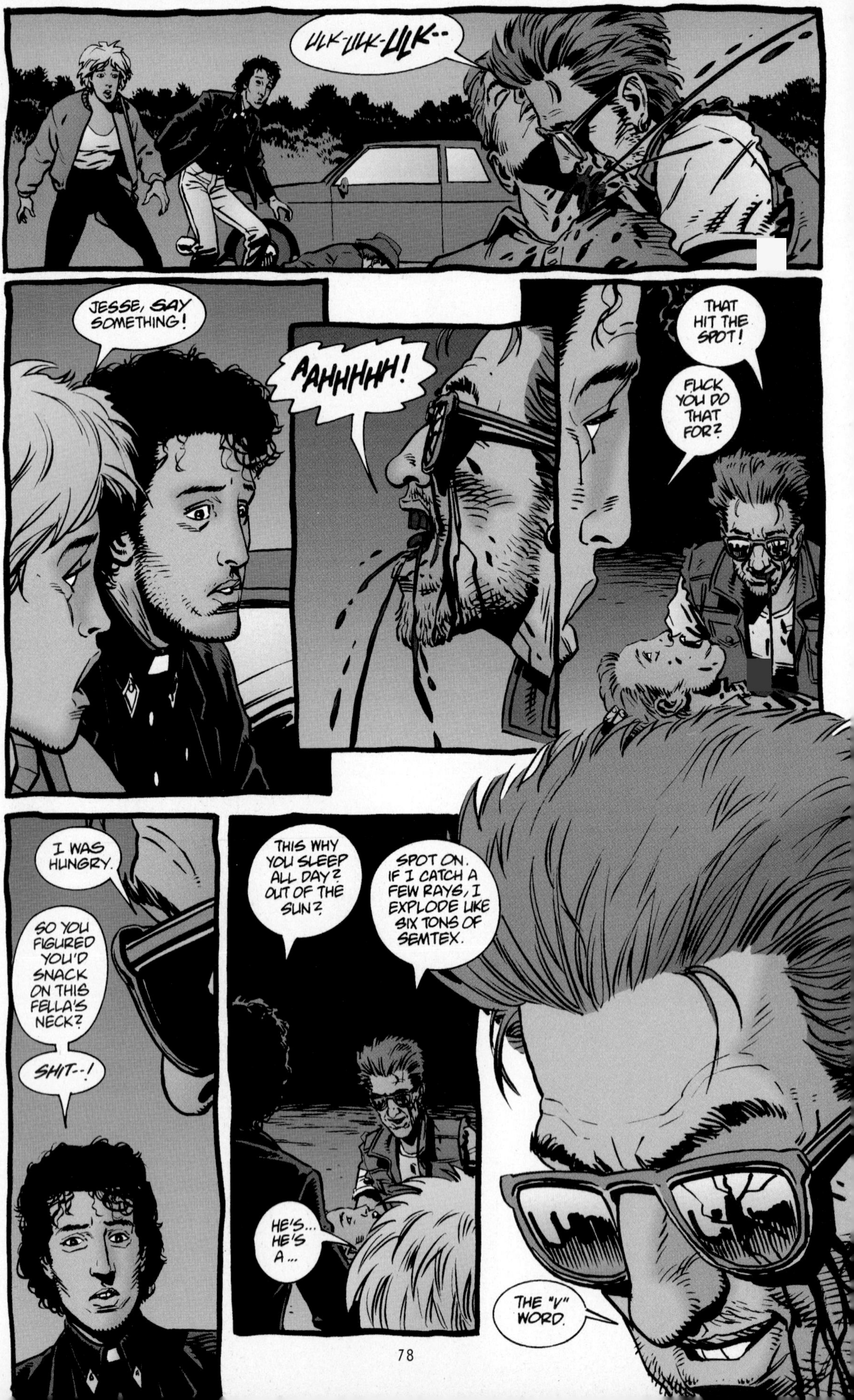
ULK-ULK-ULK--
JESSE, SAY SOMETHING!
AAHHHHH!
THAT HIT THE SPOT!
FUCK YOU DO THAT FOR?
I WAS HUNGRY.
SO YOU FIGURED YOU'D SNACK ON THIS FELLA'S NECK?
SHIT--!
THIS WHY YOU SLEEP ALL DAY? OUT OF THE SUN?
SPOT ON. IF I CATCH A FEW RAYS, I EXPLODE LIKE SIX TONS OF SEMTEX.
HE'S... HE'S A...
THE "V" WORD.

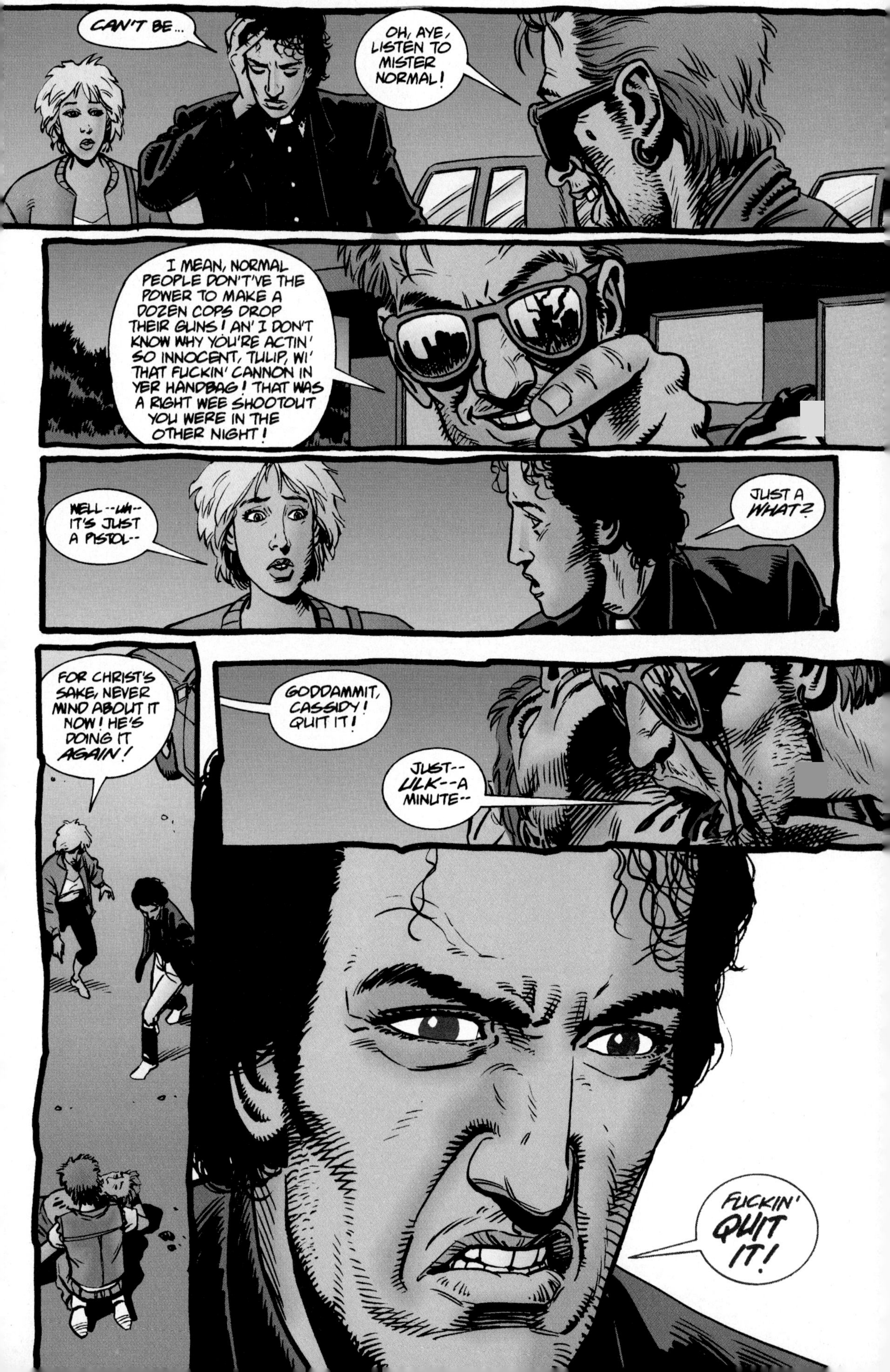
CAN'T BE...
OH, AYE, LISTEN TO MISTER NORMAL!
I MEAN, NORMAL PEOPLE DON'T'VE THE POWER TO MAKE A DOZEN COPS DROP THEIR GUNS! AN' I DON'T KNOW WHY YOU'RE ACTIN' SO INNOCENT, TULIP, WI' THAT FUCKIN' CANNON IN YER HANDBAG! THAT WAS A RIGHT WEE SHOOTOUT YOU WERE IN THE OTHER NIGHT!
WELL--UH--IT'S JUST A PISTOL--
JUST A WHAT?
FOR CHRIST'S SAKE, NEVER MIND ABOUT IT NOW! HE'S DOING IT AGAIN!
GODDAMMIT, CASSIDY! QUIT IT!
JUST--ULK--A MINUTE--
FUCKIN' QUIT IT!

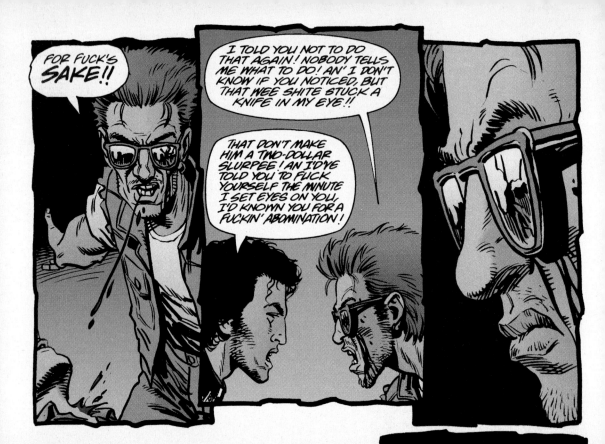

FOR FUCK'S SAKE!!

I TOLD YOU NOT TO DO THAT AGAIN! NOBODY TELLS ME WHAT TO DO! AN' I DON'T KNOW IF YOU NOTICED, BUT THAT WEE SHITE STUCK A KNIFE IN MY EYE!!

THAT DON'T MAKE HIM A TWO-DOLLAR SLURPEE! AN' I'D'VE TOLD YOU TO FUCK YOURSELF THE MINUTE I SET EYES ON YOU, I'D KNOWN YOU FOR A FUCKIN' ABOMINATION!

AND THE HORSE YOU RODE IN ON

GARTH ENNIS – WRITER
STEVE DILLON – ARTIST
MATT HOLLINGSWORTH – COLORIST
CLEM ROBINS – LETTERER
JULIE ROTTENBERG – ASSOC. EDITOR
STUART MOORE – EDITOR
PREACHER CREATED BY
GARTH ENNIS AND **STEVE DILLON**

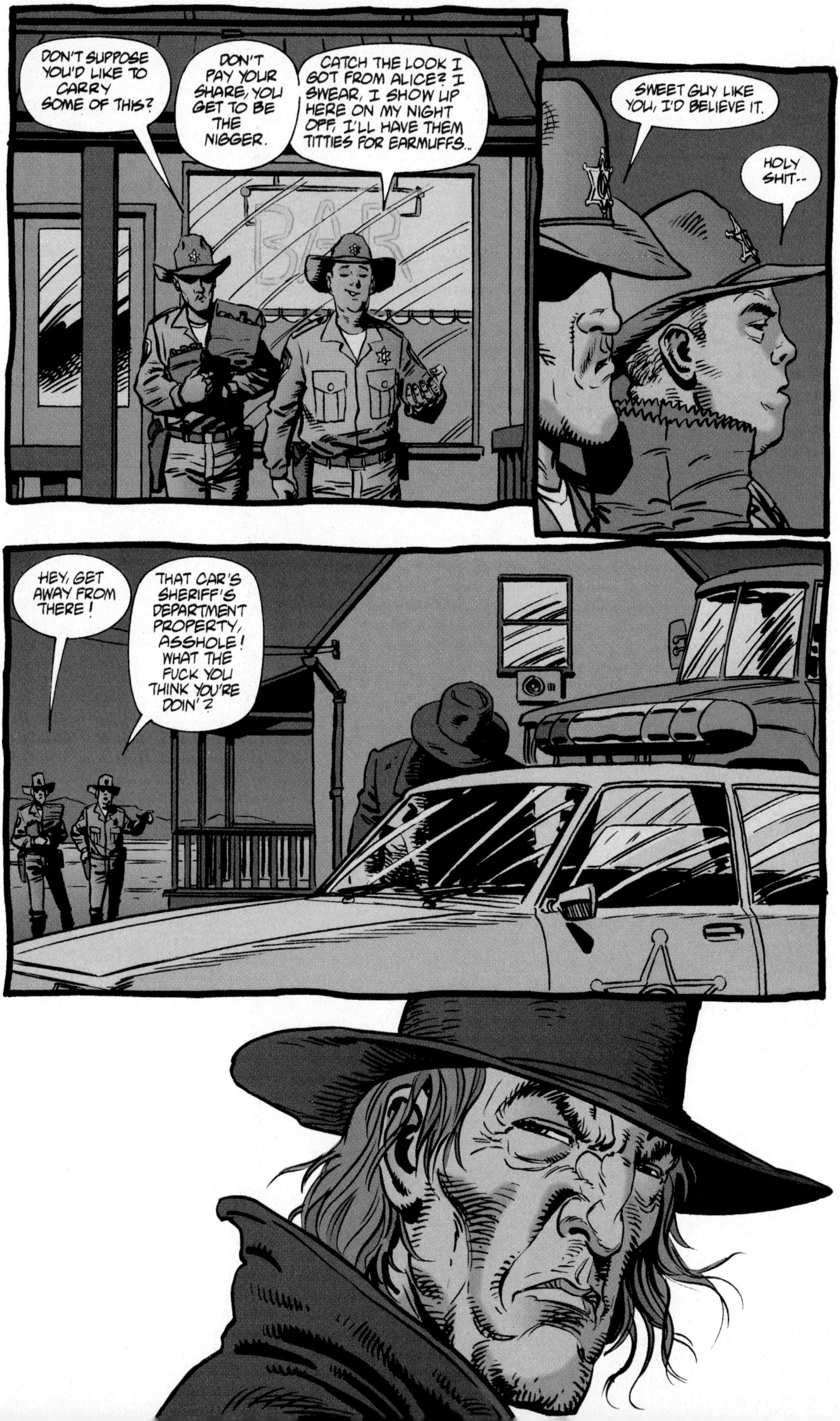
DON'T SUPPOSE YOU'D LIKE TO CARRY SOME OF THIS?
DON'T PAY YOUR SHARE, YOU GET TO BE THE NIGGER.
CATCH THE LOOK I GOT FROM ALICE? I SWEAR, I SHOW UP HERE ON MY NIGHT OFF, I'LL HAVE THEM TITTIES FOR EARMUFFS...
BAR
SWEET GUY LIKE YOU, I'D BELIEVE IT.
HOLY SHIT--
HEY, GET AWAY FROM THERE!
THAT CAR'S SHERIFF'S DEPARTMENT PROPERTY, ASSHOLE! WHAT THE FUCK YOU THINK YOU'RE DOIN'?

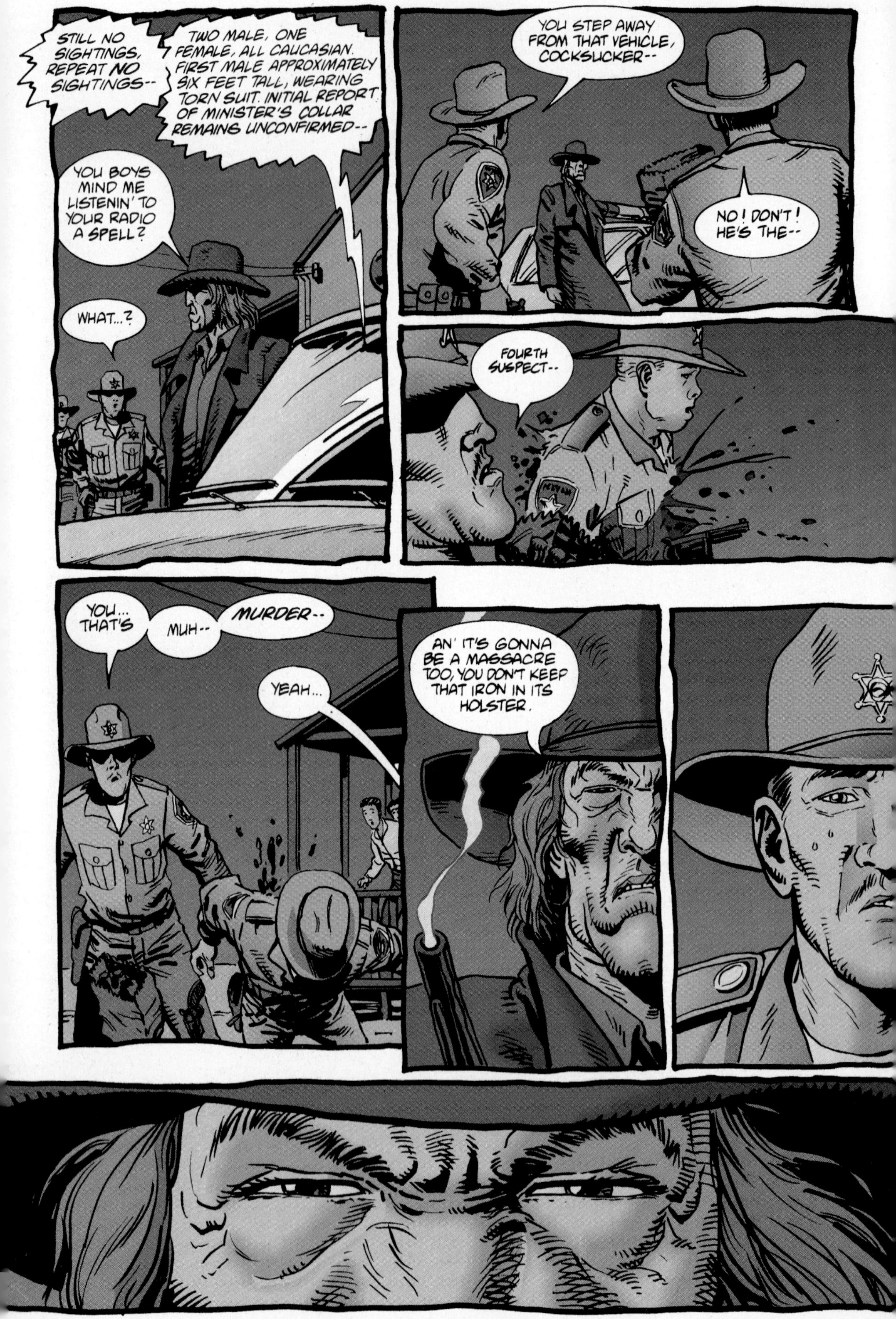
STILL NO SIGHTINGS, REPEAT **NO** SIGHTINGS--
TWO MALE, ONE FEMALE, ALL CAUCASIAN. FIRST MALE APPROXIMATELY SIX FEET TALL, WEARING TORN SUIT. INITIAL REPORT OF MINISTER'S COLLAR REMAINS UNCONFIRMED--
YOU BOYS MIND ME LISTENIN' TO YOUR RADIO A SPELL?
WHAT...?
YOU STEP AWAY FROM THAT VEHICLE, COCKSUCKER--
NO! DON'T! HE'S THE--
FOURTH SUSPECT--
YOU... THAT'S
MUH--
MURDER--
YEAH...
AN' IT'S GONNA BE A MASSACRE TOO, YOU DON'T KEEP THAT IRON IN ITS HOLSTER.

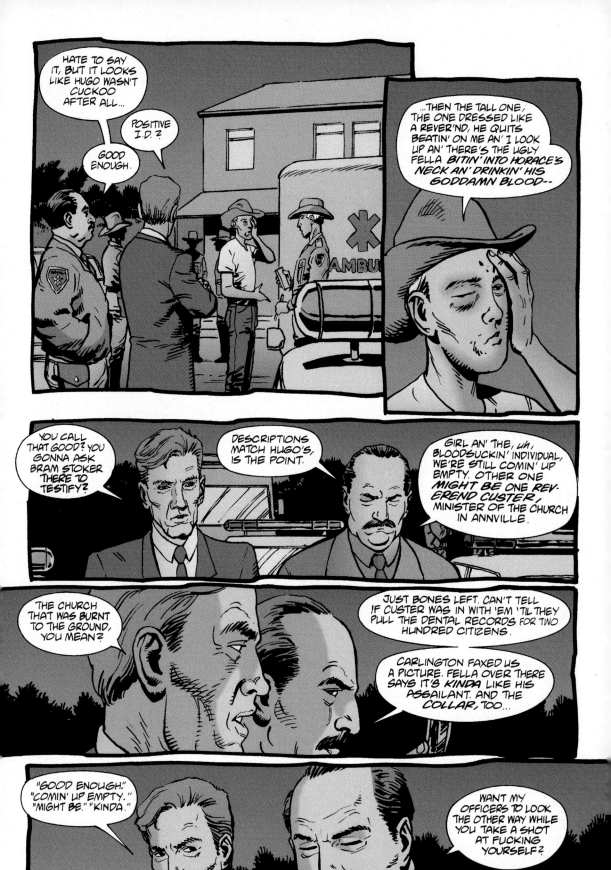

HATE TO SAY IT, BUT IT LOOKS LIKE HUGO WASN'T CUCKOO AFTER ALL...

POSITIVE I.D.?

GOOD ENOUGH.

...THEN THE TALL ONE, THE ONE DRESSED LIKE A REVER'ND, HE QUITS BEATIN' ON ME AN' I LOOK UP AN' THERE'S THE UGLY FELLA *BITIN' INTO HORACE'S NECK AN' DRINKIN' HIS GODDAMN BLOOD*--

YOU CALL THAT GOOD? YOU GONNA ASK BRAM STOKER THERE TO TESTIFY?

DESCRIPTIONS MATCH HUGO'S, IS THE POINT.

GIRL AN' THE, *UH*, BLOODSUCKIN' INDIVIDUAL, WE'RE STILL COMIN' UP EMPTY. OTHER ONE *MIGHT BE* ONE REVEREND CUSTER, MINISTER OF THE CHURCH IN ANNVILLE.

THE CHURCH THAT WAS BURNT TO THE GROUND, YOU MEAN?

JUST BONES LEFT. CAN'T TELL IF CUSTER WAS IN WITH 'EM 'TIL THEY PULL THE DENTAL RECORDS FOR TWO HUNDRED CITIZENS.

CARLINGTON FAXED US A PICTURE. FELLA OVER THERE SAYS IT'S *KINDA* LIKE HIS ASSAILANT. AND THE *COLLAR*, TOO...

"GOOD ENOUGH." "COMIN' UP EMPTY." "MIGHT BE." "KINDA."

WANT MY OFFICERS TO LOOK THE OTHER WAY WHILE YOU TAKE A SHOT AT FUCKING YOURSELF?

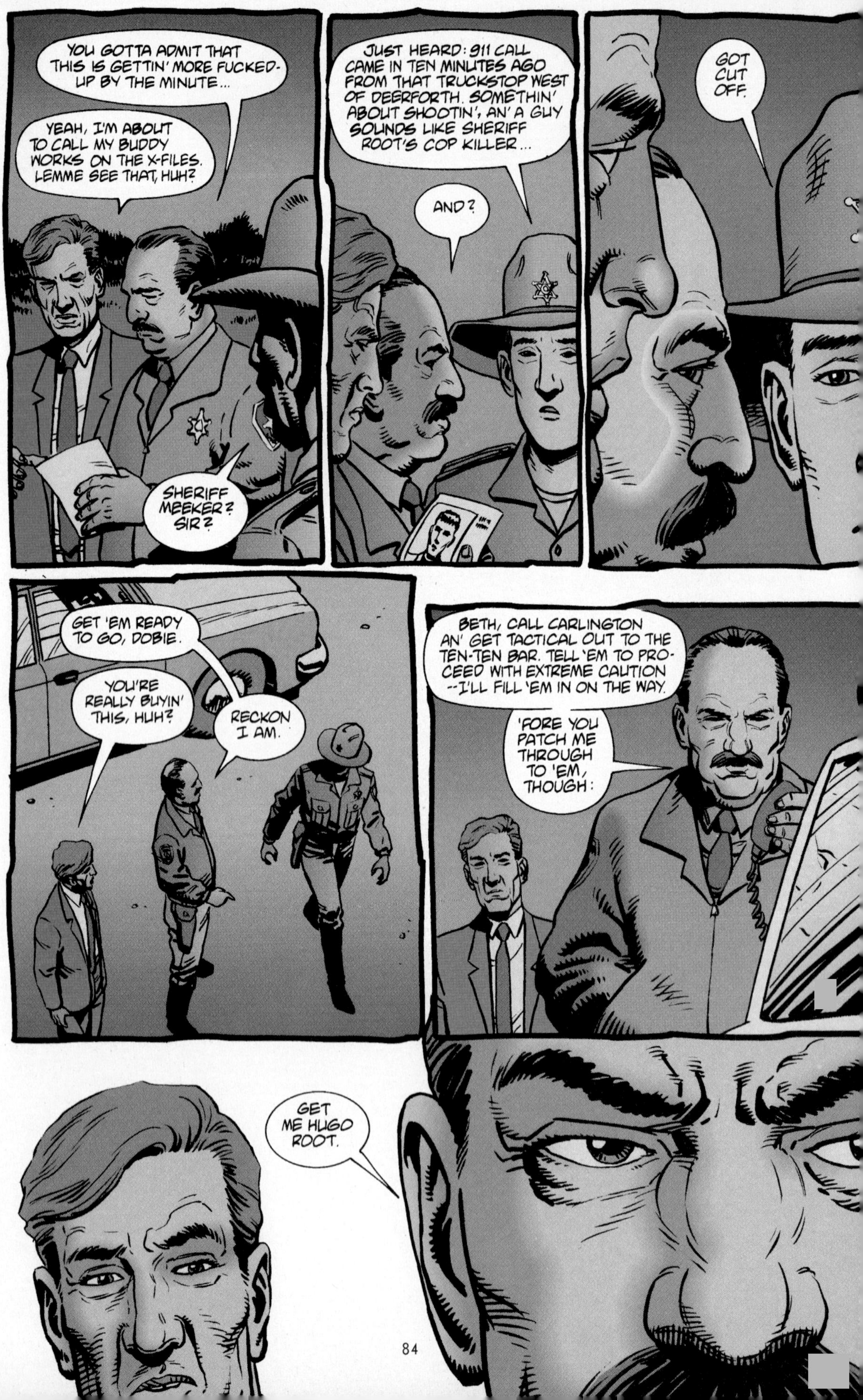
YOU GOTTA ADMIT THAT THIS IS GETTIN' MORE FUCKED-UP BY THE MINUTE...
YEAH, I'M ABOUT TO CALL MY BUDDY WORKS ON THE X-FILES. LEMME SEE THAT, HUH?
SHERIFF MEEKER? SIR?
JUST HEARD: 911 CALL CAME IN TEN MINUTES AGO FROM THAT TRUCKSTOP WEST OF DEERFORTH. SOMETHIN' ABOUT SHOOTIN', AN' A GUY SOUNDS LIKE SHERIFF ROOT'S COP KILLER...
AND?
GOT CUT OFF.
GET 'EM READY TO GO, DOBIE.
YOU'RE REALLY BUYIN' THIS, HUH?
RECKON I AM.
BETH, CALL CARLINGTON AN' GET TACTICAL OUT TO THE TEN-TEN BAR. TELL 'EM TO PROCEED WITH EXTREME CAUTION --I'LL FILL 'EM IN ON THE WAY.
'FORE YOU PATCH ME THROUGH TO 'EM, THOUGH:
GET ME HUGO ROOT.

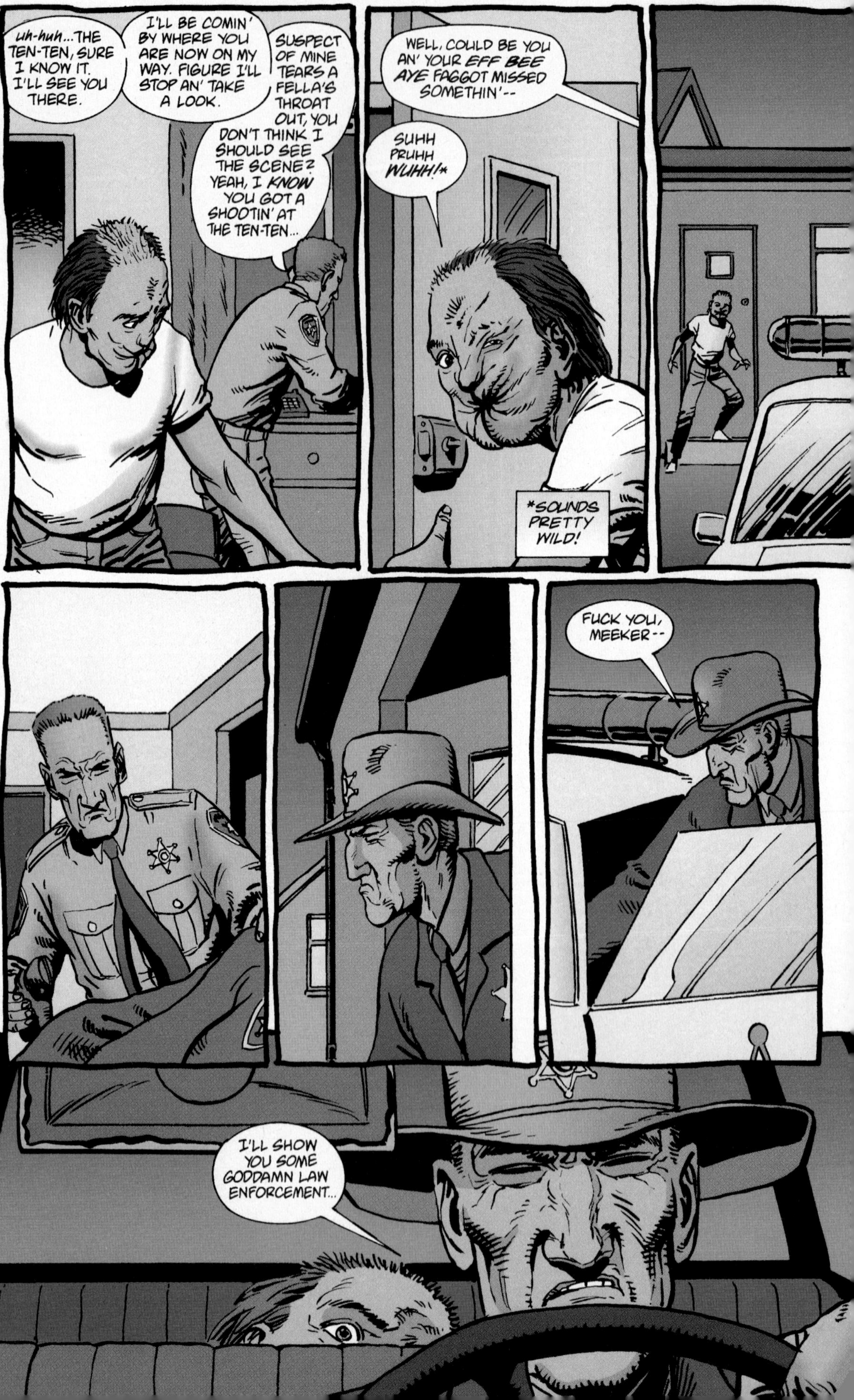

uh-huh... THE TEN-TEN, SURE I KNOW IT. I'LL SEE YOU THERE.
I'LL BE COMIN' BY WHERE YOU ARE NOW ON MY WAY. FIGURE I'LL STOP AN' TAKE A LOOK.
SUSPECT OF MINE TEARS A FELLA'S THROAT OUT, YOU DON'T THINK I SHOULD SEE THE SCENE? YEAH, I KNOW YOU GOT A SHOOTIN' AT THE TEN-TEN...
WELL, COULD BE YOU AN' YOUR EFF BEE AYE FAGGOT MISSED SOMETHIN'--
SUHH PRUHH WUHH!*
*SOUNDS PRETTY WILD!
FUCK YOU, MEEKER--
I'LL SHOW YOU SOME GODDAMN LAW ENFORCEMENT...

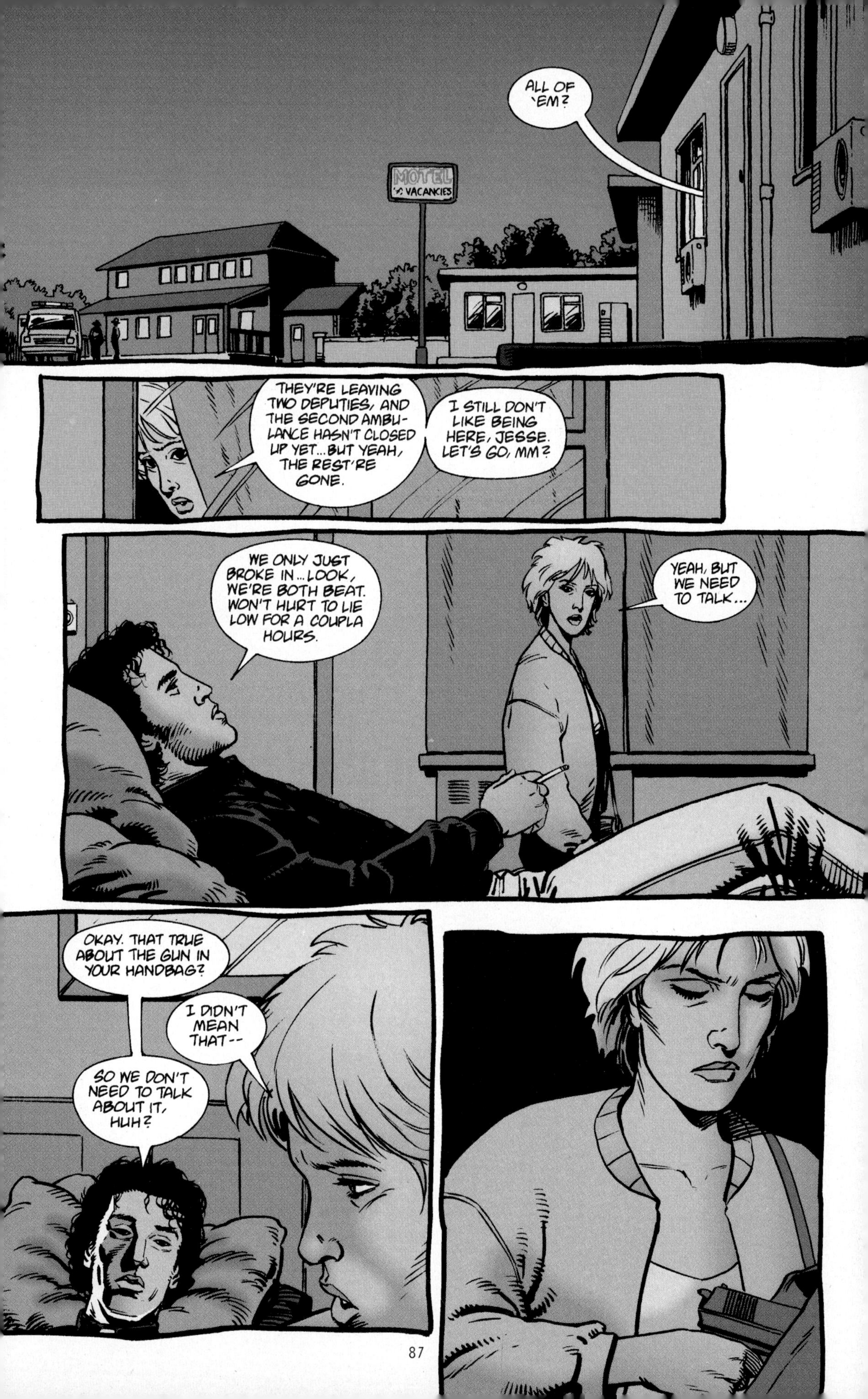
MOTEL
VACANCIES
ALL OF 'EM?
THEY'RE LEAVING TWO DEPUTIES, AND THE SECOND AMBULANCE HASN'T CLOSED UP YET... BUT YEAH, THE REST'RE GONE.
I STILL DON'T LIKE BEING HERE, JESSE. LET'S GO, MM?
WE ONLY JUST BROKE IN... LOOK, WE'RE BOTH BEAT. WON'T HURT TO LIE LOW FOR A COUPLA HOURS.
YEAH, BUT WE NEED TO TALK...
OKAY. THAT TRUE ABOUT THE GUN IN YOUR HANDBAG?
I DIDN'T MEAN THAT--
SO WE DON'T NEED TO TALK ABOUT IT, HUH?

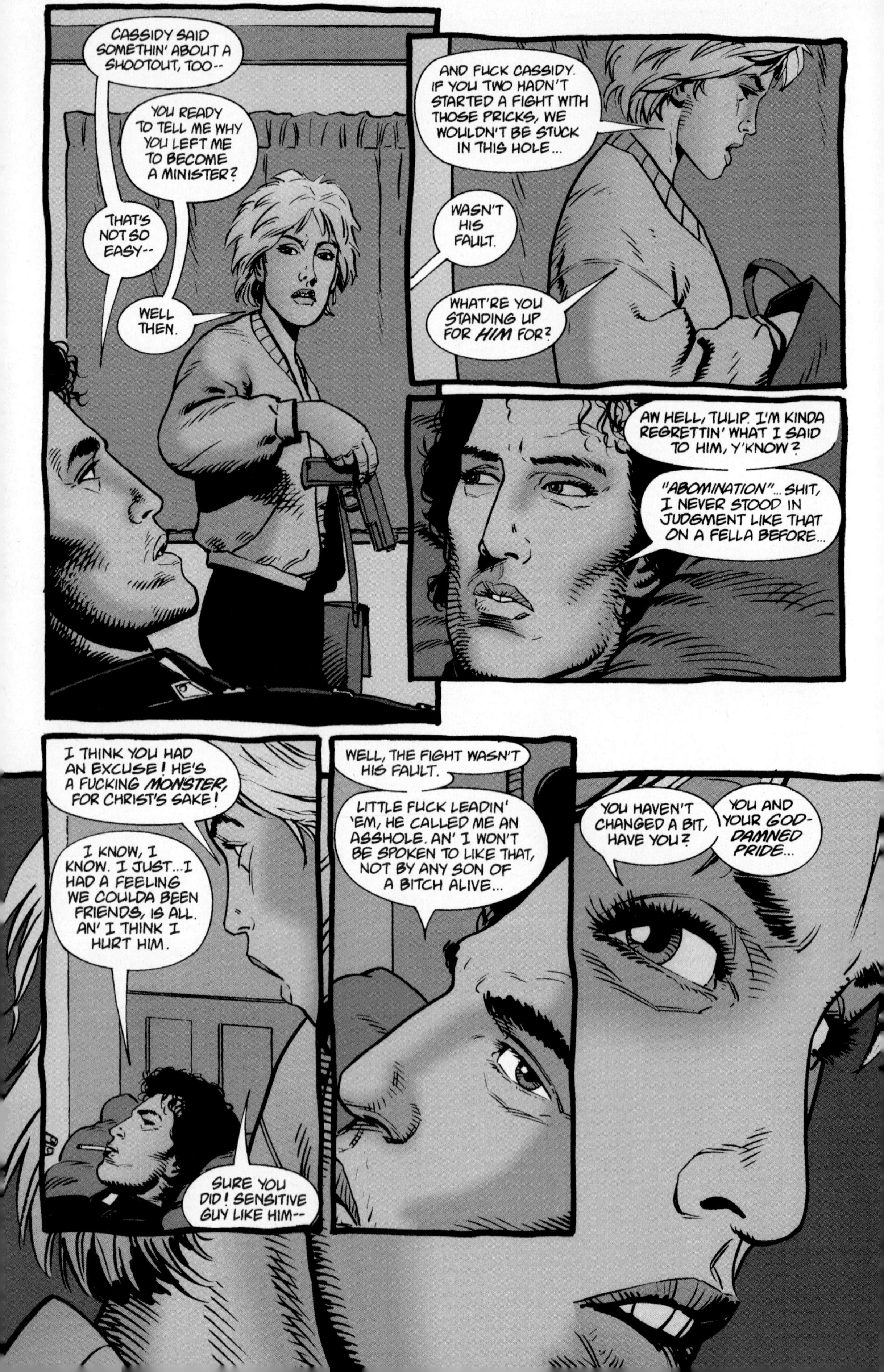

CASSIDY SAID SOMETHIN' ABOUT A SHOOTOUT, TOO--
YOU READY TO TELL ME WHY YOU LEFT ME TO BECOME A MINISTER?
THAT'S NOT SO EASY--
WELL THEN.
AND FUCK CASSIDY. IF YOU TWO HADN'T STARTED A FIGHT WITH THOSE PRICKS, WE WOULDN'T BE STUCK IN THIS HOLE...
WASN'T HIS FAULT.
WHAT'RE YOU STANDING UP FOR *HIM* FOR?
AW HELL, TULIP. I'M KINDA REGRETTIN' WHAT I SAID TO HIM, Y'KNOW?
"*ABOMINATION*"... SHIT, I NEVER STOOD IN JUDGMENT LIKE THAT ON A FELLA BEFORE...
I THINK YOU HAD AN EXCUSE! HE'S A FUCKING *MONSTER*, FOR CHRIST'S SAKE!
I KNOW, I KNOW. I JUST...I HAD A FEELING WE COULDA BEEN FRIENDS, IS ALL. AN' I THINK I HURT HIM.
SURE YOU DID! SENSITIVE GUY LIKE HIM--
WELL, THE FIGHT WASN'T HIS FAULT.
LITTLE FUCK LEADIN' 'EM, HE CALLED ME AN ASSHOLE. AN' I WON'T BE SPOKEN TO LIKE THAT, NOT BY ANY SON OF A BITCH ALIVE...
YOU HAVEN'T CHANGED A BIT, HAVE YOU?
YOU AND YOUR *GOD-DAMNED* PRIDE...

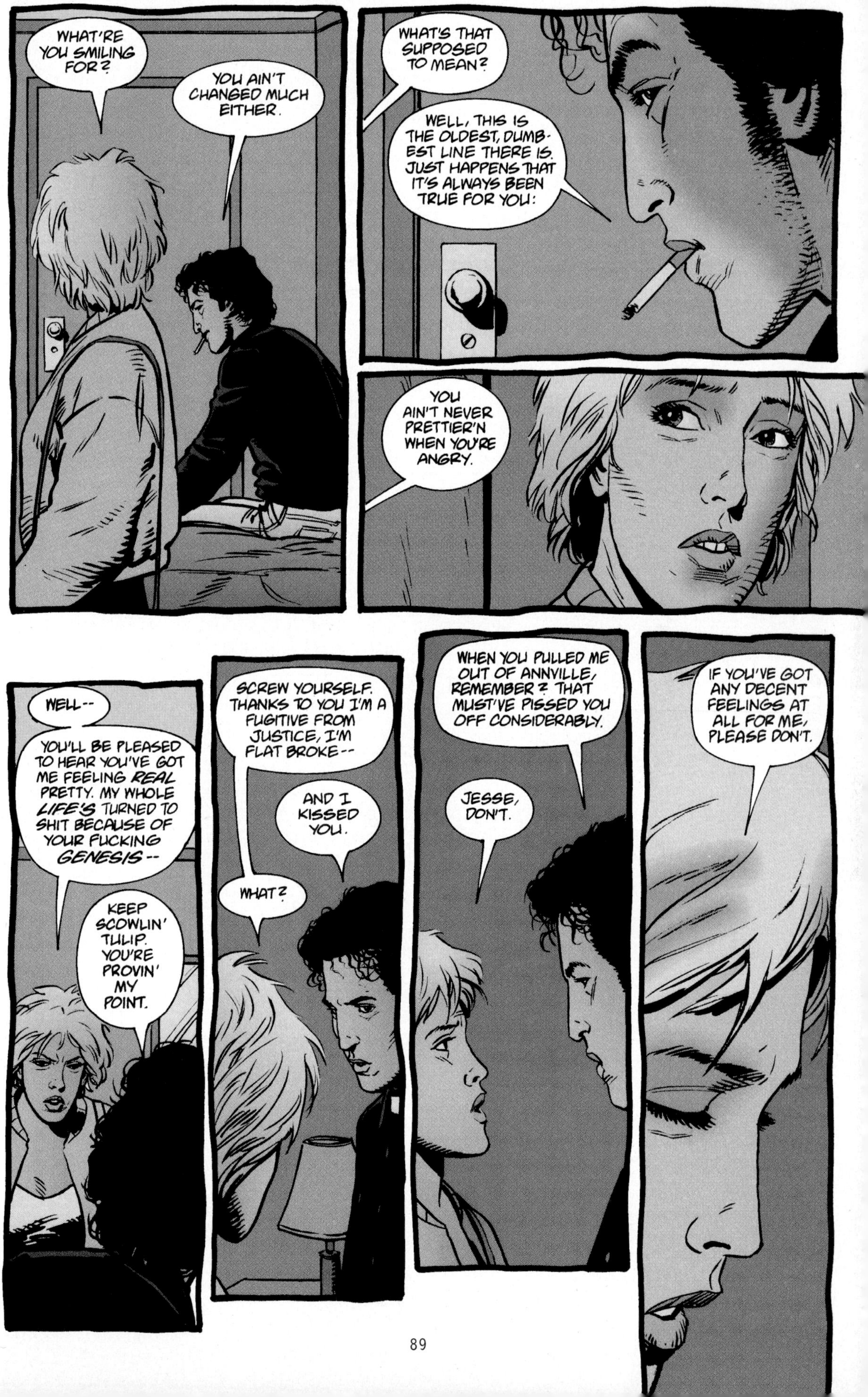
WHAT'RE YOU SMILING FOR?
YOU AIN'T CHANGED MUCH EITHER.
WHAT'S THAT SUPPOSED TO MEAN?
WELL, THIS IS THE OLDEST, DUMB-EST LINE THERE IS. JUST HAPPENS THAT IT'S ALWAYS BEEN TRUE FOR YOU:
YOU AIN'T NEVER PRETTIER'N WHEN YOU'RE ANGRY.
WELL--
YOU'LL BE PLEASED TO HEAR YOU'VE GOT ME FEELING REAL PRETTY. MY WHOLE LIFE'S TURNED TO SHIT BECAUSE OF YOUR FUCKING GENESIS--
KEEP SCOWLIN' TULIP. YOU'RE PROVIN' MY POINT.
SCREW YOURSELF. THANKS TO YOU I'M A FUGITIVE FROM JUSTICE, I'M FLAT BROKE--
WHAT?
AND I KISSED YOU.
WHEN YOU PULLED ME OUT OF ANNVILLE, REMEMBER? THAT MUST'VE PISSED YOU OFF CONSIDERABLY.
JESSE, DON'T.
IF YOU'VE GOT ANY DECENT FEELINGS AT ALL FOR ME, PLEASE DON'T.

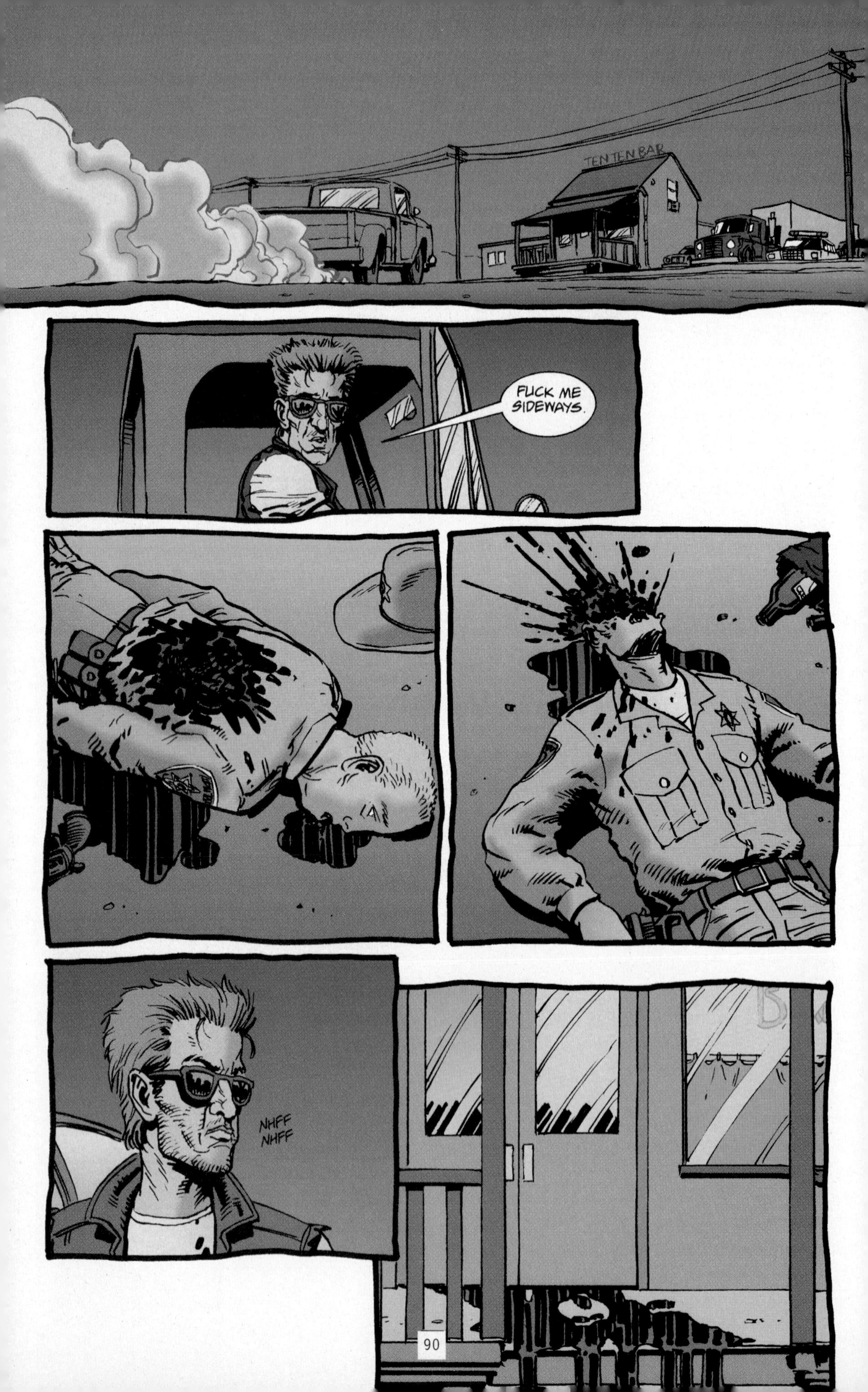
TEN TEN BAR
FUCK ME SIDEWAYS.
NHFF NHFF

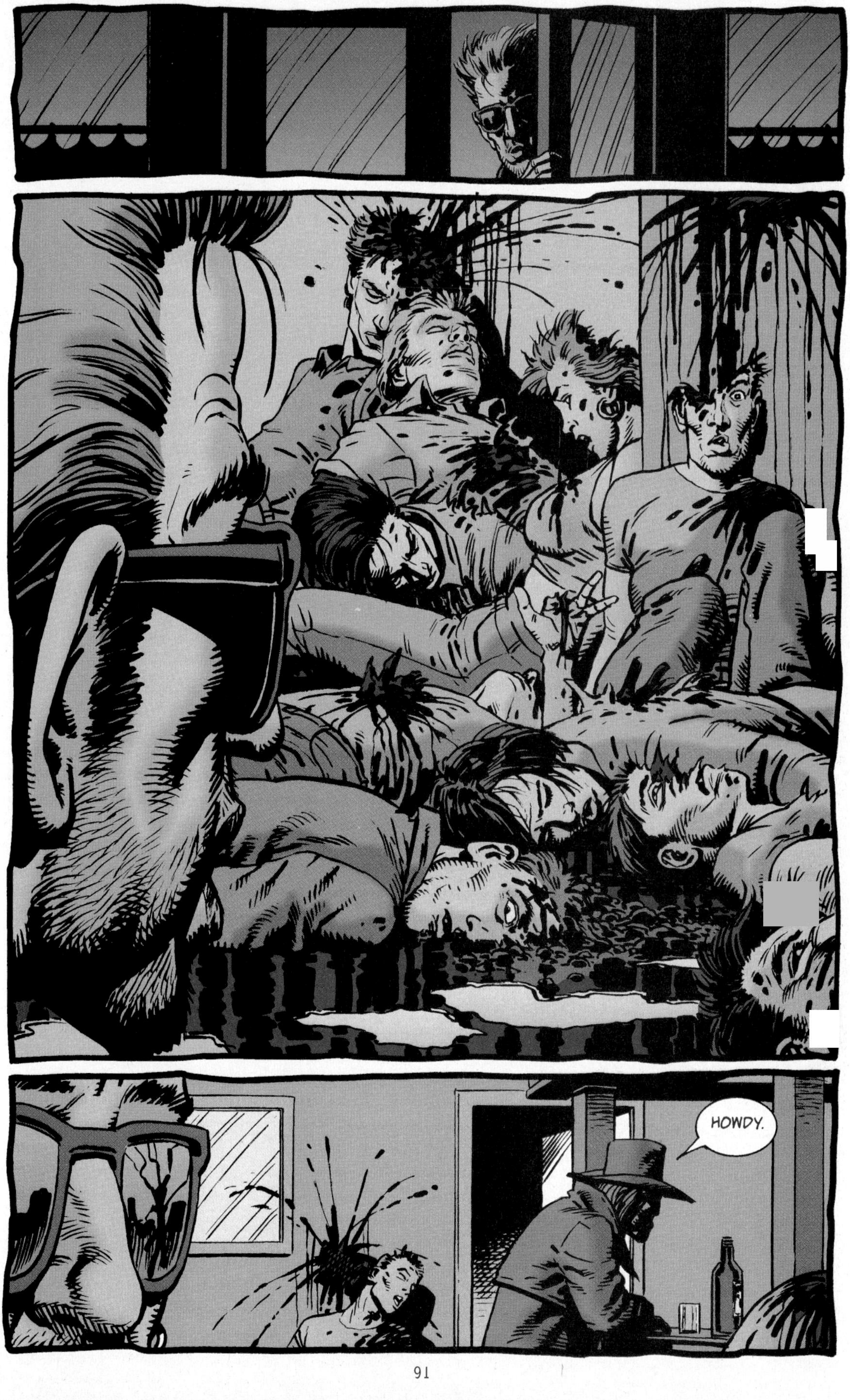
HOWDY.

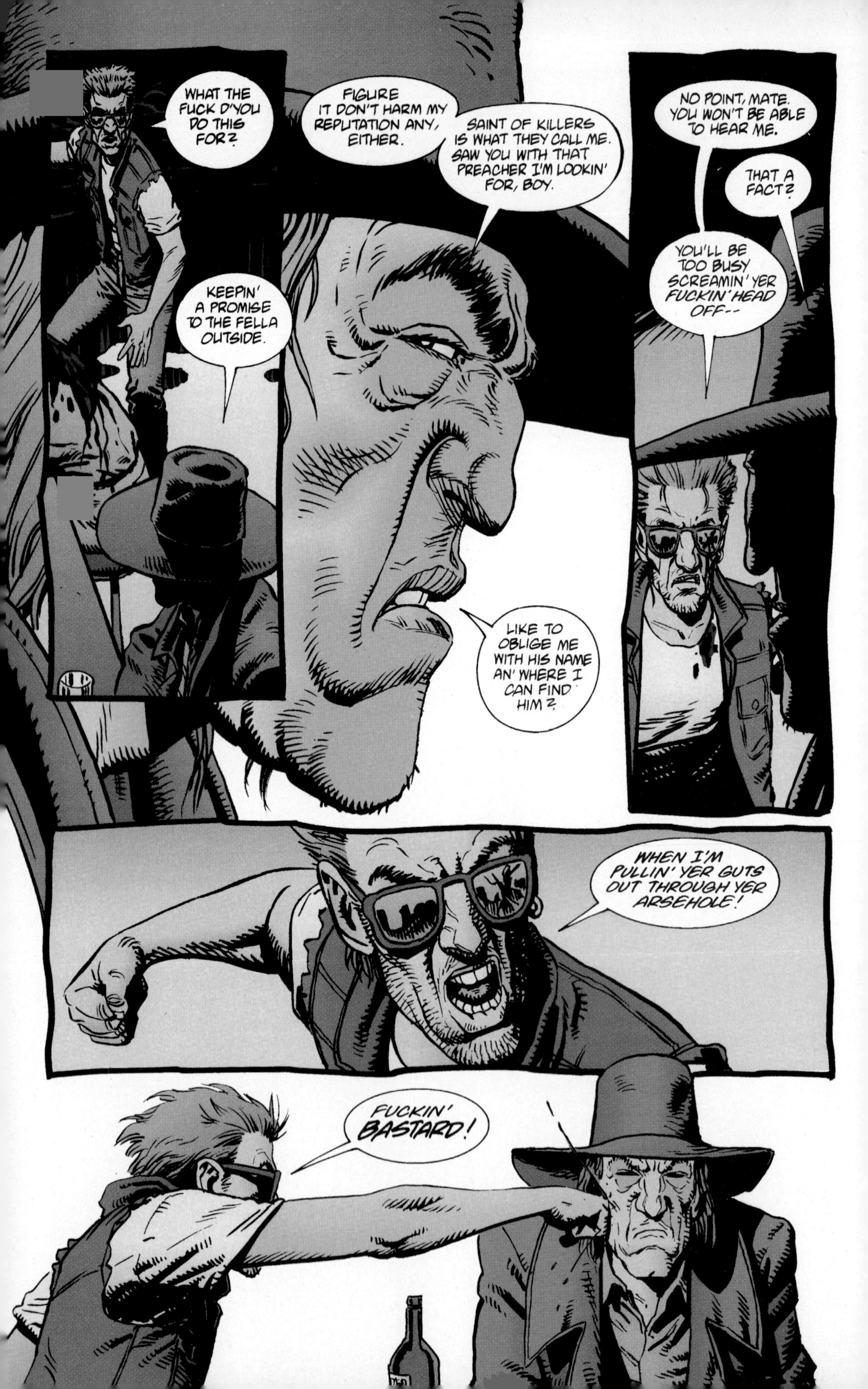
WHAT THE FUCK D'YOU DO THIS FOR?
KEEPIN' A PROMISE TO THE FELLA OUTSIDE.
FIGURE IT DON'T HARM MY REPUTATION ANY, EITHER.
SAINT OF KILLERS IS WHAT THEY CALL ME. SAW YOU WITH THAT PREACHER I'M LOOKIN' FOR, BOY.
LIKE TO OBLIGE ME WITH HIS NAME AN' WHERE I CAN FIND HIM?
NO POINT, MATE. YOU WON'T BE ABLE TO HEAR ME.
THAT A FACT?
YOU'LL BE TOO BUSY SCREAMIN' YER FUCKIN' HEAD OFF--
WHEN I'M PULLIN' YER GUTS OUT THROUGH YER ARSEHOLE!
FUCKIN' BASTARD!

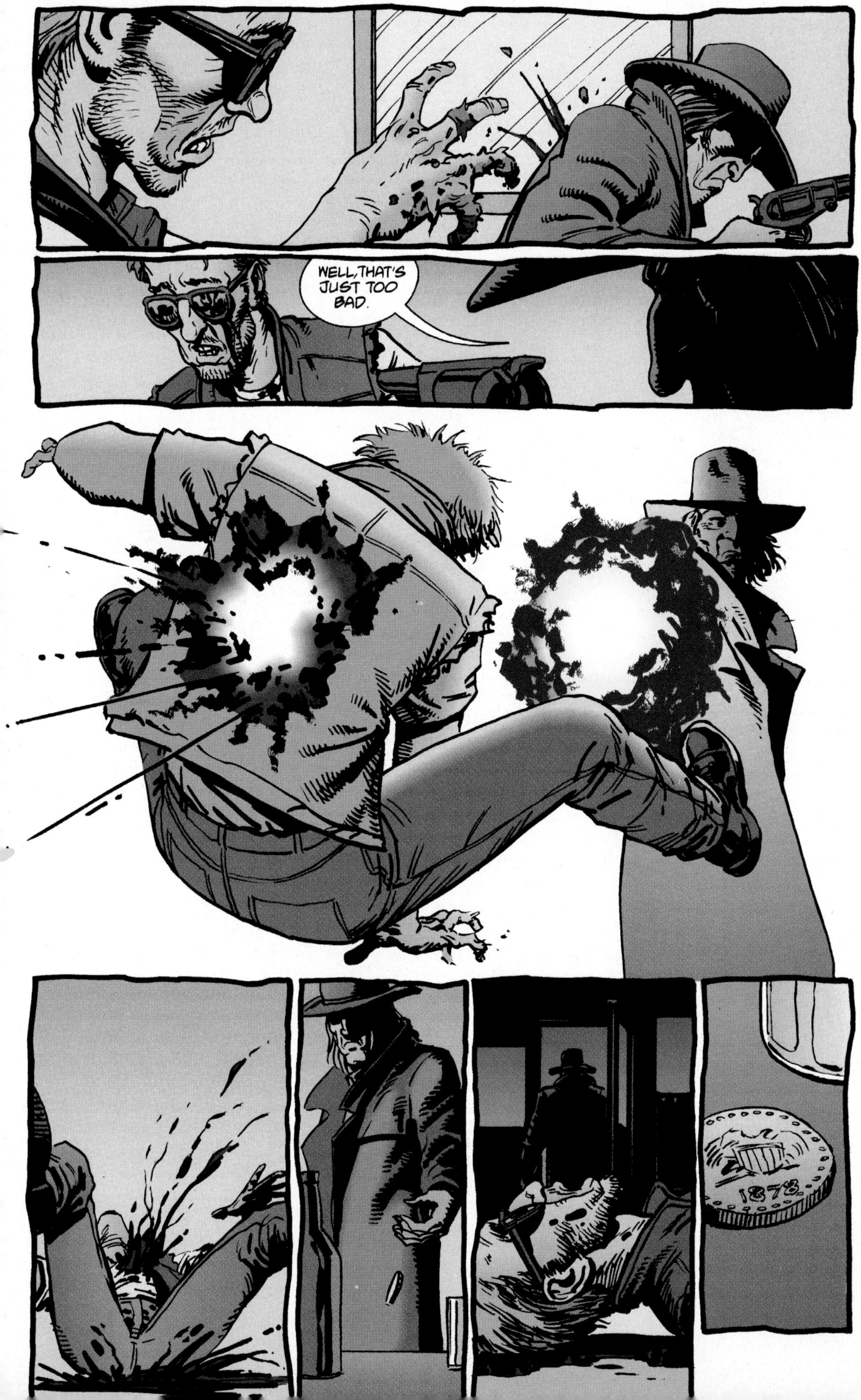
WELL, THAT'S JUST TOO BAD.
1878

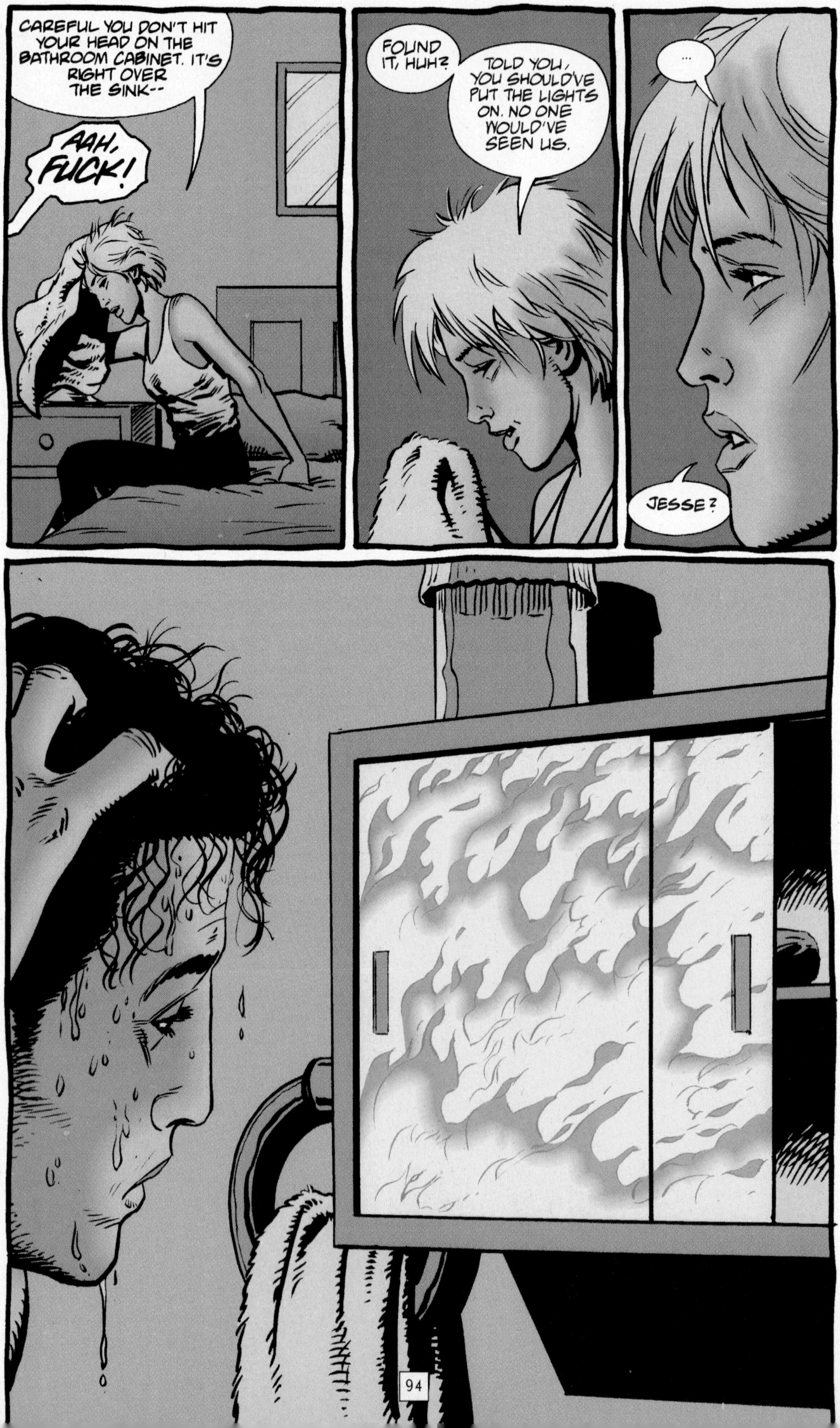
CAREFUL YOU DON'T HIT YOUR HEAD ON THE BATHROOM CABINET. IT'S RIGHT OVER THE SINK--
AAH, FUCK!
FOUND IT, HUH?
TOLD YOU, YOU SHOULD'VE PUT THE LIGHTS ON. NO ONE WOULD'VE SEEN US.
...
JESSE?

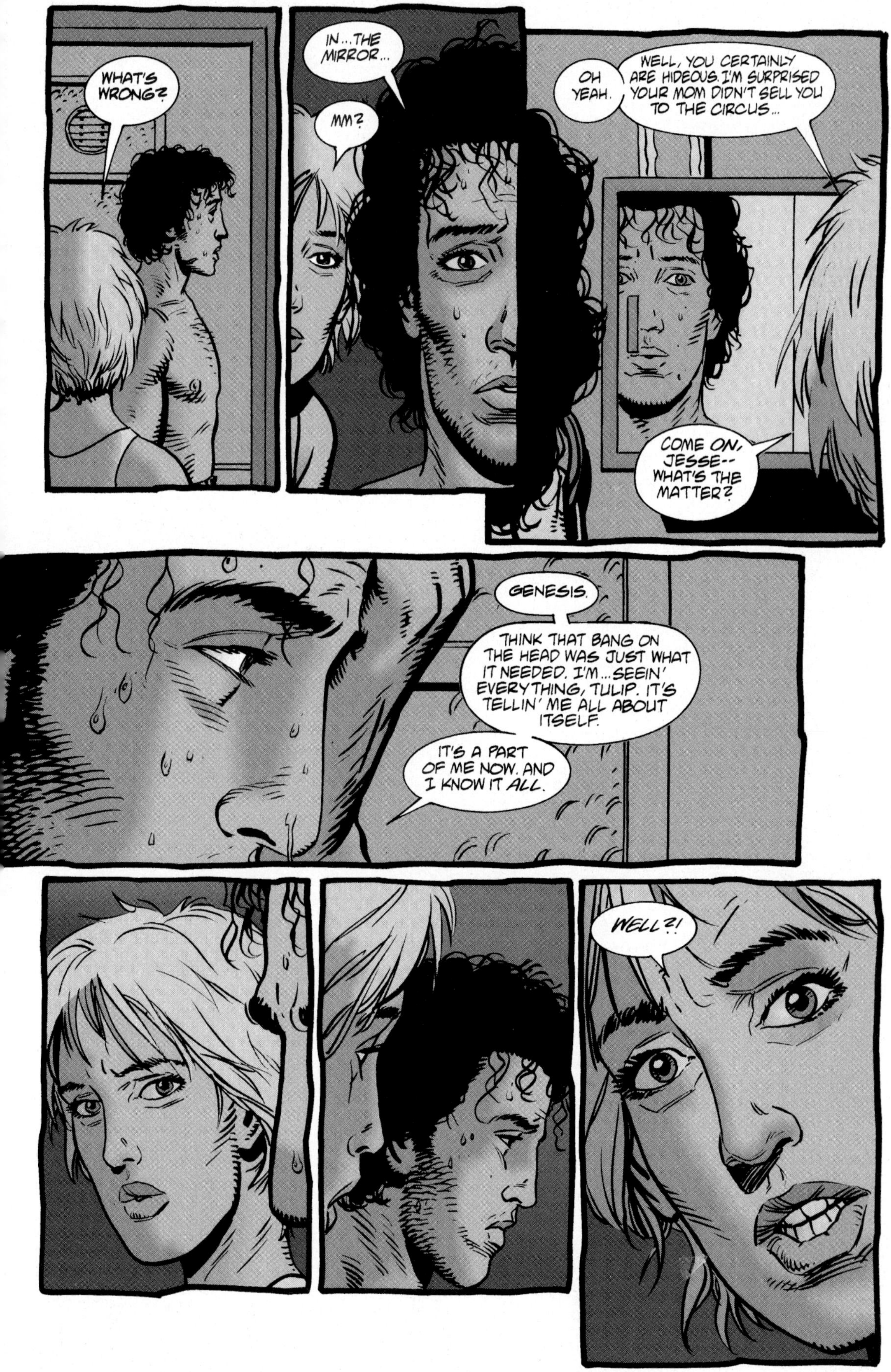
WHAT'S WRONG?
IN...THE MIRROR...
MM?
OH YEAH.
WELL, YOU CERTAINLY ARE HIDEOUS. I'M SURPRISED YOUR MOM DIDN'T SELL YOU TO THE CIRCUS...
COME ON, JESSE-- WHAT'S THE MATTER?
GENESIS.
THINK THAT BANG ON THE HEAD WAS JUST WHAT IT NEEDED. I'M...SEEIN' EVERYTHING, TULIP. IT'S TELLIN' ME ALL ABOUT ITSELF.
IT'S A PART OF ME NOW. AND I KNOW IT ALL.
WELL?!

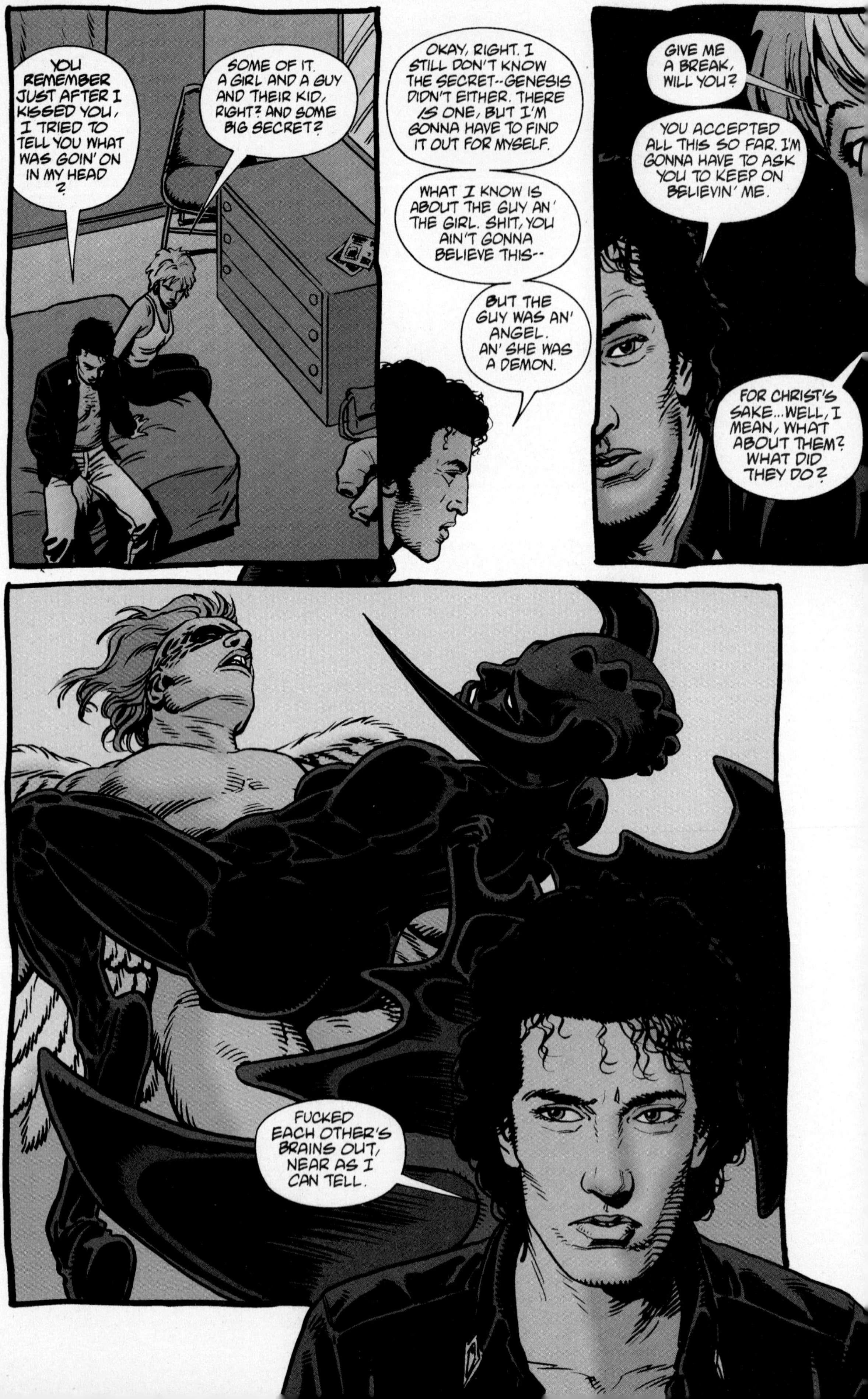
YOU REMEMBER JUST AFTER I KISSED YOU, I TRIED TO TELL YOU WHAT WAS GOIN' ON IN MY HEAD?
SOME OF IT. A GIRL AND A GUY AND THEIR KID, RIGHT? AND SOME BIG SECRET?
OKAY, RIGHT. I STILL DON'T KNOW THE SECRET--GENESIS DIDN'T EITHER. THERE IS ONE, BUT I'M GONNA HAVE TO FIND IT OUT FOR MYSELF.
WHAT I KNOW IS ABOUT THE GUY AN' THE GIRL. SHIT, YOU AIN'T GONNA BELIEVE THIS--
BUT THE GUY WAS AN' ANGEL. AN' SHE WAS A DEMON.
GIVE ME A BREAK, WILL YOU?
YOU ACCEPTED ALL THIS SO FAR. I'M GONNA HAVE TO ASK YOU TO KEEP ON BELIEVIN' ME.
FOR CHRIST'S SAKE...WELL, I MEAN, WHAT ABOUT THEM? WHAT DID THEY DO?
FUCKED EACH OTHER'S BRAINS OUT, NEAR AS I CAN TELL.

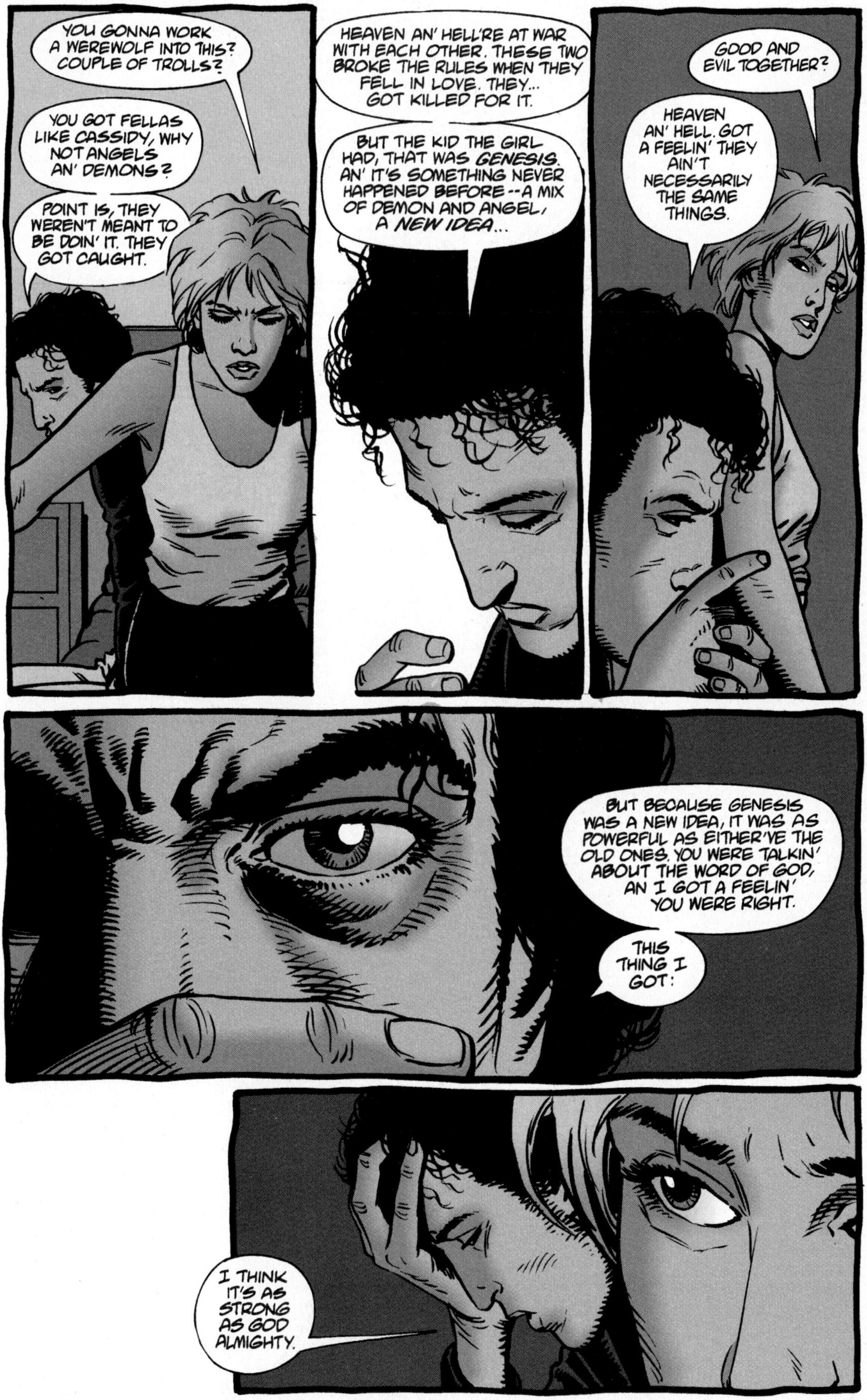
YOU GONNA WORK A WEREWOLF INTO THIS? COUPLE OF TROLLS?
YOU GOT FELLAS LIKE CASSIDY, WHY NOT ANGELS AN' DEMONS?
POINT IS, THEY WEREN'T MEANT TO BE DOIN' IT. THEY GOT CAUGHT.
HEAVEN AN' HELL'RE AT WAR WITH EACH OTHER. THESE TWO BROKE THE RULES WHEN THEY FELL IN LOVE. THEY... GOT KILLED FOR IT.
BUT THE KID THE GIRL HAD, THAT WAS GENESIS. AN' IT'S SOMETHING NEVER HAPPENED BEFORE--A MIX OF DEMON AND ANGEL, A NEW IDEA...
GOOD AND EVIL TOGETHER?
HEAVEN AN' HELL. GOT A FEELIN' THEY AIN'T NECESSARILY THE SAME THINGS.
BUT BECAUSE GENESIS WAS A NEW IDEA, IT WAS AS POWERFUL AS EITHER'VE THE OLD ONES. YOU WERE TALKIN' ABOUT THE WORD OF GOD, AN I GOT A FEELIN' YOU WERE RIGHT.
THIS THING I GOT:
I THINK IT'S AS STRONG AS GOD ALMIGHTY.

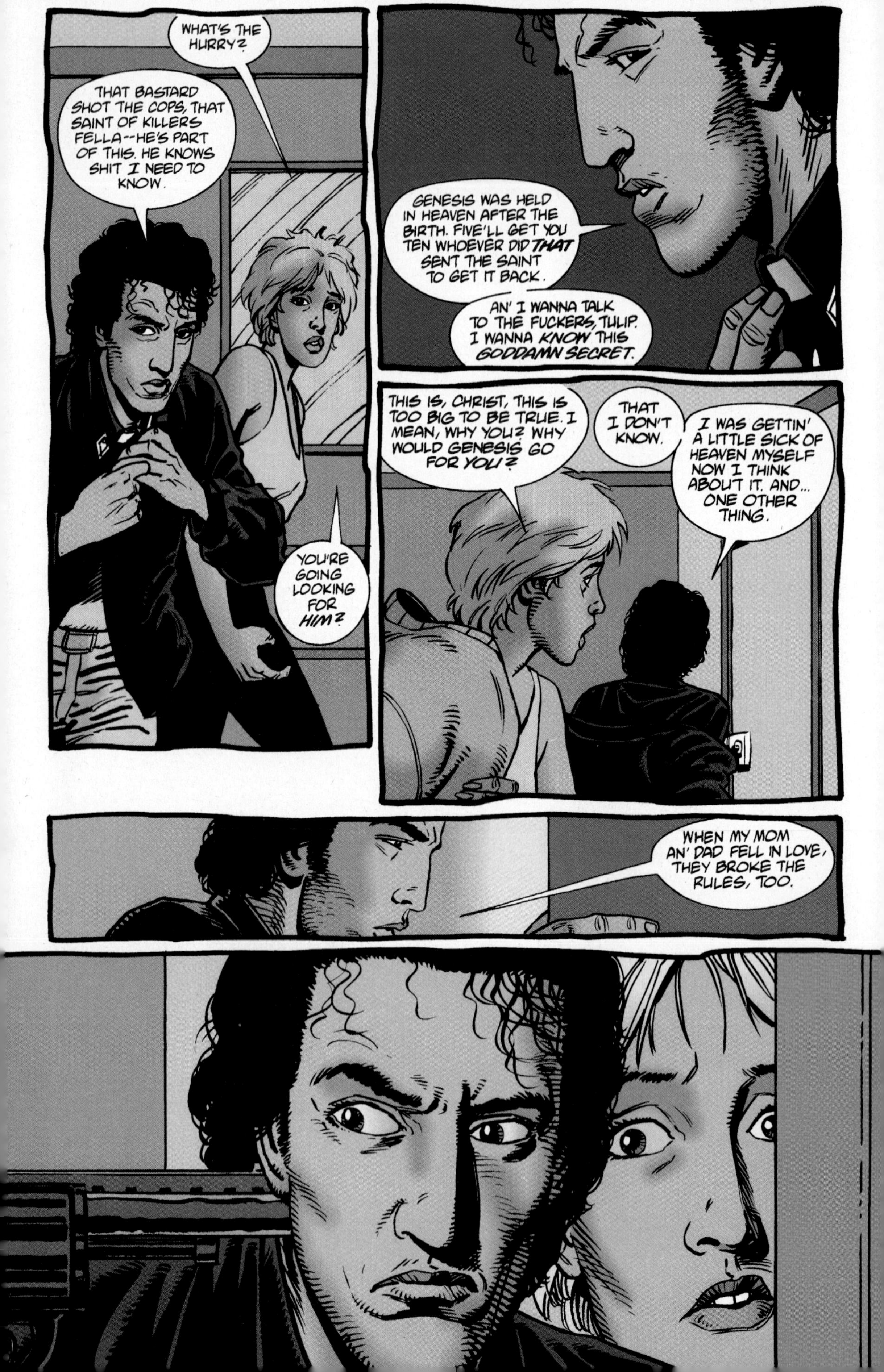
WHAT'S THE HURRY?
THAT BASTARD SHOT THE COPS, THAT SAINT OF KILLERS FELLA--HE'S PART OF THIS. HE KNOWS SHIT I NEED TO KNOW.
YOU'RE GOING LOOKING FOR HIM?
GENESIS WAS HELD IN HEAVEN AFTER THE BIRTH. FIVE'LL GET YOU TEN WHOEVER DID THAT SENT THE SAINT TO GET IT BACK.
AN' I WANNA TALK TO THE FUCKERS, TULIP. I WANNA KNOW THIS GODDAMN SECRET.
THIS IS, CHRIST, THIS IS TOO BIG TO BE TRUE. I MEAN, WHY YOU? WHY WOULD GENESIS GO FOR YOU?
THAT I DON'T KNOW.
I WAS GETTIN' A LITTLE SICK OF HEAVEN MYSELF NOW I THINK ABOUT IT. AND... ONE OTHER THING.
WHEN MY MOM AN' DAD FELL IN LOVE, THEY BROKE THE RULES, TOO.

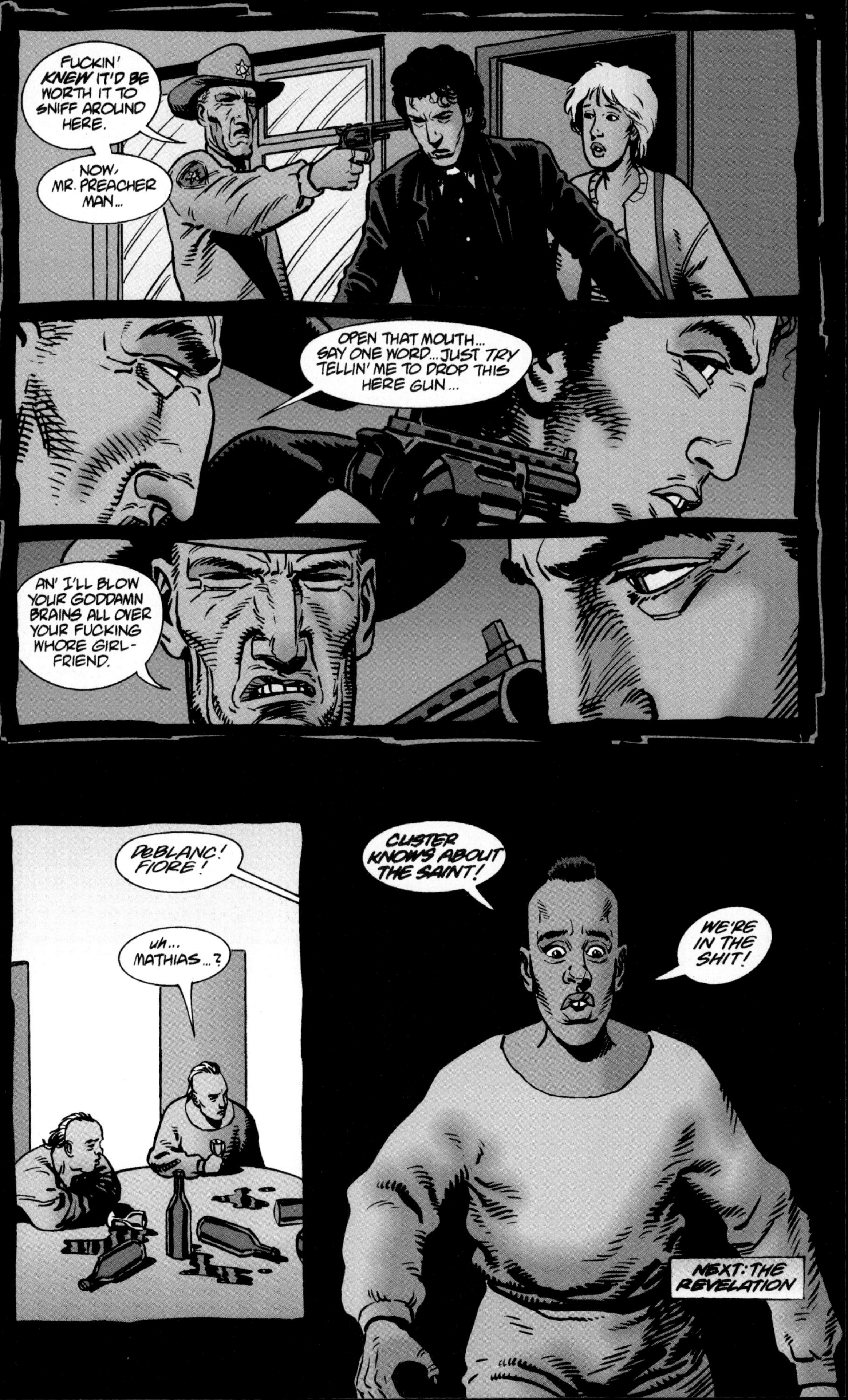
FUCKIN' KNEW IT'D BE WORTH IT TO SNIFF AROUND HERE.
NOW, MR. PREACHER MAN...
OPEN THAT MOUTH... SAY ONE WORD... JUST TRY TELLIN' ME TO DROP THIS HERE GUN...
AN' I'LL BLOW YOUR GODDAMN BRAINS ALL OVER YOUR FUCKING WHORE GIRL-FRIEND.
DeBLANC! FIORE!
uh... MATHIAS...?
CUSTER KNOWS ABOUT THE SAINT!
WE'RE IN THE SHIT!
NEXT: THE REVELATION

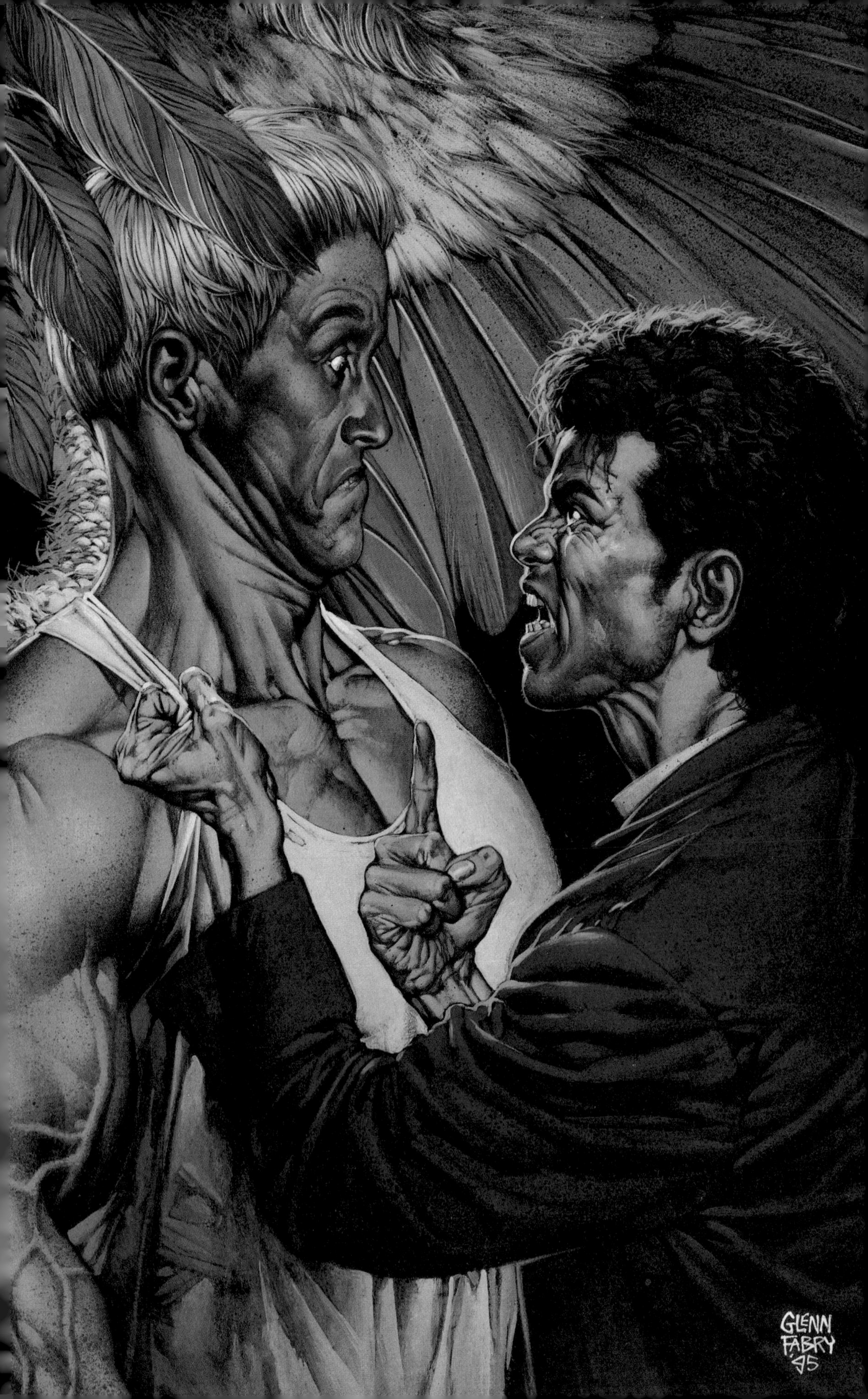
GLENN
FABRY
'95

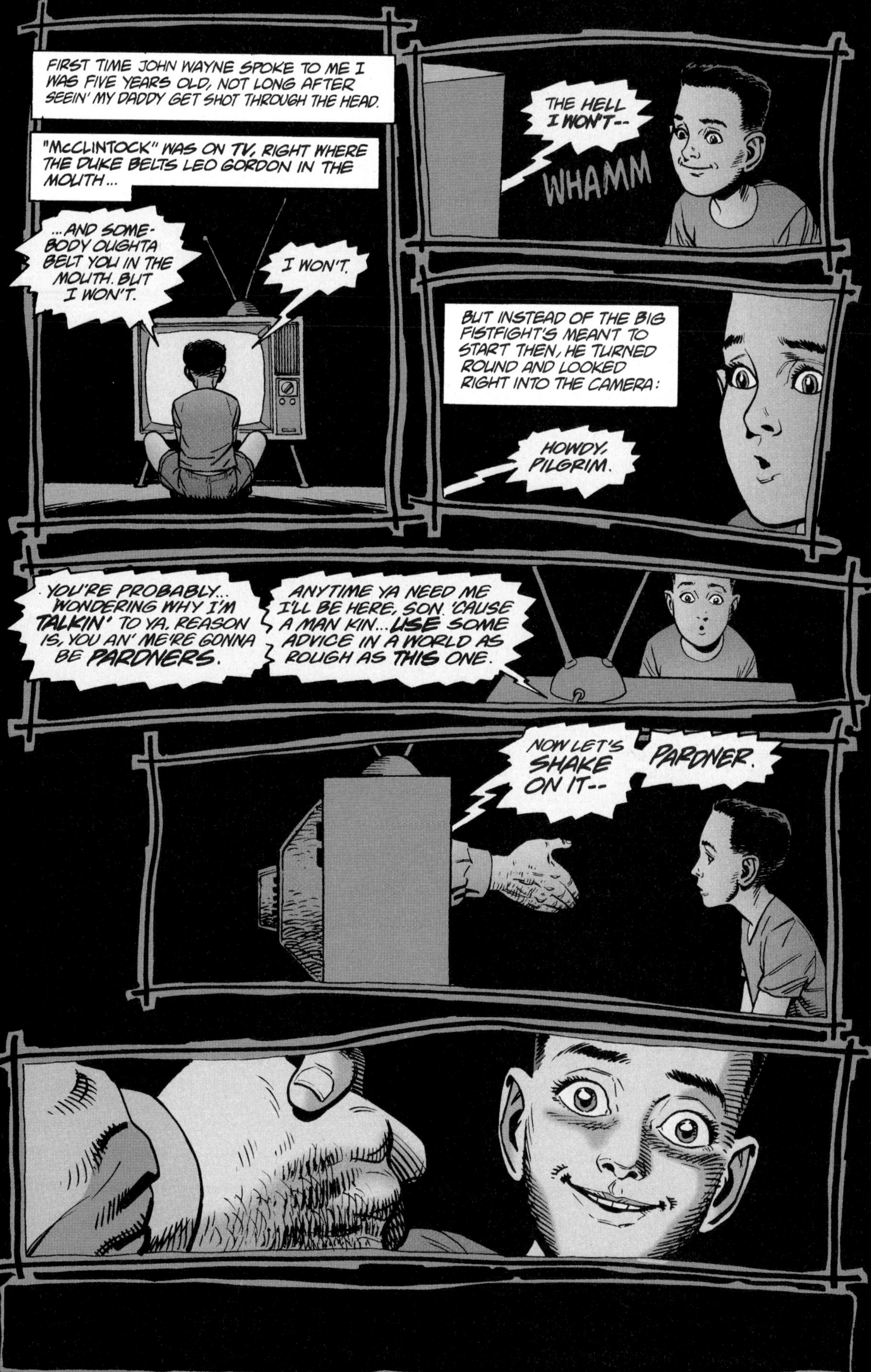
FIRST TIME JOHN WAYNE SPOKE TO ME I WAS FIVE YEARS OLD, NOT LONG AFTER SEEIN' MY DADDY GET SHOT THROUGH THE HEAD.
"McCLINTOCK" WAS ON TV, RIGHT WHERE THE DUKE BELTS LEO GORDON IN THE MOUTH...
...AND SOMEBODY OUGHTA BELT YOU IN THE MOUTH. BUT I WON'T.
I WON'T.
THE HELL I WON'T--
WHAMM
BUT INSTEAD OF THE BIG FISTFIGHT'S MEANT TO START THEN, HE TURNED ROUND AND LOOKED RIGHT INTO THE CAMERA:
HOWDY, PILGRIM.
YOU'RE PROBABLY... WONDERING WHY I'M TALKIN' TO YA. REASON IS, YOU AN' ME'RE GONNA BE PARDNERS.
ANYTIME YA NEED ME I'LL BE HERE, SON. 'CAUSE A MAN KIN... USE SOME ADVICE IN A WORLD AS ROUGH AS THIS ONE.
NOW LET'S SHAKE ON IT--
PARDNER.

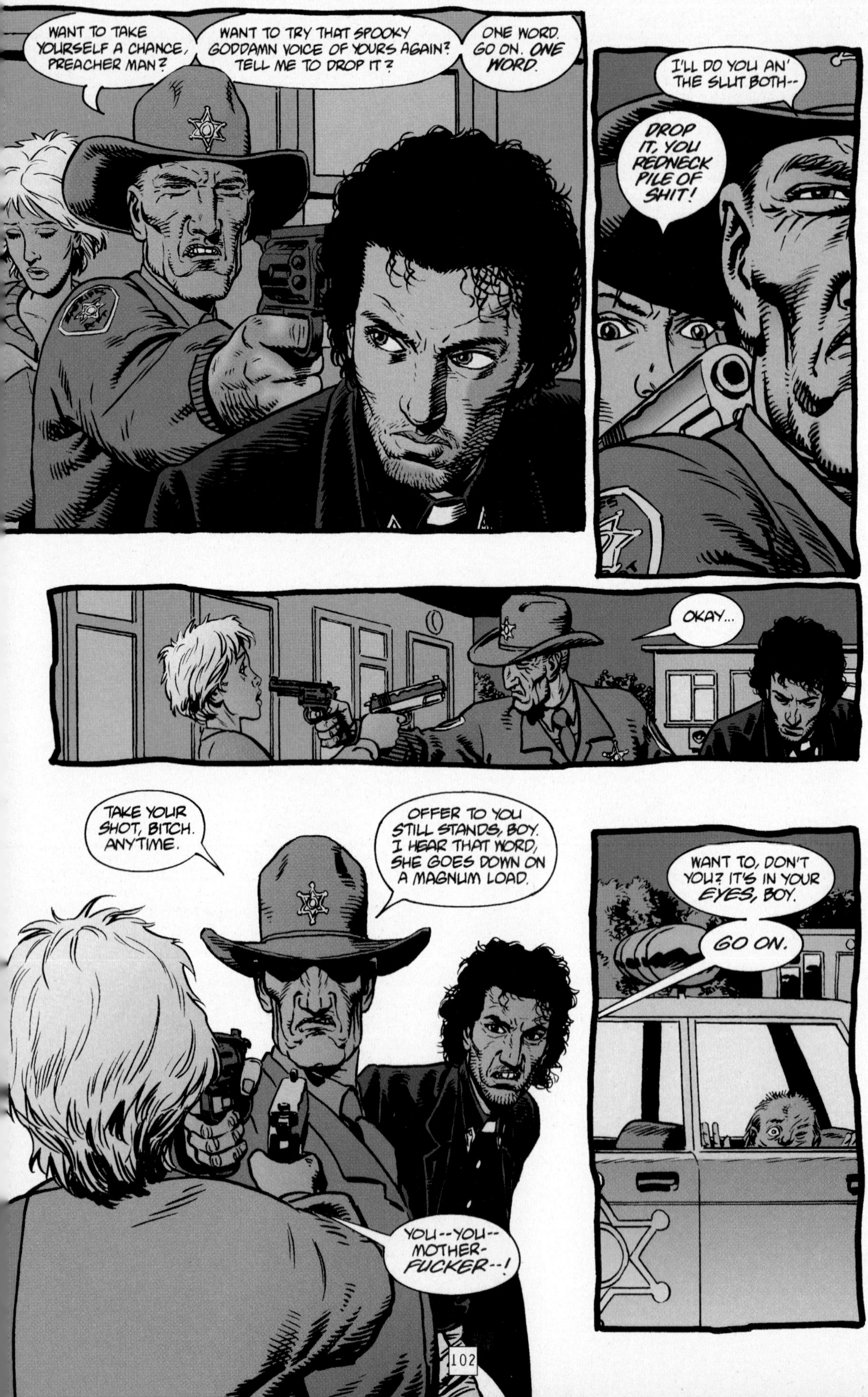
WANT TO TAKE YOURSELF A CHANCE, PREACHER MAN?
WANT TO TRY THAT SPOOKY GODDAMN VOICE OF YOURS AGAIN? TELL ME TO DROP IT?
ONE WORD. GO ON. ONE WORD.
I'LL DO YOU AN' THE SLUT BOTH--
DROP IT, YOU REDNECK PILE OF SHIT!
OKAY...
TAKE YOUR SHOT, BITCH. ANYTIME.
OFFER TO YOU STILL STANDS, BOY. I HEAR THAT WORD, SHE GOES DOWN ON A MAGNUM LOAD.
YOU--YOU--MOTHER-FUCKER--!
WANT TO, DON'T YOU? IT'S IN YOUR EYES, BOY.
GO ON.

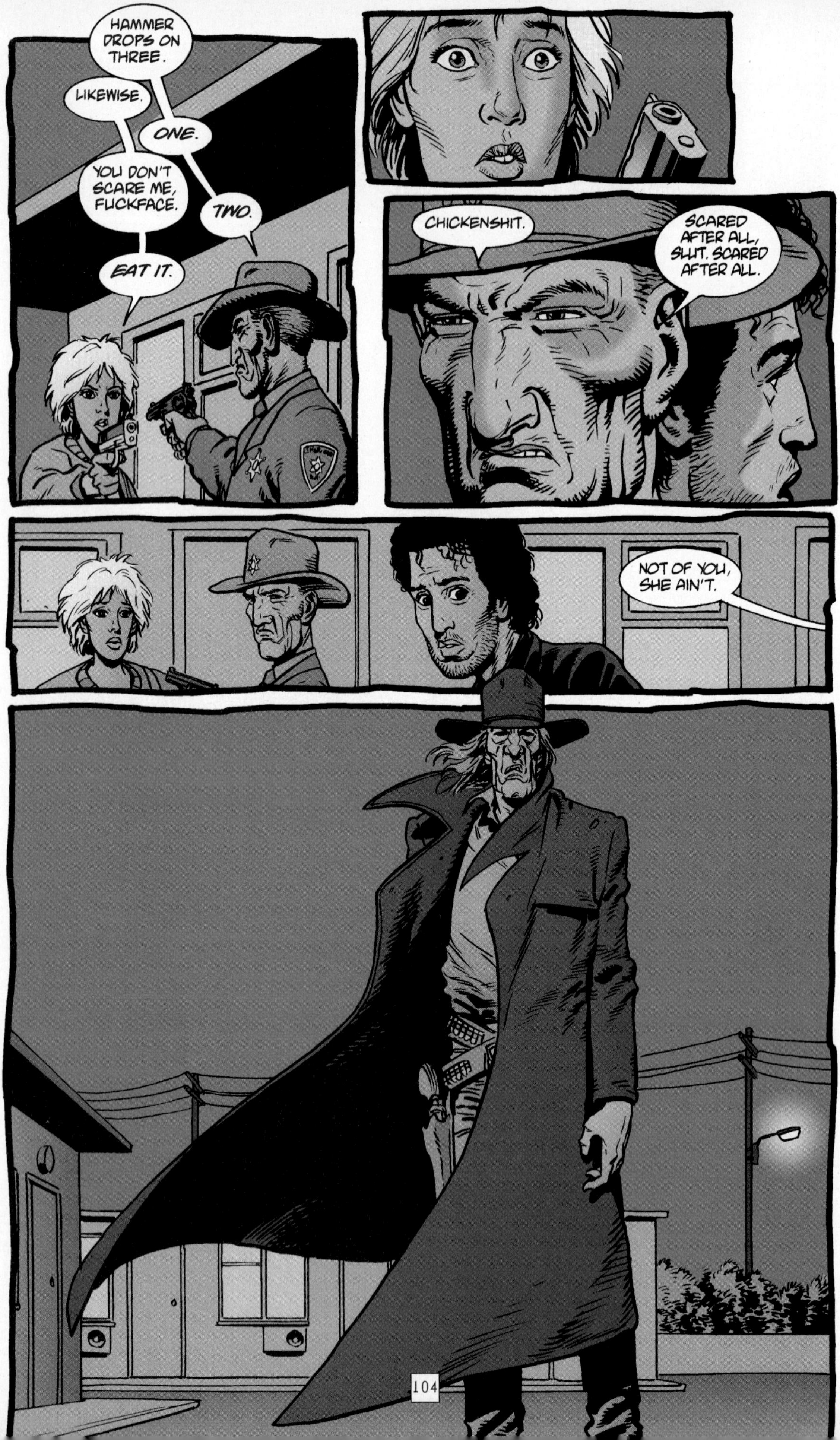

HAMMER DROPS ON THREE.
LIKEWISE.
ONE.
YOU DON'T SCARE ME, FUCKFACE.
TWO.
EAT IT.
CHICKENSHIT.
SCARED AFTER ALL, SLUT. SCARED AFTER ALL.
NOT OF YOU, SHE AIN'T.

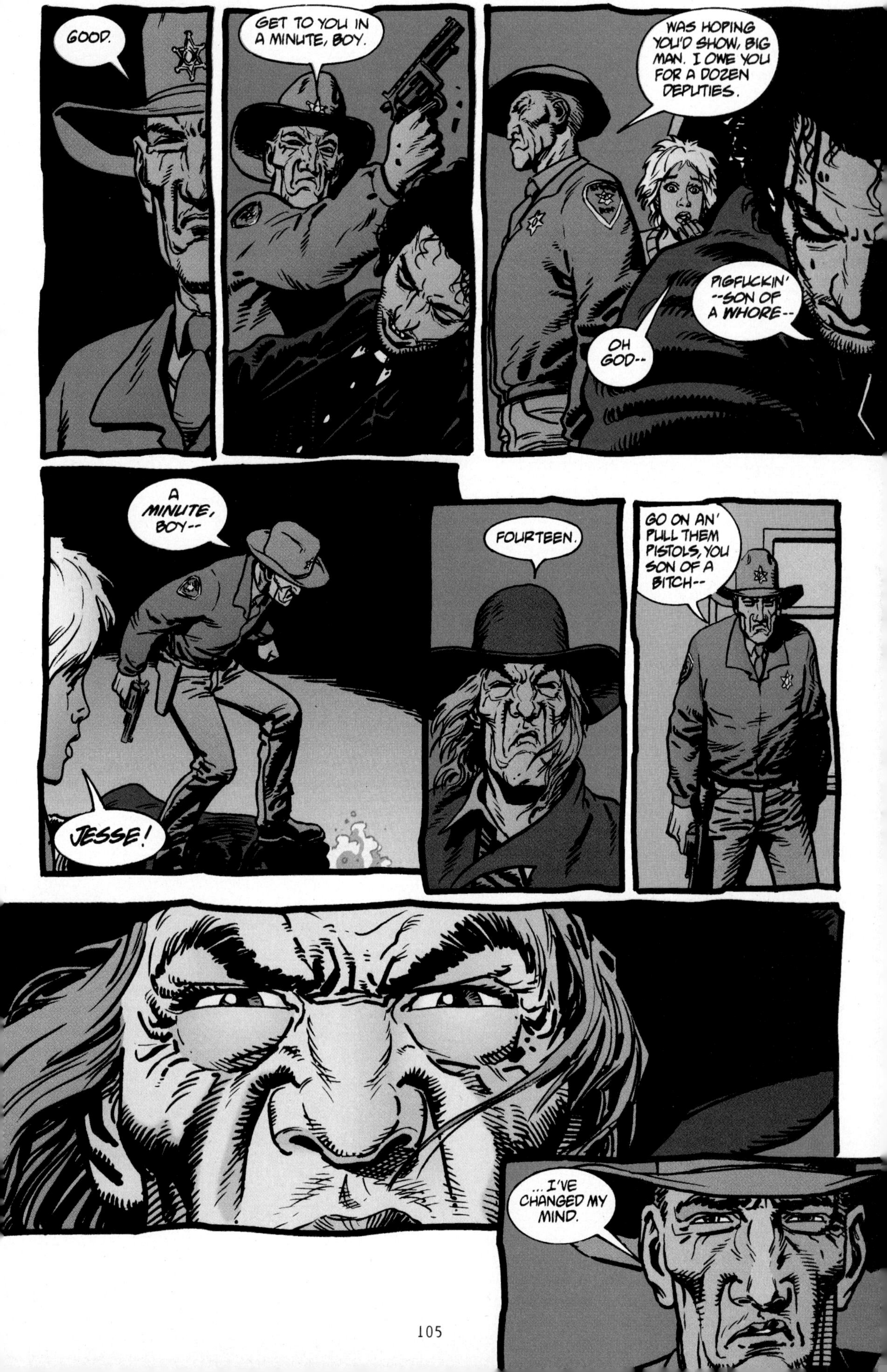
GOOD.
GET TO YOU IN A MINUTE, BOY.
WAS HOPING YOU'D SHOW, BIG MAN. I OWE YOU FOR A DOZEN DEPUTIES.
PIGFUCKIN' --SON OF A WHORE--
OH GOD--
A MINUTE, BOY--
JESSE!
FOURTEEN.
GO ON AN' PULL THEM PISTOLS, YOU SON OF A BITCH--
...I'VE CHANGED MY MIND.

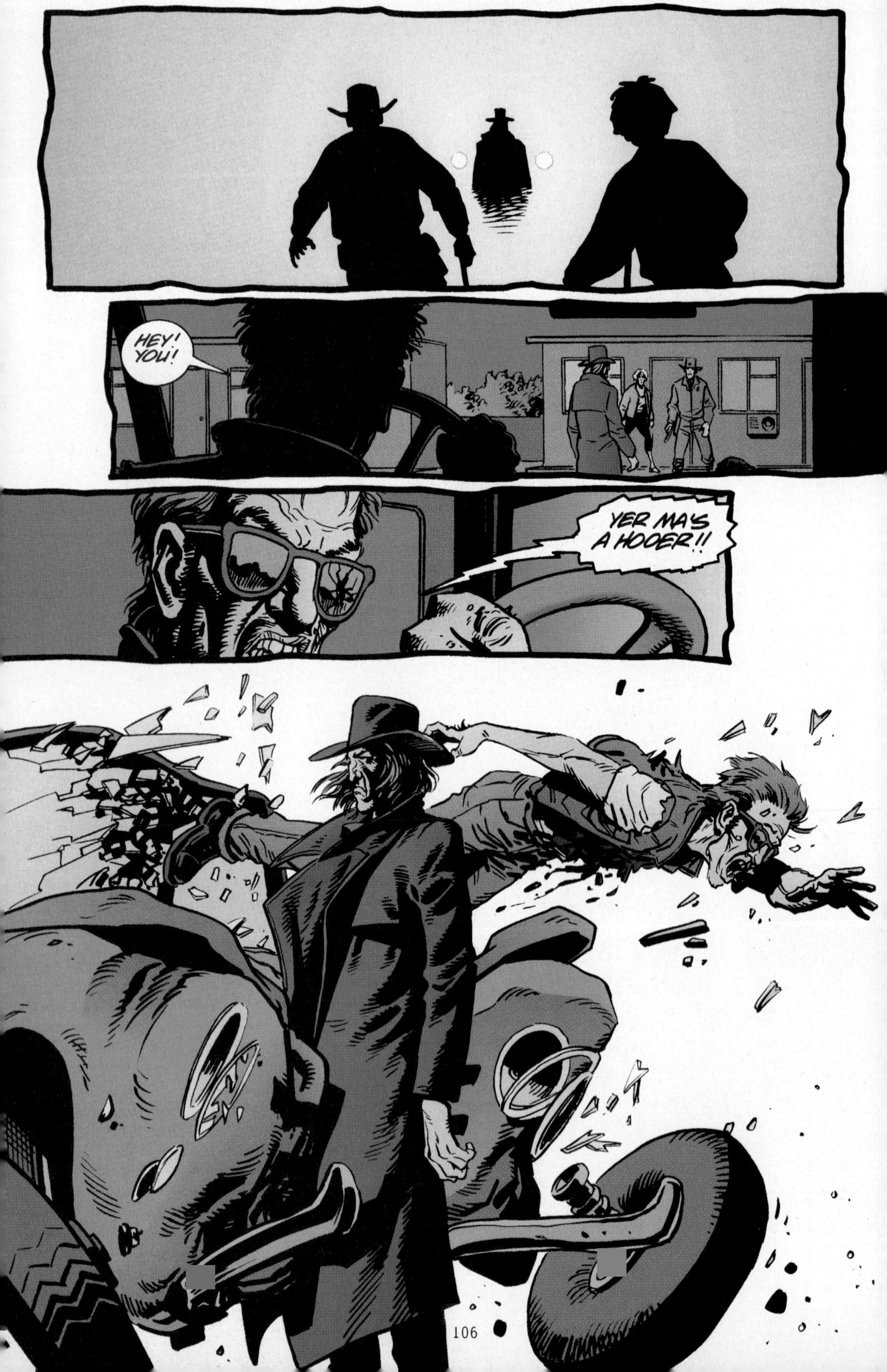
HEY! YOU!
YER MA'S A HOOER!!

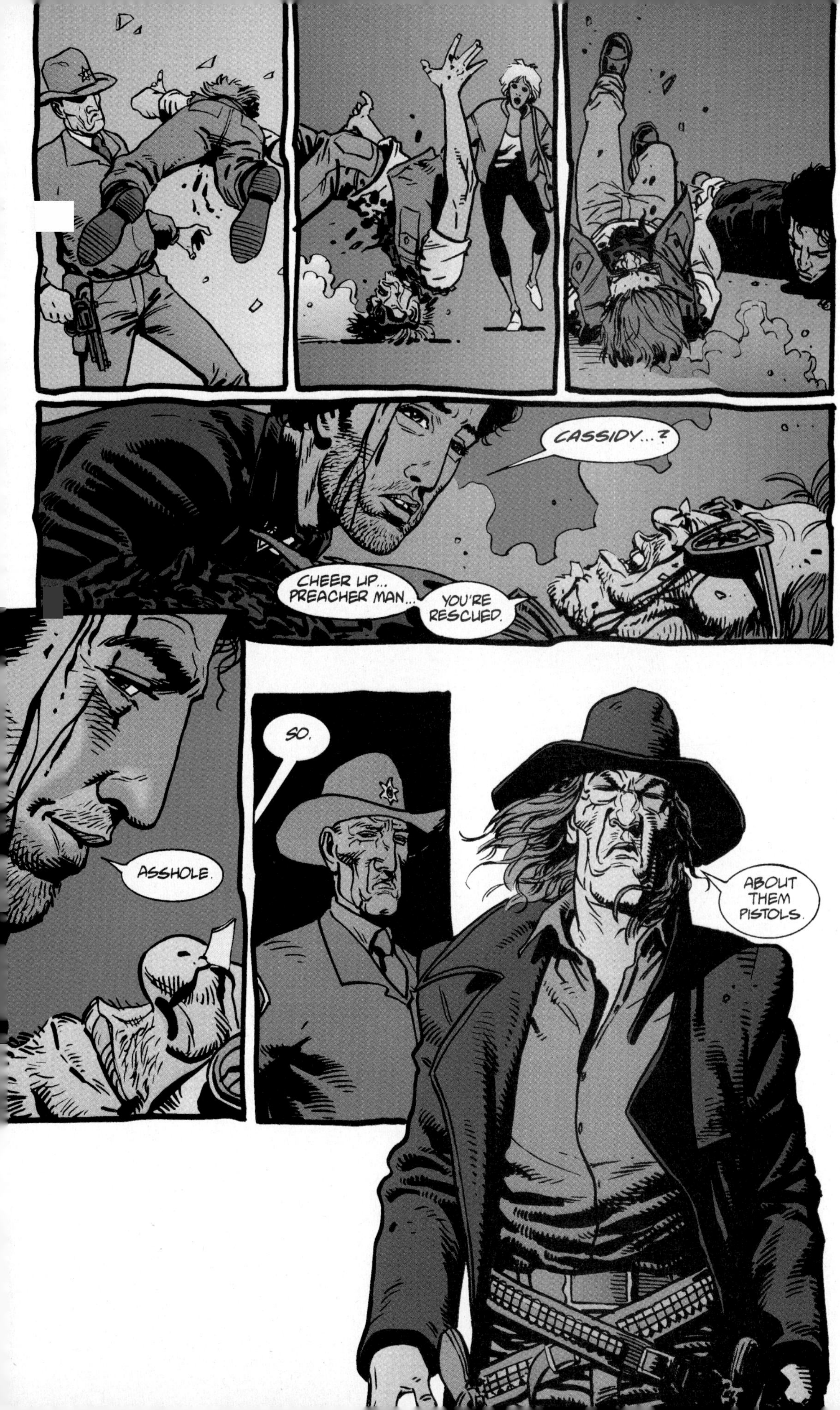
CASSIDY...?
CHEER UP... PREACHER MAN...
YOU'RE RESCUED.
ASSHOLE.
SO.
ABOUT THEM PISTOLS.

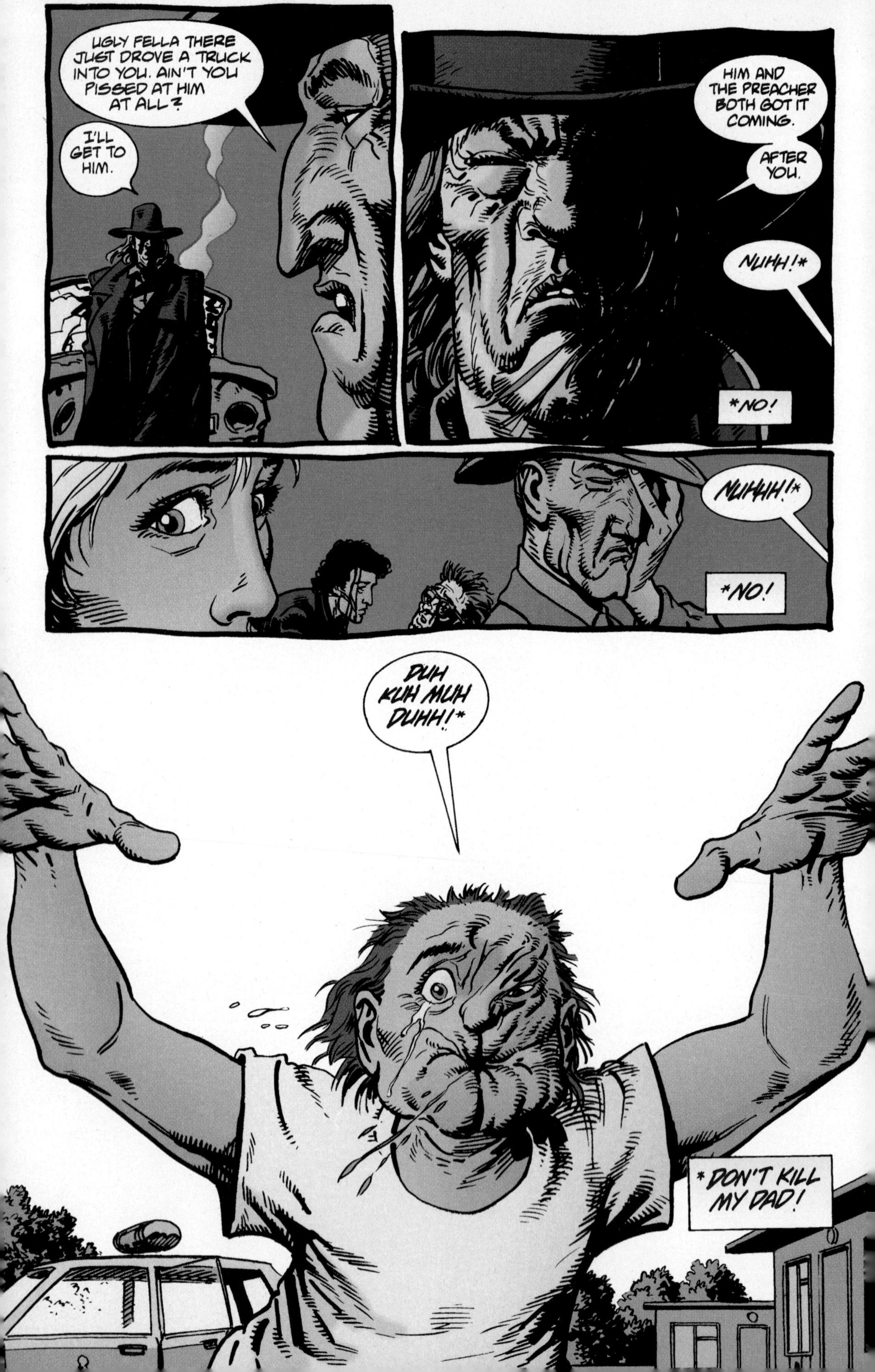
UGLY FELLA THERE JUST DROVE A TRUCK INTO YOU. AIN'T YOU PISSED AT HIM AT ALL?
I'LL GET TO HIM.
HIM AND THE PREACHER BOTH GOT IT COMING.
AFTER YOU.
NUHH!*
*NO!
NUHHH!*
*NO!
DUH KUH MUH DUHH!*
*DON'T KILL MY DAD!

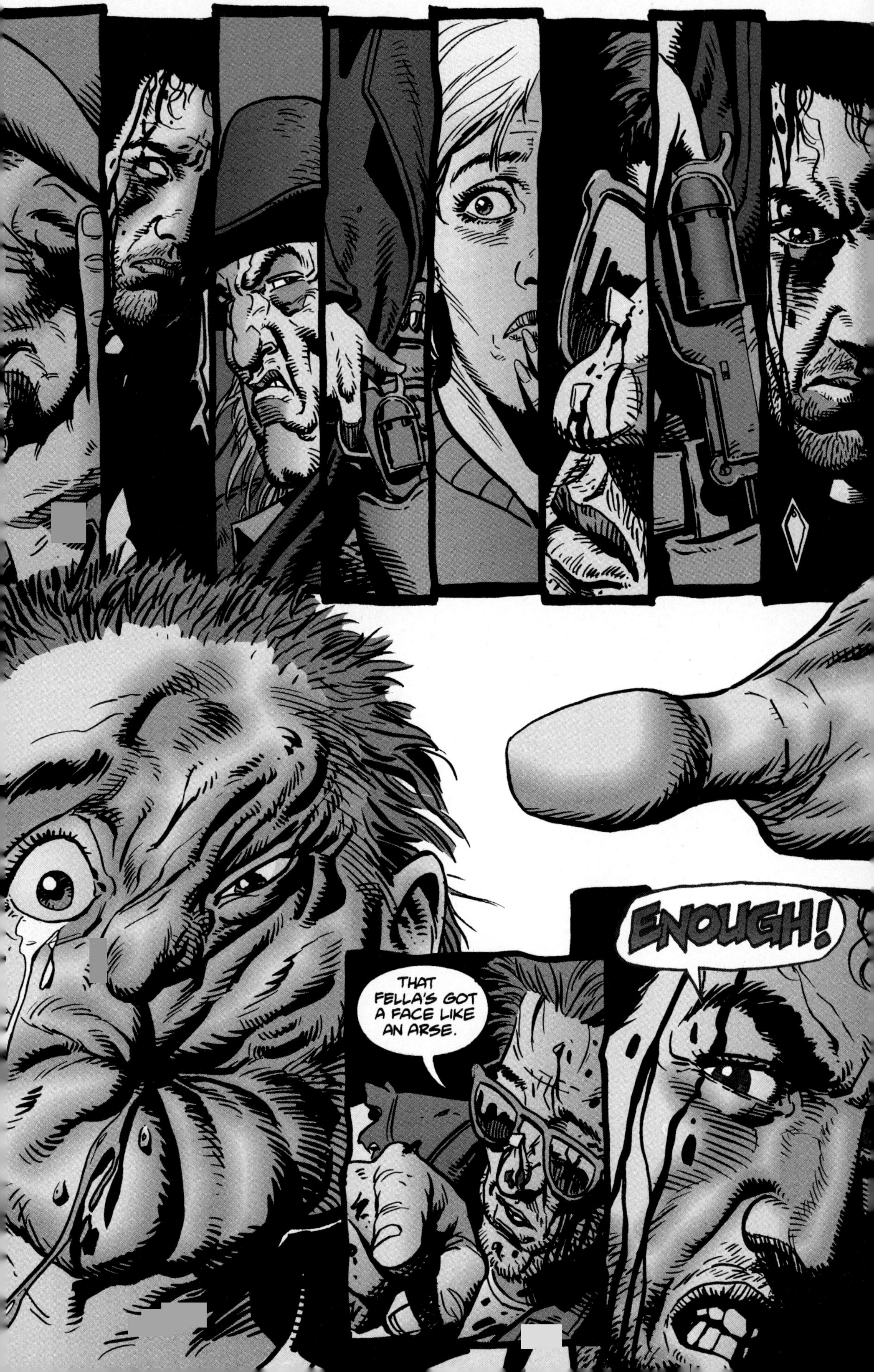
ENOUGH!
THAT FELLA'S GOT A FACE LIKE AN ARSE.

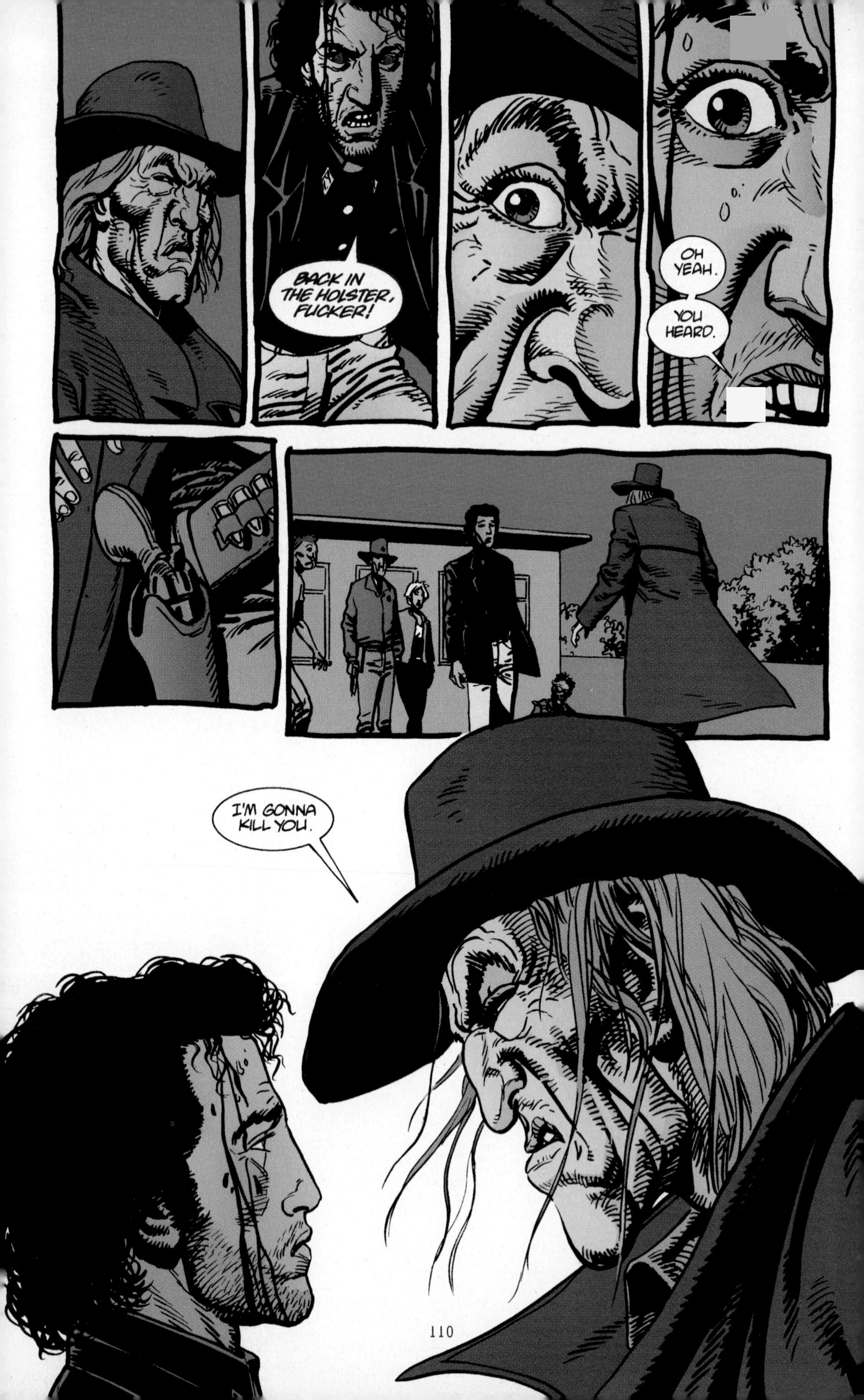
BACK IN THE HOLSTER, FUCKER!
OH YEAH.
YOU HEARD.
I'M GONNA KILL YOU.

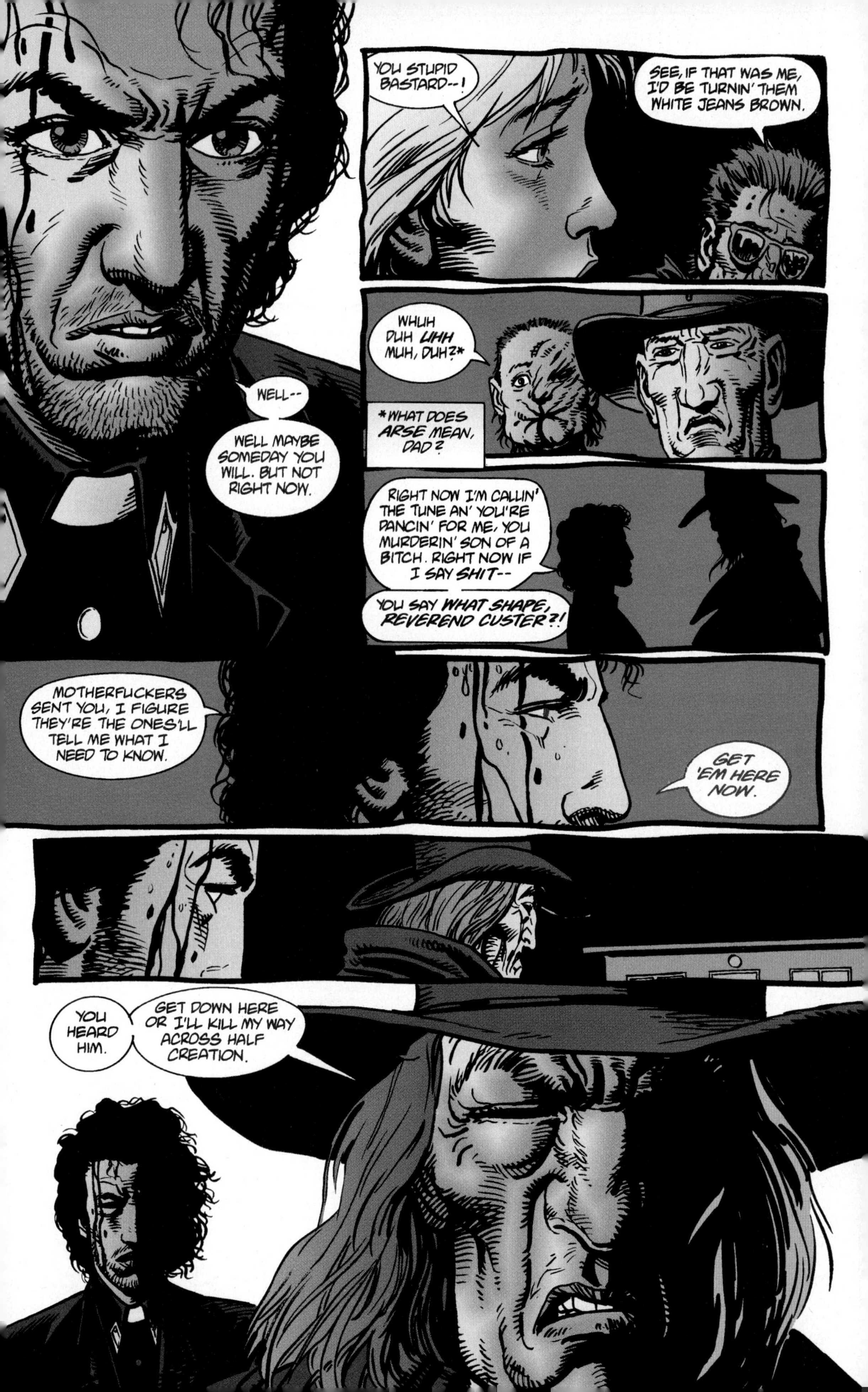
YOU STUPID BASTARD--!
SEE, IF THAT WAS ME, I'D BE TURNIN' THEM WHITE JEANS BROWN.
WHUH DUH UHH MUH, DUH?*
*WHAT DOES ARSE MEAN, DAD?
WELL--
WELL MAYBE SOMEDAY YOU WILL. BUT NOT RIGHT NOW.
RIGHT NOW I'M CALLIN' THE TUNE AN' YOU'RE DANCIN' FOR ME, YOU MURDERIN' SON OF A BITCH. RIGHT NOW IF I SAY SHIT--
YOU SAY WHAT SHAPE, REVEREND CUSTER?!
MOTHERFUCKERS SENT YOU, I FIGURE THEY'RE THE ONES'LL TELL ME WHAT I NEED TO KNOW.
GET 'EM HERE NOW.
YOU HEARD HIM.
GET DOWN HERE OR I'LL KILL MY WAY ACROSS HALF CREATION.

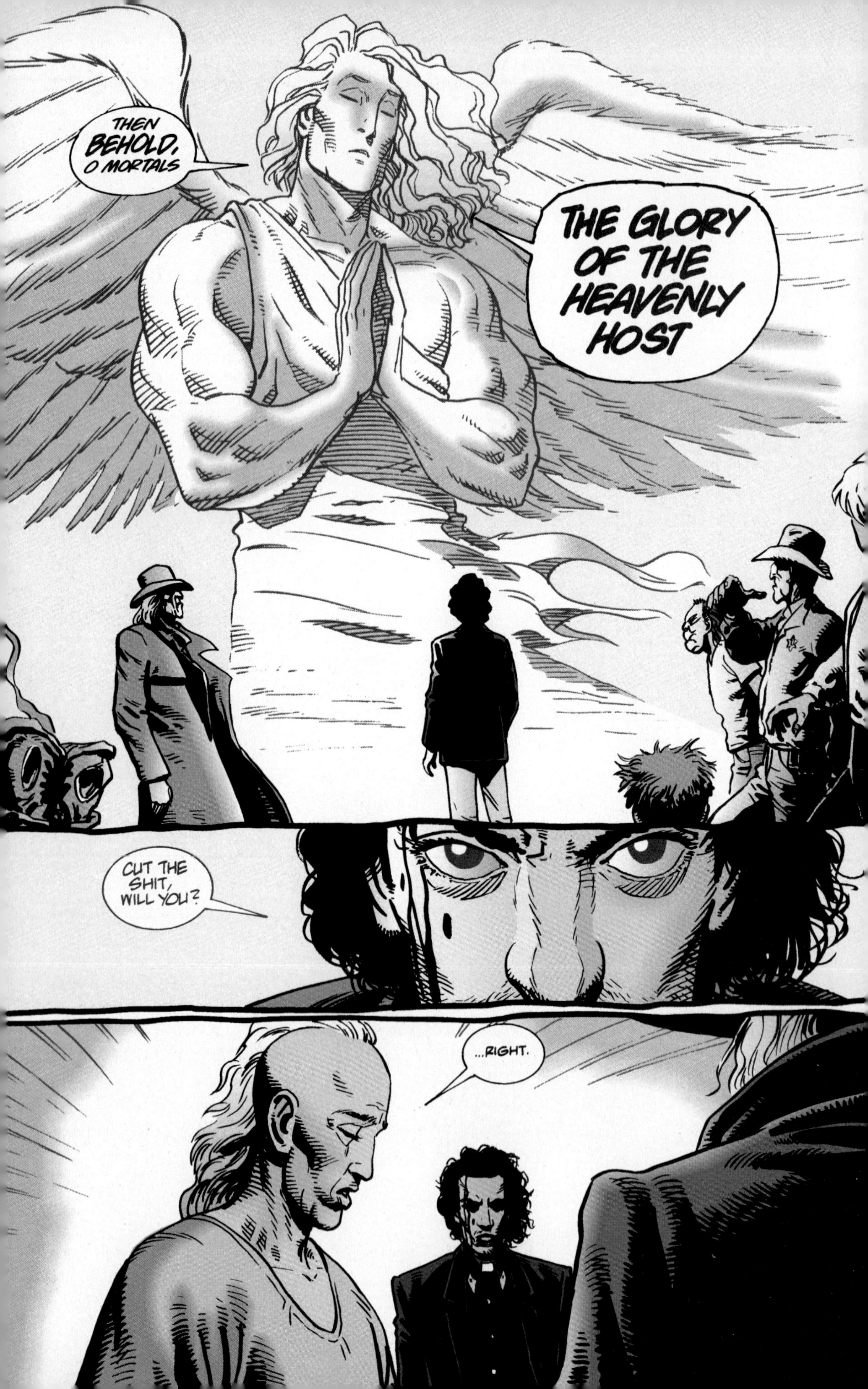
THEN BEHOLD, O MORTALS
THE GLORY OF THE HEAVENLY HOST
CUT THE SHIT, WILL YOU?
...RIGHT.

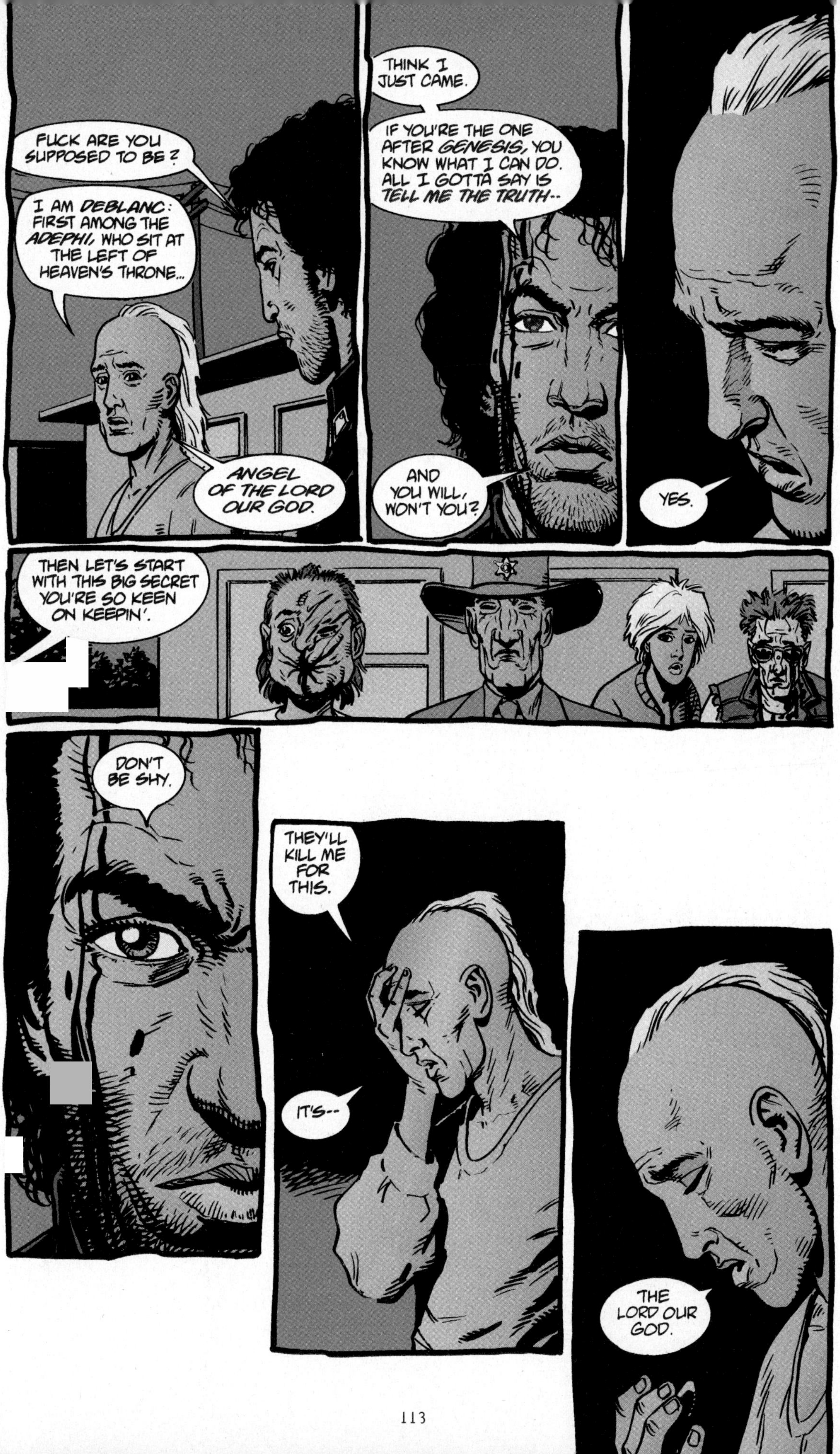
FUCK ARE YOU SUPPOSED TO BE?
I AM DEBLANC: FIRST AMONG THE ADEPHI, WHO SIT AT THE LEFT OF HEAVEN'S THRONE...
ANGEL OF THE LORD OUR GOD.
THINK I JUST CAME.
IF YOU'RE THE ONE AFTER GENESIS, YOU KNOW WHAT I CAN DO. ALL I GOTTA SAY IS TELL ME THE TRUTH--
AND YOU WILL, WON'T YOU?
YES.
THEN LET'S START WITH THIS BIG SECRET YOU'RE SO KEEN ON KEEPIN'.
DON'T BE SHY.
THEY'LL KILL ME FOR THIS.
IT'S--
THE LORD OUR GOD.

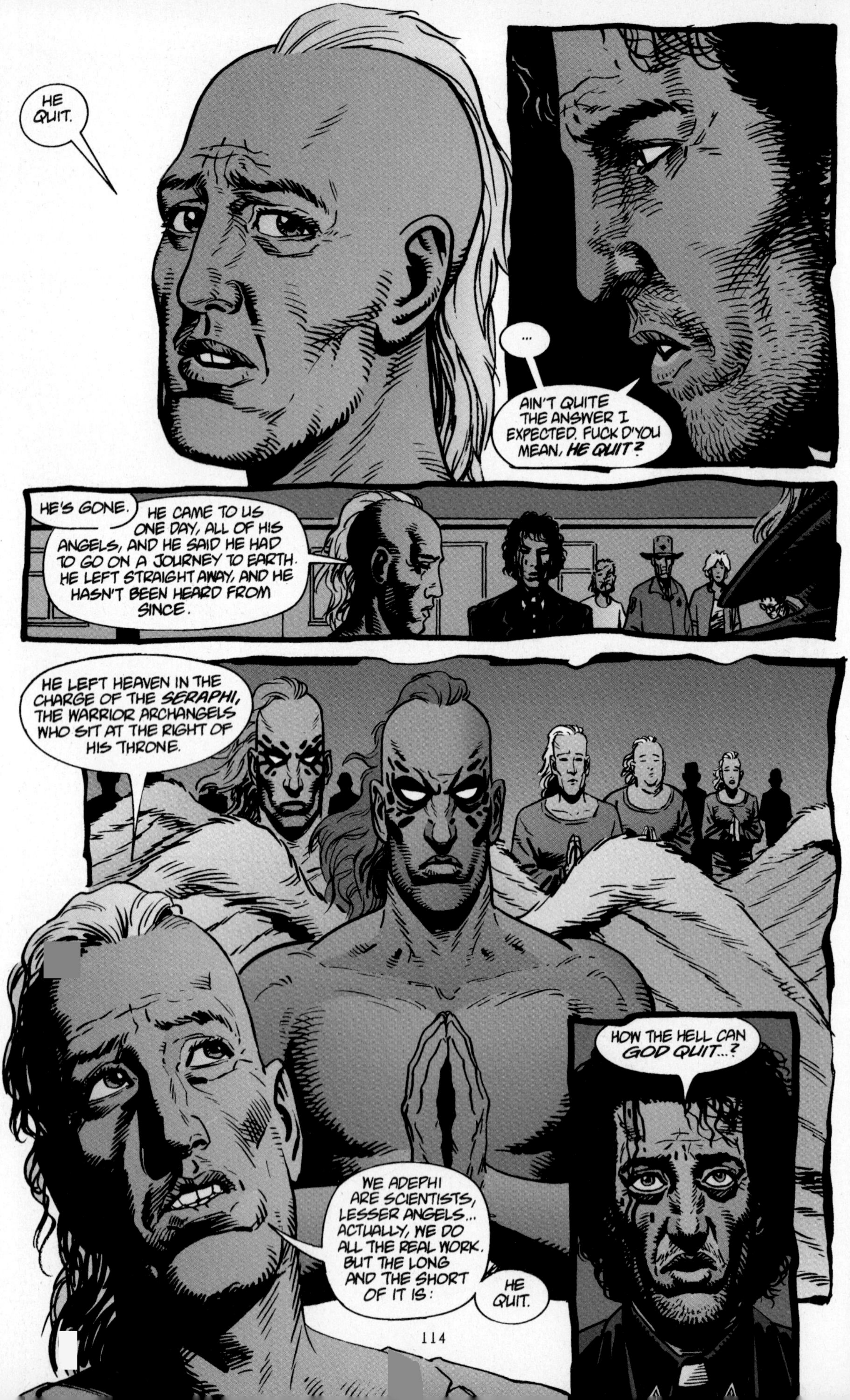
HE QUIT.
...
AIN'T QUITE THE ANSWER I EXPECTED. FUCK D'YOU MEAN, HE QUIT?
HE'S GONE.
HE CAME TO US ONE DAY, ALL OF HIS ANGELS, AND HE SAID HE HAD TO GO ON A JOURNEY TO EARTH. HE LEFT STRAIGHT AWAY, AND HE HASN'T BEEN HEARD FROM SINCE.
HE LEFT HEAVEN IN THE CHARGE OF THE SERAPHI, THE WARRIOR ARCHANGELS WHO SIT AT THE RIGHT OF HIS THRONE.
HOW THE HELL CAN GOD QUIT...?
WE ADEPHI ARE SCIENTISTS, LESSER ANGELS... ACTUALLY, WE DO ALL THE REAL WORK. BUT THE LONG AND THE SHORT OF IT IS:
HE QUIT.

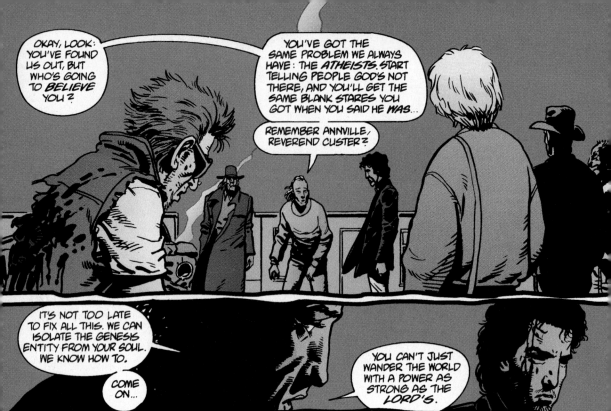

OKAY, LOOK: YOU'VE FOUND US OUT, BUT WHO'S GOING TO *BELIEVE* YOU?

YOU'VE GOT THE SAME PROBLEM WE ALWAYS HAVE: THE *ATHEISTS.* START TELLING PEOPLE GOD'S NOT THERE, AND YOU'LL GET THE SAME BLANK STARES YOU GOT WHEN YOU SAID HE *WAS...*

REMEMBER ANNVILLE, REVEREND CUSTER?

IT'S NOT TOO LATE TO FIX ALL THIS. WE CAN ISOLATE THE GENESIS ENTITY FROM YOUR SOUL. WE KNOW HOW TO.

COME ON...

YOU CAN'T JUST WANDER THE WORLD WITH A POWER AS STRONG AS THE *LORD'S.*

IT *IS* AS STRONG AS HIM, HUH?

AH-- WELL--

RECKON YOU'RE RIGHT. NO ONE'S GONNA BELIEVE *ANY OF THIS* --UNLESS THEY HEAR IT FROM THE LORD HIMSELF...

YOU KNOW WHAT? I'M GONNA GO LOOKIN' FOR HIM. I DON'T CARE HOW LONG IT TAKES OR WHERE I HAVE TO GO. I'M GONNA *FIND HIM.*

AN' I'M GONNA *MAKE HIM* TELL HIS PEOPLE WHAT HE'S DONE.

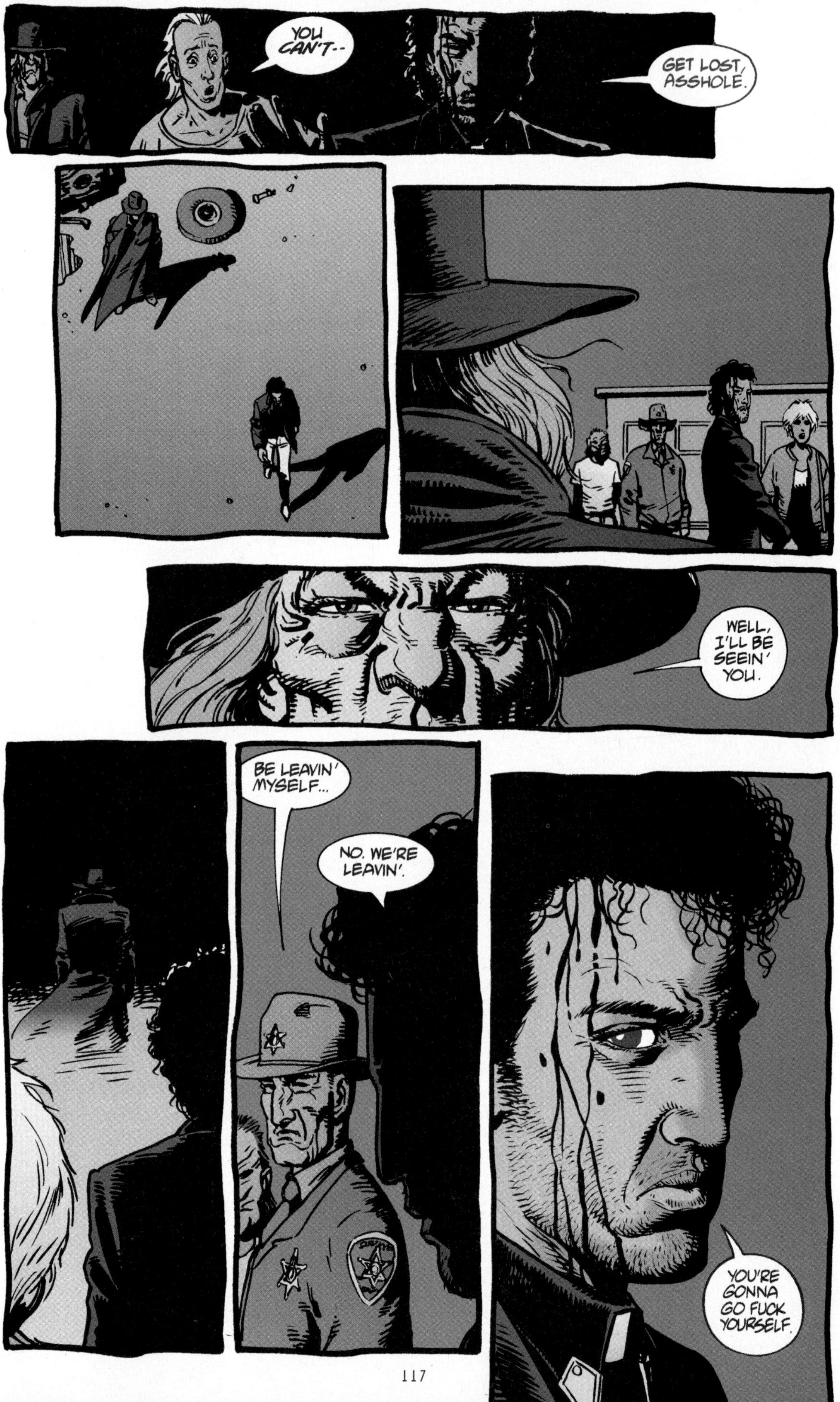
YOU CAN'T--
GET LOST, ASSHOLE.
WELL, I'LL BE SEEIN' YOU.
BE LEAVIN' MYSELF...
NO. WE'RE LEAVIN'.
YOU'RE GONNA GO FUCK YOURSELF.

FIGURE WE MISSED ALL THE ACTION HERE, TOO.

IF IT WAS ANYTHING LIKE THE ACTION AT THE TEN-TEN, I'M NOT TOO UNHAPPY ABOUT THAT.

YOU KNOW, EVER SINCE I CROSSED THE MASON-DIXON I'VE BEEN DRINKING UNIFORMLY SHITTY COFFEE. OR DID YOU GET ALL EXCITED AGAIN?

BLOW ME. HEY, THIS OUGHTA BE TOUCHING...

UH MUH DUH GUHBUH UKAH?*

*IS MY DAD GONNA BE OKAY?

WELL, UH--

LOOK, NO OFFENSE, BUT IS THERE ANY CHANCE YOU COULD FACE THE OTHER WAY WHILE I'M TALKING TO YOU? YOUR FACE IS MAKING ME NAUSEOUS, IS ALL.

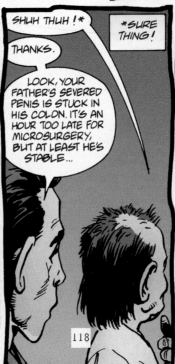

SHUH THUH !*

*SURE THING!

THANKS.

LOOK, YOUR FATHER'S SEVERED PENIS IS STUCK IN HIS COLON. IT'S AN HOUR TOO LATE FOR MICROSURGERY, BUT AT LEAST HE'S STABLE...

WE'RE TAKING HIM TO THE HOSPITAL NOW--

S...SON...?

DUHH!*

*DAD!

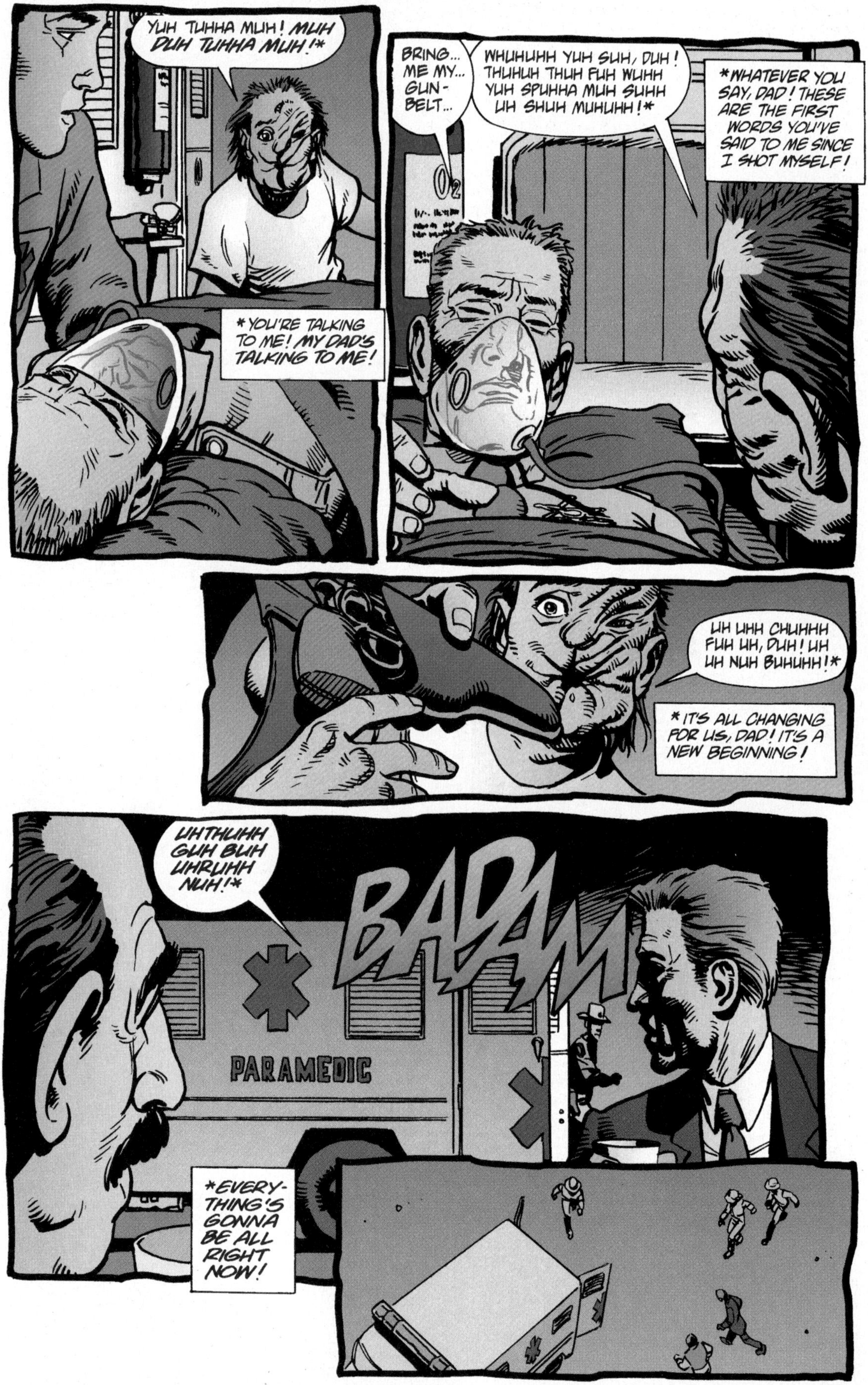
YUH TUHHA MUH! MUH DUH TUHHA MUH!*
*YOU'RE TALKING TO ME! MY DAD'S TALKING TO ME!
BRING... ME MY... GUN-BELT...
WHUHUHH YUH SUH, DUH! THUHUH THUH FUH WUHH YUH SPUHHA MUH SUHH UH SHUH MUHUHH!*
*WHATEVER YOU SAY, DAD! THESE ARE THE FIRST WORDS YOU'VE SAID TO ME SINCE I SHOT MYSELF!
UH UHH CHUHHH FUH UH, DUH! UH UH NUH BUHUHH!*
*IT'S ALL CHANGING FOR US, DAD! IT'S A NEW BEGINNING!
UHTHUHH GUH BUH UHRUHH NUH!*
BADAM
PARAMEDIC
*EVERY-THING'S GONNA BE ALL RIGHT NOW!

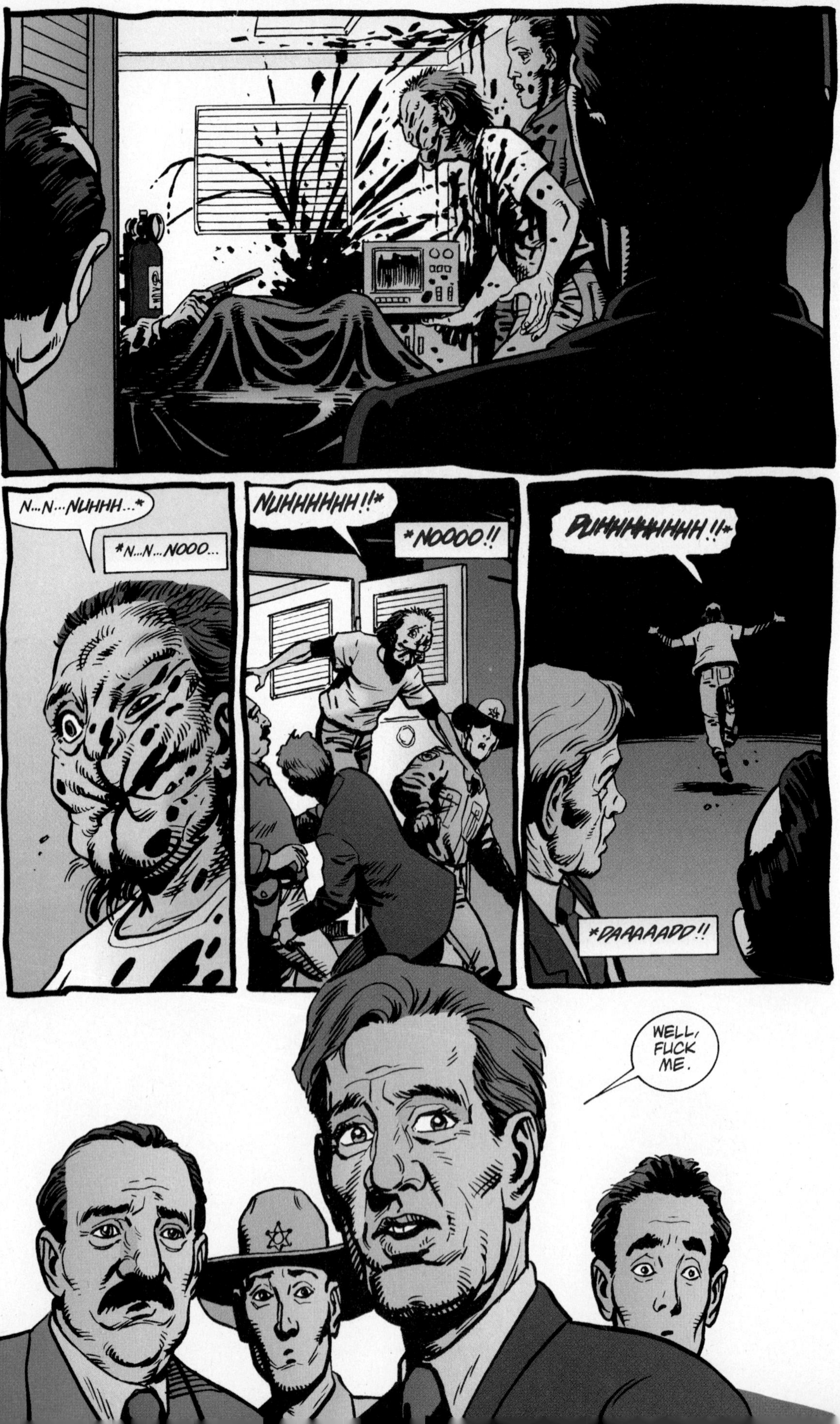
N...N...NUHHH...*
*N...N...NOOO...
NUHHHHHHH!!*
*NOOOO!!
DUHHHHHHHH!!*
*DAAAAADD!!
WELL, FUCK ME.

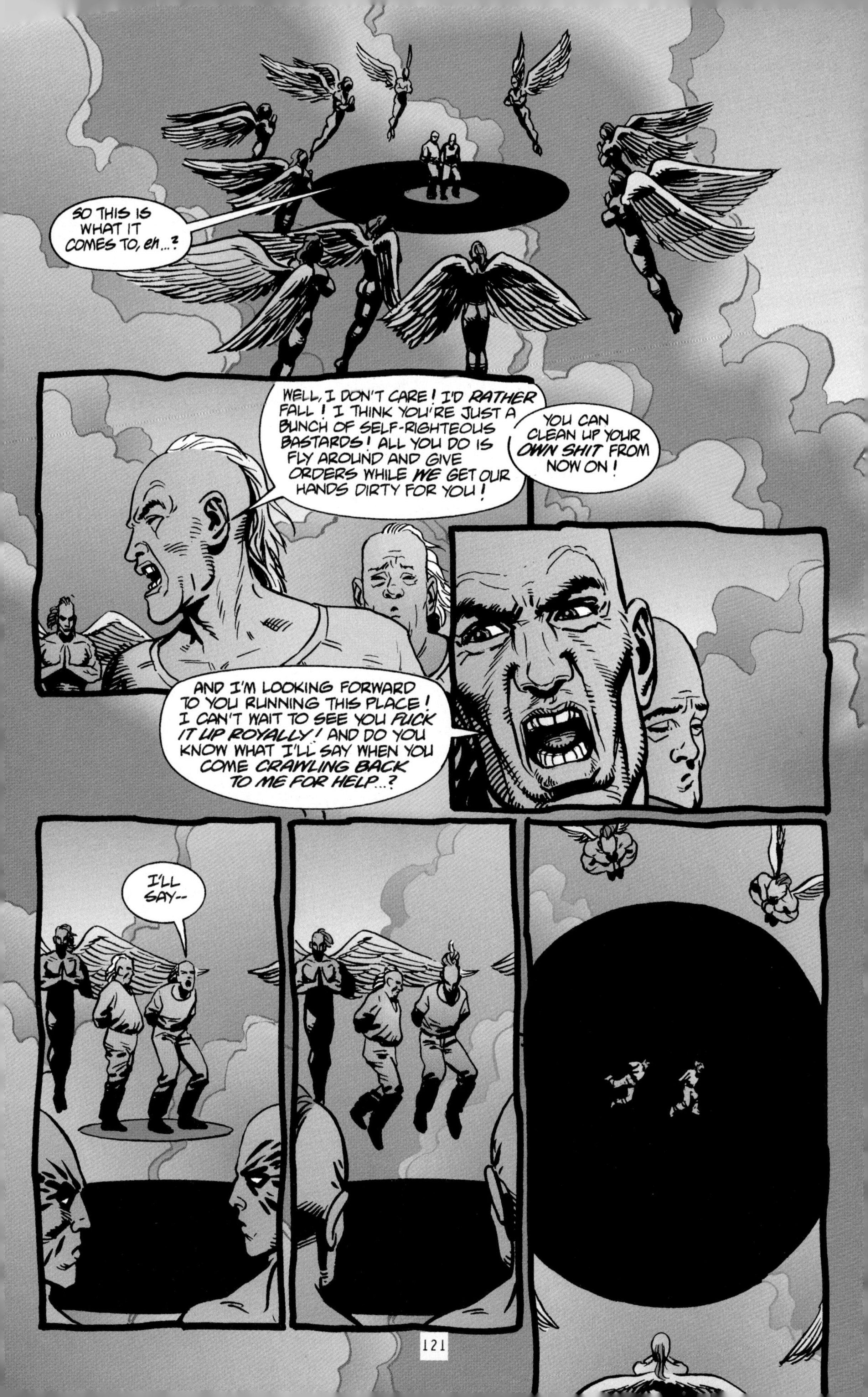
SO THIS IS WHAT IT COMES TO, eh...?
WELL, I DON'T CARE! I'D RATHER FALL! I THINK YOU'RE JUST A BUNCH OF SELF-RIGHTEOUS BASTARDS! ALL YOU DO IS FLY AROUND AND GIVE ORDERS WHILE WE GET OUR HANDS DIRTY FOR YOU!
YOU CAN CLEAN UP YOUR OWN SHIT FROM NOW ON!
AND I'M LOOKING FORWARD TO YOU RUNNING THIS PLACE! I CAN'T WAIT TO SEE YOU FUCK IT UP ROYALLY! AND DO YOU KNOW WHAT I'LL SAY WHEN YOU COME CRAWLING BACK TO ME FOR HELP...?
I'LL SAY--

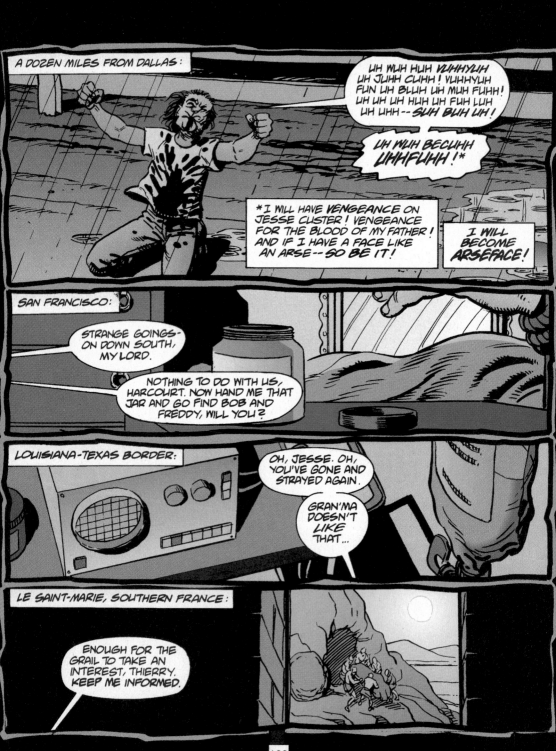

A DOZEN MILES FROM DALLAS:

UH WUH HUH *VUHHYUH* UH JUHH CUHH! *VUHHYUH* FUN UH BLUH UH MUH FUHH! UH UH UH HUH UH FUH LUH UH UHH-- *SUH BUH UH!*

UH WUH BECUHH *UHHFUHH!*

*I WILL HAVE *VENGEANCE* ON JESSE CUSTER! VENGEANCE FOR THE BLOOD OF MY FATHER! AND IF I HAVE A FACE LIKE AN ARSE-- *SO BE IT!*

I WILL BECOME *ARSEFACE!*

SAN FRANCISCO:

STRANGE GOINGS-ON DOWN SOUTH, MY LORD.

NOTHING TO DO WITH US, HARCOURT. NOW HAND ME THAT JAR AND GO FIND BOB AND FREDDY, WILL YOU?

LOUISIANA-TEXAS BORDER:

OH, JESSE. OH, YOU'VE GONE AND STRAYED AGAIN.

GRAN'MA DOESN'T LIKE THAT...

LE SAINT-MARIE, SOUTHERN FRANCE:

ENOUGH FOR THE GRAIL TO TAKE AN INTEREST, THIERRY. KEEP ME INFORMED.

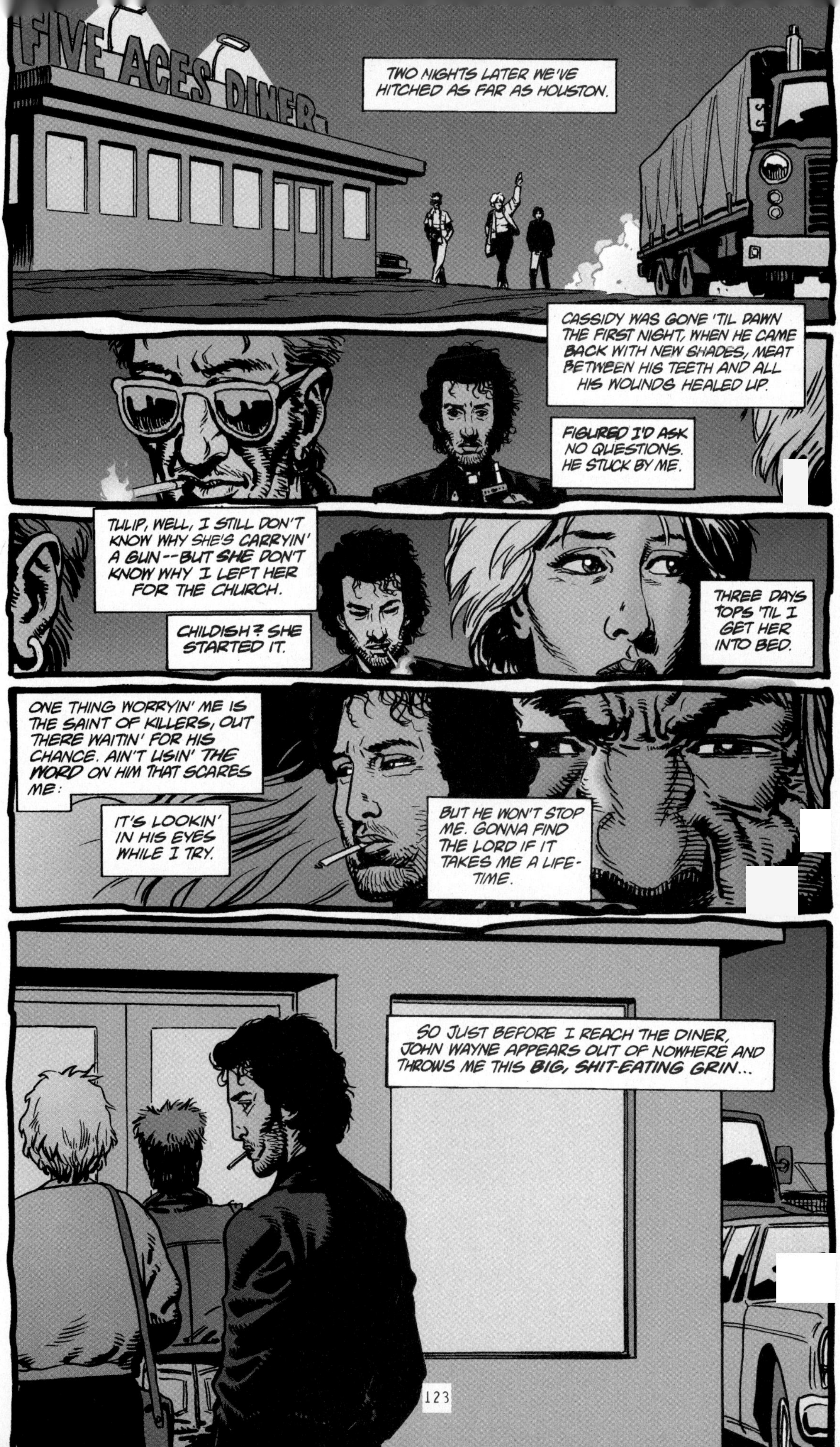
FIVE ACES DINER
TWO NIGHTS LATER WE'VE HITCHED AS FAR AS HOUSTON.
CASSIDY WAS GONE 'TIL DAWN THE FIRST NIGHT, WHEN HE CAME BACK WITH NEW SHADES, MEAT BETWEEN HIS TEETH AND ALL HIS WOUNDS HEALED UP.
FIGURED I'D ASK NO QUESTIONS. HE STUCK BY ME.
TULIP, WELL, I STILL DON'T KNOW WHY SHE'S CARRYIN' A GUN--BUT SHE DON'T KNOW WHY I LEFT HER FOR THE CHURCH.
CHILDISH? SHE STARTED IT.
THREE DAYS TOPS 'TIL I GET HER INTO BED.
ONE THING WORRYIN' ME IS THE SAINT OF KILLERS, OUT THERE WAITIN' FOR HIS CHANCE. AIN'T USIN' THE WORD ON HIM THAT SCARES ME:
IT'S LOOKIN' IN HIS EYES WHILE I TRY.
BUT HE WON'T STOP ME. GONNA FIND THE LORD IF IT TAKES ME A LIFE-TIME.
SO JUST BEFORE I REACH THE DINER, JOHN WAYNE APPEARS OUT OF NOWHERE AND THROWS ME THIS BIG, SHIT-EATING GRIN...

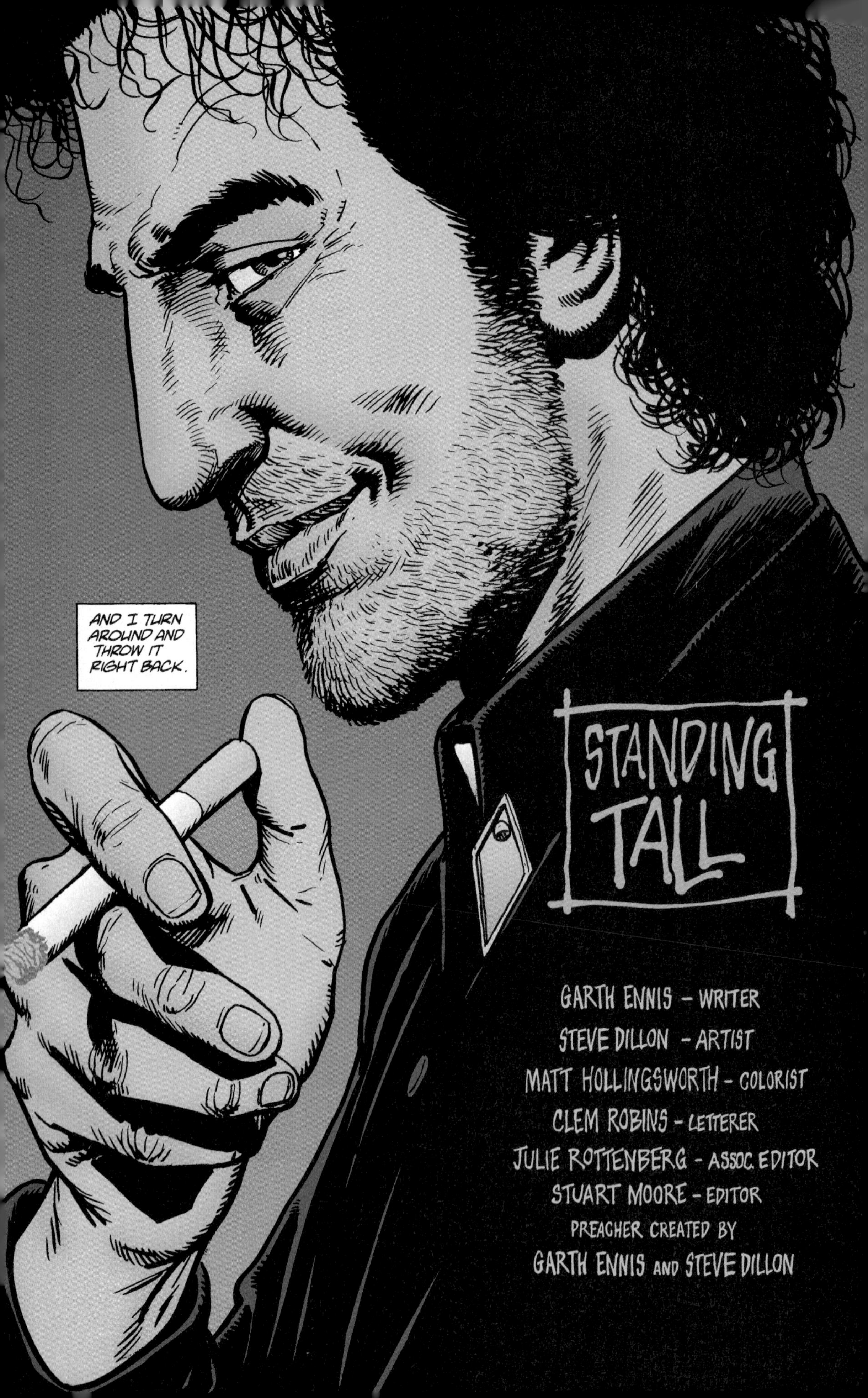
AND I TURN AROUND AND THROW IT RIGHT BACK.
STANDING TALL
GARTH ENNIS - WRITER
STEVE DILLON - ARTIST
MATT HOLLINGSWORTH - COLORIST
CLEM ROBINS - LETTERER
JULIE ROTTENBERG - ASSOC. EDITOR
STUART MOORE - EDITOR
PREACHER CREATED BY
GARTH ENNIS AND STEVE DILLON

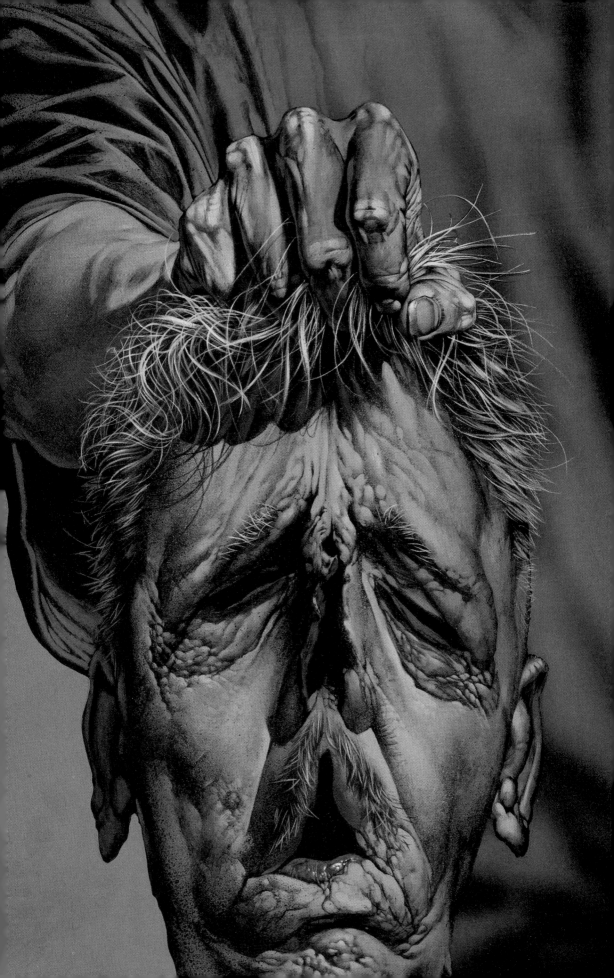

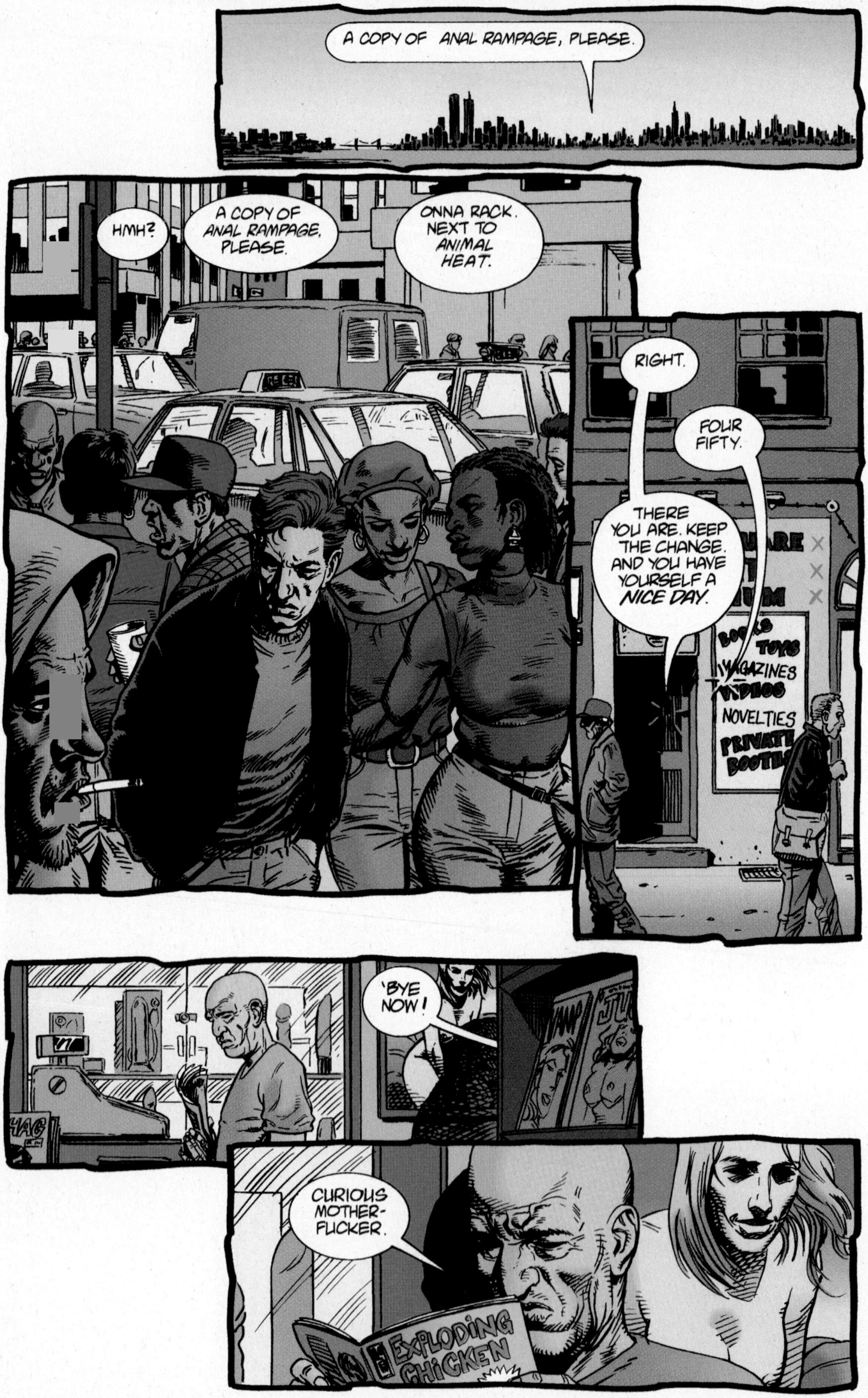
A COPY OF ANAL RAMPAGE, PLEASE.
HMH?
A COPY OF ANAL RAMPAGE, PLEASE.
ONNA RACK. NEXT TO ANIMAL HEAT.
RIGHT.
FOUR FIFTY.
THERE YOU ARE. KEEP THE CHANGE. AND YOU HAVE YOURSELF A NICE DAY.
BOOKS
TOYS
MAGAZINES
VIDEOS
NOVELTIES
PRIVATE BOOTHS
'BYE NOW!
CURIOUS MOTHER-FUCKER.
EXPLODING CHICKEN

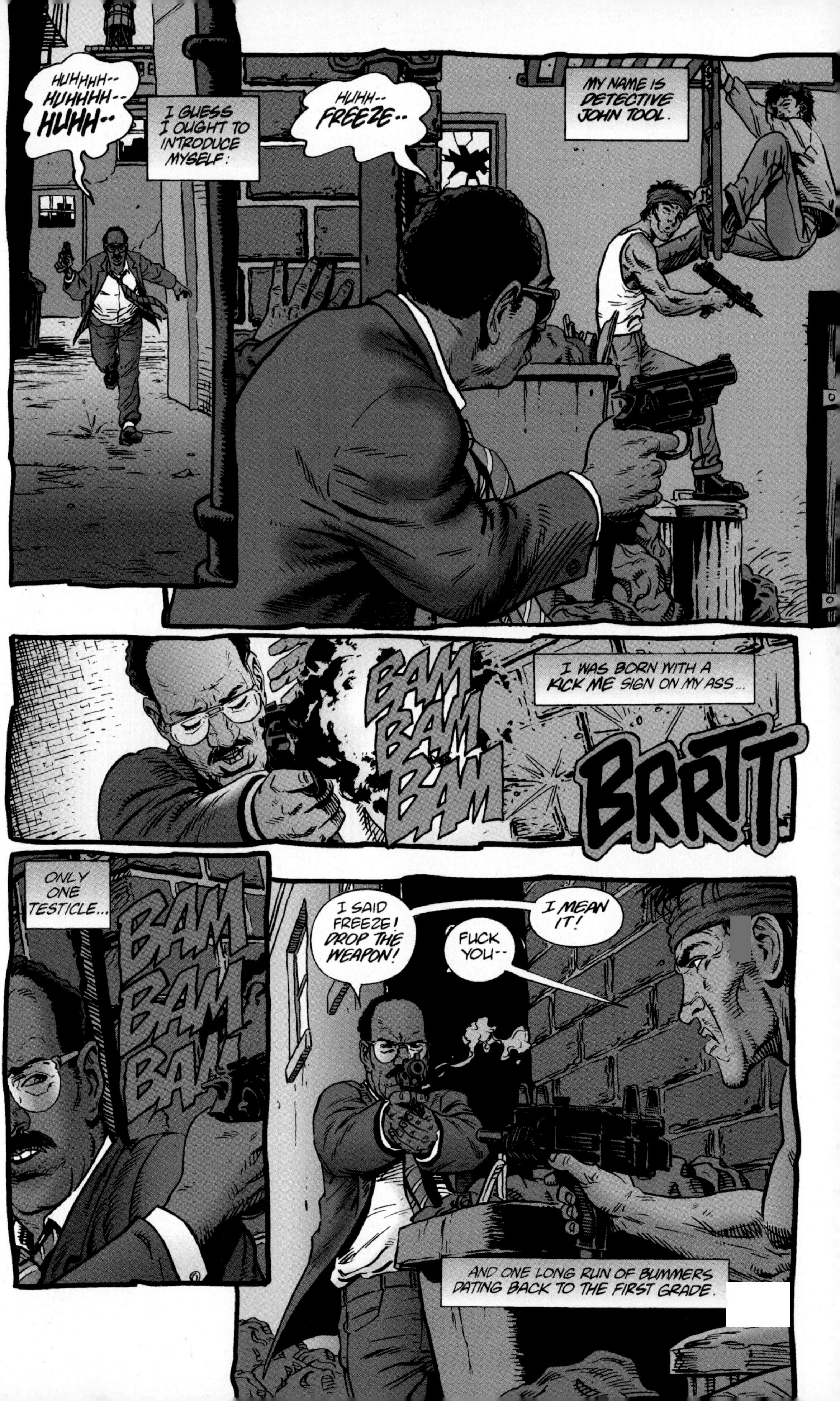
HUHHHH--
HUHHHH--
HUHH--
I GUESS I OUGHT TO INTRODUCE MYSELF:
HUHH--
FREEZE--
MY NAME IS DETECTIVE JOHN TOOL.
BAM BAM BAM
I WAS BORN WITH A KICK ME SIGN ON MY ASS...
BRRTT
ONLY ONE TESTICLE...
BAM BAM BA
I SAID FREEZE! DROP THE WEAPON!
I MEAN IT!
FUCK YOU--
AND ONE LONG RUN OF BUMMERS DATING BACK TO THE FIRST GRADE.

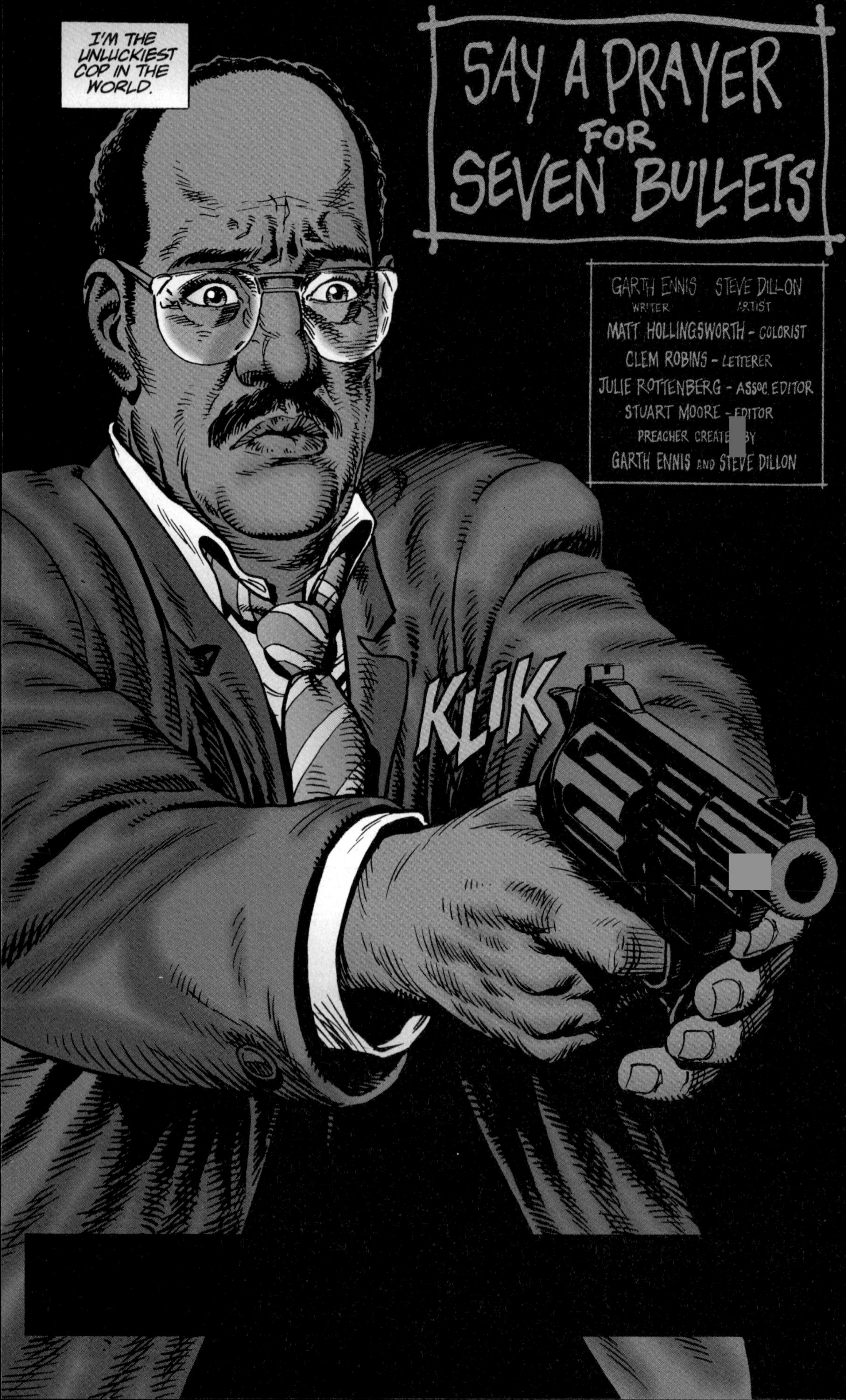

I'M THE UNLUCKIEST COP IN THE WORLD.
SAY A PRAYER FOR SEVEN BULLETS
GARTH ENNIS WRITER
STEVE DILLON ARTIST
MATT HOLLINGSWORTH - COLORIST
CLEM ROBINS - LETTERER
JULIE ROTTENBERG - ASSOC. EDITOR
STUART MOORE - EDITOR
PREACHER CREATE BY
GARTH ENNIS AND STEVE DILLON
KLIK
[redacted]

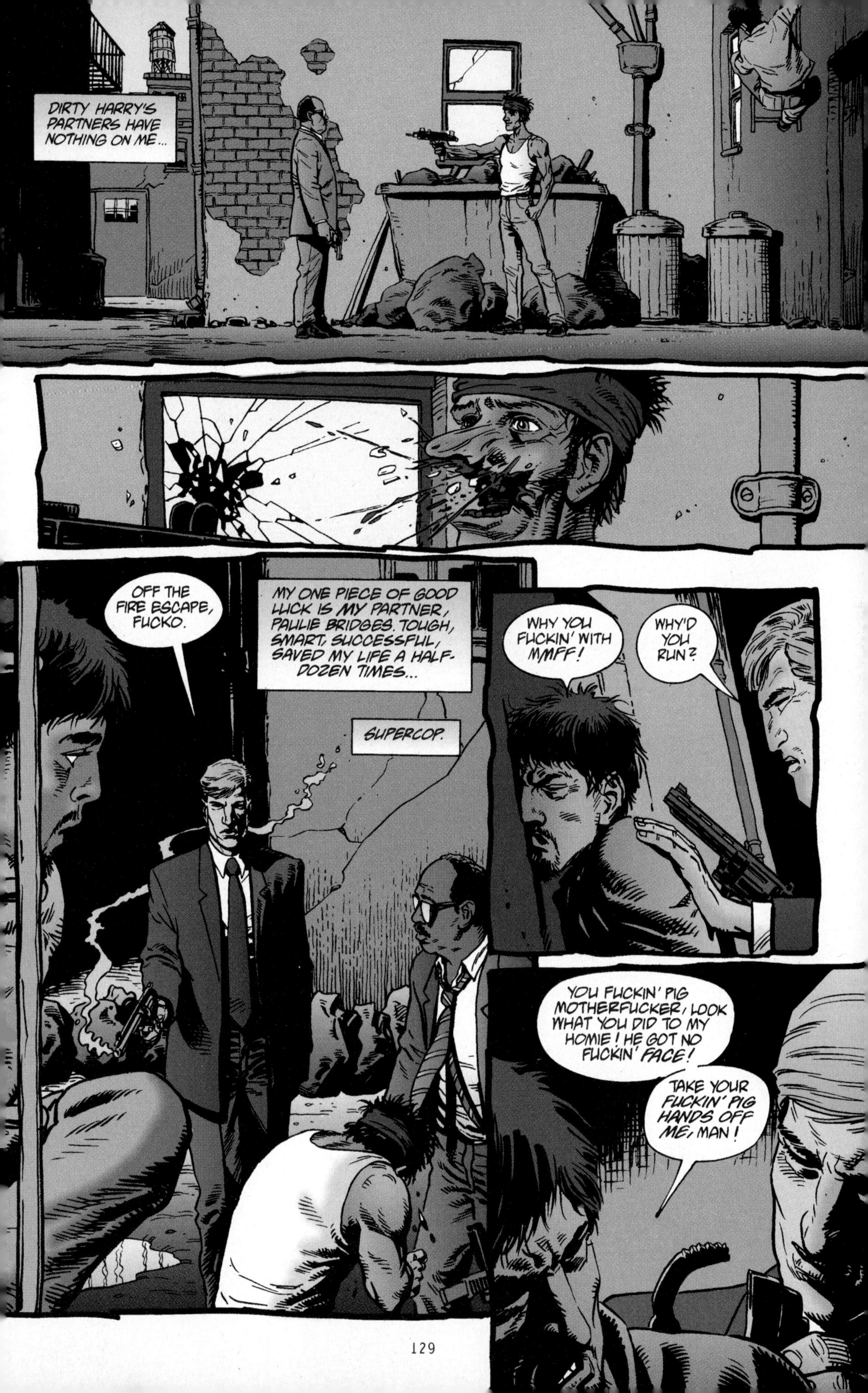
DIRTY HARRY'S PARTNERS HAVE NOTHING ON ME...
OFF THE FIRE ESCAPE, FUCKO.
MY ONE PIECE OF GOOD LUCK IS MY PARTNER, PAULIE BRIDGES. TOUGH, SMART, SUCCESSFUL, SAVED MY LIFE A HALF-DOZEN TIMES...
SUPERCOP.
WHY YOU FUCKIN' WITH MMFF!
WHY'D YOU RUN?
YOU FUCKIN' PIG MOTHERFUCKER, LOOK WHAT YOU DID TO MY HOMIE! HE GOT NO FUCKIN' FACE!
TAKE YOUR FUCKIN' PIG HANDS OFF ME, MAN!

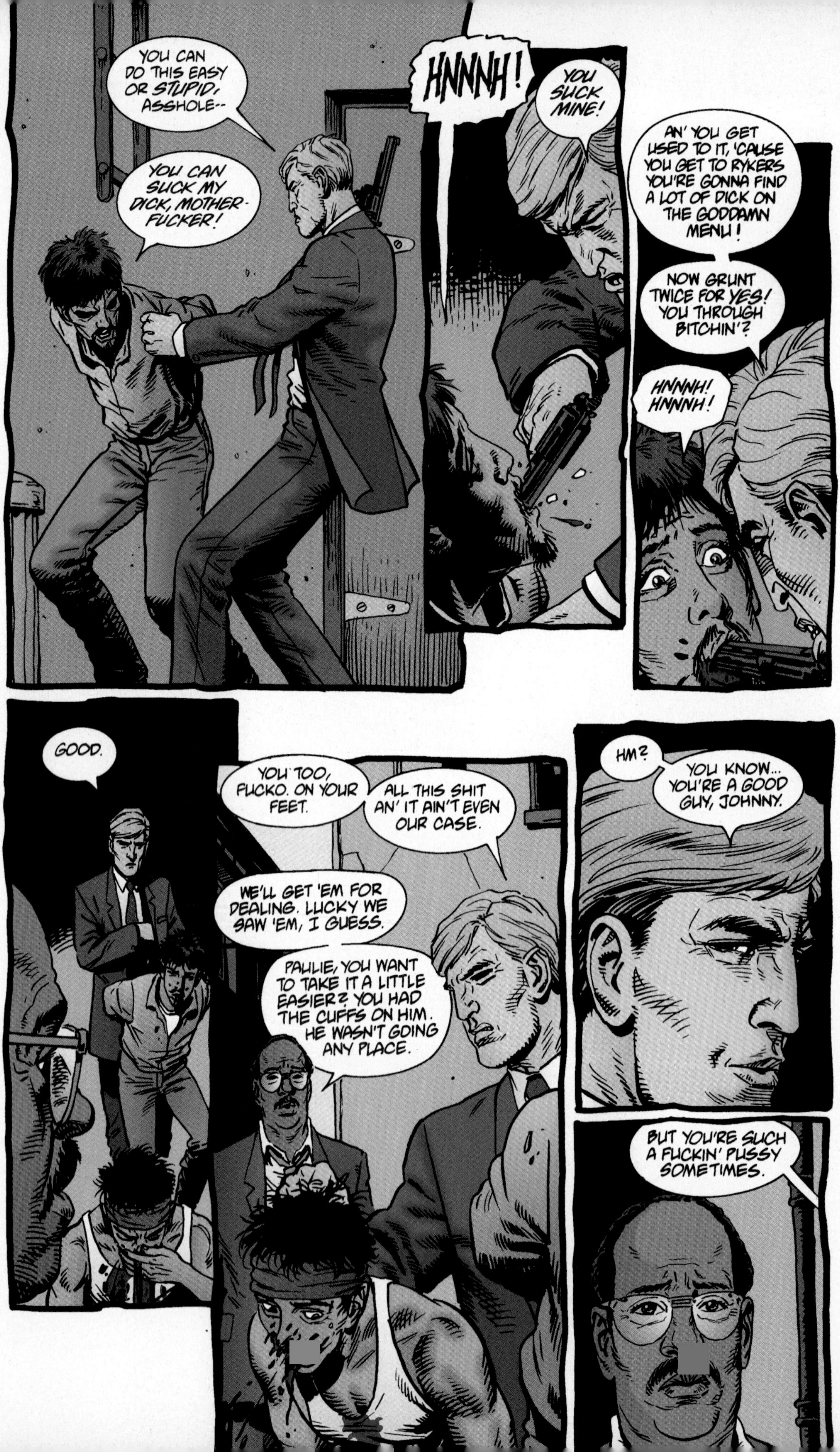
YOU CAN DO THIS EASY OR STUPID, ASSHOLE--
YOU CAN SUCK MY DICK, MOTHER-FUCKER!
HNNNH!
YOU SUCK MINE!
AN' YOU GET USED TO IT, 'CAUSE YOU GET TO RYKERS YOU'RE GONNA FIND A LOT OF DICK ON THE GODDAMN MENU!
NOW GRUNT TWICE FOR YES! YOU THROUGH BITCHIN'?
HNNNH! HNNNH!
GOOD.
YOU TOO, FUCKO. ON YOUR FEET.
ALL THIS SHIT AN' IT AIN'T EVEN OUR CASE.
WE'LL GET 'EM FOR DEALING. LUCKY WE SAW 'EM, I GUESS.
PAULIE, YOU WANT TO TAKE IT A LITTLE EASIER? YOU HAD THE CUFFS ON HIM. HE WASN'T GOING ANY PLACE.
HM?
YOU KNOW... YOU'RE A GOOD GUY, JOHNNY.
BUT YOU'RE SUCH A FUCKIN' PUSSY SOMETIMES.

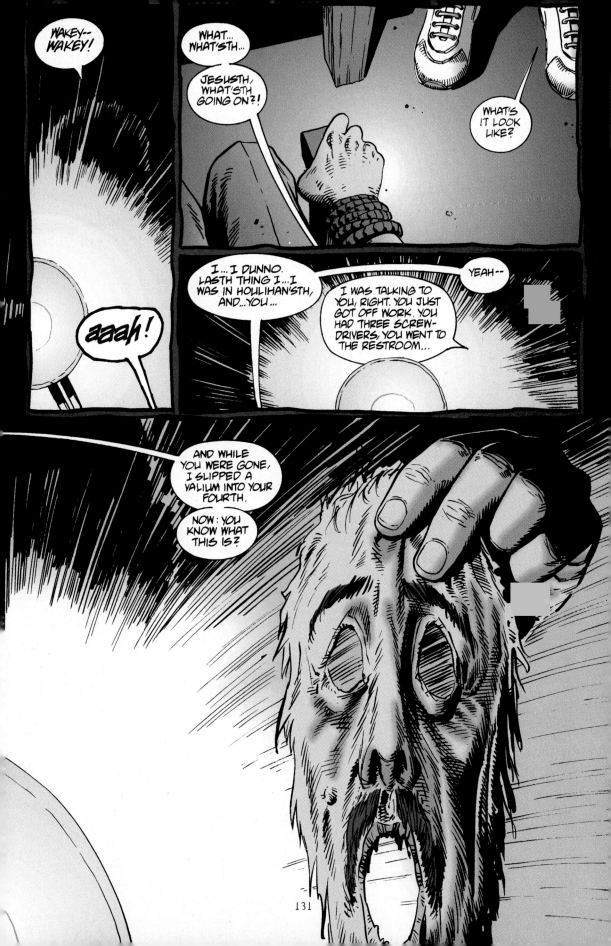

WAKEY--WAKEY!

WHAT... WHAT'STH...

JESUSTH, WHAT'STH GOING ON?!

WHAT'S IT LOOK LIKE?

aaah!

I... I DUNNO. LASTH THING I...I WAS IN HOULIHAN'STH, AND...YOU...

YEAH--

I WAS TALKING TO YOU, RIGHT. YOU JUST GOT OFF WORK. YOU HAD THREE SCREW-DRIVERS, YOU WENT TO THE RESTROOM...

AND WHILE YOU WERE GONE, I SLIPPED A VALIUM INTO YOUR FOURTH.

NOW: YOU KNOW WHAT THIS IS?

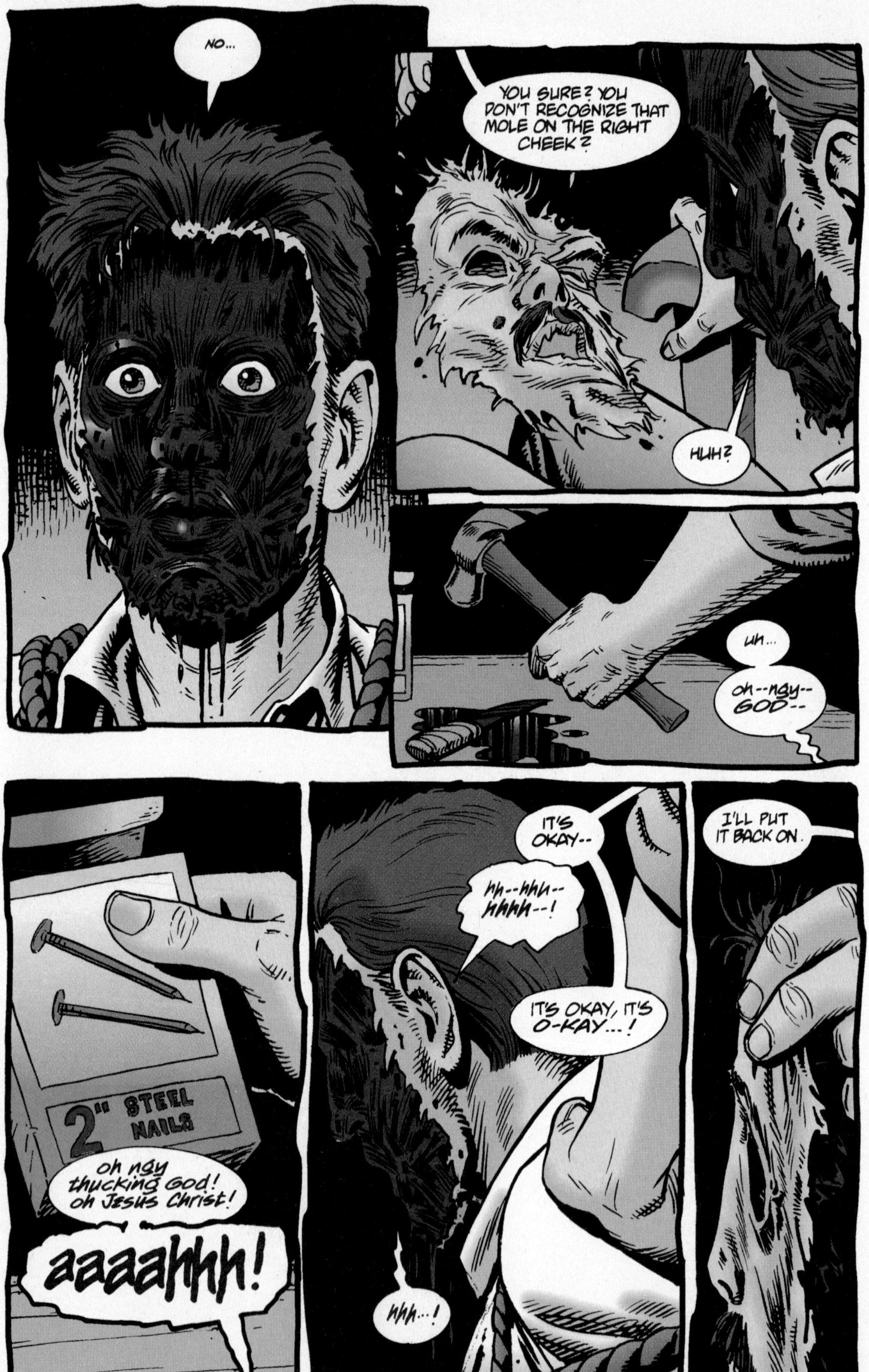
NO...
YOU SURE? YOU DON'T RECOGNIZE THAT MOLE ON THE RIGHT CHEEK?
HUH?
uh...
oh--ngy--GOD--
2" STEEL NAILS
oh ngy thucking God! oh Jesus Christ!
aaaaahhh!
IT'S OKAY--
hh--hhh--hhhh--!
IT'S OKAY, IT'S O-KAY...!
hhh...!
I'LL PUT IT BACK ON.

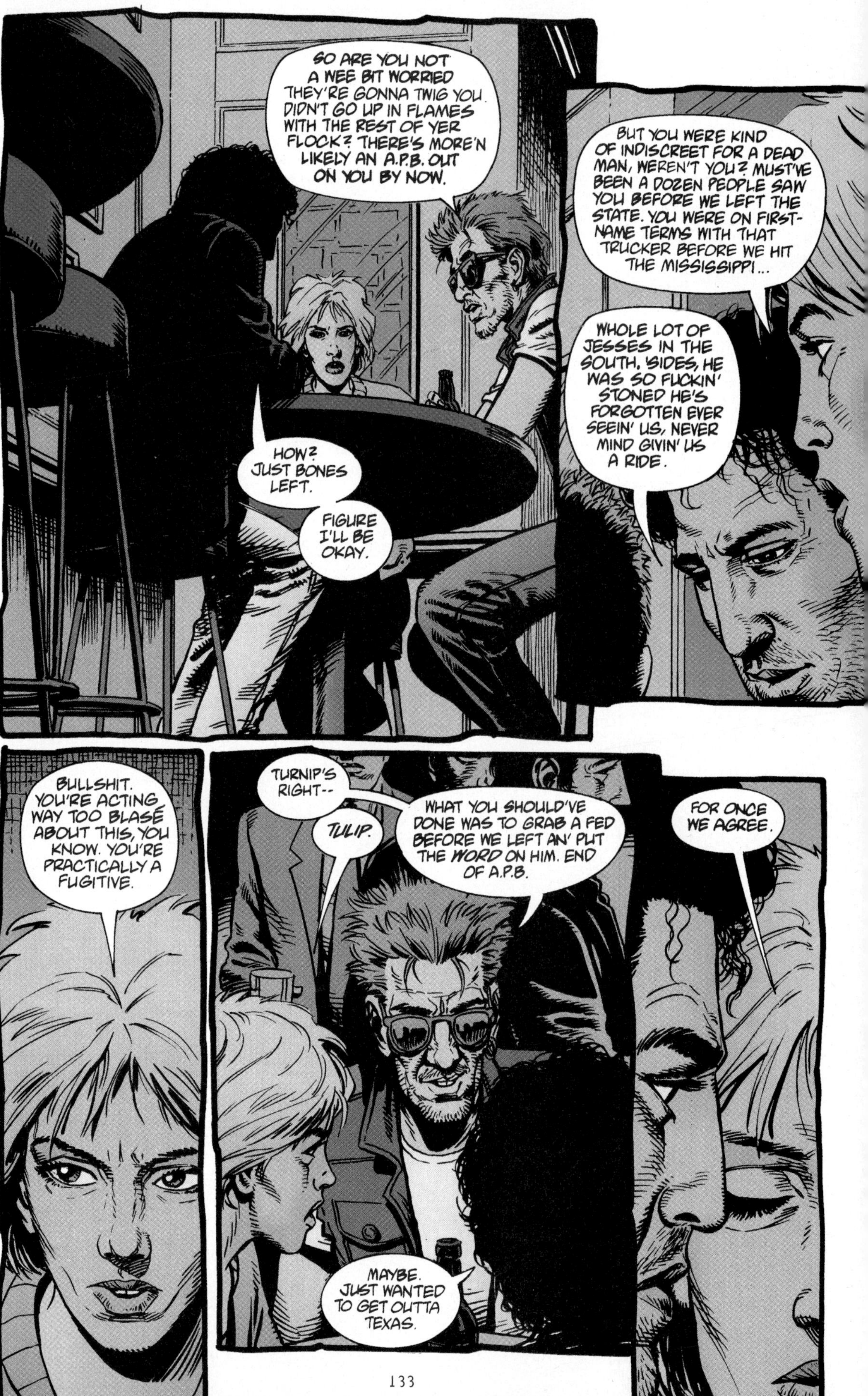
SO ARE YOU NOT A WEE BIT WORRIED THEY'RE GONNA TWIG YOU DIDN'T GO UP IN FLAMES WITH THE REST OF YER FLOCK? THERE'S MORE'N LIKELY AN A.P.B. OUT ON YOU BY NOW.
HOW? JUST BONES LEFT.
FIGURE I'LL BE OKAY.
BUT YOU WERE KIND OF INDISCREET FOR A DEAD MAN, WEREN'T YOU? MUST'VE BEEN A DOZEN PEOPLE SAW YOU BEFORE WE LEFT THE STATE. YOU WERE ON FIRST-NAME TERMS WITH THAT TRUCKER BEFORE WE HIT THE MISSISSIPPI...
WHOLE LOT OF JESSES IN THE SOUTH, 'SIDES, HE WAS SO FUCKIN' STONED HE'S FORGOTTEN EVER SEEIN' US, NEVER MIND GIVIN' US A RIDE.
BULLSHIT. YOU'RE ACTING WAY TOO BLASÉ ABOUT THIS, YOU KNOW. YOU'RE PRACTICALLY A FUGITIVE.
TURNIP'S RIGHT--
TULIP.
WHAT YOU SHOULD'VE DONE WAS TO GRAB A FED BEFORE WE LEFT AN' PUT THE WORD ON HIM. END OF A.P.B.
FOR ONCE WE AGREE.
MAYBE. JUST WANTED TO GET OUTTA TEXAS.

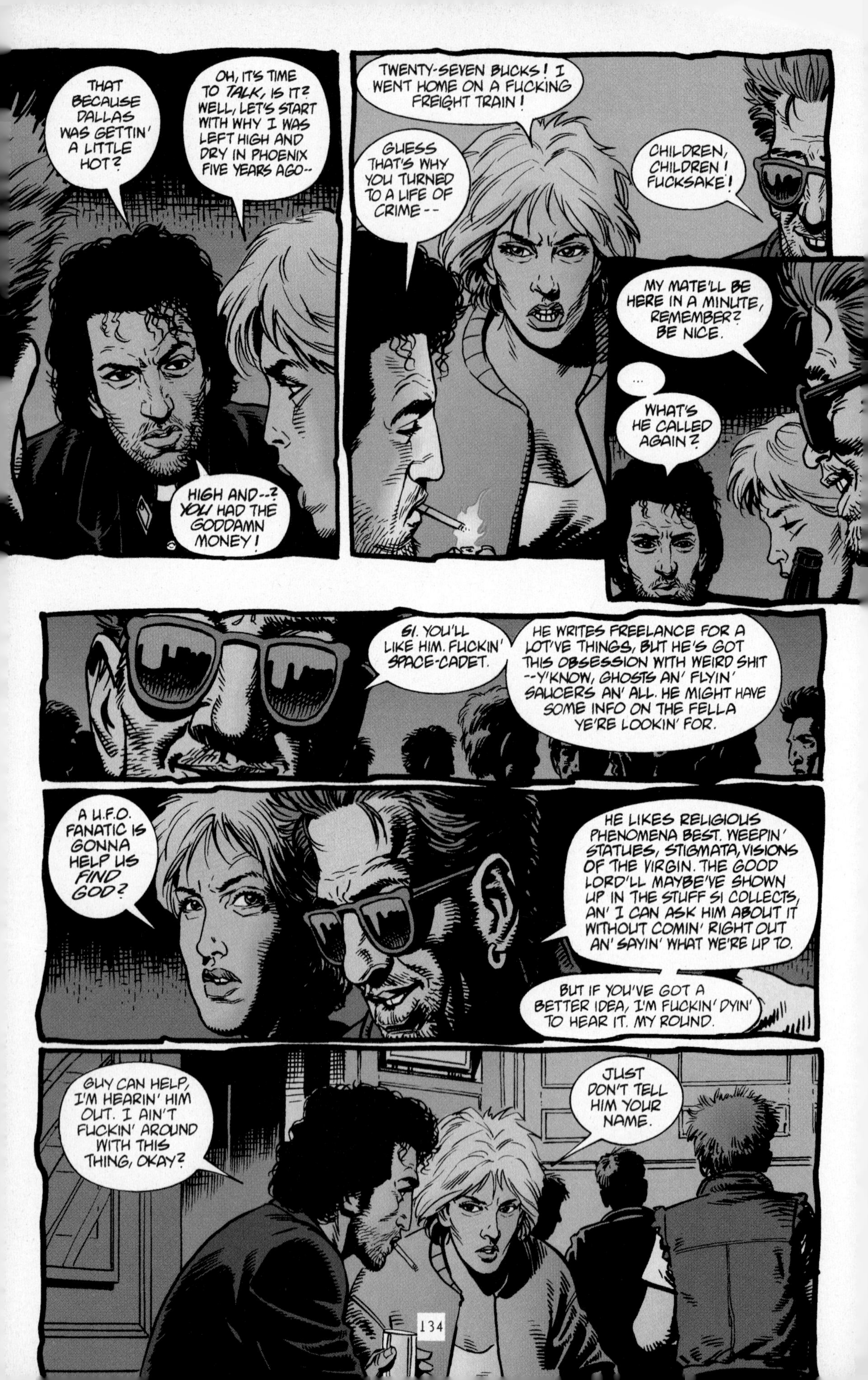
THAT BECAUSE DALLAS WAS GETTIN' A LITTLE HOT?
OH, IT'S TIME TO TALK, IS IT? WELL, LET'S START WITH WHY I WAS LEFT HIGH AND DRY IN PHOENIX FIVE YEARS AGO--
HIGH AND--? YOU HAD THE GODDAMN MONEY!
TWENTY-SEVEN BUCKS! I WENT HOME ON A FUCKING FREIGHT TRAIN!
GUESS THAT'S WHY YOU TURNED TO A LIFE OF CRIME--
CHILDREN, CHILDREN! FUCKSAKE!
MY MATE'LL BE HERE IN A MINUTE, REMEMBER? BE NICE.
...
WHAT'S HE CALLED AGAIN?
SI. YOU'LL LIKE HIM. FUCKIN' SPACE-CADET.
HE WRITES FREELANCE FOR A LOT'VE THINGS, BUT HE'S GOT THIS OBSESSION WITH WEIRD SHIT --Y'KNOW, GHOSTS AN' FLYIN' SAUCERS AN' ALL. HE MIGHT HAVE SOME INFO ON THE FELLA YE'RE LOOKIN' FOR.
A U.F.O. FANATIC IS GONNA HELP US FIND GOD?
HE LIKES RELIGIOUS PHENOMENA BEST. WEEPIN' STATUES, STIGMATA, VISIONS OF THE VIRGIN. THE GOOD LORD'LL MAYBE'VE SHOWN UP IN THE STUFF SI COLLECTS, AN' I CAN ASK HIM ABOUT IT WITHOUT COMIN' RIGHT OUT AN' SAYIN' WHAT WE'RE UP TO.
BUT IF YOU'VE GOT A BETTER IDEA, I'M FUCKIN' DYIN' TO HEAR IT. MY ROUND.
GUY CAN HELP, I'M HEARIN' HIM OUT. I AIN'T FUCKIN' AROUND WITH THIS THING, OKAY?
JUST DON'T TELL HIM YOUR NAME.

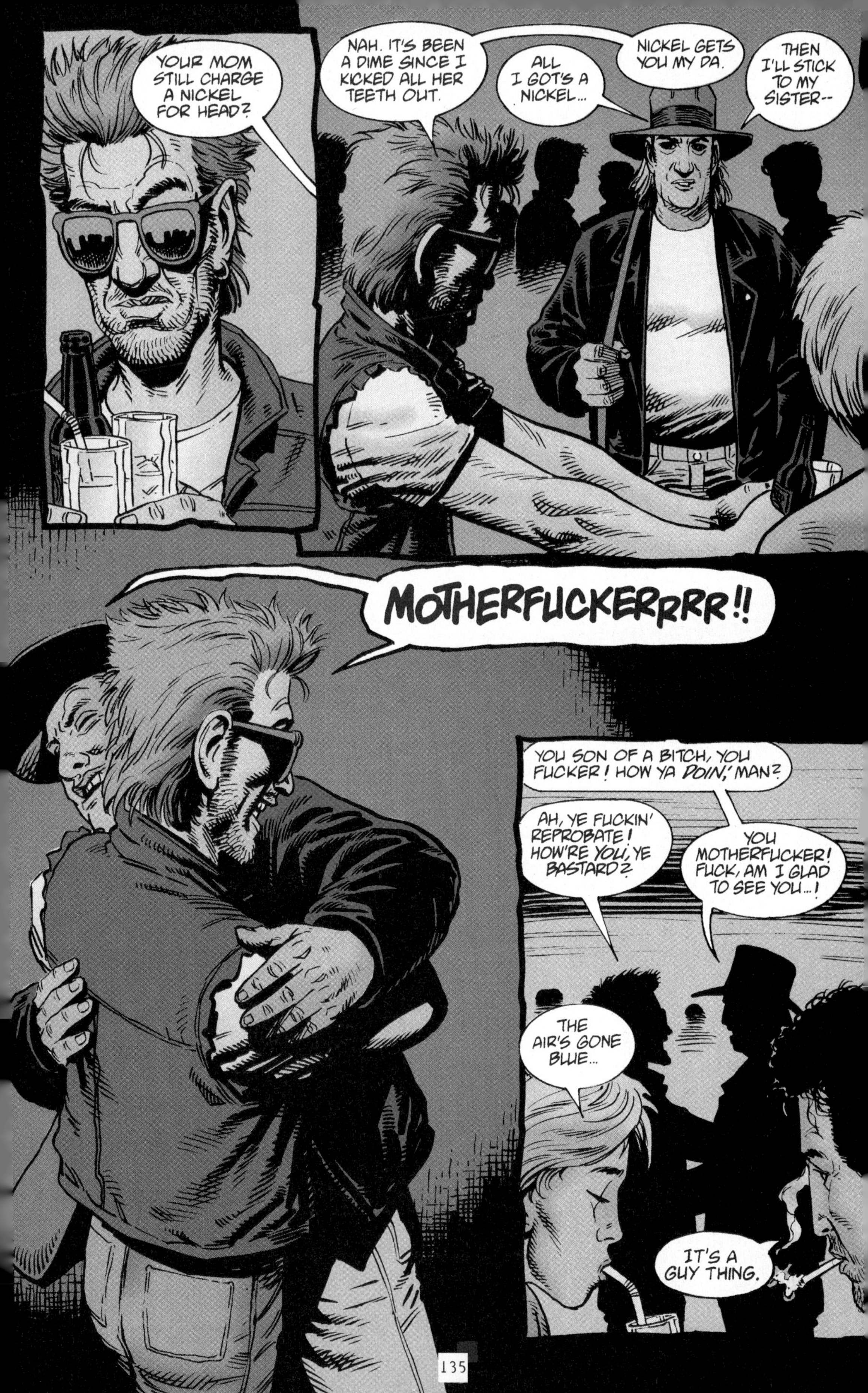
YOUR MOM STILL CHARGE A NICKEL FOR HEAD?
NAH. IT'S BEEN A DIME SINCE I KICKED ALL HER TEETH OUT.
ALL I GOT'S A NICKEL...
NICKEL GETS YOU MY DA.
THEN I'LL STICK TO MY SISTER--
MOTHERFUCKERRRR!!
YOU SON OF A BITCH, YOU FUCKER! HOW YA DOIN,' MAN?
AH, YE FUCKIN' REPROBATE! HOW'RE YOU, YE BASTARD?
YOU MOTHERFUCKER! FUCK, AM I GLAD TO SEE YOU...!
THE AIR'S GONE BLUE...
IT'S A GUY THING.

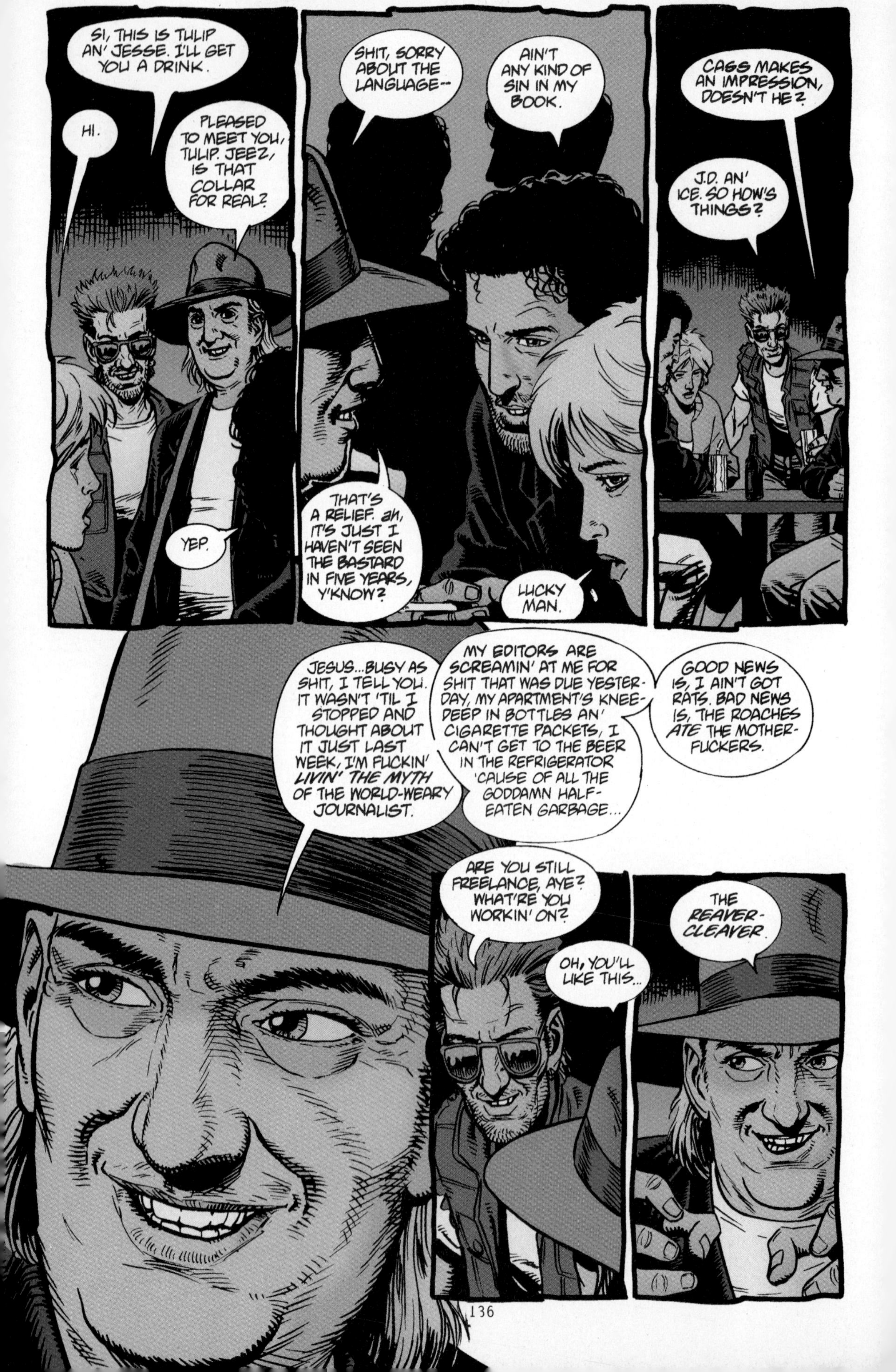
SI, THIS IS TULIP AN' JESSE. I'LL GET YOU A DRINK.
HI.
PLEASED TO MEET YOU, TULIP. JEEZ, IS THAT COLLAR FOR REAL?
YEP.
SHIT, SORRY ABOUT THE LANGUAGE--
AIN'T ANY KIND OF SIN IN MY BOOK.
THAT'S A RELIEF. AH, IT'S JUST I HAVEN'T SEEN THE BASTARD IN FIVE YEARS, Y'KNOW?
LUCKY MAN.
CASS MAKES AN IMPRESSION, DOESN'T HE?
J.D. AN' ICE. SO HOW'S THINGS?
JESUS...BUSY AS SHIT, I TELL YOU. IT WASN'T 'TIL I STOPPED AND THOUGHT ABOUT IT JUST LAST WEEK, I'M FUCKIN' *LIVIN' THE MYTH* OF THE WORLD-WEARY JOURNALIST.
MY EDITORS ARE SCREAMIN' AT ME FOR SHIT THAT WAS DUE YESTERDAY, MY APARTMENT'S KNEE-DEEP IN BOTTLES AN' CIGARETTE PACKETS, I CAN'T GET TO THE BEER IN THE REFRIGERATOR 'CAUSE OF ALL THE GODDAMN HALF-EATEN GARBAGE...
GOOD NEWS IS, I AIN'T GOT RATS. BAD NEWS IS, THE ROACHES *ATE* THE MOTHERFUCKERS.
ARE YOU STILL FREELANCE, AYE? WHAT'RE YOU WORKIN' ON?
OH, YOU'LL LIKE THIS...
THE *REAVER-CLEAVER*.

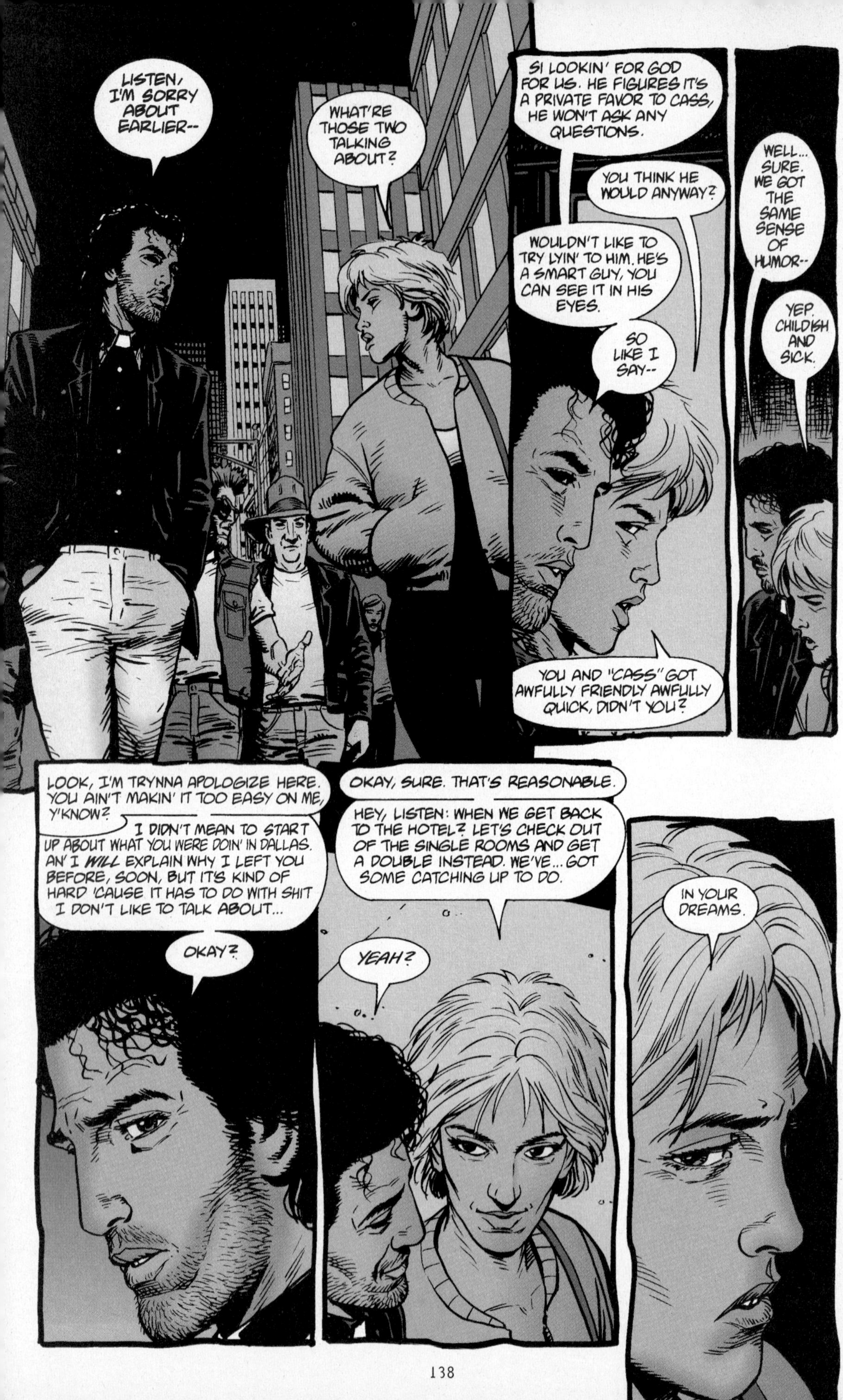
LISTEN, I'M SORRY ABOUT EARLIER--
WHAT'RE THOSE TWO TALKING ABOUT?
SI LOOKIN' FOR GOD FOR US. HE FIGURES IT'S A PRIVATE FAVOR TO CASS, HE WON'T ASK ANY QUESTIONS.
YOU THINK HE WOULD ANYWAY?
WOULDN'T LIKE TO TRY LYIN' TO HIM. HE'S A SMART GUY, YOU CAN SEE IT IN HIS EYES.
SO LIKE I SAY--
YOU AND "CASS" GOT AWFULLY FRIENDLY AWFULLY QUICK, DIDN'T YOU?
WELL... SURE. WE GOT THE SAME SENSE OF HUMOR--
YEP. CHILDISH AND SICK.
LOOK, I'M TRYNNA APOLOGIZE HERE. YOU AIN'T MAKIN' IT TOO EASY ON ME, Y'KNOW?
I DIDN'T MEAN TO START UP ABOUT WHAT YOU WERE DOIN' IN DALLAS. AN' I WILL EXPLAIN WHY I LEFT YOU BEFORE, SOON, BUT IT'S KIND OF HARD 'CAUSE IT HAS TO DO WITH SHIT I DON'T LIKE TO TALK ABOUT...
OKAY?
OKAY, SURE. THAT'S REASONABLE.
HEY, LISTEN: WHEN WE GET BACK TO THE HOTEL? LET'S CHECK OUT OF THE SINGLE ROOMS AND GET A DOUBLE INSTEAD. WE'VE... GOT SOME CATCHING UP TO DO.
YEAH?
IN YOUR DREAMS.

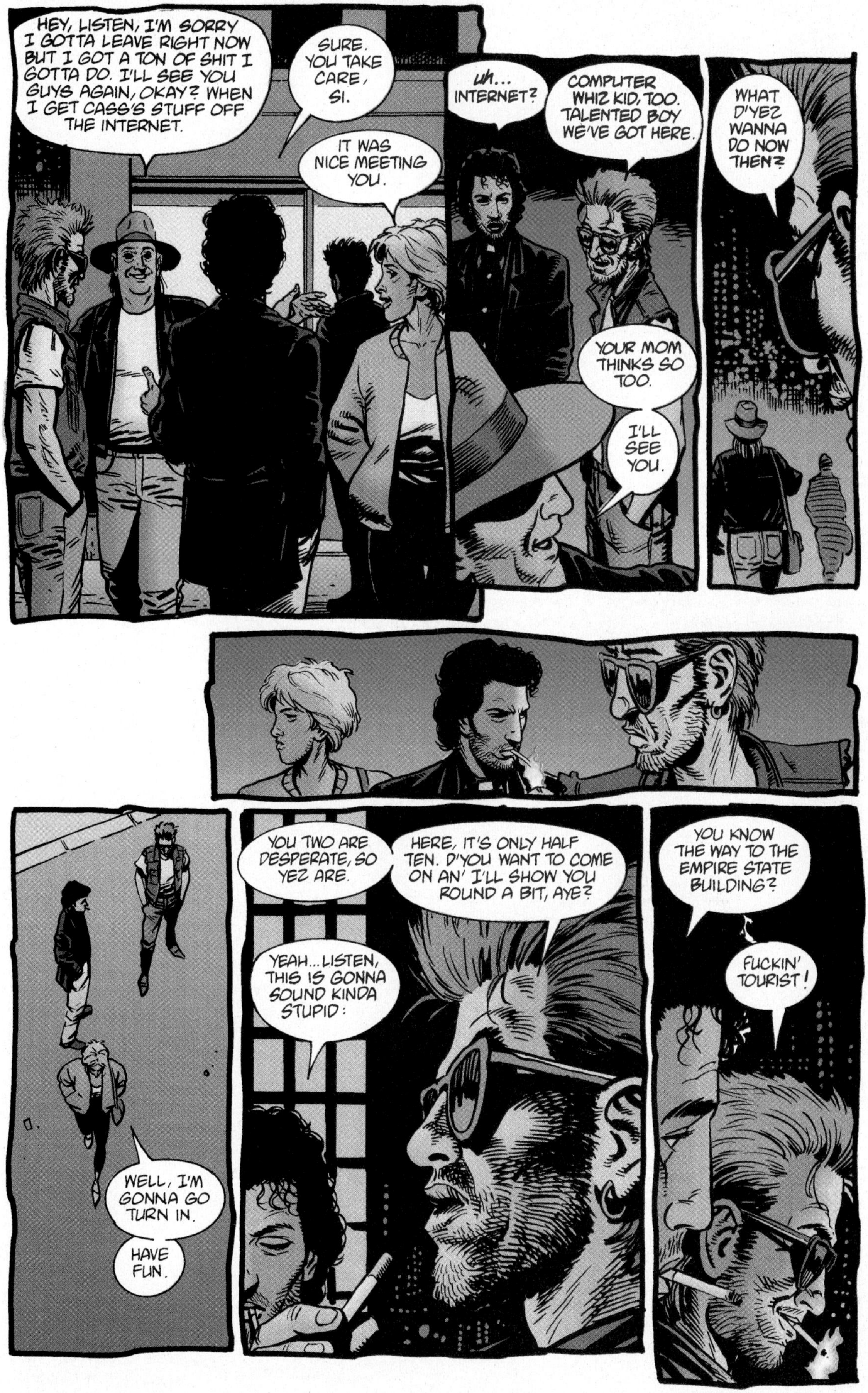
HEY, LISTEN, I'M SORRY I GOTTA LEAVE RIGHT NOW BUT I GOT A TON OF SHIT I GOTTA DO. I'LL SEE YOU GUYS AGAIN, OKAY? WHEN I GET CASS'S STUFF OFF THE INTERNET.
SURE. YOU TAKE CARE, SI.
IT WAS NICE MEETING YOU.
uh... INTERNET?
COMPUTER WHIZ KID, TOO. TALENTED BOY WE'VE GOT HERE.
YOUR MOM THINKS SO TOO.
I'LL SEE YOU.
WHAT D'YEZ WANNA DO NOW THEN?
WELL, I'M GONNA GO TURN IN.
HAVE FUN.
YOU TWO ARE DESPERATE, SO YEZ ARE.
HERE, IT'S ONLY HALF TEN. D'YOU WANT TO COME ON AN' I'LL SHOW YOU ROUND A BIT, AYE?
YEAH... LISTEN, THIS IS GONNA SOUND KINDA STUPID:
YOU KNOW THE WAY TO THE EMPIRE STATE BUILDING?
FUCKIN' TOURIST!

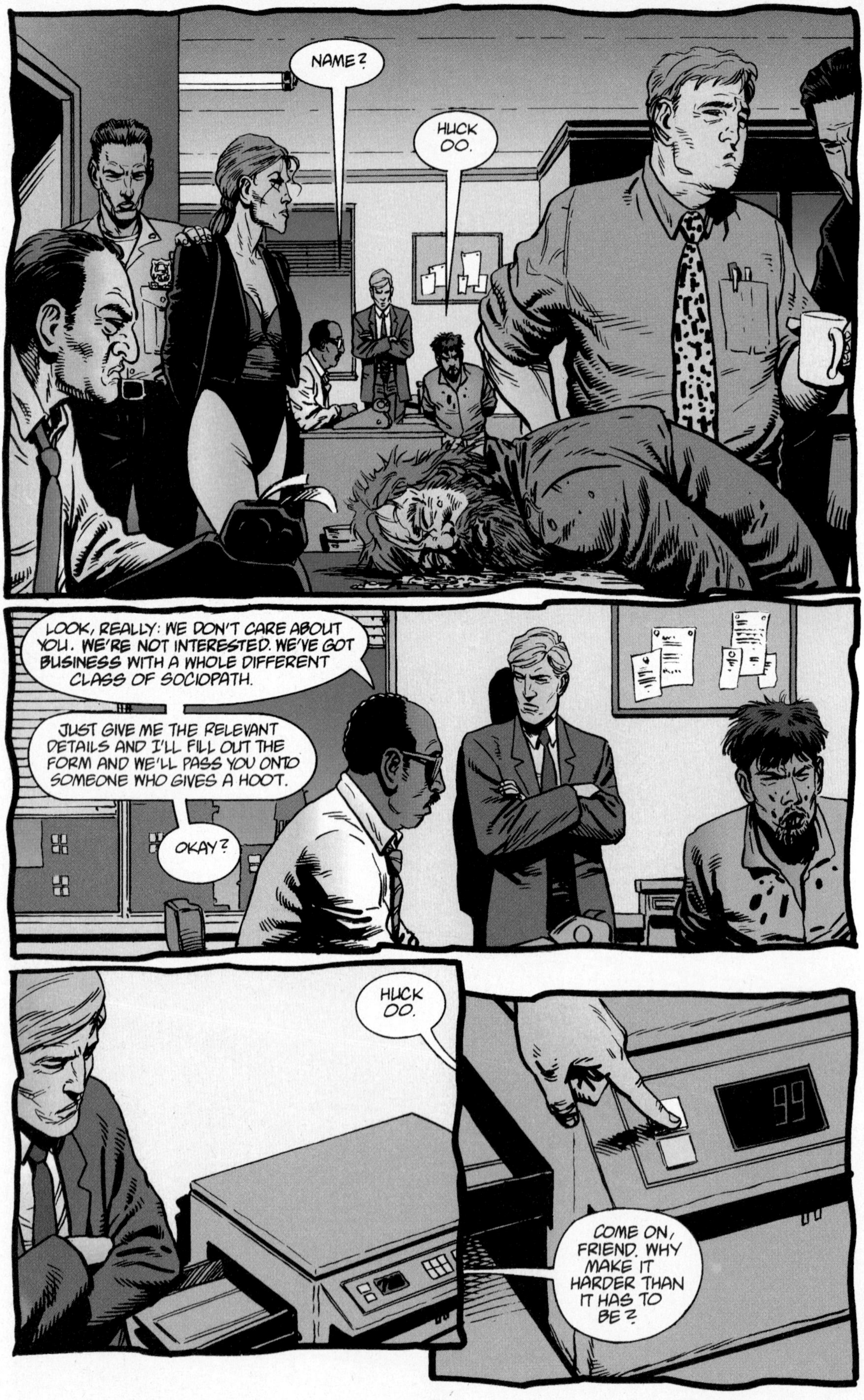
NAME?
HUCK OO.
LOOK, REALLY: WE DON'T CARE ABOUT YOU. WE'RE NOT INTERESTED. WE'VE GOT BUSINESS WITH A WHOLE DIFFERENT CLASS OF SOCIOPATH.
JUST GIVE ME THE RELEVANT DETAILS AND I'LL FILL OUT THE FORM AND WE'LL PASS YOU ONTO SOMEONE WHO GIVES A HOOT.
OKAY?
HUCK OO.
99
COME ON, FRIEND. WHY MAKE IT HARDER THAN IT HAS TO BE?

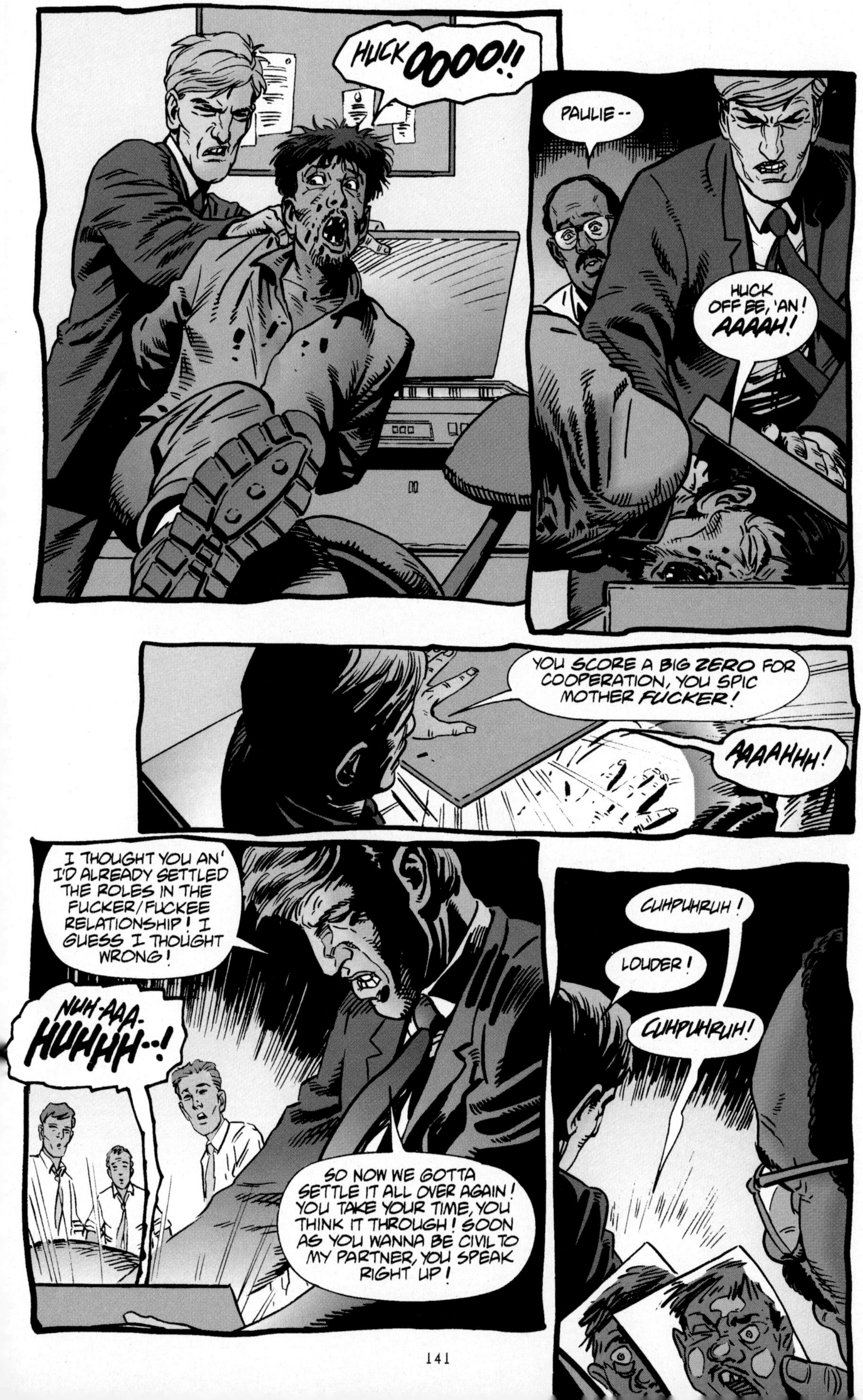
HUCK OOOO!!
PAULIE --
HUCK OFF BE, 'AN! AAAAH!
YOU SCORE A BIG ZERO FOR COOPERATION, YOU SPIC MOTHER FUCKER!
AAAAHHH!
I THOUGHT YOU AN' I'D ALREADY SETTLED THE ROLES IN THE FUCKER/FUCKEE RELATIONSHIP! I GUESS I THOUGHT WRONG!
NUH-AAA-HUHHH--!
SO NOW WE GOTTA SETTLE IT ALL OVER AGAIN! YOU TAKE YOUR TIME, YOU THINK IT THROUGH! SOON AS YOU WANNA BE CIVIL TO MY PARTNER, YOU SPEAK RIGHT UP!
CUHPUHRUH!
LOUDER!
CUHPUHRUH!

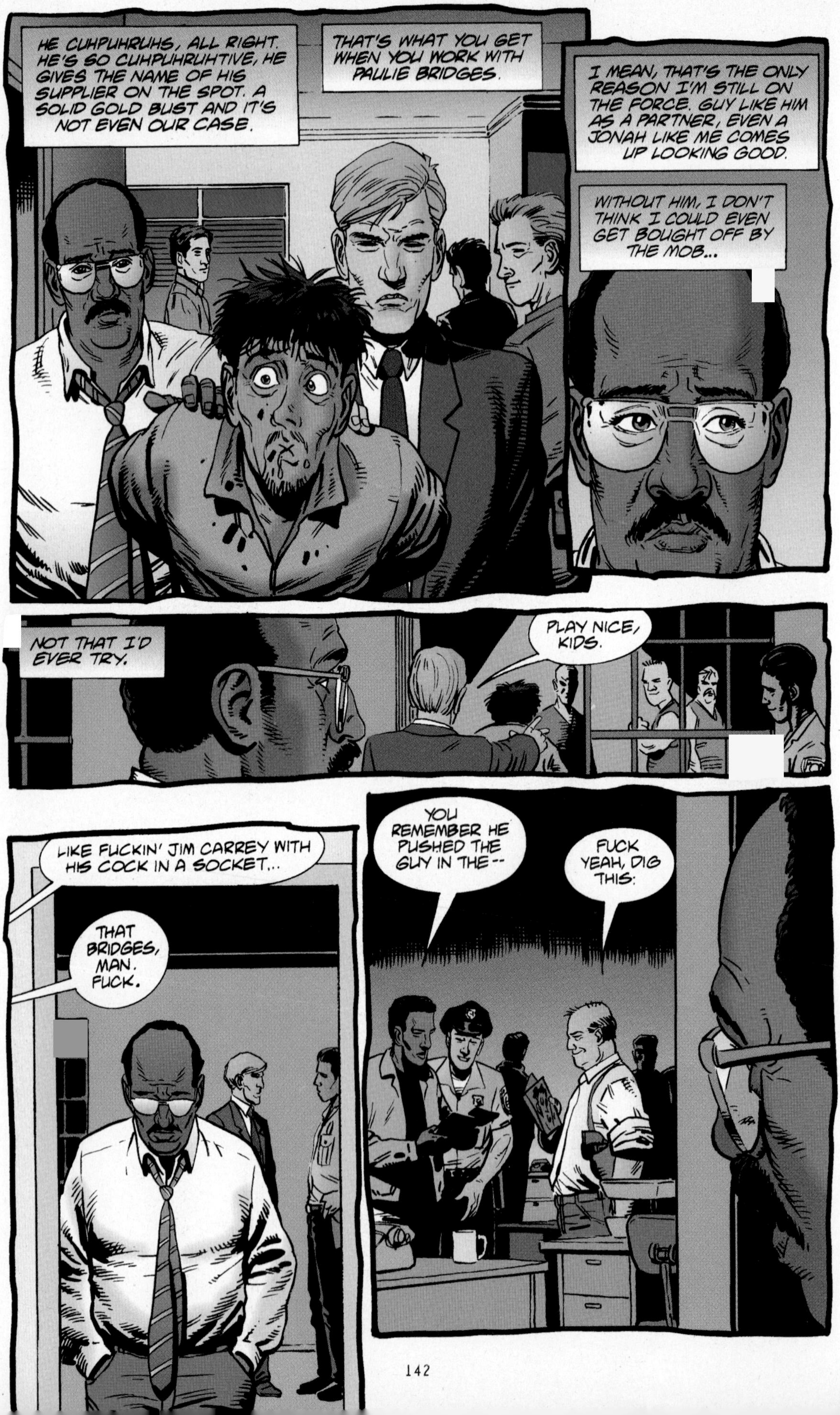
HE CUHPUHRUHS, ALL RIGHT. HE'S SO CUHPUHRUHTIVE, HE GIVES THE NAME OF HIS SUPPLIER ON THE SPOT. A SOLID GOLD BUST AND IT'S NOT EVEN OUR CASE.
THAT'S WHAT YOU GET WHEN YOU WORK WITH PAULIE BRIDGES.
I MEAN, THAT'S THE ONLY REASON I'M STILL ON THE FORCE. GUY LIKE HIM AS A PARTNER, EVEN A JONAH LIKE ME COMES UP LOOKING GOOD.
WITHOUT HIM, I DON'T THINK I COULD EVEN GET BOUGHT OFF BY THE MOB...
NOT THAT I'D EVER TRY.
PLAY NICE, KIDS.
LIKE FUCKIN' JIM CARREY WITH HIS COCK IN A SOCKET...
THAT BRIDGES, MAN. FUCK.
YOU REMEMBER HE PUSHED THE GUY IN THE --
FUCK YEAH, DIG THIS:

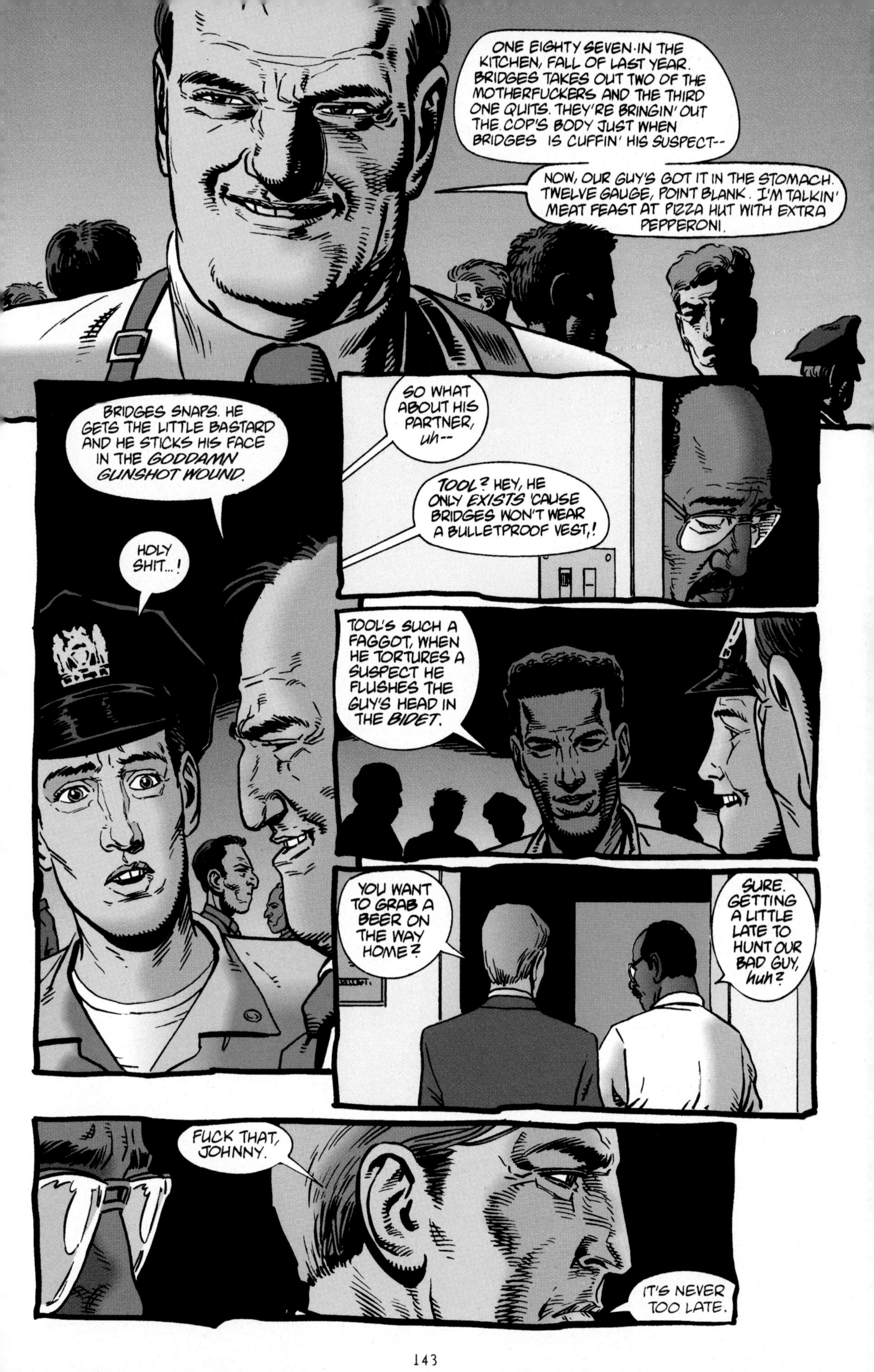
ONE EIGHTY SEVEN IN THE KITCHEN, FALL OF LAST YEAR. BRIDGES TAKES OUT TWO OF THE MOTHERFUCKERS AND THE THIRD ONE QUITS. THEY'RE BRINGIN' OUT THE COP'S BODY JUST WHEN BRIDGES IS CUFFIN' HIS SUSPECT--
NOW, OUR GUY'S GOT IT IN THE STOMACH. TWELVE GAUGE, POINT BLANK. I'M TALKIN' MEAT FEAST AT PIZZA HUT WITH EXTRA PEPPERONI.
BRIDGES SNAPS. HE GETS THE LITTLE BASTARD AND HE STICKS HIS FACE IN THE GODDAMN GUNSHOT WOUND.
HOLY SHIT...!
SO WHAT ABOUT HIS PARTNER, uh--
TOOL? HEY, HE ONLY EXISTS 'CAUSE BRIDGES WON'T WEAR A BULLETPROOF VEST,!
TOOL'S SUCH A FAGGOT, WHEN HE TORTURES A SUSPECT HE FLUSHES THE GUY'S HEAD IN THE BIDET.
YOU WANT TO GRAB A BEER ON THE WAY HOME?
SURE. GETTING A LITTLE LATE TO HUNT OUR BAD GUY, huh?
FUCK THAT, JOHNNY.
IT'S NEVER TOO LATE.

ALL THEY HAD WAS BUD.

'COURSE, YOU COULD NIP IN THERE AN' ORDER THEM TO GO OUT AN' GET US A MAGNUM OF KRUG AN' THEY'D HAVE TO OBEY YOU, Y'KNOW.

MM.

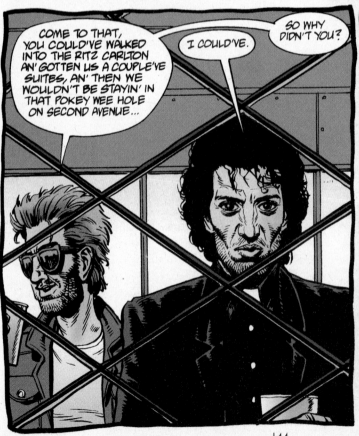

COME TO THAT, YOU COULD'VE WALKED INTO THE RITZ CARLTON AN' GOTTEN US A COUPLE'VE SUITES, AN' THEN WE WOULDN'T BE STAYIN' IN THAT POKEY WEE HOLE ON SECOND AVENUE...

I COULD'VE.

SO WHY DIDN'T YOU?

'CAUSE THAT JUST AIN'T THE WAY IT WORKS.

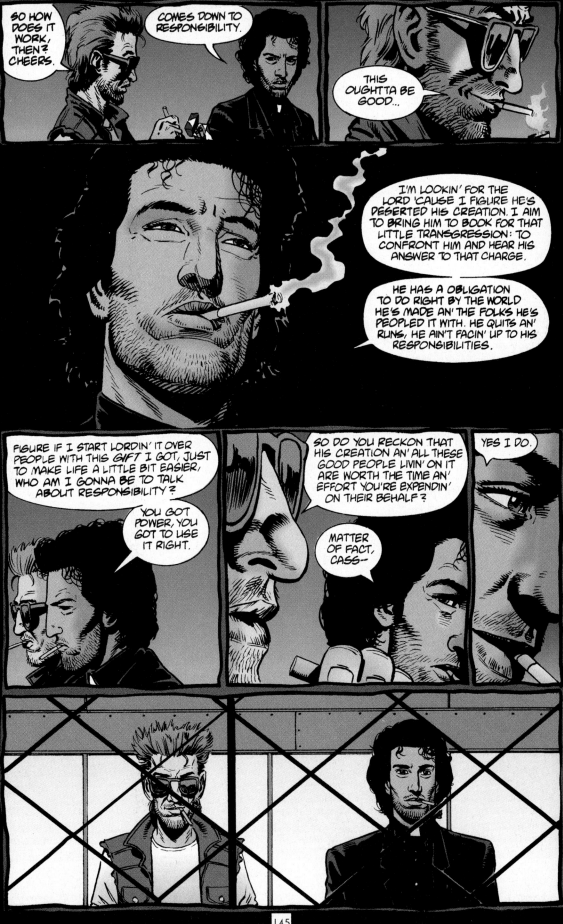

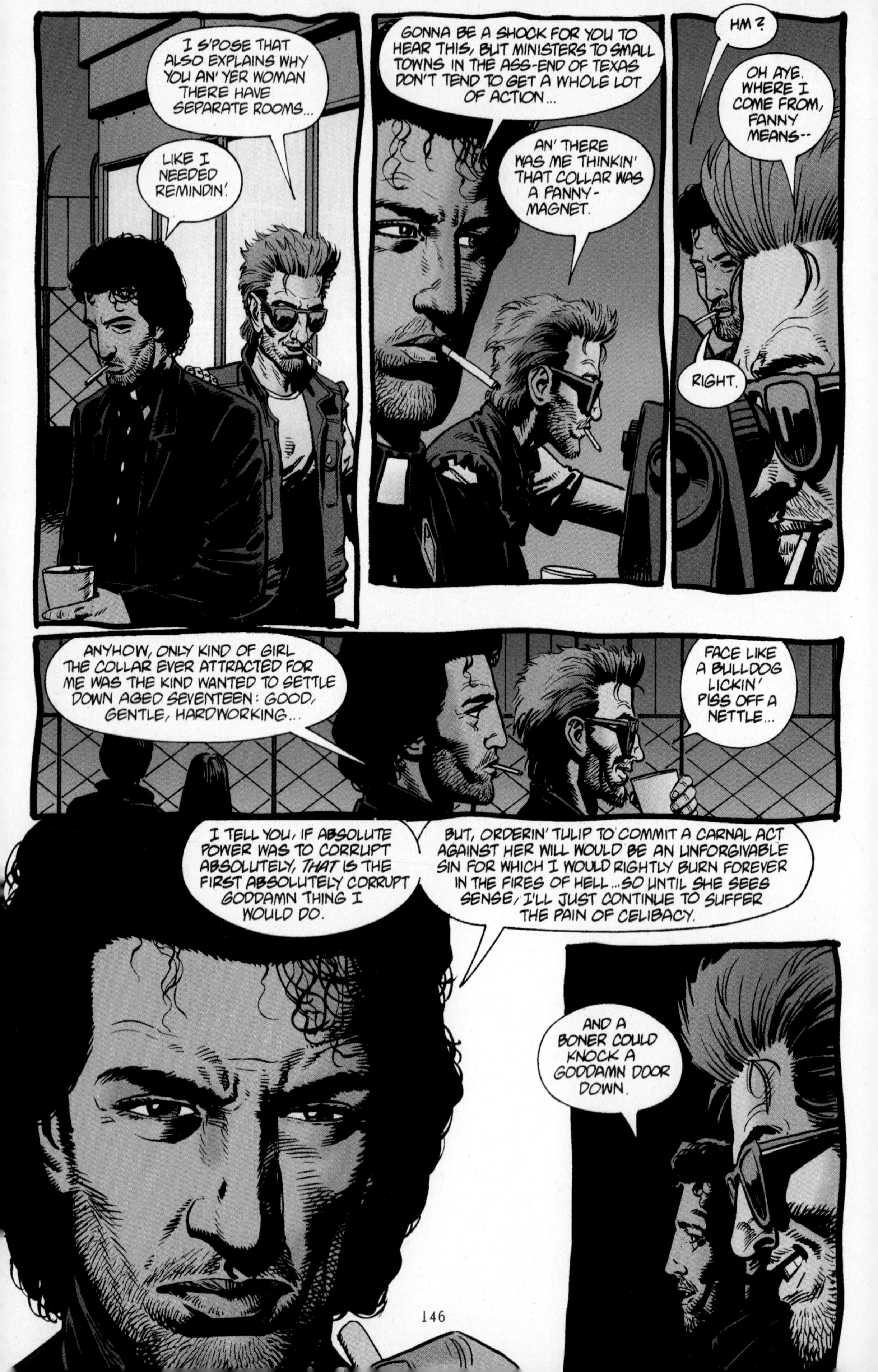
I S'POSE THAT ALSO EXPLAINS WHY YOU AN' YER WOMAN THERE HAVE SEPARATE ROOMS...
LIKE I NEEDED REMINDIN'.
GONNA BE A SHOCK FOR YOU TO HEAR THIS, BUT MINISTERS TO SMALL TOWNS IN THE ASS-END OF TEXAS DON'T TEND TO GET A WHOLE LOT OF ACTION...
AN' THERE WAS ME THINKIN' THAT COLLAR WAS A FANNY-MAGNET.
HM?
OH AYE. WHERE I COME FROM, FANNY MEANS--
RIGHT.
ANYHOW, ONLY KIND OF GIRL THE COLLAR EVER ATTRACTED FOR ME WAS THE KIND WANTED TO SETTLE DOWN AGED SEVENTEEN: GOOD, GENTLE, HARDWORKING...
FACE LIKE A BULLDOG LICKIN' PISS OFF A NETTLE...
I TELL YOU, IF ABSOLUTE POWER WAS TO CORRUPT ABSOLUTELY, *THAT* IS THE FIRST ABSOLUTELY CORRUPT GODDAMN THING I WOULD DO.
BUT, ORDERIN' TULIP TO COMMIT A CARNAL ACT AGAINST HER WILL WOULD BE AN UNFORGIVABLE SIN FOR WHICH I WOULD RIGHTLY BURN FOREVER IN THE FIRES OF HELL...SO UNTIL SHE SEES SENSE, I'LL JUST CONTINUE TO SUFFER THE PAIN OF CELIBACY.
AND A BONER COULD KNOCK A GODDAMN DOOR DOWN.

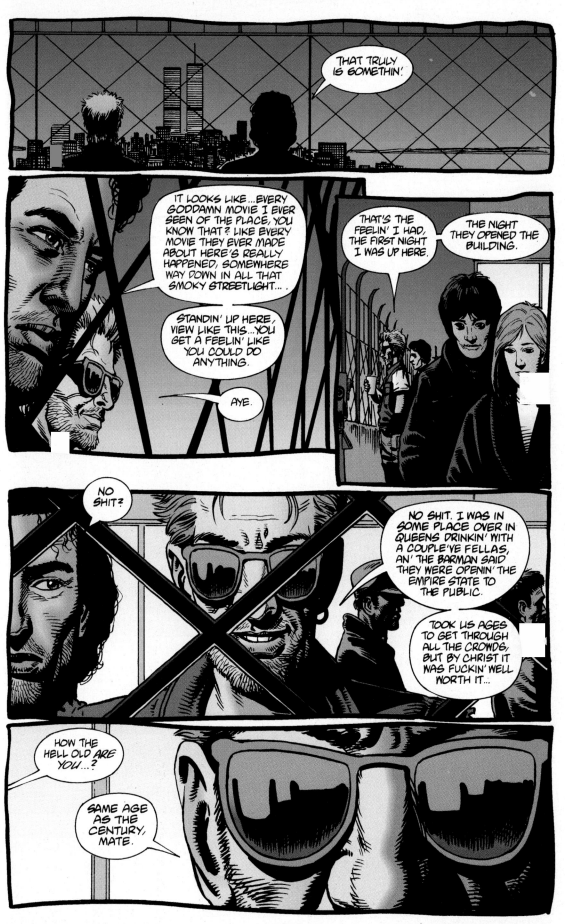

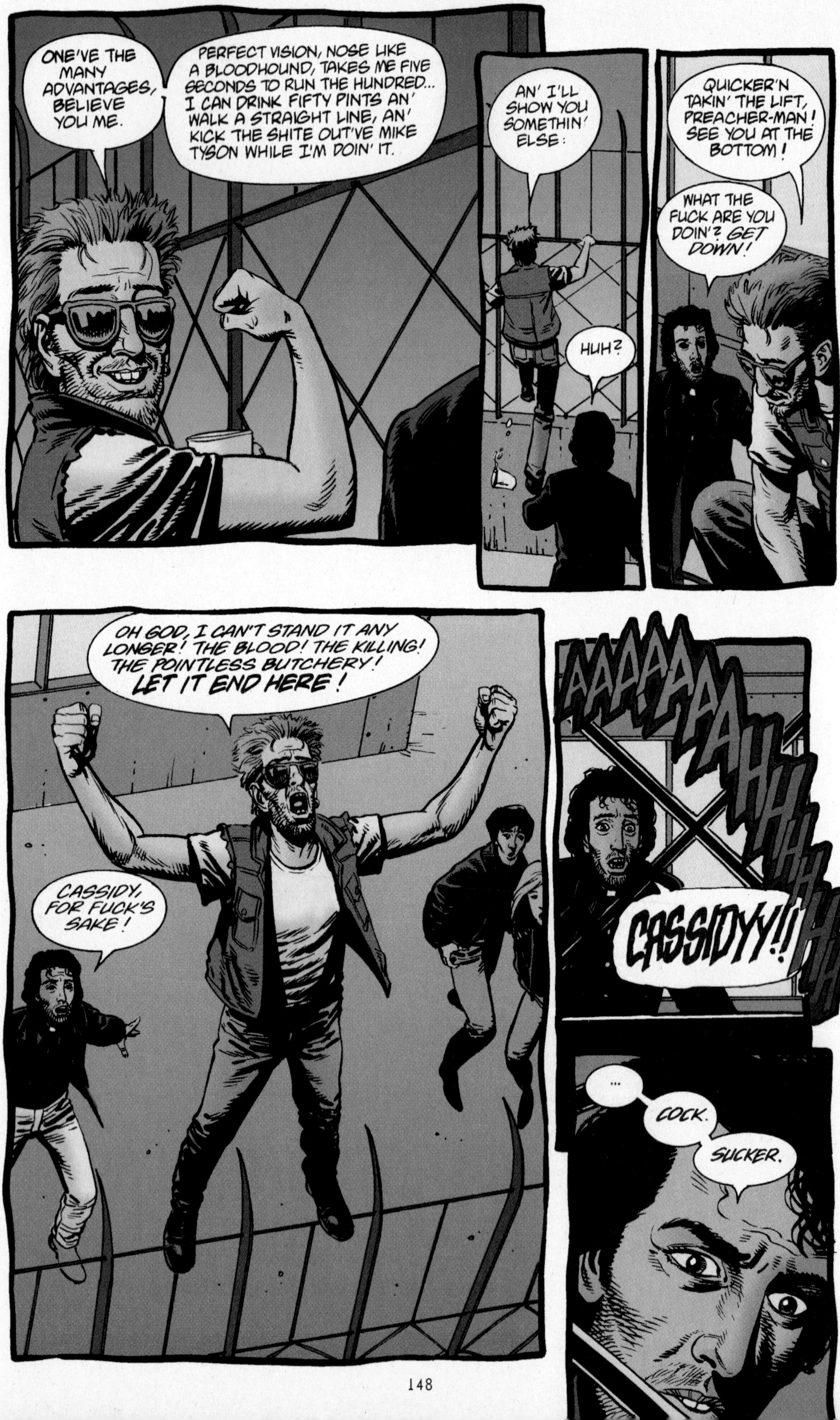
ONE'VE THE MANY ADVANTAGES, BELIEVE YOU ME.
PERFECT VISION, NOSE LIKE A BLOODHOUND, TAKES ME FIVE SECONDS TO RUN THE HUNDRED... I CAN DRINK FIFTY PINTS AN' WALK A STRAIGHT LINE, AN' KICK THE SHITE OUT'VE MIKE TYSON WHILE I'M DOIN' IT.
AN' I'LL SHOW YOU SOMETHIN' ELSE:
HUH?
QUICKER'N TAKIN' THE LIFT, PREACHER-MAN! SEE YOU AT THE BOTTOM!
WHAT THE FUCK ARE YOU DOIN'? GET DOWN!
OH GOD, I CAN'T STAND IT ANY LONGER! THE BLOOD! THE KILLING! THE POINTLESS BUTCHERY! LET IT END HERE!
CASSIDY, FOR FUCK'S SAKE!
AAAAAAAHHHHHHHH
CASSIDYY!!
...
COCK.
SUCKER.

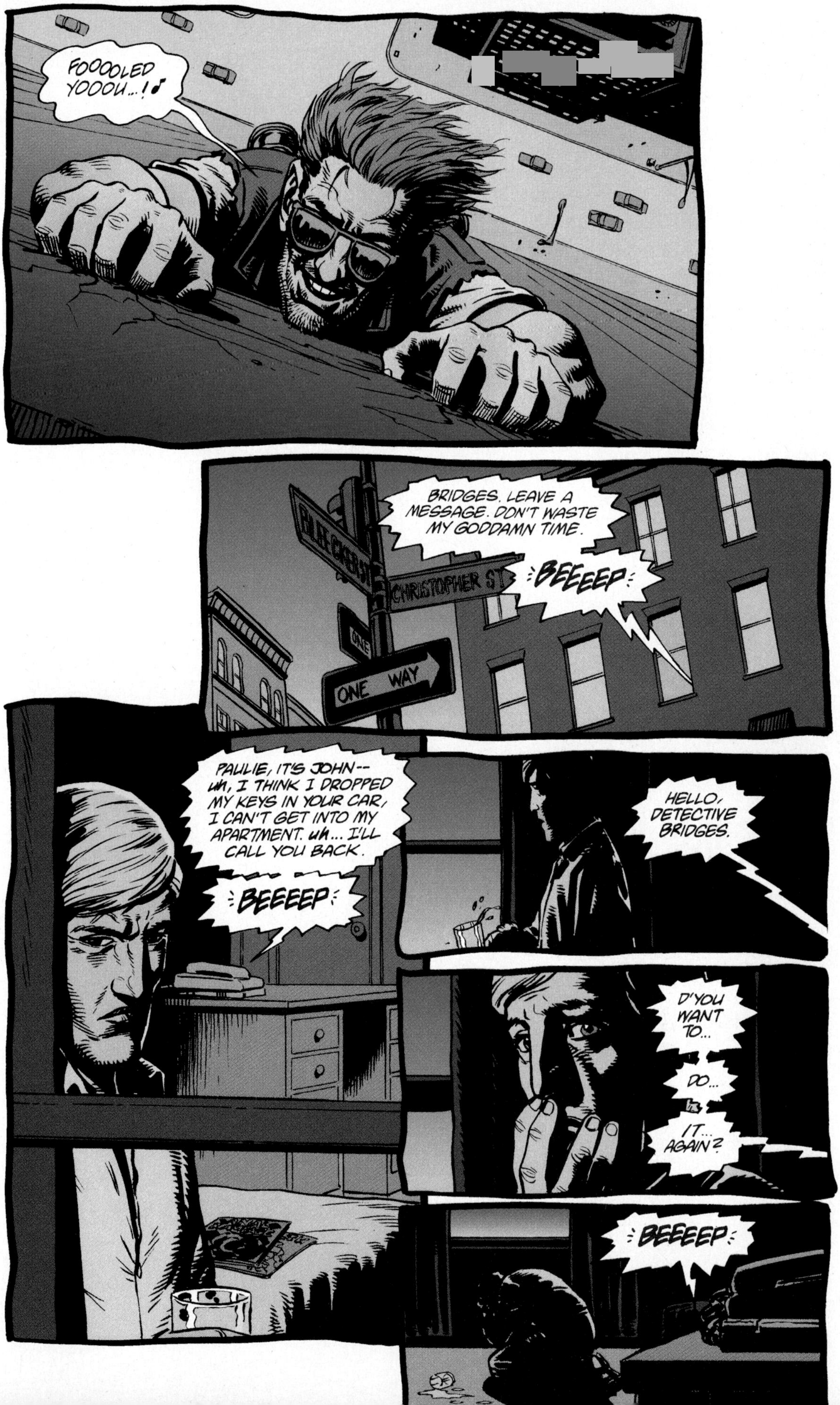
FOOOOLED YOOOU...!♪
BRIDGES. LEAVE A MESSAGE. DON'T WASTE MY GODDAMN TIME.
BEEEEP
CHRISTOPHER ST
ONE
ONE WAY
PAULIE, IT'S JOHN-- uh, I THINK I DROPPED MY KEYS IN YOUR CAR, I CAN'T GET INTO MY APARTMENT. uh... I'LL CALL YOU BACK.
BEEEEP
HELLO, DETECTIVE BRIDGES.
D'YOU WANT TO...
DO...
IT... AGAIN?
BEEEEP

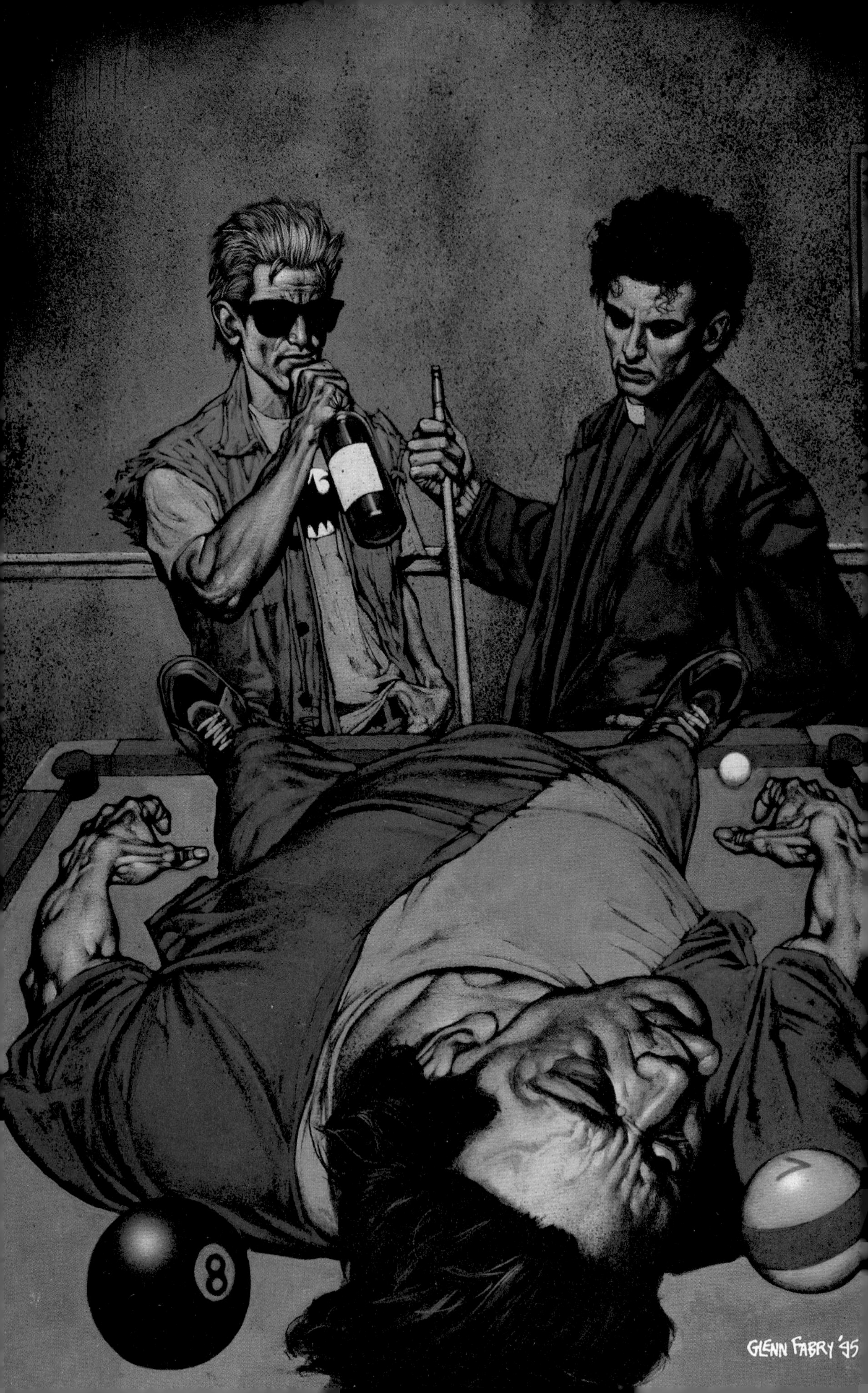
GLENN FABRY '95

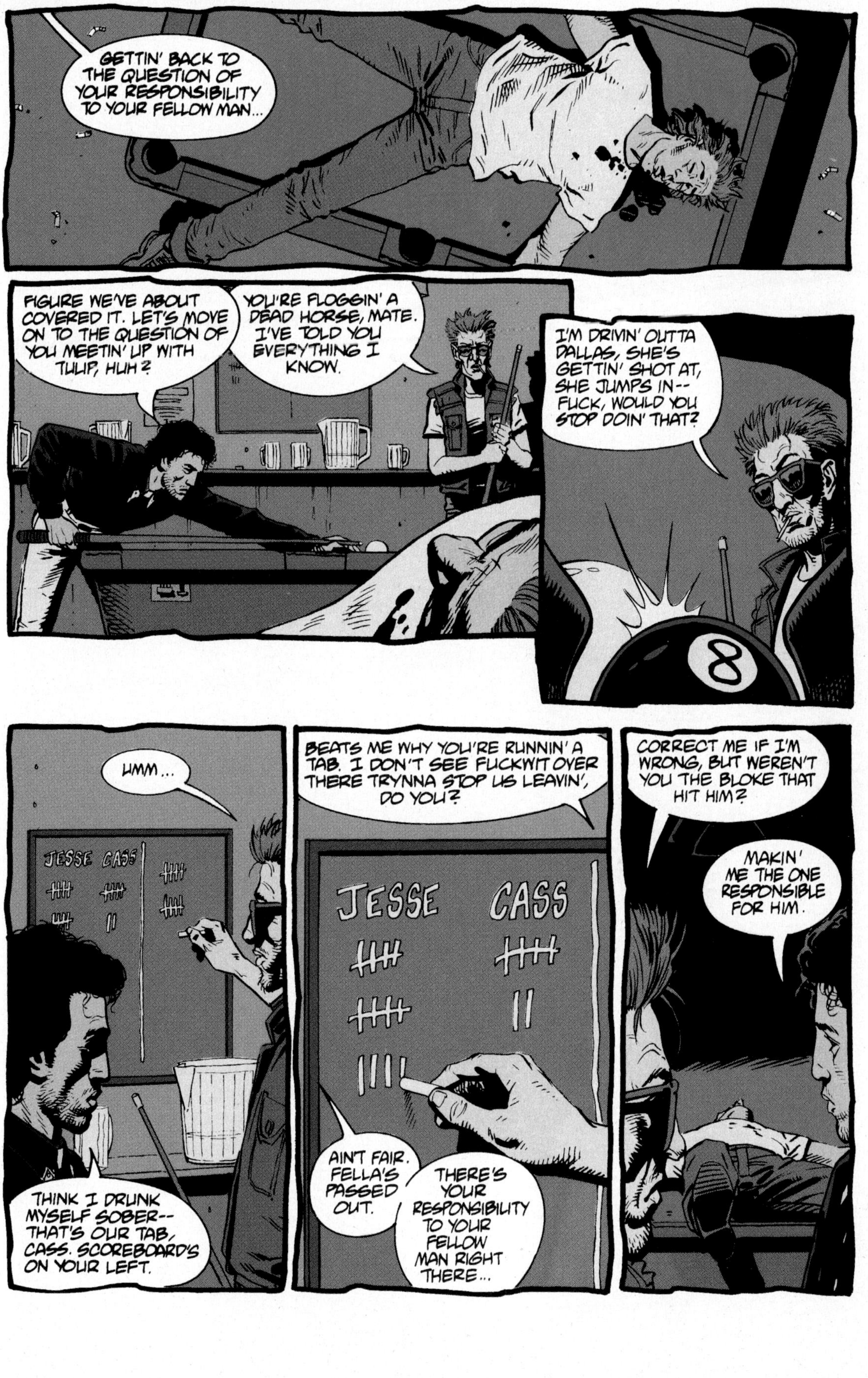
GETTIN' BACK TO THE QUESTION OF YOUR RESPONSIBILITY TO YOUR FELLOW MAN...
FIGURE WE'VE ABOUT COVERED IT. LET'S MOVE ON TO THE QUESTION OF YOU MEETIN' UP WITH TULIP, HUH?
YOU'RE FLOGGIN' A DEAD HORSE, MATE. I'VE TOLD YOU EVERYTHING I KNOW.
I'M DRIVIN' OUTTA DALLAS, SHE'S GETTIN' SHOT AT, SHE JUMPS IN-- FUCK, WOULD YOU STOP DOIN' THAT?
8
UMM...
JESSE CASS
THINK I DRUNK MYSELF SOBER-- THAT'S OUR TAB, CASS. SCOREBOARD'S ON YOUR LEFT.
BEATS ME WHY YOU'RE RUNNIN' A TAB. I DON'T SEE FUCKWIT OVER THERE TRYNNA STOP US LEAVIN', DO YOU?
JESSE CASS
AIN'T FAIR. FELLA'S PASSED OUT.
THERE'S YOUR RESPONSIBILITY TO YOUR FELLOW MAN RIGHT THERE...
CORRECT ME IF I'M WRONG, BUT WEREN'T YOU THE BLOKE THAT HIT HIM?
MAKIN' ME THE ONE RESPONSIBLE FOR HIM.

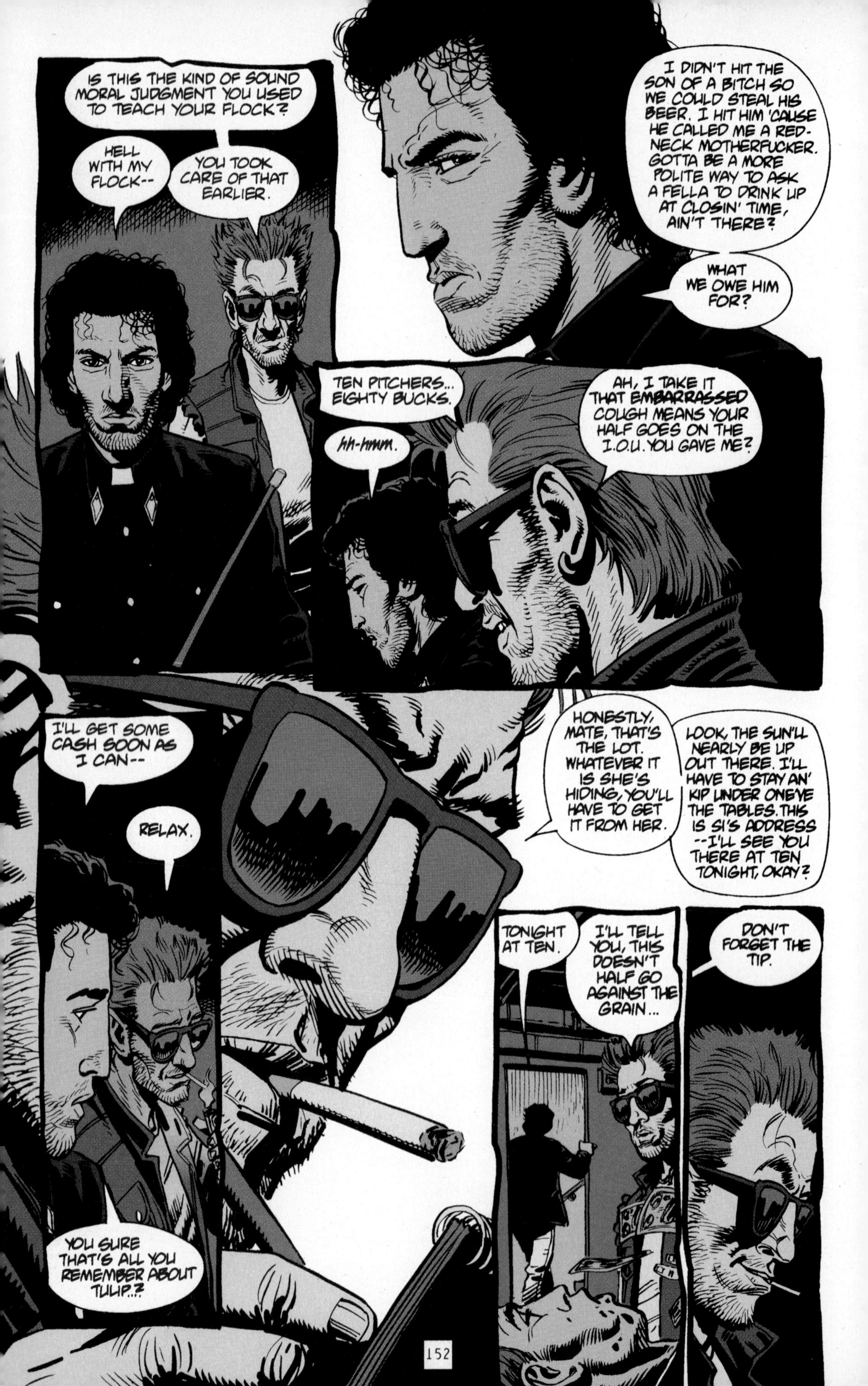
IS THIS THE KIND OF SOUND MORAL JUDGMENT YOU USED TO TEACH YOUR FLOCK?
HELL WITH MY FLOCK--
YOU TOOK CARE OF THAT EARLIER.
I DIDN'T HIT THE SON OF A BITCH SO WE COULD STEAL HIS BEER. I HIT HIM 'CAUSE HE CALLED ME A RED-NECK MOTHERFUCKER. GOTTA BE A MORE POLITE WAY TO ASK A FELLA TO DRINK UP AT CLOSIN' TIME, AIN'T THERE?
WHAT WE OWE HIM FOR?
TEN PITCHERS... EIGHTY BUCKS.
hh-hmm.
AH, I TAKE IT THAT EMBARRASSED COUGH MEANS YOUR HALF GOES ON THE I.O.U. YOU GAVE ME?
I'LL GET SOME CASH SOON AS I CAN--
RELAX.
YOU SURE THAT'S ALL YOU REMEMBER ABOUT TULIP...?
HONESTLY, MATE, THAT'S THE LOT. WHATEVER IT IS SHE'S HIDING, YOU'LL HAVE TO GET IT FROM HER.
LOOK, THE SUN'LL NEARLY BE UP OUT THERE. I'LL HAVE TO STAY AN' KIP UNDER ONE'YE THE TABLES. THIS IS SI'S ADDRESS --I'LL SEE YOU THERE AT TEN TONIGHT, OKAY?
TONIGHT AT TEN.
I'LL TELL YOU, THIS DOESN'T HALF GO AGAINST THE GRAIN...
DON'T FORGET THE TIP.

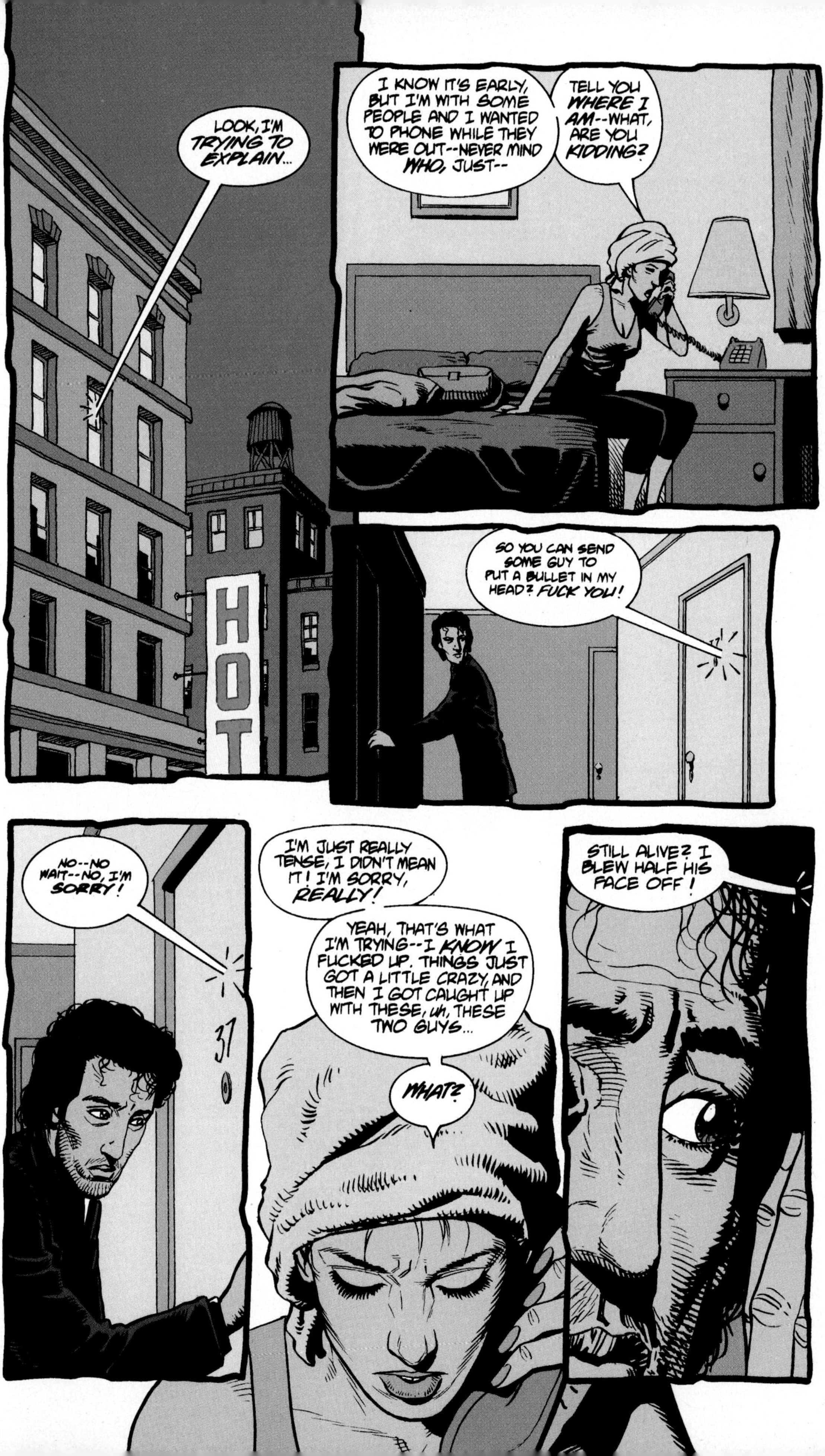

LOOK, I'M TRYING TO EXPLAIN...
I KNOW IT'S EARLY, BUT I'M WITH SOME PEOPLE AND I WANTED TO PHONE WHILE THEY WERE OUT--NEVER MIND WHO, JUST--
TELL YOU WHERE I AM--WHAT, ARE YOU KIDDING?
SO YOU CAN SEND SOME GUY TO PUT A BULLET IN MY HEAD? FUCK YOU!
HOT
NO--NO WAIT--NO, I'M SORRY!
I'M JUST REALLY TENSE, I DIDN'T MEAN IT! I'M SORRY, REALLY!
YEAH, THAT'S WHAT I'M TRYING--I KNOW I FUCKED UP. THINGS JUST GOT A LITTLE CRAZY, AND THEN I GOT CAUGHT UP WITH THESE, uh, THESE TWO GUYS...
37
WHAT?
STILL ALIVE? I BLEW HALF HIS FACE OFF!

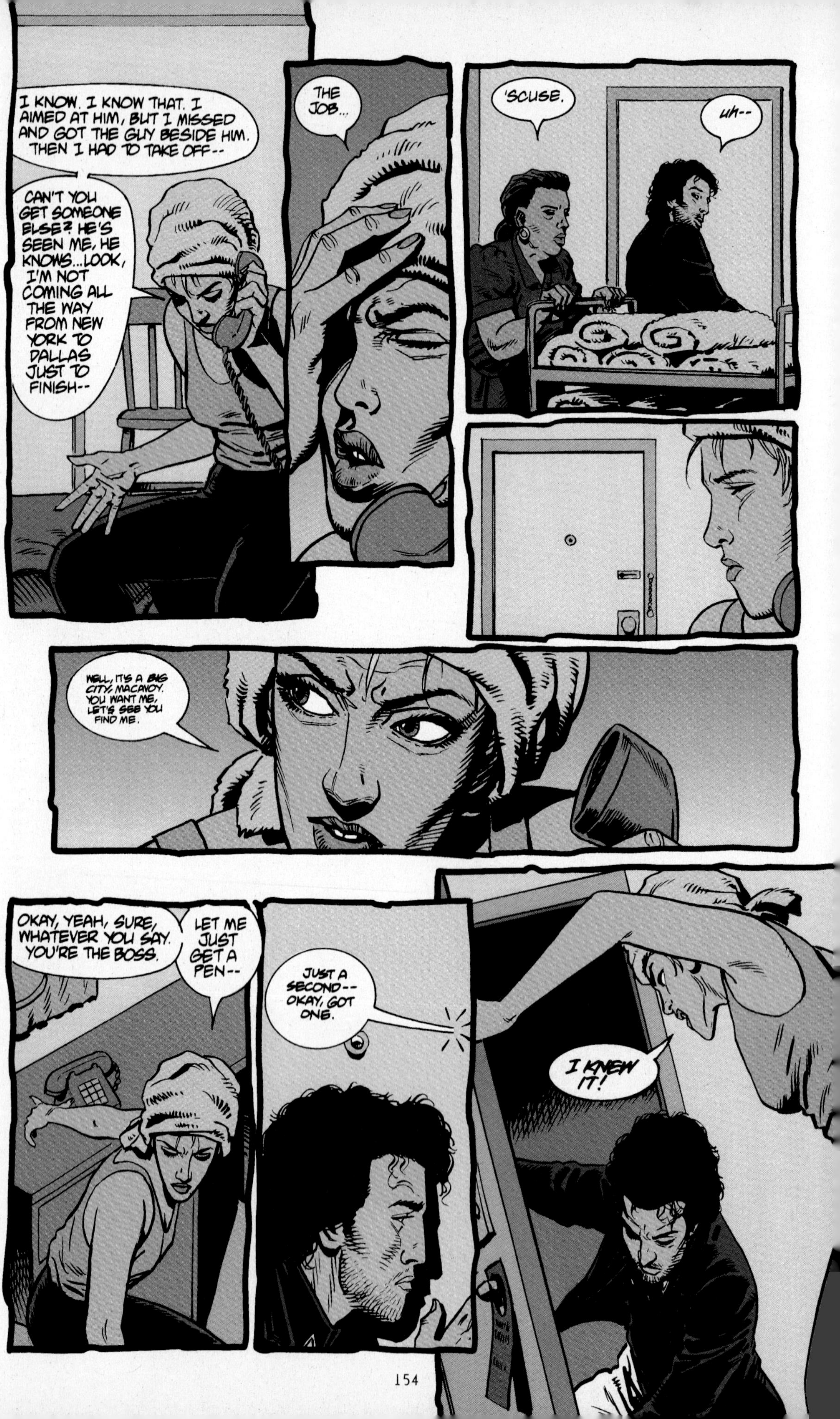
I KNOW. I KNOW THAT. I AIMED AT HIM, BUT I MISSED AND GOT THE GUY BESIDE HIM. THEN I HAD TO TAKE OFF--
CAN'T YOU GET SOMEONE ELSE? HE'S SEEN ME, HE KNOWS...LOOK, I'M NOT COMING ALL THE WAY FROM NEW YORK TO DALLAS JUST TO FINISH--
THE JOB...
'SCUSE.
uh--
WELL, IT'S A BIG CITY, MACAVOY. YOU WANT ME, LET'S SEE YOU FIND ME.
OKAY, YEAH, SURE, WHATEVER YOU SAY. YOU'RE THE BOSS.
LET ME JUST GET A PEN--
JUST A SECOND-- OKAY, GOT ONE.
I KNEW IT!

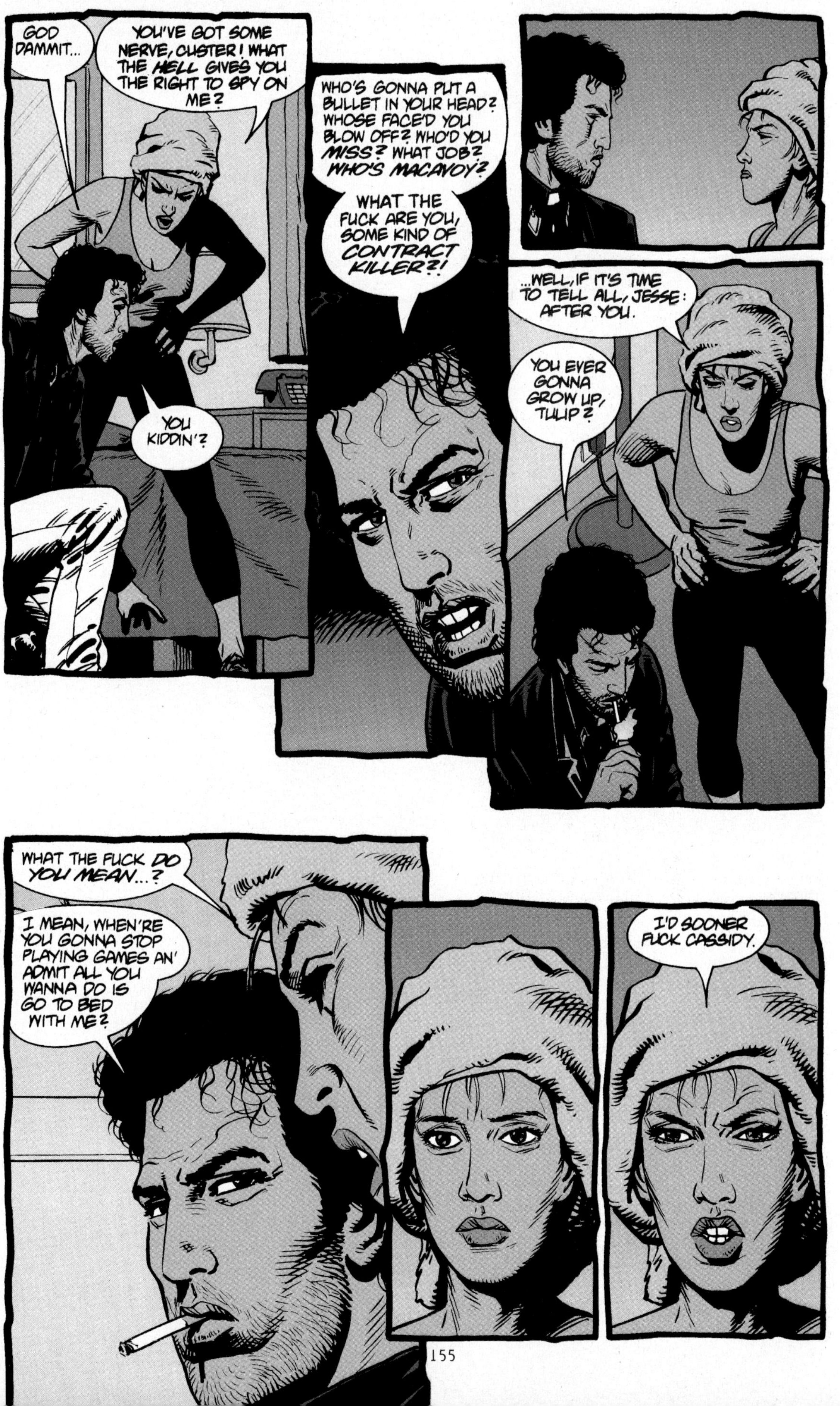
GOD DAMMIT...
YOU'VE GOT SOME NERVE, CUSTER! WHAT THE HELL GIVES YOU THE RIGHT TO SPY ON ME?
YOU KIDDIN'?
WHO'S GONNA PUT A BULLET IN YOUR HEAD? WHOSE FACE'D YOU BLOW OFF? WHO'D YOU MISS? WHAT JOB? WHO'S MACAVOY?
WHAT THE FUCK ARE YOU, SOME KIND OF CONTRACT KILLER?!
...WELL, IF IT'S TIME TO TELL ALL, JESSE: AFTER YOU.
YOU EVER GONNA GROW UP, TULIP?
WHAT THE FUCK DO YOU MEAN...?
I MEAN, WHEN'RE YOU GONNA STOP PLAYING GAMES AN' ADMIT ALL YOU WANNA DO IS GO TO BED WITH ME?
I'D SOONER FUCK CASSIDY.

HURTS, BUT I'LL BE SURE TO TELL HIM.

DON'T YOU DARE!

WHERE DO YOU GET OFF, SAYING A THING LIKE THAT?

AW, CUT THE HORSESHIT! IF IT AIN'T TRUE, WHY'RE YOU STICKIN' AROUND? WHAT'S KEEPIN' YOU WITH ME?

I TOLD YOU—

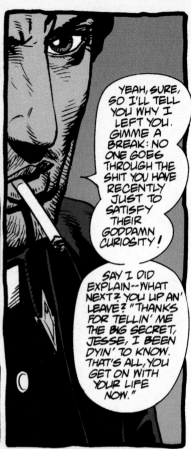

YEAH, SURE, SO I'LL TELL YOU WHY I LEFT YOU. GIMME A BREAK: NO ONE GOES THROUGH THE SHIT YOU HAVE RECENTLY JUST TO SATISFY THEIR GODDAMN CURIOSITY!

SAY I DID EXPLAIN-- WHAT NEXT? YOU UP AN' LEAVE? "THANKS FOR TELLIN' ME THE BIG SECRET, JESSE, I BEEN DYIN' TO KNOW. THAT'S ALL, YOU GET ON WITH YOUR LIFE NOW."

SO WHAT'S YOUR EXCUSE? WHY'RE YOU SO INTERESTED IN MY SECRET?

HEY, I'M CURIOUS TOO. DIFFERENCE IS, I AIN'T USIN' THE FACT TO COVER UP WHAT I REALLY WANT.

OUT.

NEARLY THERE, PILGRIM.

uh-huh.

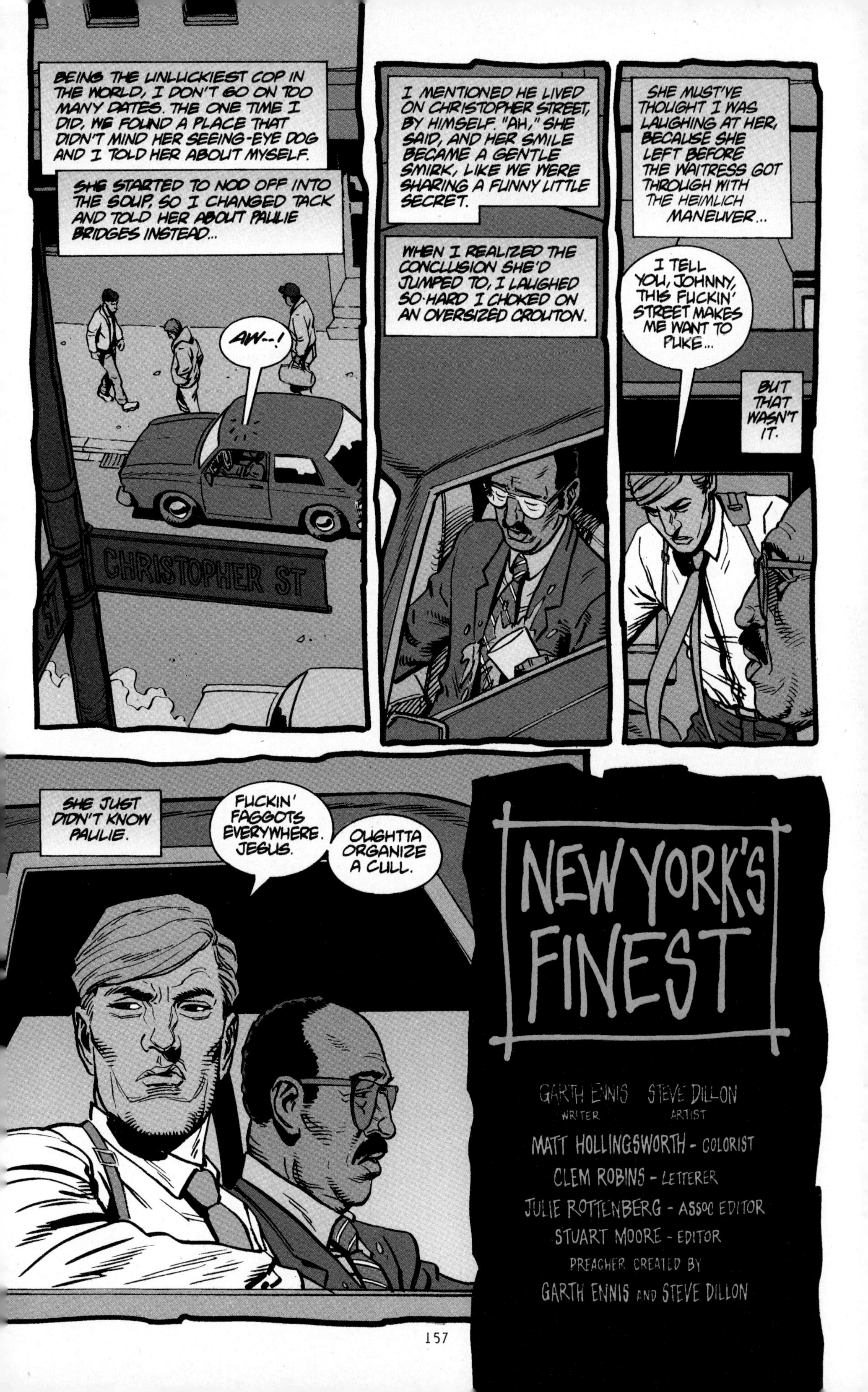
BEING THE UNLUCKIEST COP IN THE WORLD, I DON'T GO ON TOO MANY DATES. THE ONE TIME I DID, WE FOUND A PLACE THAT DIDN'T MIND HER SEEING-EYE DOG AND I TOLD HER ABOUT MYSELF.
SHE STARTED TO NOD OFF INTO THE SOUP, SO I CHANGED TACK AND TOLD HER ABOUT PAULIE BRIDGES INSTEAD...
AW--!
CHRISTOPHER ST
I MENTIONED HE LIVED ON CHRISTOPHER STREET, BY HIMSELF. "AH," SHE SAID, AND HER SMILE BECAME A GENTLE SMIRK, LIKE WE WERE SHARING A FUNNY LITTLE SECRET.
WHEN I REALIZED THE CONCLUSION SHE'D JUMPED TO, I LAUGHED SO HARD I CHOKED ON AN OVERSIZED CROUTON.
SHE MUST'VE THOUGHT I WAS LAUGHING AT HER, BECAUSE SHE LEFT BEFORE THE WAITRESS GOT THROUGH WITH THE HEIMLICH MANEUVER...
I TELL YOU, JOHNNY, THIS FUCKIN' STREET MAKES ME WANT TO PUKE...
BUT THAT WASN'T IT.
SHE JUST DIDN'T KNOW PAULIE.
FUCKIN' FAGGOTS EVERYWHERE. JESUS.
OUGHTTA ORGANIZE A CULL.
NEW YORK'S FINEST
GARTH ENNIS WRITER
STEVE DILLON ARTIST
MATT HOLLINGSWORTH - COLORIST
CLEM ROBINS - LETTERER
JULIE ROTTENBERG - ASSOC EDITOR
STUART MOORE - EDITOR
PREACHER CREATED BY
GARTH ENNIS AND STEVE DILLON

THEY'RE NOT HURTING ANY- BODY, PAULIE--

WHAT'S THE ADDRESS?

EIGHTY- FIRST AND LEX.

DID A YUPPIE AT LAST, HUH?

MAYBE NOW WE'LL RATE SOME BACKUP.

HEARD A HALF HOUR AGO. LADY CALLS IN--HUSBAND'S BEEN GONE TWO NIGHTS RUNNING, THEN THIS PACKAGE SHOWS UP IN THE MAIL. SHE STARTS TO OPEN IT WHEN SHE REALIZES IT'S *LEAKING BLOOD.*

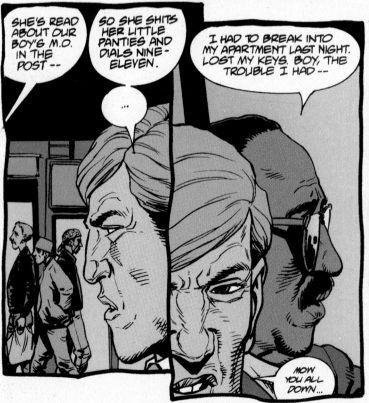

SHE'S READ ABOUT OUR BOY'S M.O. IN THE POST --

SO SHE SHITS HER LITTLE PANTIES AND DIALS NINE- ELEVEN.

...

I HAD TO BREAK INTO MY APARTMENT LAST NIGHT. LOST MY KEYS. BOY, THE TROUBLE I HAD --

MOW YOU ALL DOWN...

PAULIE? WHAT'D YOU SAY?

WAKE ME WHEN YOU GET THERE.

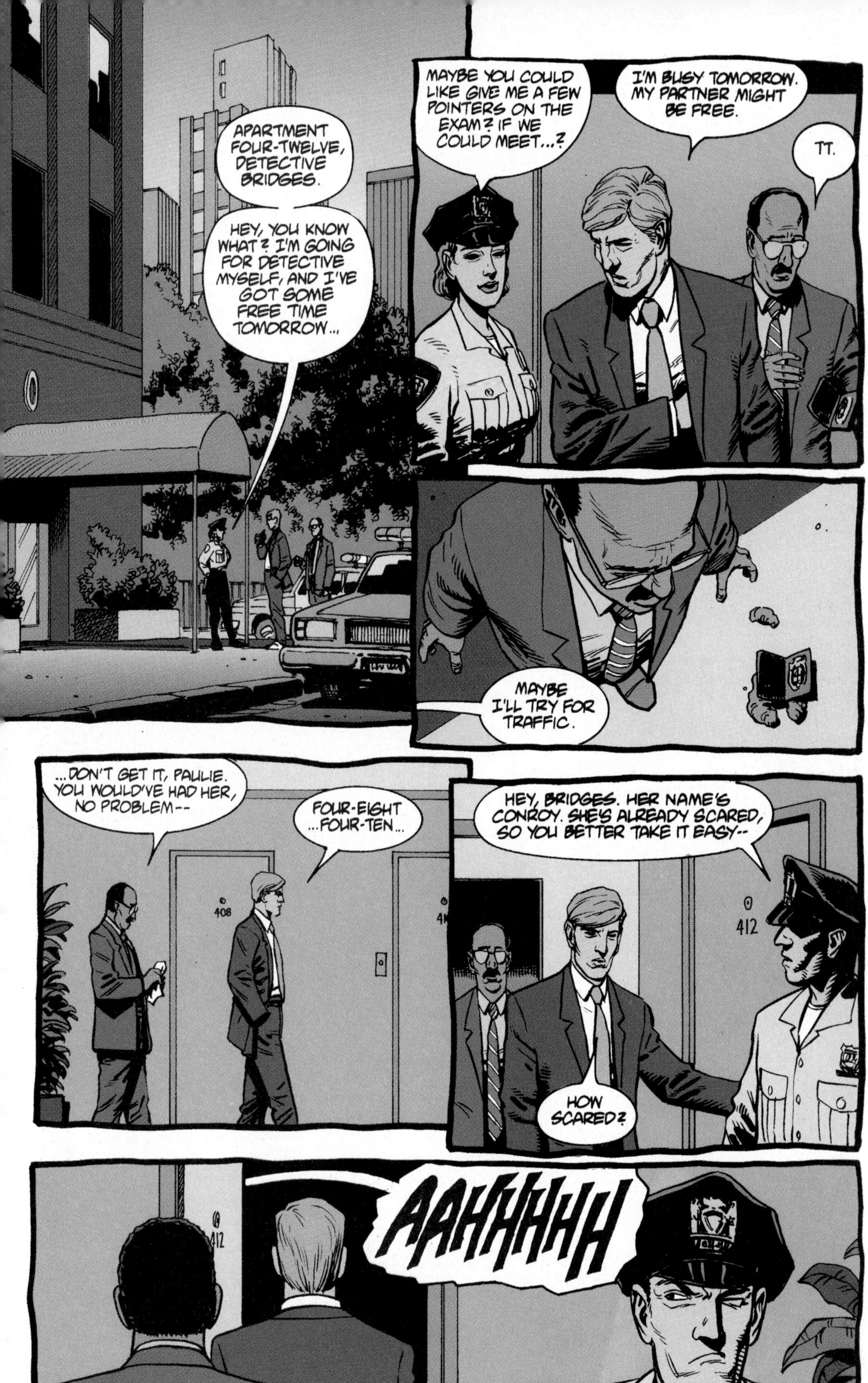
APARTMENT FOUR-TWELVE, DETECTIVE BRIDGES.
HEY, YOU KNOW WHAT? I'M GOING FOR DETECTIVE MYSELF, AND I'VE GOT SOME FREE TIME TOMORROW...
MAYBE YOU COULD LIKE GIVE ME A FEW POINTERS ON THE EXAM? IF WE COULD MEET...?
I'M BUSY TOMORROW. MY PARTNER MIGHT BE FREE.
TT.
MAYBE I'LL TRY FOR TRAFFIC.
...DON'T GET IT, PAULIE. YOU WOULD'VE HAD HER, NO PROBLEM--
FOUR-EIGHT ...FOUR-TEN...
408
HEY, BRIDGES. HER NAME'S CONROY. SHE'S ALREADY SCARED, SO YOU BETTER TAKE IT EASY--
412
HOW SCARED?
412
AAHHHHH

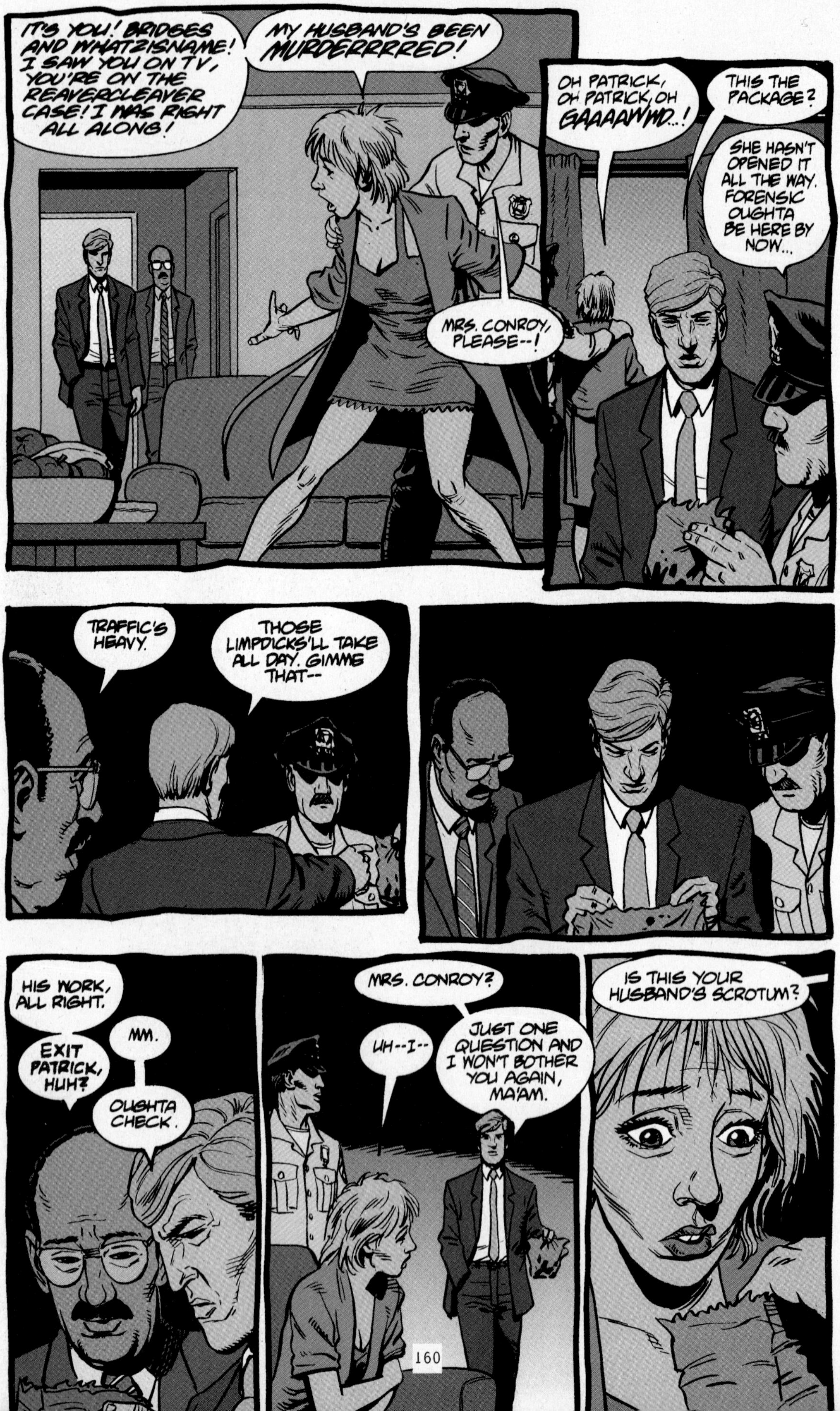
IT'S YOU! BRIDGES AND WHATZISNAME! I SAW YOU ON TV, YOU'RE ON THE REAVERCLEAVER CASE! I WAS RIGHT ALL ALONG!
MY HUSBAND'S BEEN MURDERRRRED!
MRS. CONROY, PLEASE--!
OH PATRICK, OH PATRICK, OH GAAAAWWD...!
THIS THE PACKAGE?
SHE HASN'T OPENED IT ALL THE WAY. FORENSIC OUGHTA BE HERE BY NOW...
TRAFFIC'S HEAVY.
THOSE LIMPDICKS'LL TAKE ALL DAY. GIMME THAT--
HIS WORK, ALL RIGHT.
EXIT PATRICK, HUH?
MM.
OUGHTA CHECK.
MRS. CONROY?
UH--I--
JUST ONE QUESTION AND I WON'T BOTHER YOU AGAIN, MA'AM.
IS THIS YOUR HUSBAND'S SCROTUM?

KNOCK IT OFF, WILL YOU?

AW, YOU GOTTA ADMIT IT'S A HELL OF A SIGHT...

NO, I DON'T. BUT THEN, I'M NOT A YOKEL ON HIS FIRST TRIP OUT OF THE BOONIES.

FOR CHRIST'S SAKE STOP IT, JESSE.. IT'S A DAMN GOOD WAY TO GET MUGGED.

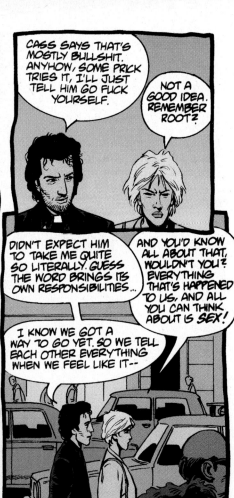

CASS SAYS THAT'S MOSTLY BULLSHIT. ANYHOW, SOME PRICK TRIES IT, I'LL JUST TELL HIM GO FUCK YOURSELF.

NOT A GOOD IDEA. REMEMBER ROOT?

DIDN'T EXPECT HIM TO TAKE ME QUITE SO LITERALLY. GUESS THE WORD BRINGS ITS OWN RESPONSIBILITIES...

AND YOU'D KNOW ALL ABOUT THAT, WOULDN'T YOU? EVERYTHING THAT'S HAPPENED TO US, AND ALL YOU CAN THINK ABOUT IS SEX!

I KNOW WE GOT A WAY TO GO YET. SO WE TELL EACH OTHER EVERYTHING WHEN WE FEEL LIKE IT--

--MEANTIME, LET'S GET BACK TO THREE TIMES A NIGHT AN' TWICE WEEKLY MATINEES...

YOU WALKED OUT ON THAT FIVE YEARS AGO--

HEY, YOU KNOW SOMETHIN'?

YOU AIN'T SMILED ALL DAY, YOU KNOW THAT? HOW ABOUT SMILIN' FOR ME, JUST ONCE. JUST TO REMIND ME WHAT IT LOOKS LIKE.

YOU--

BASTARD...

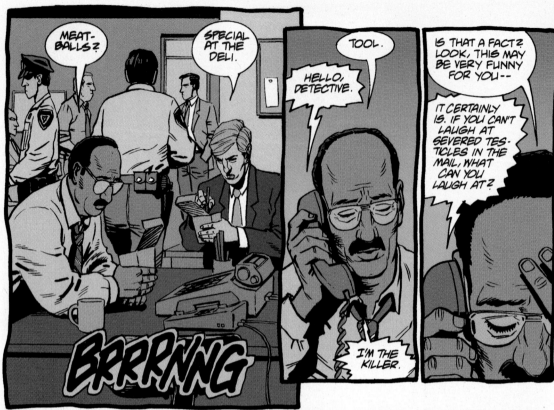

MEAT-BALLS?

SPECIAL AT THE DELI.

HELLO, DETECTIVE.

TOOL.

IS THAT A FACT? LOOK, THIS MAY BE VERY FUNNY FOR YOU--

IT CERTAINLY IS. IF YOU CAN'T LAUGH AT SEVERED TESTICLES IN THE MAIL, WHAT CAN YOU LAUGH AT?

BRRRNNG

I'M THE KILLER.

NOW SEEING AS THAT JUICY LITTLE DETAIL HASN'T YET BEEN MADE PUBLIC, I FIGURE YOU'RE CONVINCED I'M ON THE LEVEL.

I JUST WANTED TO ESTABLISH THAT FOR WHEN I CALL AGAIN...

IT'S HIM! VENUCCI, I'VE GOT HIM ON THE LINE! TAP IT!

HUH?

HOW THE FUCK CAN I? YOUR PHONE ISN'T HOOKED UP! AND DON'T FUCKING SHOUT AT ME, TOOL!

BUT-- BUT--

'BYE FOR NOW.

...GOD'STH STHAKE, KILL ME...

162

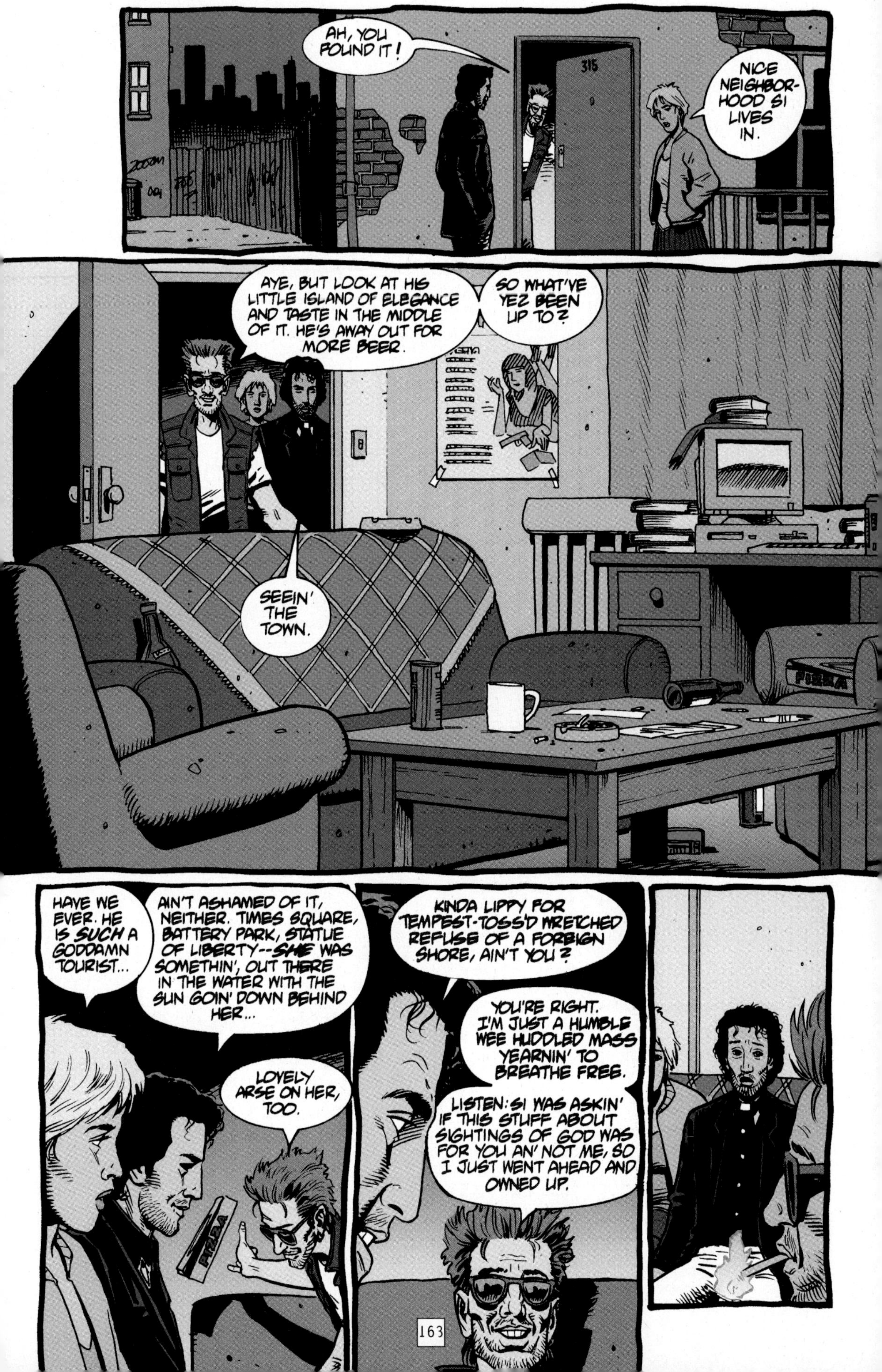
AH, YOU FOUND IT!
315
NICE NEIGHBOR-HOOD SI LIVES IN.
AYE, BUT LOOK AT HIS LITTLE ISLAND OF ELEGANCE AND TASTE IN THE MIDDLE OF IT. HE'S AWAY OUT FOR MORE BEER.
SO WHAT'VE YEZ BEEN UP TO?
SEEIN' THE TOWN.
PIZZA
HAVE WE EVER. HE IS *SUCH* A GODDAMN TOURIST...
AIN'T ASHAMED OF IT, NEITHER. TIMES SQUARE, BATTERY PARK, STATUE OF LIBERTY--*SHE* WAS SOMETHIN', OUT THERE IN THE WATER WITH THE SUN GOIN' DOWN BEHIND HER...
LOVELY ARSE ON HER, TOO.
PIZZA
KINDA LIPPY FOR TEMPEST-TOSS'D WRETCHED REFUSE OF A FOREIGN SHORE, AIN'T YOU?
YOU'RE RIGHT. I'M JUST A HUMBLE WEE HUDDLED MASS YEARNIN' TO BREATHE FREE.
LISTEN: SI WAS ASKIN' IF THIS STUFF ABOUT SIGHTINGS OF GOD WAS FOR YOU AN' NOT ME, SO I JUST WENT AHEAD AND OWNED UP.

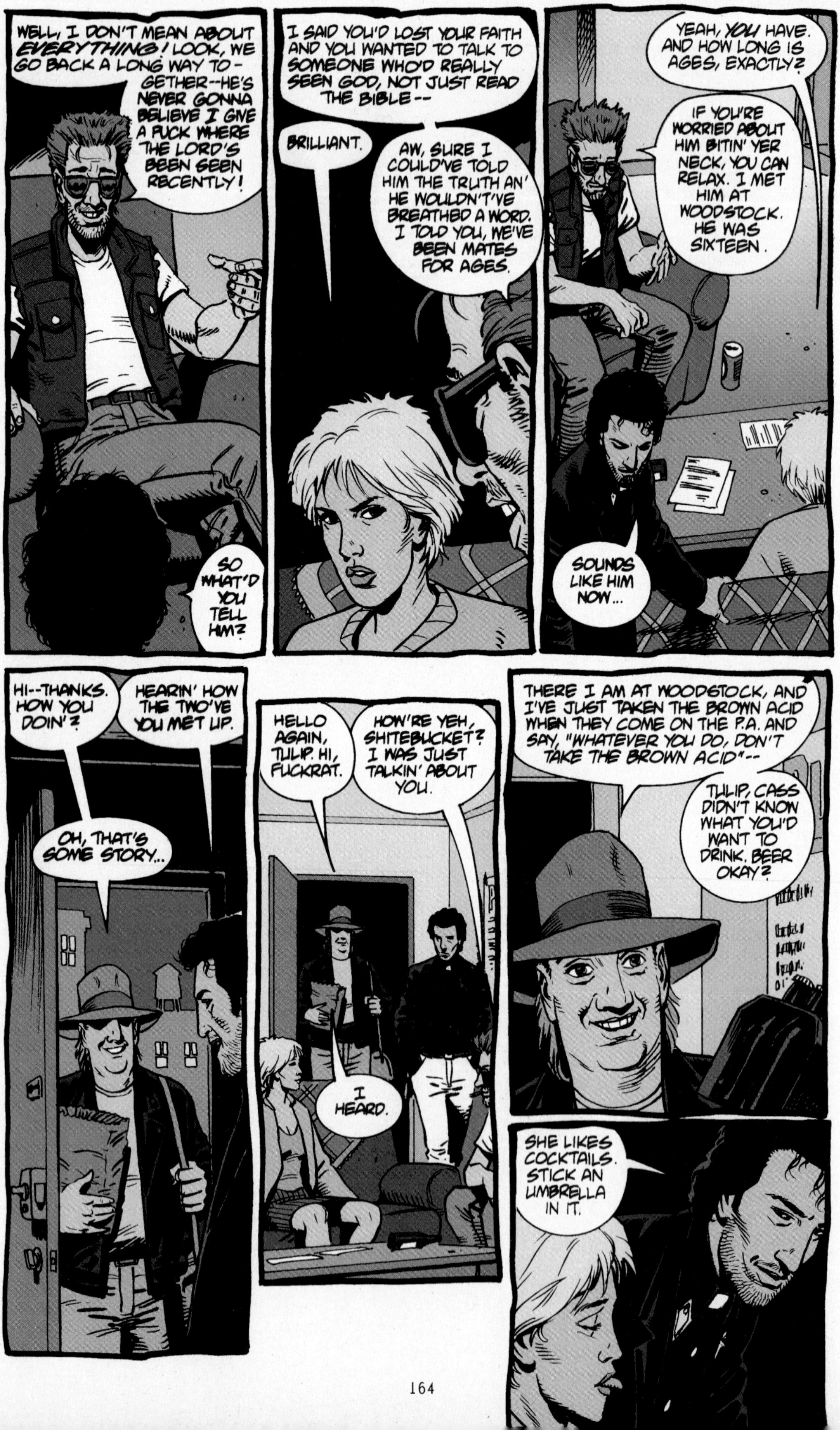
WELL, I DON'T MEAN ABOUT EVERYTHING! LOOK, WE GO BACK A LONG WAY TO-GETHER--HE'S NEVER GONNA BELIEVE I GIVE A FUCK WHERE THE LORD'S BEEN SEEN RECENTLY!
SO WHAT'D YOU TELL HIM?
I SAID YOU'D LOST YOUR FAITH AND YOU WANTED TO TALK TO SOMEONE WHO'D REALLY SEEN GOD, NOT JUST READ THE BIBLE--
BRILLIANT.
AW, SURE I COULD'VE TOLD HIM THE TRUTH AN' HE WOULDN'T'VE BREATHED A WORD. I TOLD YOU, WE'VE BEEN MATES FOR AGES.
YEAH, YOU HAVE. AND HOW LONG IS AGES, EXACTLY?
IF YOU'RE WORRIED ABOUT HIM BITIN' YER NECK, YOU CAN RELAX. I MET HIM AT WOODSTOCK. HE WAS SIXTEEN.
SOUNDS LIKE HIM NOW...
HI--THANKS. HOW YOU DOIN'?
HEARIN' HOW THE TWO'VE YOU MET UP.
OH, THAT'S SOME STORY...
HELLO AGAIN, TULIP. HI, FUCKRAT.
HOW'RE YEH, SHITEBUCKET? I WAS JUST TALKIN' ABOUT YOU.
I HEARD.
THERE I AM AT WOODSTOCK, AND I'VE JUST TAKEN THE BROWN ACID WHEN THEY COME ON THE P.A. AND SAY, "WHATEVER YOU DO, DON'T TAKE THE BROWN ACID"--
TULIP, CASS DIDN'T KNOW WHAT YOU'D WANT TO DRINK. BEER OKAY?
SHE LIKES COCKTAILS. STICK AN UMBRELLA IN IT.

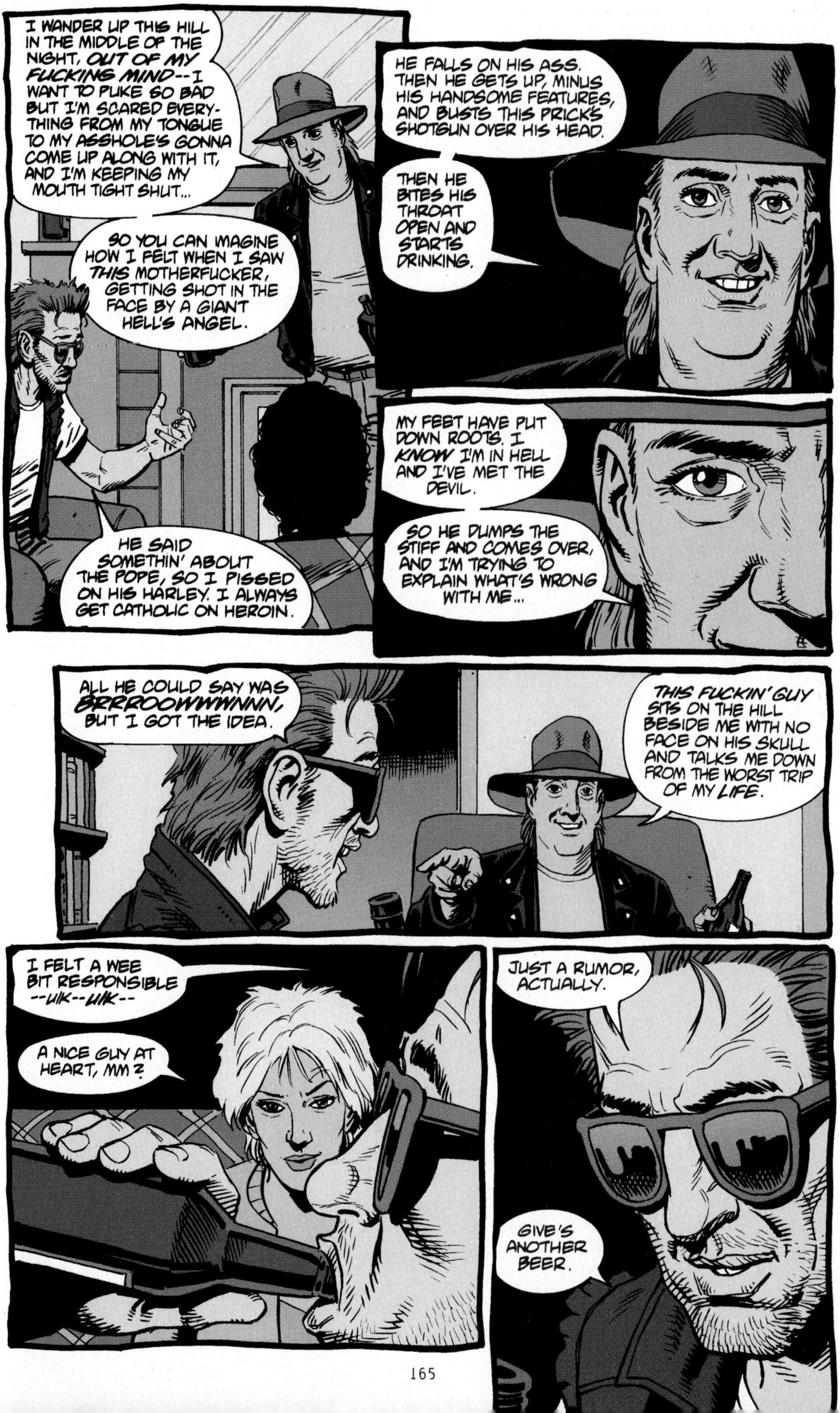
I WANDER UP THIS HILL IN THE MIDDLE OF THE NIGHT, OUT OF MY FUCKING MIND--I WANT TO PUKE SO BAD BUT I'M SCARED EVERYTHING FROM MY TONGUE TO MY ASSHOLE'S GONNA COME UP ALONG WITH IT, AND I'M KEEPING MY MOUTH TIGHT SHUT...
SO YOU CAN IMAGINE HOW I FELT WHEN I SAW THIS MOTHERFUCKER, GETTING SHOT IN THE FACE BY A GIANT HELL'S ANGEL.
HE SAID SOMETHIN' ABOUT THE POPE, SO I PISSED ON HIS HARLEY. I ALWAYS GET CATHOLIC ON HEROIN.
HE FALLS ON HIS ASS. THEN HE GETS UP, MINUS HIS HANDSOME FEATURES, AND BUSTS THIS PRICK'S SHOTGUN OVER HIS HEAD.
THEN HE BITES HIS THROAT OPEN AND STARTS DRINKING.
MY FEET HAVE PUT DOWN ROOTS. I KNOW I'M IN HELL AND I'VE MET THE DEVIL.
SO HE DUMPS THE STIFF AND COMES OVER, AND I'M TRYING TO EXPLAIN WHAT'S WRONG WITH ME...
ALL HE COULD SAY WAS BRRROOWWWNNN, BUT I GOT THE IDEA.
THIS FUCKIN' GUY SITS ON THE HILL BESIDE ME WITH NO FACE ON HIS SKULL AND TALKS ME DOWN FROM THE WORST TRIP OF MY LIFE.
I FELT A WEE BIT RESPONSIBLE --UIK--UIK--
A NICE GUY AT HEART, MM?
JUST A RUMOR, ACTUALLY.
GIVE'S ANOTHER BEER.

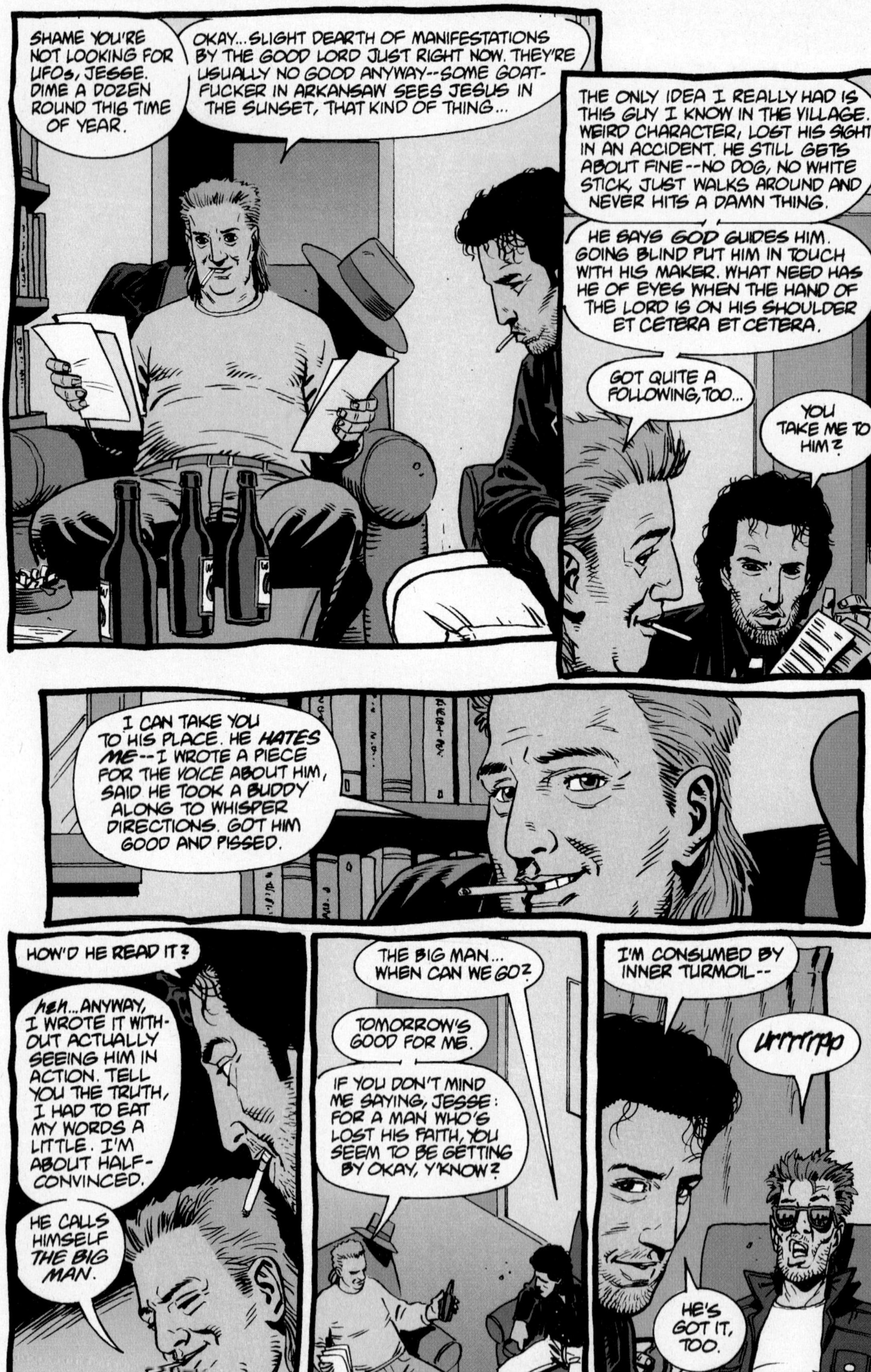
SHAME YOU'RE NOT LOOKING FOR UFOs, JESSE. DIME A DOZEN ROUND THIS TIME OF YEAR.
OKAY... SLIGHT DEARTH OF MANIFESTATIONS BY THE GOOD LORD JUST RIGHT NOW. THEY'RE USUALLY NO GOOD ANYWAY--SOME GOAT-FUCKER IN ARKANSAW SEES JESUS IN THE SUNSET, THAT KIND OF THING...
THE ONLY IDEA I REALLY HAD IS THIS GUY I KNOW IN THE VILLAGE. WEIRD CHARACTER, LOST HIS SIGHT IN AN ACCIDENT. HE STILL GETS ABOUT FINE--NO DOG, NO WHITE STICK, JUST WALKS AROUND AND NEVER HITS A DAMN THING.
HE SAYS GOD GUIDES HIM. GOING BLIND PUT HIM IN TOUCH WITH HIS MAKER. WHAT NEED HAS HE OF EYES WHEN THE HAND OF THE LORD IS ON HIS SHOULDER ET CETERA ET CETERA.
GOT QUITE A FOLLOWING, TOO...
YOU TAKE ME TO HIM?
I CAN TAKE YOU TO HIS PLACE. HE HATES ME--I WROTE A PIECE FOR THE VOICE ABOUT HIM, SAID HE TOOK A BUDDY ALONG TO WHISPER DIRECTIONS. GOT HIM GOOD AND PISSED.
HOW'D HE READ IT?
heh... ANYWAY, I WROTE IT WITHOUT ACTUALLY SEEING HIM IN ACTION. TELL YOU THE TRUTH, I HAD TO EAT MY WORDS A LITTLE. I'M ABOUT HALF-CONVINCED.
HE CALLS HIMSELF THE BIG MAN.
THE BIG MAN... WHEN CAN WE GO?
TOMORROW'S GOOD FOR ME.
IF YOU DON'T MIND ME SAYING, JESSE: FOR A MAN WHO'S LOST HIS FAITH, YOU SEEM TO BE GETTING BY OKAY, Y'KNOW?
I'M CONSUMED BY INNER TURMOIL--
Urrrrrpp
HE'S GOT IT, TOO.

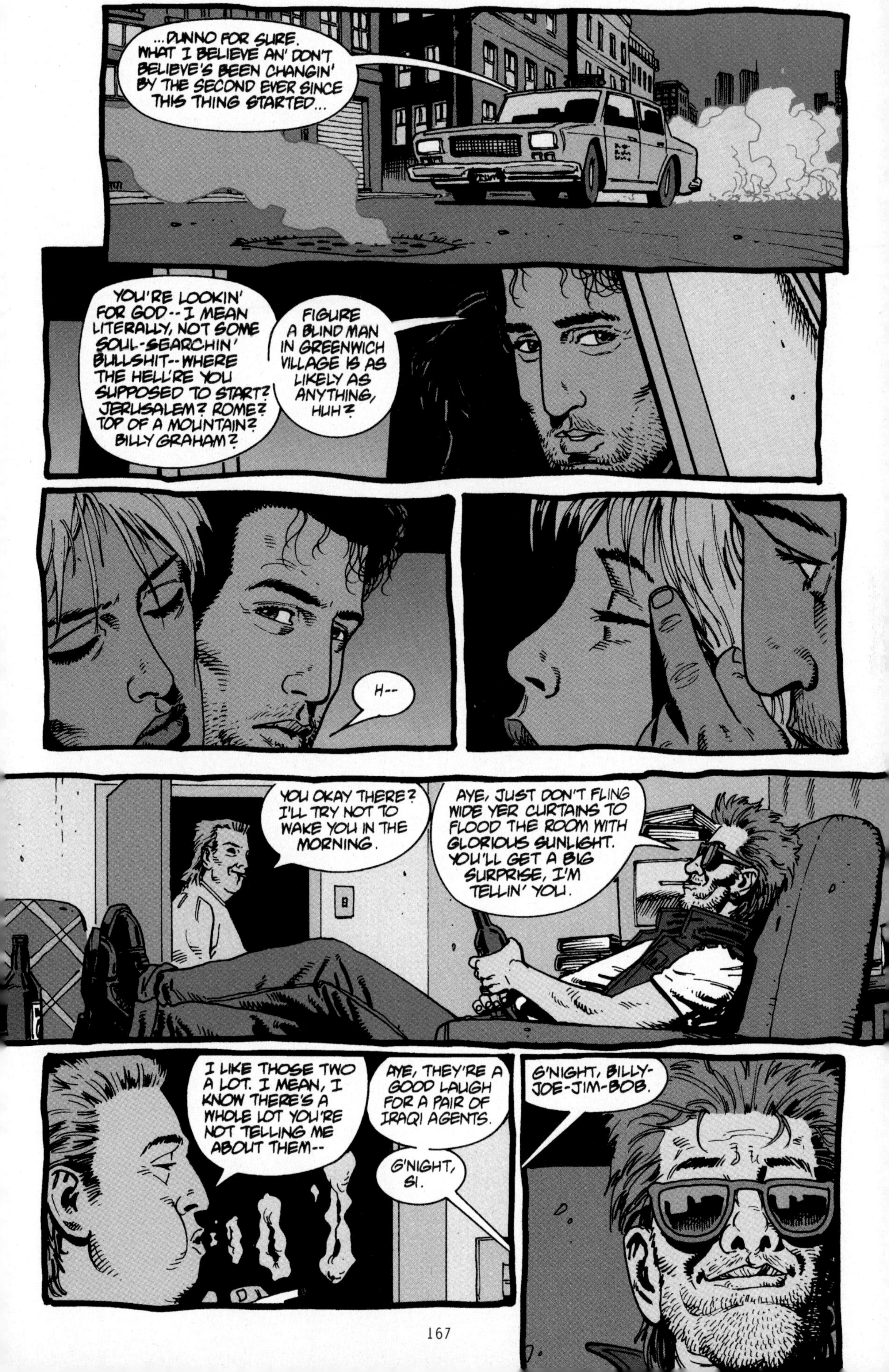
...DUNNO FOR SURE. WHAT I BELIEVE AN' DON'T BELIEVE'S BEEN CHANGIN' BY THE SECOND EVER SINCE THIS THING STARTED...
YOU'RE LOOKIN' FOR GOD--I MEAN LITERALLY, NOT SOME SOUL-SEARCHIN' BULLSHIT--WHERE THE HELL'RE YOU SUPPOSED TO START? JERUSALEM? ROME? TOP OF A MOUNTAIN? BILLY GRAHAM?
FIGURE A BLIND MAN IN GREENWICH VILLAGE IS AS LIKELY AS ANYTHING, HUH?
H--
YOU OKAY THERE? I'LL TRY NOT TO WAKE YOU IN THE MORNING.
AYE, JUST DON'T FLING WIDE YER CURTAINS TO FLOOD THE ROOM WITH GLORIOUS SUNLIGHT. YOU'LL GET A BIG SURPRISE, I'M TELLIN' YOU.
I LIKE THOSE TWO A LOT. I MEAN, I KNOW THERE'S A WHOLE LOT YOU'RE NOT TELLING ME ABOUT THEM--
AYE, THEY'RE A GOOD LAUGH FOR A PAIR OF IRAQI AGENTS.
G'NIGHT, SI.
G'NIGHT, BILLY-JOE-JIM-BOB.

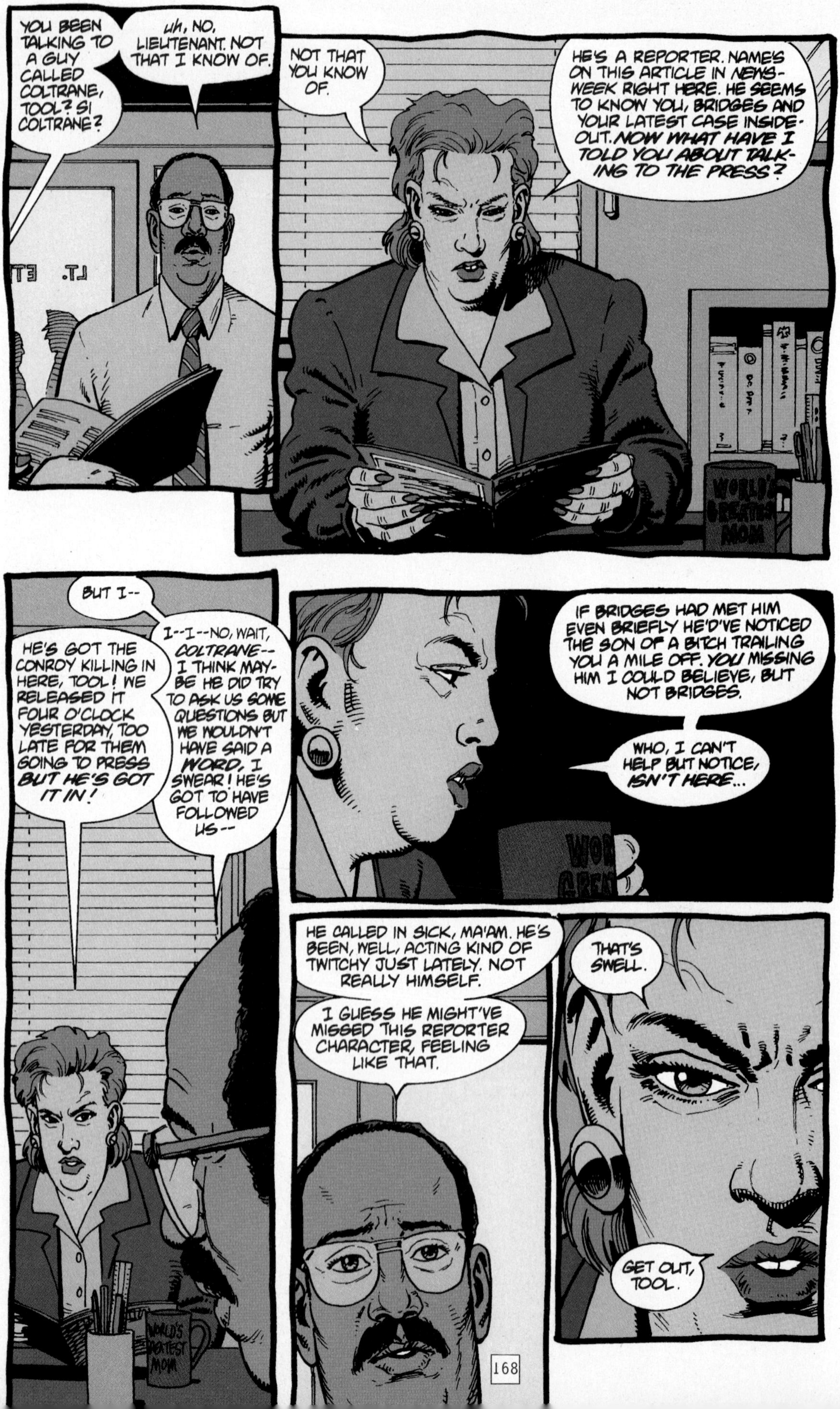
YOU BEEN TALKING TO A GUY CALLED COLTRANE, TOOL? SI COLTRANE?
UH, NO, LIEUTENANT. NOT THAT I KNOW OF.
NOT THAT YOU KNOW OF.
HE'S A REPORTER. NAME'S ON THIS ARTICLE IN NEWSWEEK RIGHT HERE. HE SEEMS TO KNOW YOU, BRIDGES AND YOUR LATEST CASE INSIDE-OUT. NOW WHAT HAVE I TOLD YOU ABOUT TALKING TO THE PRESS?
WORLD'S GREATEST MOM
BUT I--
HE'S GOT THE CONROY KILLING IN HERE, TOOL! WE RELEASED IT FOUR O'CLOCK YESTERDAY, TOO LATE FOR THEM GOING TO PRESS BUT HE'S GOT IT IN!
I--I--NO, WAIT, COLTRANE-- I THINK MAYBE HE DID TRY TO ASK US SOME QUESTIONS BUT WE WOULDN'T HAVE SAID A WORD, I SWEAR! HE'S GOT TO HAVE FOLLOWED US--
IF BRIDGES HAD MET HIM EVEN BRIEFLY HE'D'VE NOTICED THE SON OF A BITCH TRAILING YOU A MILE OFF. YOU MISSING HIM I COULD BELIEVE, BUT NOT BRIDGES.
WHO, I CAN'T HELP BUT NOTICE, ISN'T HERE...
HE CALLED IN SICK, MA'AM. HE'S BEEN, WELL, ACTING KIND OF TWITCHY JUST LATELY. NOT REALLY HIMSELF.
I GUESS HE MIGHT'VE MISSED THIS REPORTER CHARACTER, FEELING LIKE THAT.
THAT'S SWELL.
GET OUT, TOOL.
WORLD'S GREATEST MOM

I CAN'T REALLY BLAME HER. THIS IS THE HIGHEST-PROFILE SERIES OF HOMICIDES EVER FACED BY THIS PRECINCT, AND THE TWO OFFICERS SHE ASSIGNS CAN'T EVEN EXERCISE AN OUNCE OF DISCRETION...

SO I'VE GOT NO LEADS, NO SUSPECT, NO PARTNER--AND BRIDGES *HAS* BEEN ACTING WEIRD; I COULD SWEAR HE WAS CRYING WHEN HE GOT OUT'VE THE CAR LAST NIGHT--

CALL FOR YOU, TOOL.

AND NO LUCK.

TOOL.

GOOD MORNING, DETECTIVE.

YES, IT'S ME AGAIN.

I'M SORRY TO NOTE THAT DETECTIVE BRIDGES IS ILL TODAY, BUT ON THE OTHER HAND HE WON'T BE THERE TO DETRACT FROM YOUR MOMENT OF GLORY...

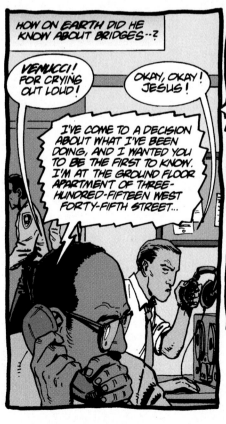

HOW ON EARTH DID HE KNOW ABOUT BRIDGES--?

VENUCCI! FOR CRYING OUT LOUD!

OKAY, OKAY! JESUS!

I'VE COME TO A DECISION ABOUT WHAT I'VE BEEN DOING, AND I WANTED YOU TO BE THE FIRST TO KNOW. I'M AT THE GROUND FLOOR APARTMENT OF THREE-HUNDRED FIFTEEN WEST FORTY-FIFTH STREET...

AND DETECTIVE?

YES?

I'VE GOT A LOT TO SAY FOR MYSELF.

BRING A *BIG* S.W.A.T. TEAM.

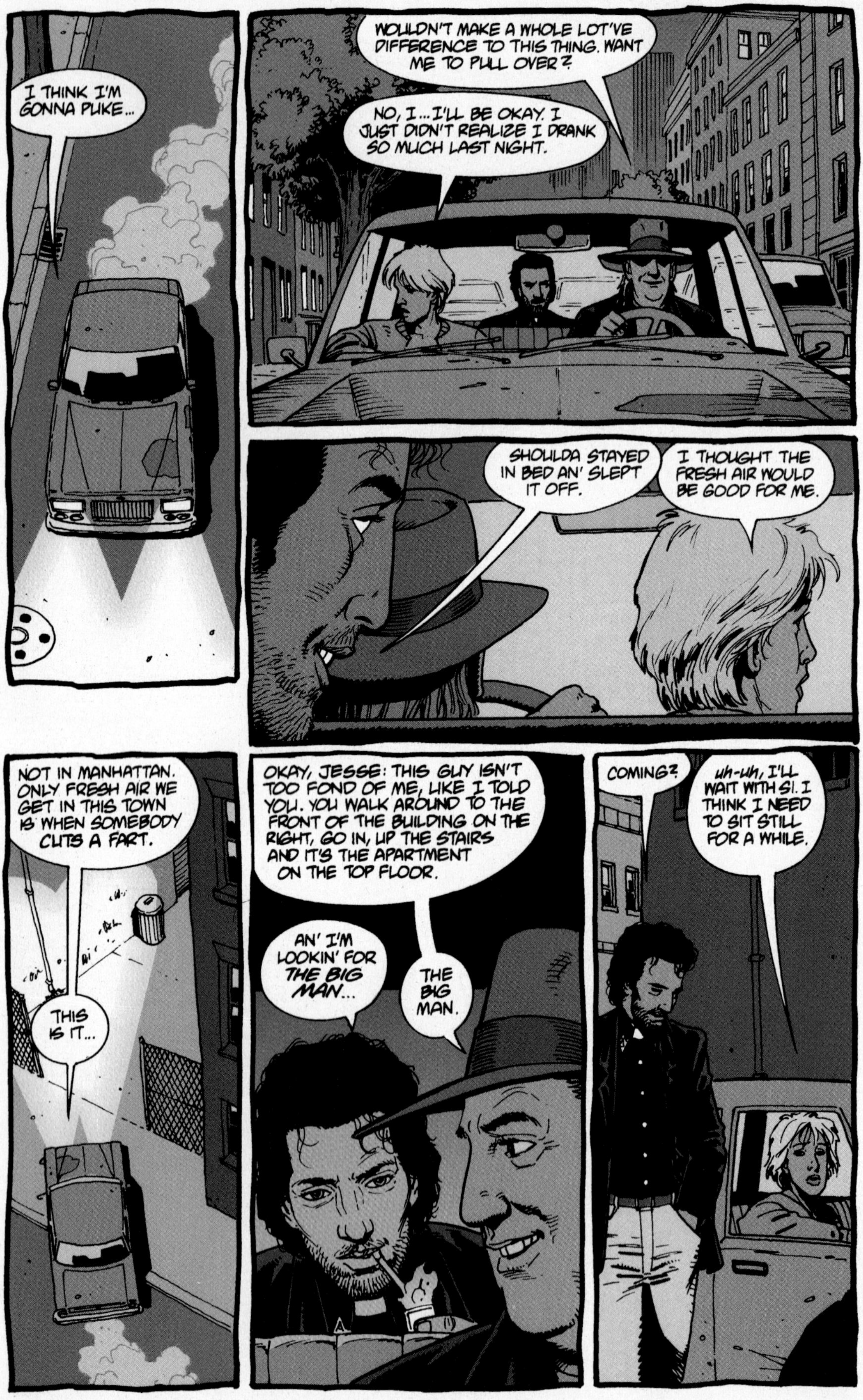
I THINK I'M GONNA PUKE...
WOULDN'T MAKE A WHOLE LOT'VE DIFFERENCE TO THIS THING. WANT ME TO PULL OVER?
NO, I...I'LL BE OKAY. I JUST DIDN'T REALIZE I DRANK SO MUCH LAST NIGHT.
SHOULDA STAYED IN BED AN' SLEPT IT OFF.
I THOUGHT THE FRESH AIR WOULD BE GOOD FOR ME.
NOT IN MANHATTAN. ONLY FRESH AIR WE GET IN THIS TOWN IS WHEN SOMEBODY CUTS A FART.
THIS IS IT...
OKAY, JESSE: THIS GUY ISN'T TOO FOND OF ME, LIKE I TOLD YOU. YOU WALK AROUND TO THE FRONT OF THE BUILDING ON THE RIGHT, GO IN, UP THE STAIRS AND IT'S THE APARTMENT ON THE TOP FLOOR.
AN' I'M LOOKIN' FOR THE BIG MAN...
THE BIG MAN.
COMING?
uh-uh, I'LL WAIT WITH SI. I THINK I NEED TO SIT STILL FOR A WHILE.

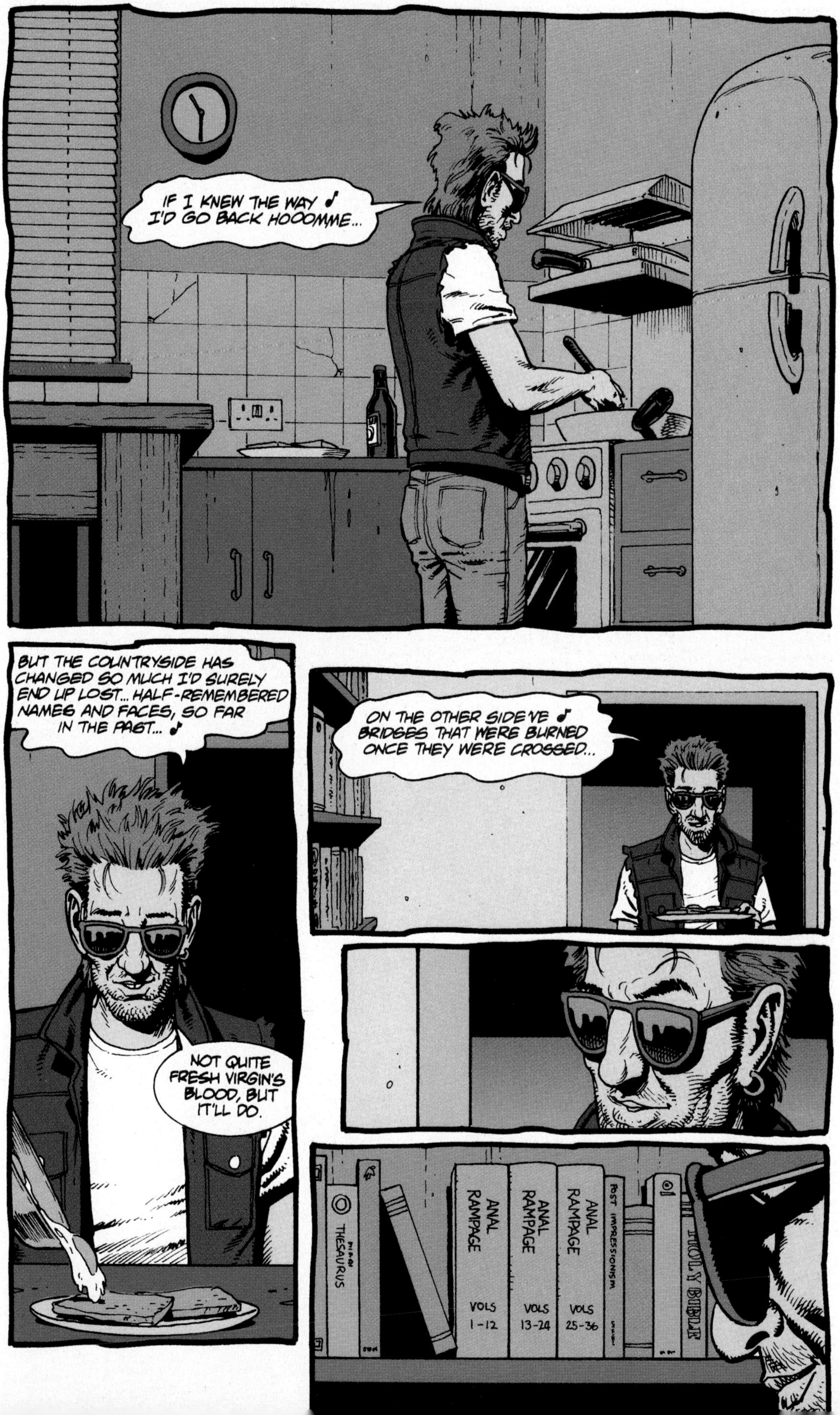
IF I KNEW THE WAY ♪ I'D GO BACK HOOOMME...
BUT THE COUNTRYSIDE HAS CHANGED SO MUCH I'D SURELY END UP LOST... HALF-REMEMBERED NAMES AND FACES, SO FAR IN THE PAST... ♪
ON THE OTHER SIDE 'VE ♪ BRIDGES THAT WERE BURNED ONCE THEY WERE CROSSED...
NOT QUITE FRESH VIRGIN'S BLOOD, BUT IT'LL DO.
THESAURUS
ANAL RAMPAGE VOLS 1-12
ANAL RAMPAGE VOLS 13-24
ANAL RAMPAGE VOLS 25-36
POST IMPRESSIONISM
HOLY BIBLE

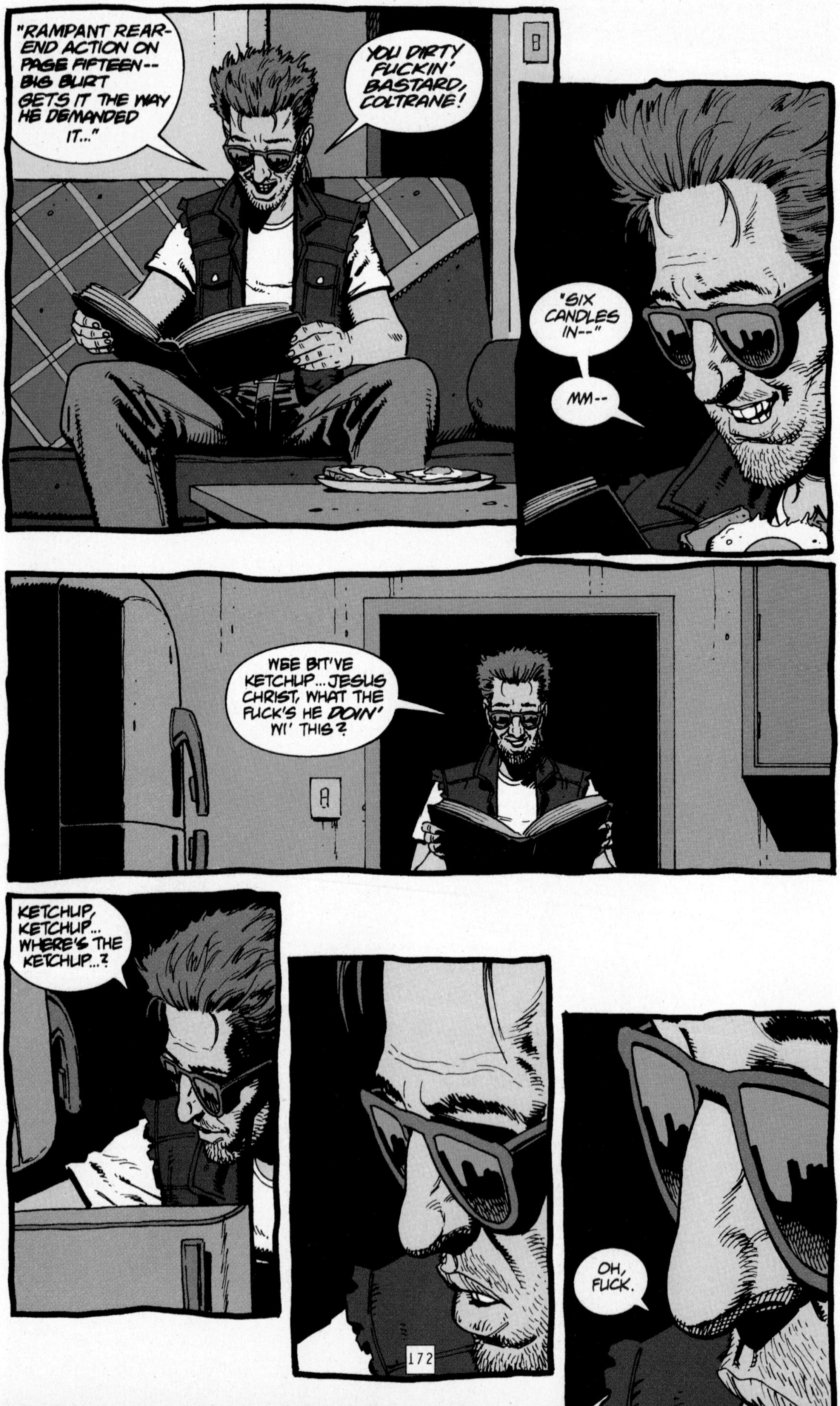
"RAMPANT REAR-END ACTION ON PAGE FIFTEEN-- BIG BURT GETS IT THE WAY HE DEMANDED IT..."
YOU DIRTY FUCKIN' BASTARD, COLTRANE!
"SIX CANDLES IN--"
MM--
WEE BIT'VE KETCHUP... JESUS CHRIST, WHAT THE FUCK'S HE DOIN' WI' THIS?
KETCHUP, KETCHUP... WHERE'S THE KETCHUP...?
OH, FUCK.

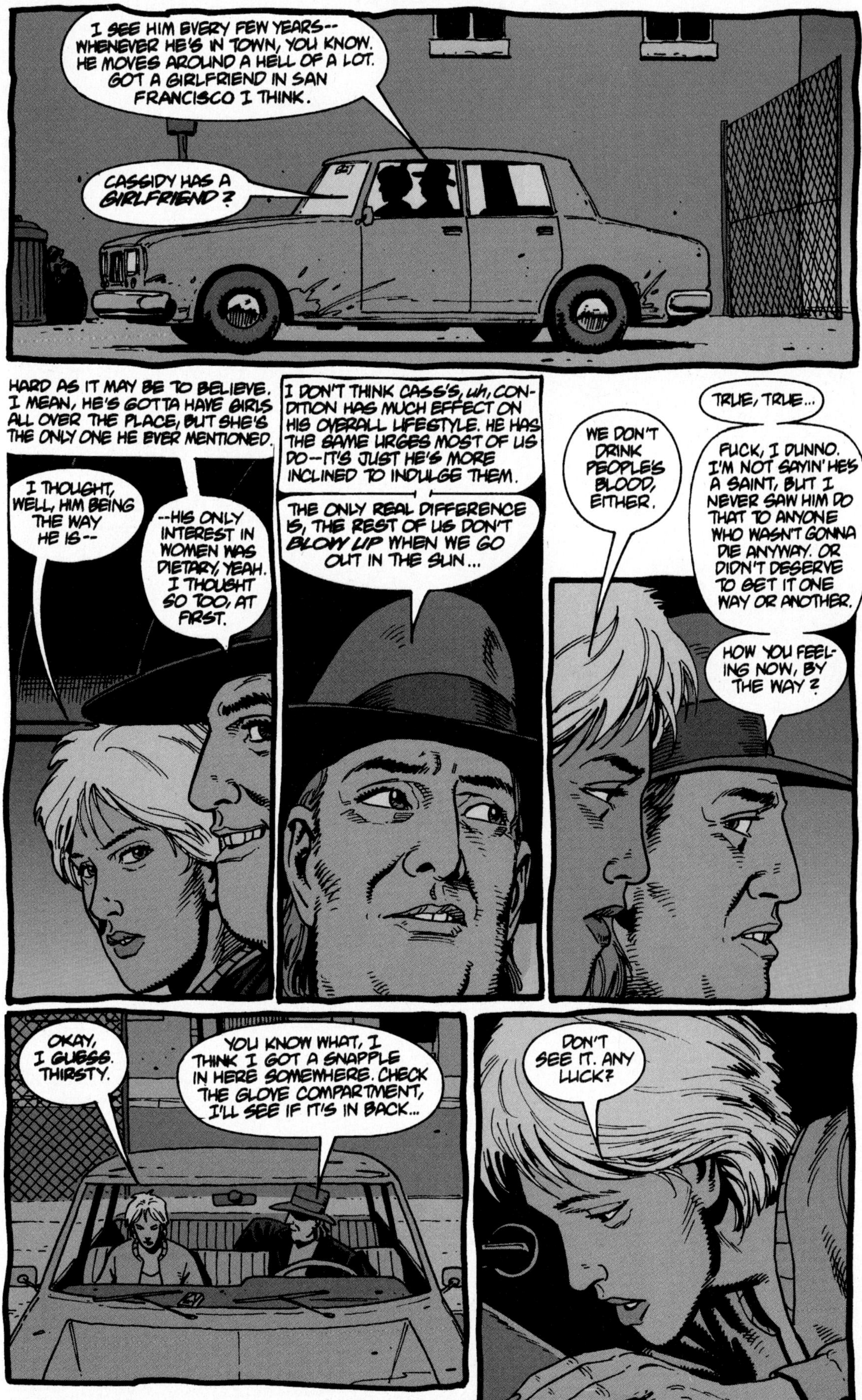
I SEE HIM EVERY FEW YEARS-- WHENEVER HE'S IN TOWN, YOU KNOW. HE MOVES AROUND A HELL OF A LOT. GOT A GIRLFRIEND IN SAN FRANCISCO I THINK.
CASSIDY HAS A GIRLFRIEND?
HARD AS IT MAY BE TO BELIEVE. I MEAN, HE'S GOTTA HAVE GIRLS ALL OVER THE PLACE, BUT SHE'S THE ONLY ONE HE EVER MENTIONED.
I THOUGHT, WELL, HIM BEING THE WAY HE IS--
--HIS ONLY INTEREST IN WOMEN WAS DIETARY, YEAH. I THOUGHT SO TOO, AT FIRST.
I DON'T THINK CASS'S, uh, CONDITION HAS MUCH EFFECT ON HIS OVERALL LIFESTYLE. HE HAS THE SAME URGES MOST OF US DO--IT'S JUST HE'S MORE INCLINED TO INDULGE THEM.
THE ONLY REAL DIFFERENCE IS, THE REST OF US DON'T BLOW UP WHEN WE GO OUT IN THE SUN...
WE DON'T DRINK PEOPLE'S BLOOD, EITHER.
TRUE, TRUE...
FUCK, I DUNNO. I'M NOT SAYIN' HE'S A SAINT, BUT I NEVER SAW HIM DO THAT TO ANYONE WHO WASN'T GONNA DIE ANYWAY. OR DIDN'T DESERVE TO GET IT ONE WAY OR ANOTHER.
HOW YOU FEELING NOW, BY THE WAY?
OKAY, I GUESS. THIRSTY.
YOU KNOW WHAT, I THINK I GOT A SNAPPLE IN HERE SOMEWHERE. CHECK THE GLOVE COMPARTMENT, I'LL SEE IF IT'S IN BACK...
DON'T SEE IT. ANY LUCK?

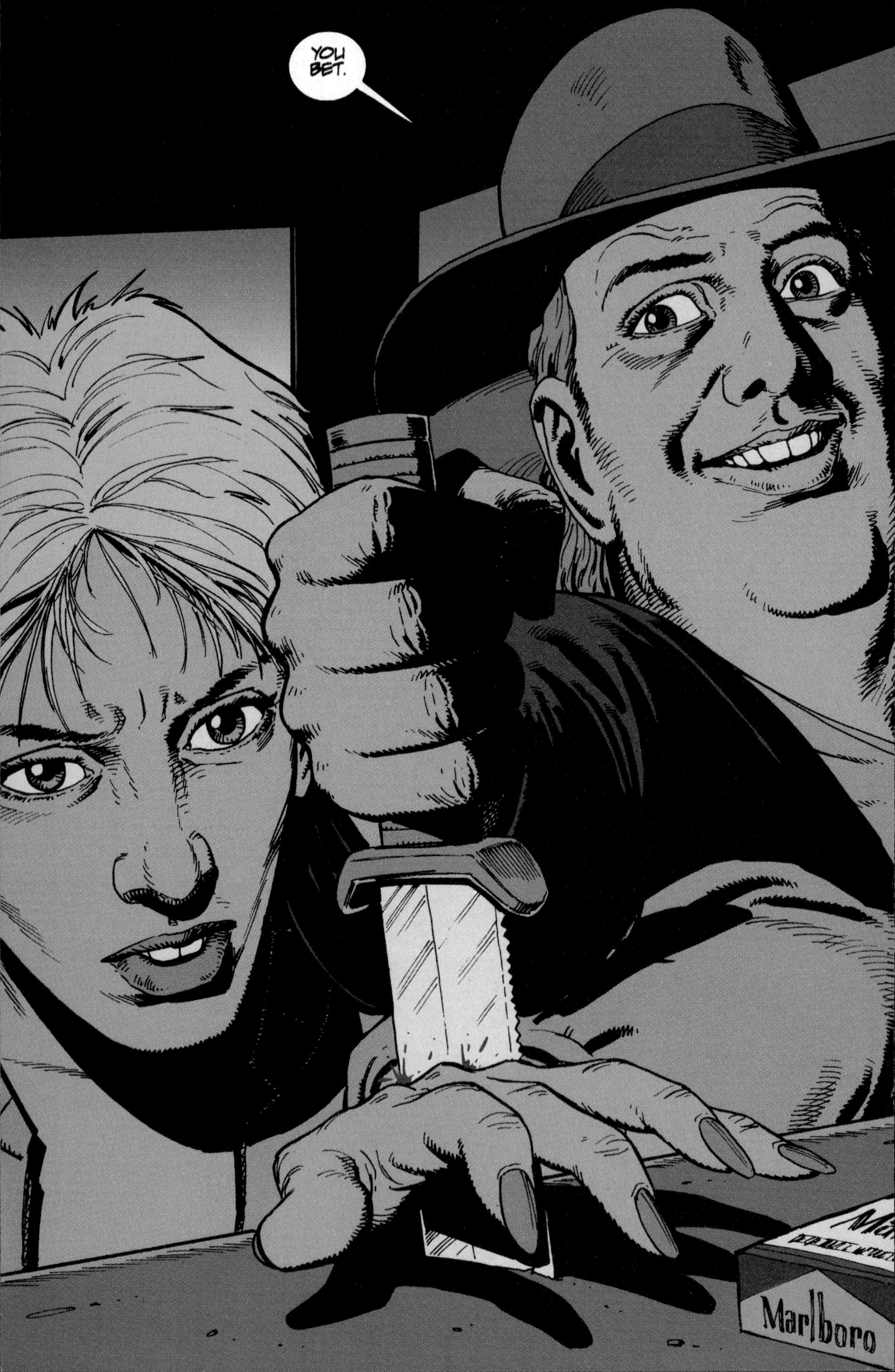
YOU BET.
Marlboro

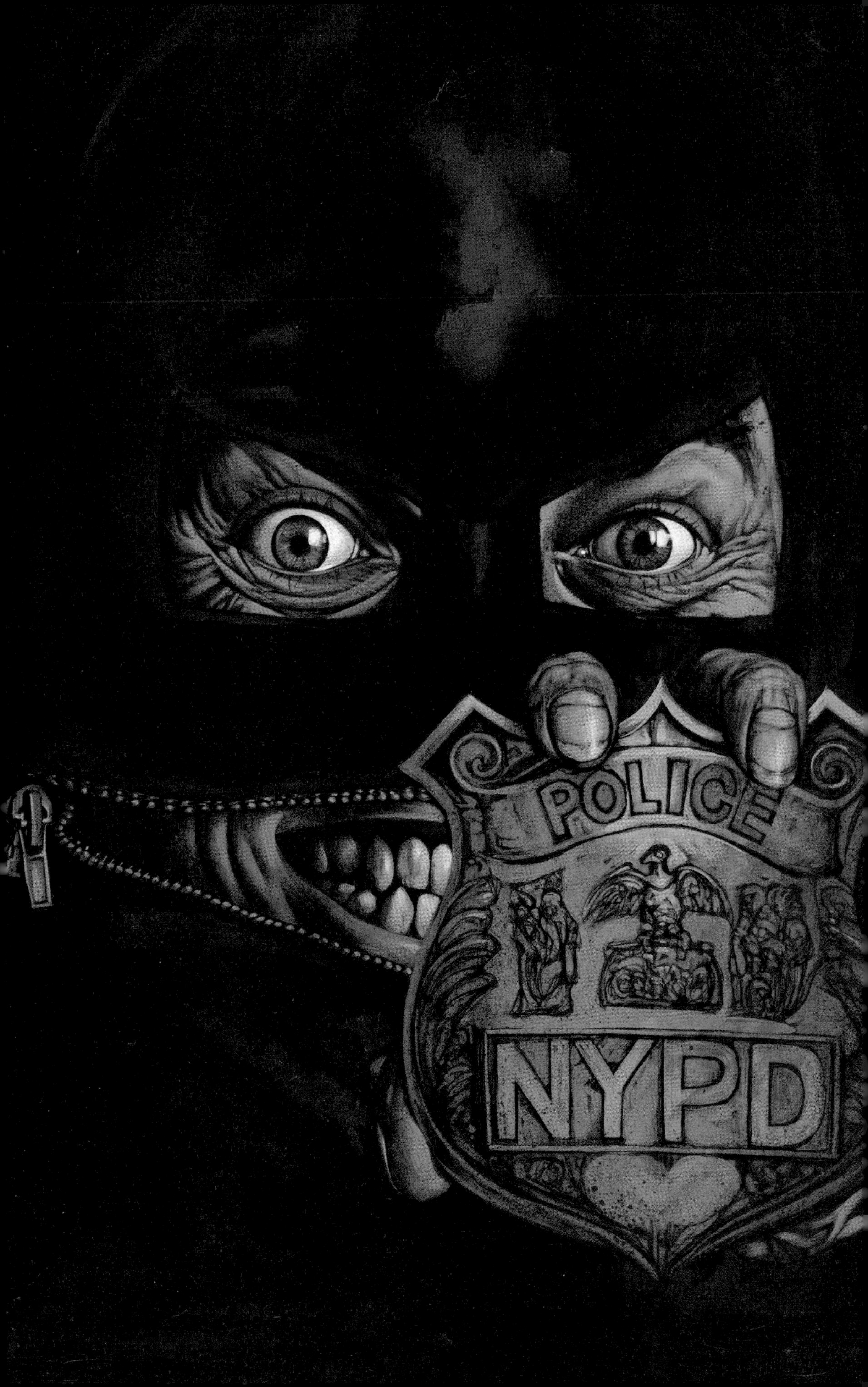
POLICE
NYPD

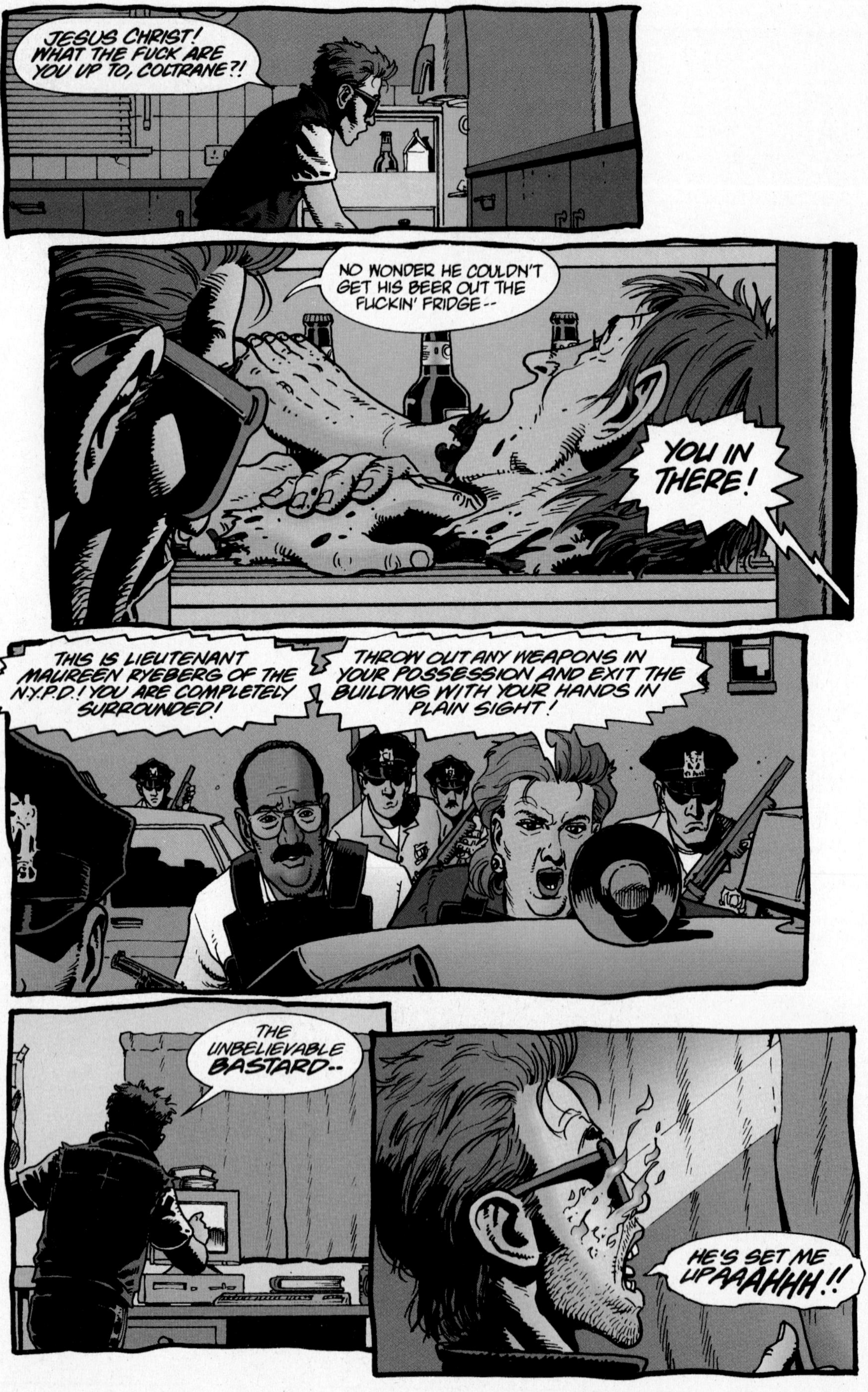
JESUS CHRIST! WHAT THE FUCK ARE YOU UP TO, COLTRANE?!
NO WONDER HE COULDN'T GET HIS BEER OUT THE FUCKIN' FRIDGE--
YOU IN THERE!
THIS IS LIEUTENANT MAUREEN RYEBERG OF THE N.Y.P.D.! YOU ARE COMPLETELY SURROUNDED!
THROW OUT ANY WEAPONS IN YOUR POSSESSION AND EXIT THE BUILDING WITH YOUR HANDS IN PLAIN SIGHT!
THE UNBELIEVABLE BASTARD--
HE'S SET ME UPAAAHHH!!

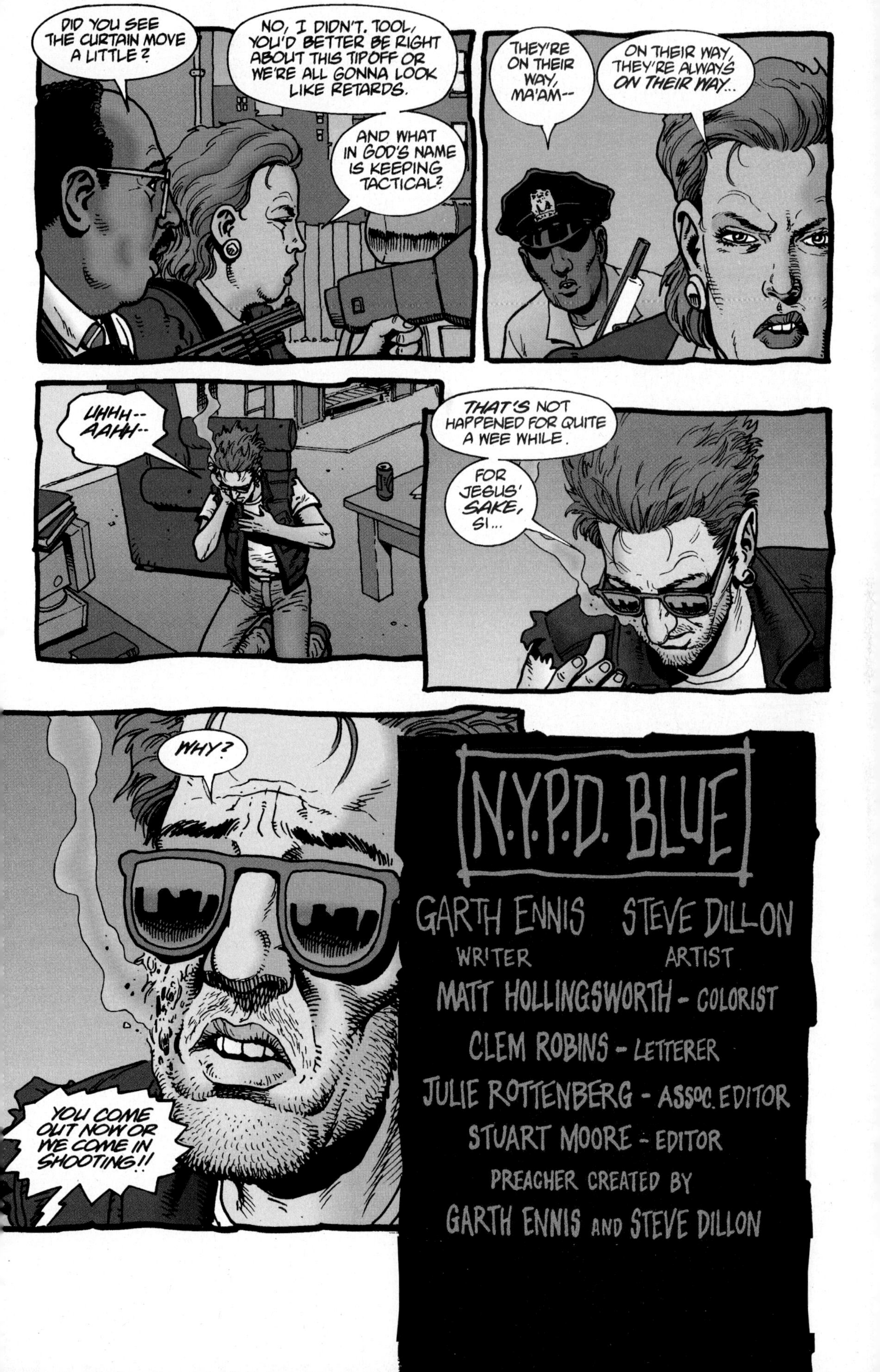

DID YOU SEE THE CURTAIN MOVE A LITTLE?
NO, I DIDN'T. TOOL, YOU'D BETTER BE RIGHT ABOUT THIS TIPOFF OR WE'RE ALL GONNA LOOK LIKE RETARDS.
AND WHAT IN GOD'S NAME IS KEEPING TACTICAL?
THEY'RE ON THEIR WAY, MA'AM--
ON THEIR WAY, THEY'RE ALWAYS ON THEIR WAY...
UHHH-- AAHH--
THAT'S NOT HAPPENED FOR QUITE A WEE WHILE.
FOR JESUS' SAKE, SI...
WHY?
YOU COME OUT NOW OR WE COME IN SHOOTING!!
N.Y.P.D. BLUE
GARTH ENNIS WRITER
STEVE DILLON ARTIST
MATT HOLLINGSWORTH - COLORIST
CLEM ROBINS - LETTERER
JULIE ROTTENBERG - ASSOC. EDITOR
STUART MOORE - EDITOR
PREACHER CREATED BY GARTH ENNIS AND STEVE DILLON

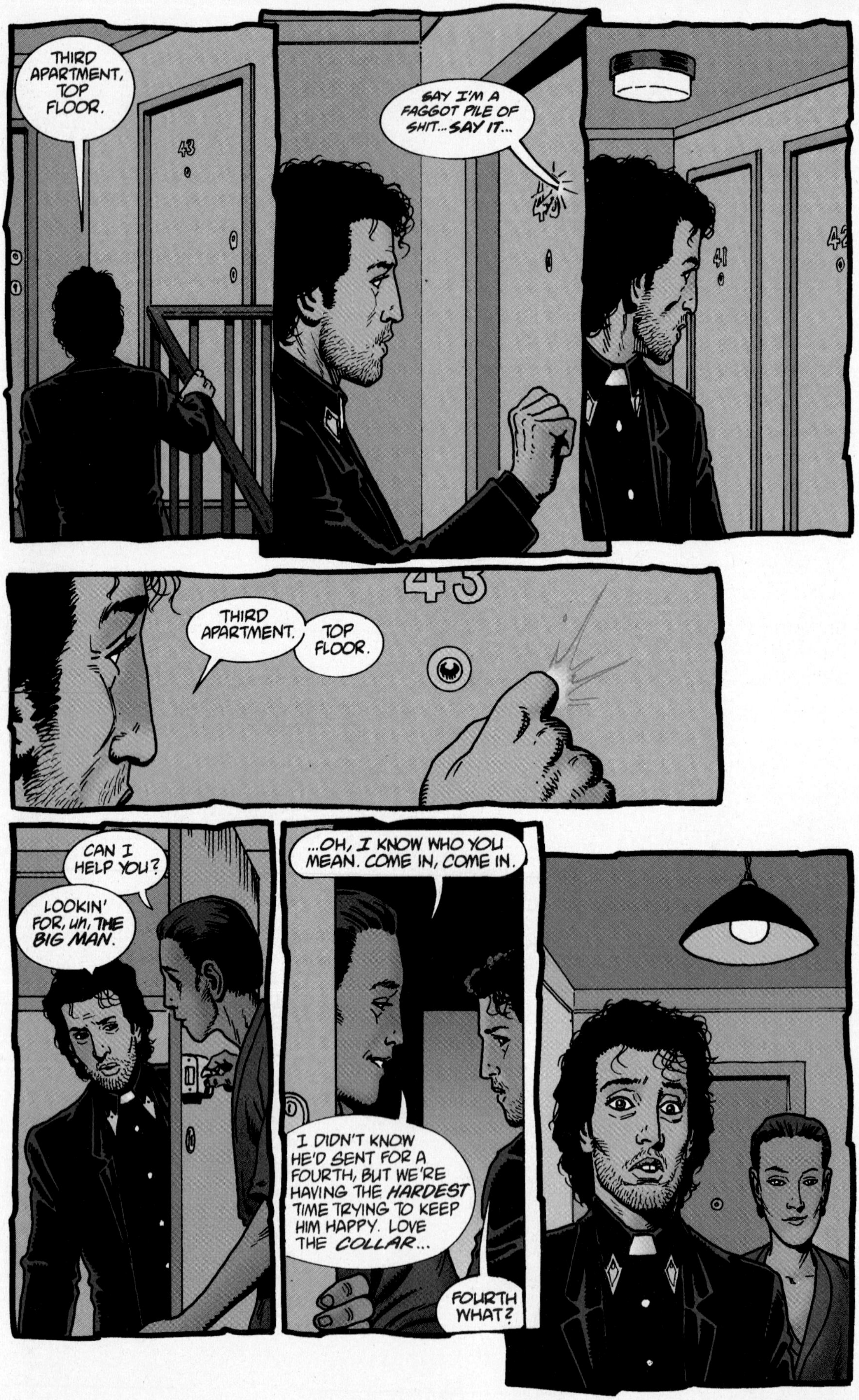
THIRD APARTMENT, TOP FLOOR.
SAY I'M A FAGGOT PILE OF SHIT... SAY IT...
43
41
42
43
THIRD APARTMENT.
TOP FLOOR.
CAN I HELP YOU?
LOOKIN' FOR, uh, THE BIG MAN.
...OH, I KNOW WHO YOU MEAN. COME IN, COME IN.
I DIDN'T KNOW HE'D SENT FOR A FOURTH, BUT WE'RE HAVING THE HARDEST TIME TRYING TO KEEP HIM HAPPY. LOVE THE COLLAR...
FOURTH WHAT?

I'M SORRY, TULIP. THIS MUST HAVE BEEN A TERRIBLE SHOCK FOR YOU.

AND THERE'S WORSE TO COME, I'M AFRAID.

YOU REMEMBER THE SERIAL KILLER STORY I'M COVERING? WELL, NOT TO PUT TOO FINE A POINT ON IT: I'M HIM.

EASIEST EXCLUSIVES I EVER GOT, BELIEVE ME.

AS WELL AS THAT, THERE IS NO "BIG MAN." THAT WAS ALL JUST BULLSHIT I MADE UP.

YOUR BOYFRIEND'S WALKING INTO THE HOME OF ONE *DETECTIVE PAULIE BRIDGES,* WHO-- YOU MIGHT REMEMBER-- IS SUPPOSED TO BE ON THE TRAIL OF THE KILLER.

WHY HAVE I DONE THIS? WELL, THE FIRST THING I FOUND WHILE HACKING THROUGH VARIOUS DATABASES--LOOKING FOR THE RELIGIOUS PHENOMENA JESSE WANTED--WAS AN *A.P.B.* LISTED IN THE F.B.I. COMPUTER...

REVEREND JESSE CUSTER, MISSING SINCE A MYSTERIOUS EXPLOSION KILLED HIS CONGREGATION IN ANNVILLE, TEXAS. *AND* SUBSEQUENT CURIOUS GOINGS-ON RESULTED IN THE DEATHS OF SEVERAL DOZEN MORE CIVILIANS AND LAW OFFICERS.

WUH-- WUH--

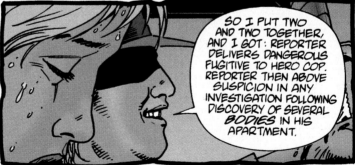

SO I PUT TWO AND TWO TOGETHER, AND I GOT: REPORTER DELIVERS DANGEROUS FUGITIVE TO HERO COP. REPORTER THEN ABOVE SUSPICION IN ANY INVESTIGATION FOLLOWING DISCOVERY OF SEVERAL *BODIES* IN HIS APARTMENT.

DANGEROUS FUGITIVE'S GIRLFRIEND TOO *DEAD* TO SAY DIFFERENT.

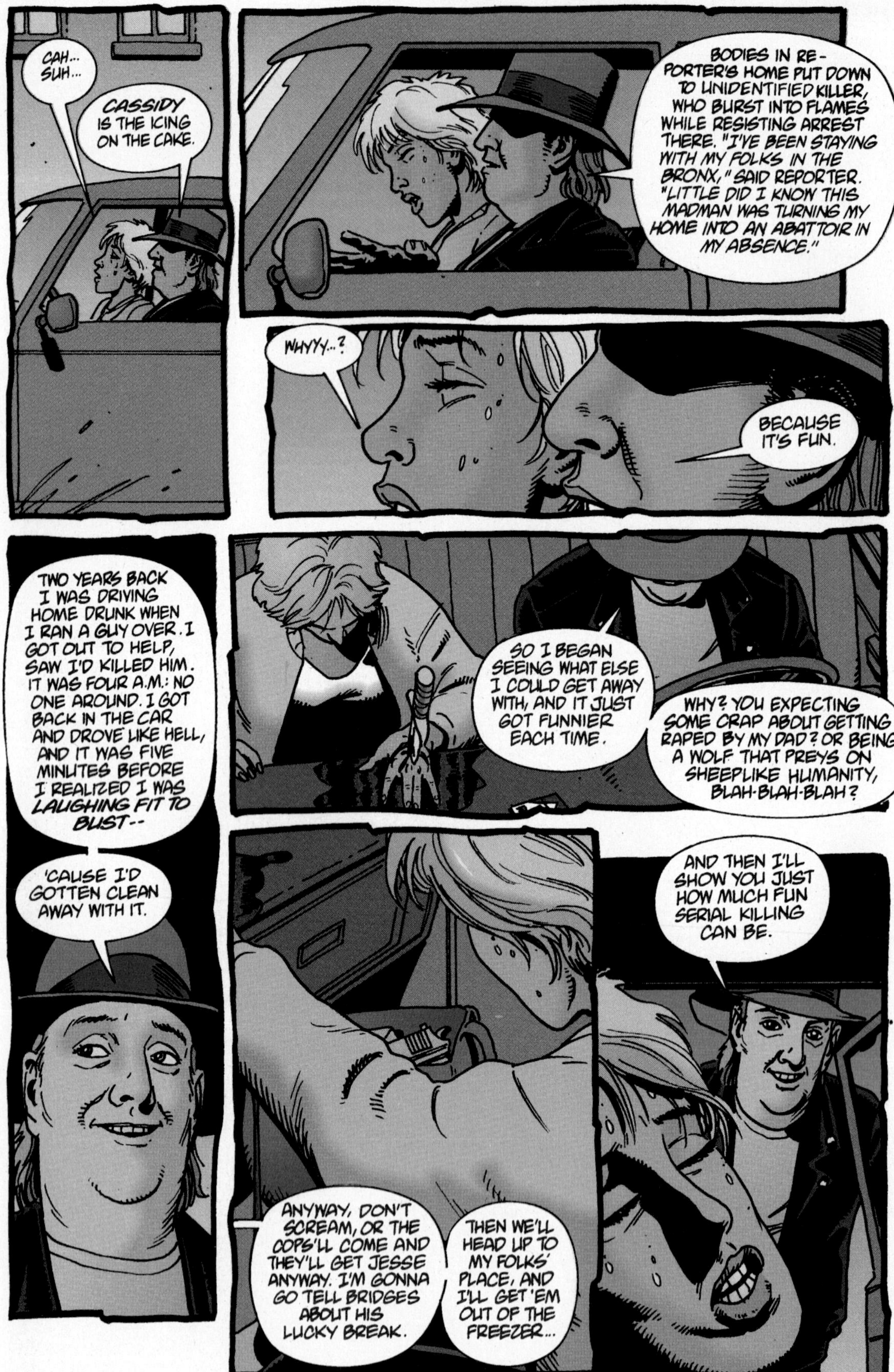
CAH... SUH...
CASSIDY IS THE ICING ON THE CAKE.
BODIES IN REPORTER'S HOME PUT DOWN TO UNIDENTIFIED KILLER, WHO BURST INTO FLAMES WHILE RESISTING ARREST THERE. "I'VE BEEN STAYING WITH MY FOLKS IN THE BRONX," SAID REPORTER. "LITTLE DID I KNOW THIS MADMAN WAS TURNING MY HOME INTO AN ABATTOIR IN MY ABSENCE."
WHYYY...?
BECAUSE IT'S FUN.
TWO YEARS BACK I WAS DRIVING HOME DRUNK WHEN I RAN A GUY OVER. I GOT OUT TO HELP, SAW I'D KILLED HIM. IT WAS FOUR A.M.: NO ONE AROUND. I GOT BACK IN THE CAR AND DROVE LIKE HELL, AND IT WAS FIVE MINUTES BEFORE I REALIZED I WAS LAUGHING FIT TO BUST--
'CAUSE I'D GOTTEN CLEAN AWAY WITH IT.
SO I BEGAN SEEING WHAT ELSE I COULD GET AWAY WITH, AND IT JUST GOT FUNNIER EACH TIME.
WHY? YOU EXPECTING SOME CRAP ABOUT GETTING RAPED BY MY DAD? OR BEING A WOLF THAT PREYS ON SHEEPLIKE HUMANITY, BLAH-BLAH-BLAH?
ANYWAY, DON'T SCREAM, OR THE COPS'LL COME AND THEY'LL GET JESSE ANYWAY. I'M GONNA GO TELL BRIDGES ABOUT HIS LUCKY BREAK.
THEN WE'LL HEAD UP TO MY FOLKS' PLACE, AND I'LL GET 'EM OUT OF THE FREEZER...
AND THEN I'LL SHOW YOU JUST HOW MUCH FUN SERIAL KILLING CAN BE.

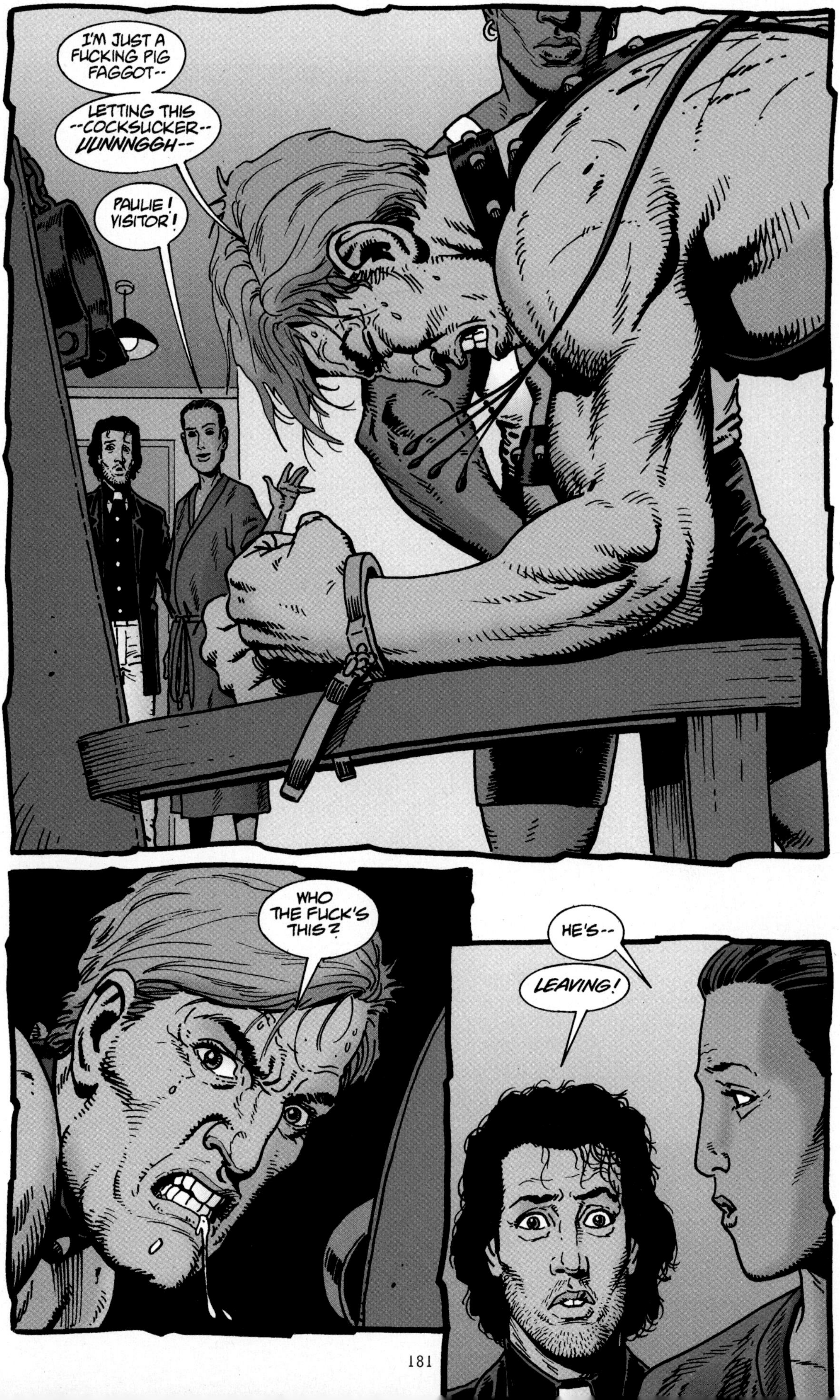
I'M JUST A FUCKING PIG FAGGOT--
LETTING THIS --COCKSUCKER-- UUNNNGGH--
PAULIE! VISITOR!
WHO THE FUCK'S THIS?
HE'S--
LEAVING!

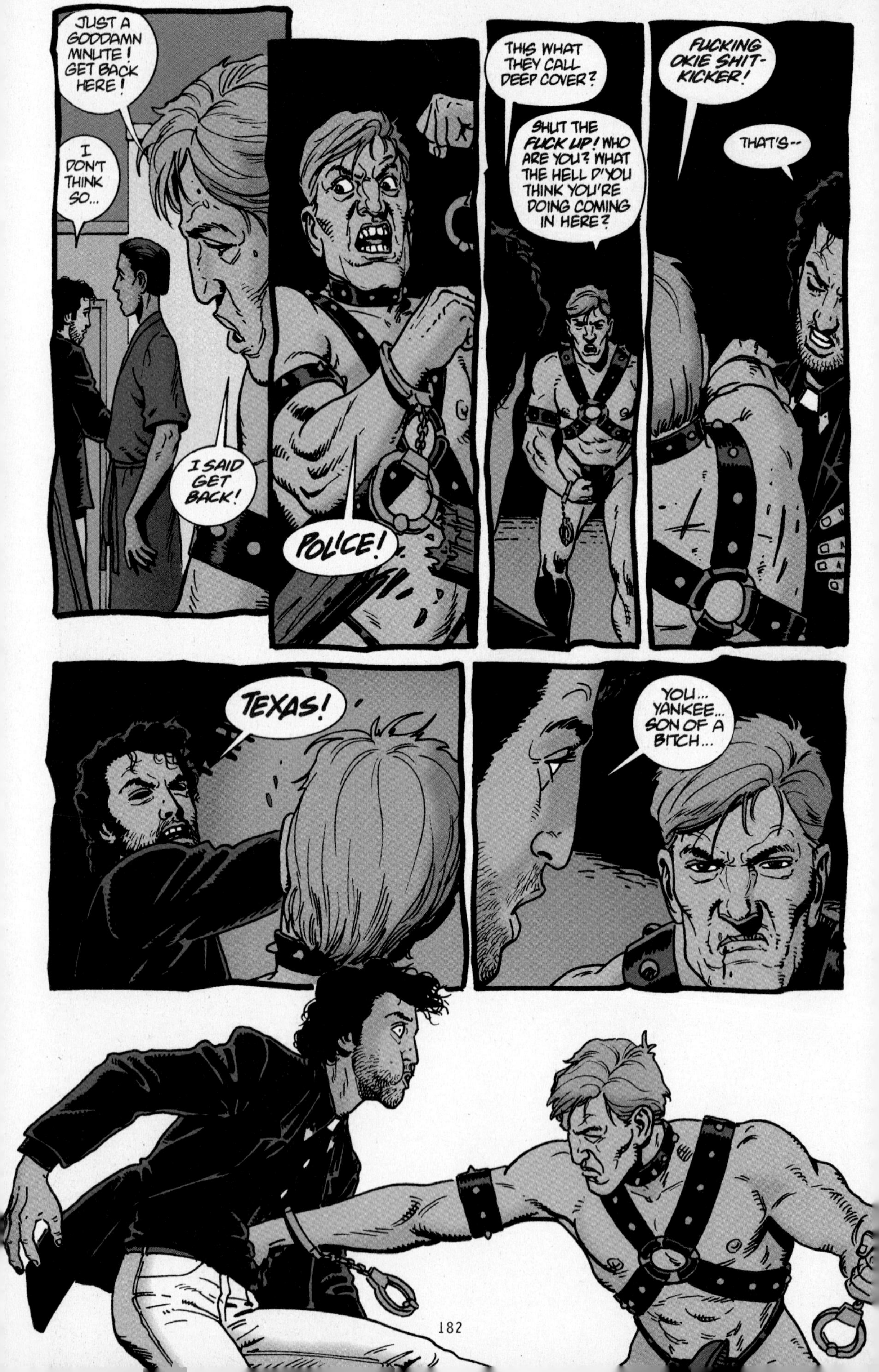
JUST A GODDAMN MINUTE! GET BACK HERE!
I DON'T THINK SO...
I SAID GET BACK!
POLICE!
THIS WHAT THEY CALL DEEP COVER?
SHUT THE FUCK UP! WHO ARE YOU? WHAT THE HELL D'YOU THINK YOU'RE DOING COMING IN HERE?
FUCKING OKIE SHIT-KICKER!
THAT'S--
TEXAS!
YOU... YANKEE... SON OF A BITCH...

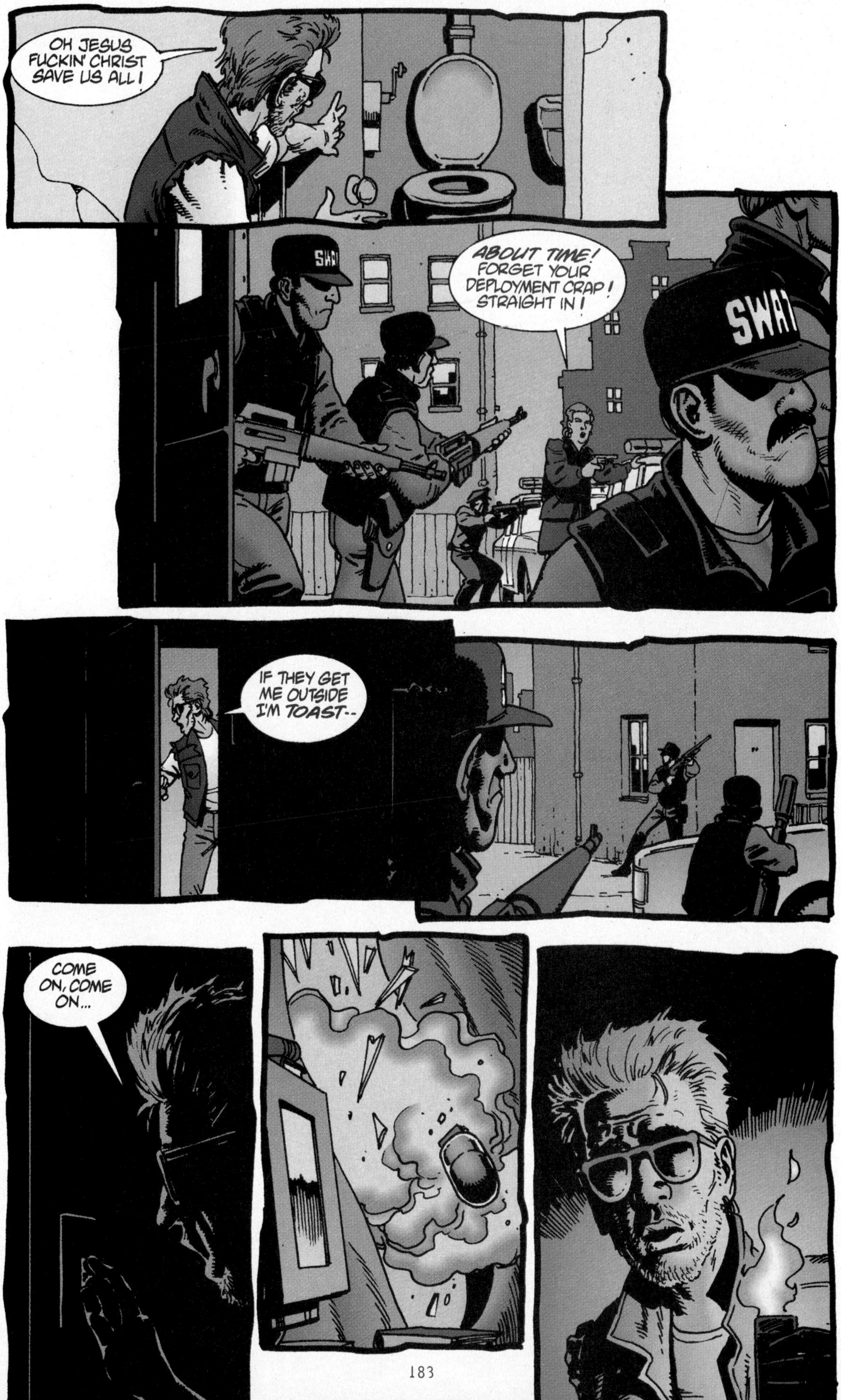
OH JESUS FUCKIN' CHRIST SAVE US ALL!
ABOUT TIME! FORGET YOUR DEPLOYMENT CRAP! STRAIGHT IN!
SWAT
IF THEY GET ME OUTSIDE I'M TOAST--
COME ON, COME ON...

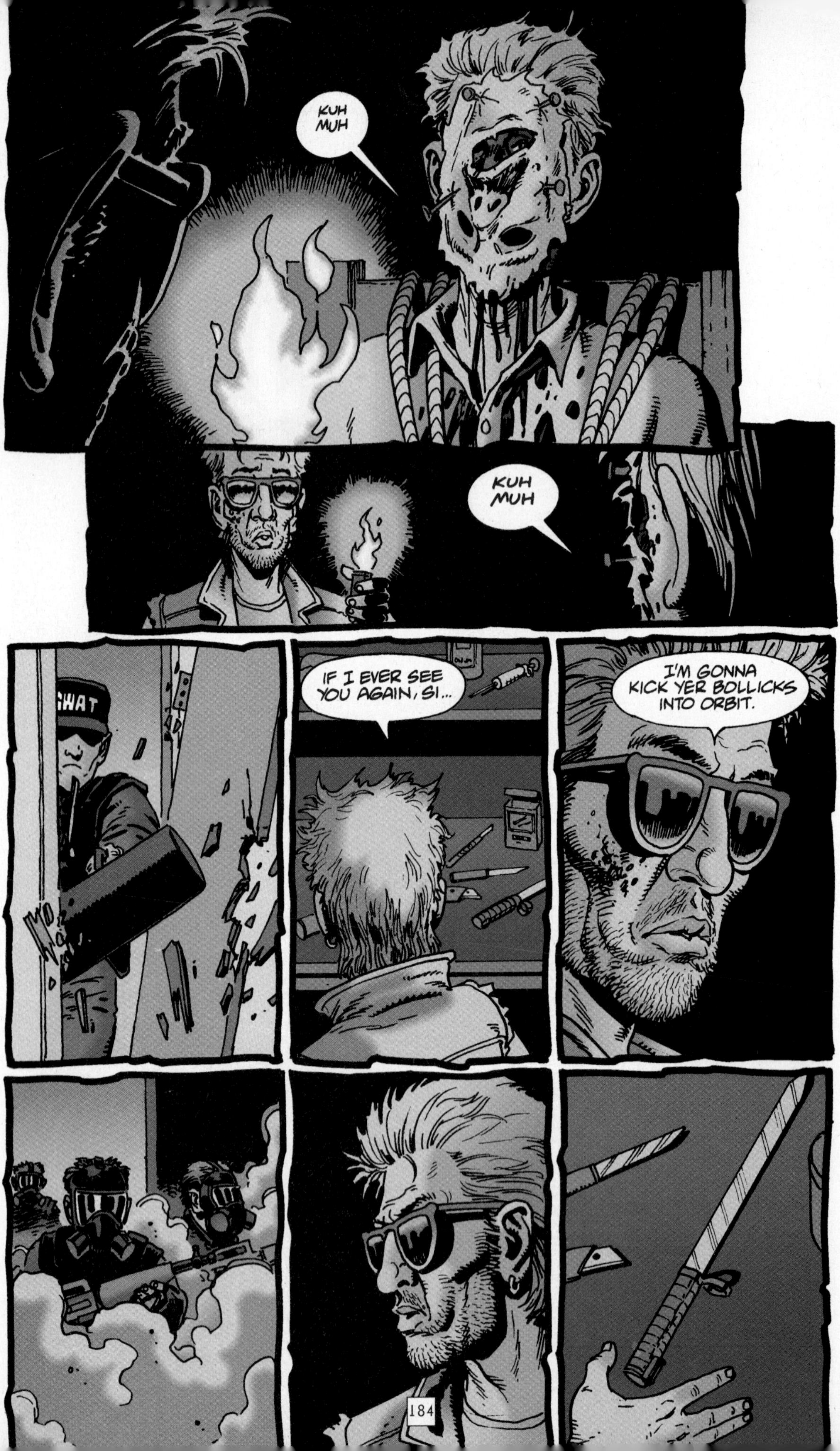
KUH MUH
KUH MUH
IF I EVER SEE YOU AGAIN, SI...
I'M GONNA KICK YER BOLLICKS INTO ORBIT.

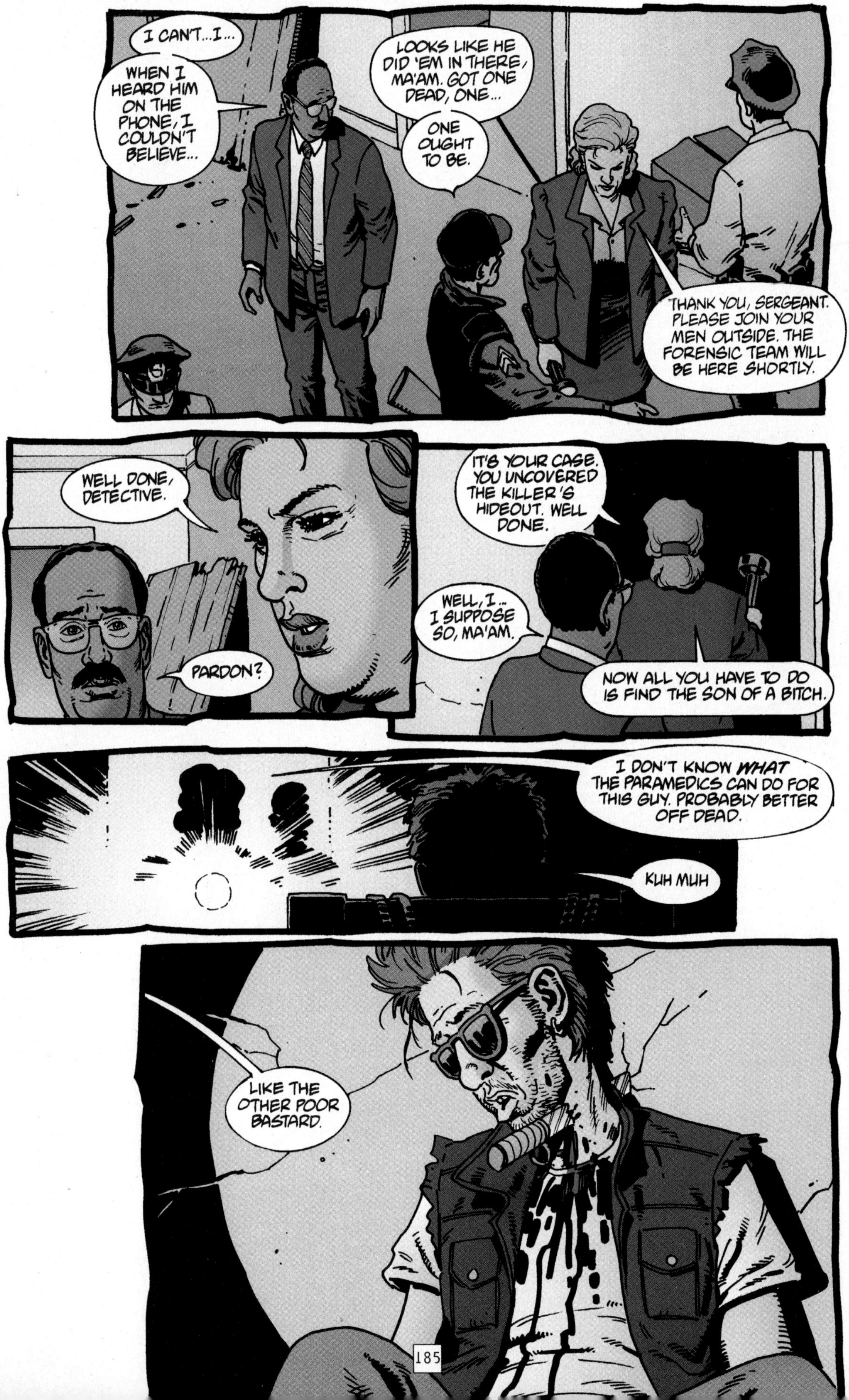
I CAN'T...I...
WHEN I HEARD HIM ON THE PHONE, I COULDN'T BELIEVE...
LOOKS LIKE HE DID 'EM IN THERE, MA'AM. GOT ONE DEAD, ONE...
ONE OUGHT TO BE.
THANK YOU, SERGEANT. PLEASE JOIN YOUR MEN OUTSIDE. THE FORENSIC TEAM WILL BE HERE SHORTLY.
WELL DONE, DETECTIVE.
PARDON?
IT'S YOUR CASE. YOU UNCOVERED THE KILLER'S HIDEOUT. WELL DONE.
WELL, I... I SUPPOSE SO, MA'AM.
NOW ALL YOU HAVE TO DO IS FIND THE SON OF A BITCH.
I DON'T KNOW *WHAT* THE PARAMEDICS CAN DO FOR THIS GUY. PROBABLY BETTER OFF DEAD.
KUH MUH
LIKE THE OTHER POOR BASTARD.

SO THEY PULLED THE BAYONET OUT OF HIS NECK AND STUFFED HIM IN A BODYBAG, AND THEN THEY STARTED TAKING BETS ON WHETHER THE OTHER GUY WOULD MAKE IT.

THE APARTMENT TURNED OUT TO BELONG TO SI COLTRANE, THE REPORTER THAT WAS TAILING US ON THE CASE--SO I FIGURED PAULIE'D FIND IT PRETTY FUNNY THAT THE CREEP *WAS* THE CASE --

NO ANSWER FROM DETECTIVE BRIDGES.

NO ANSWER?

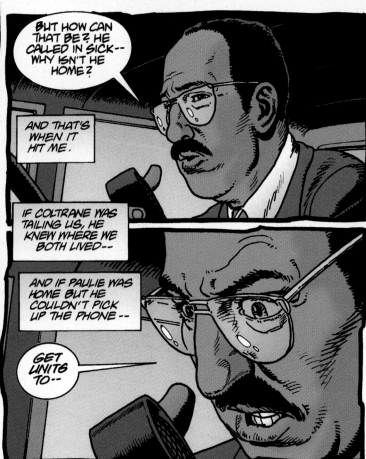

BUT HOW CAN THAT BE? HE CALLED IN SICK-- WHY ISN'T HE HOME?

AND THAT'S WHEN IT HIT ME.

IF COLTRANE WAS TAILING US, HE KNEW WHERE WE BOTH LIVED--

AND IF PAULIE WAS HOME BUT HE COULDN'T PICK UP THE PHONE--

GET UNITS TO--

AND THAT'S HOW I RAN THE INTERSECTION--

AND THAT'S WHY THE UNLUCKIEST COP IN THE WORLD HAD TO HANDLE THIS ONE BY HIMSELF.

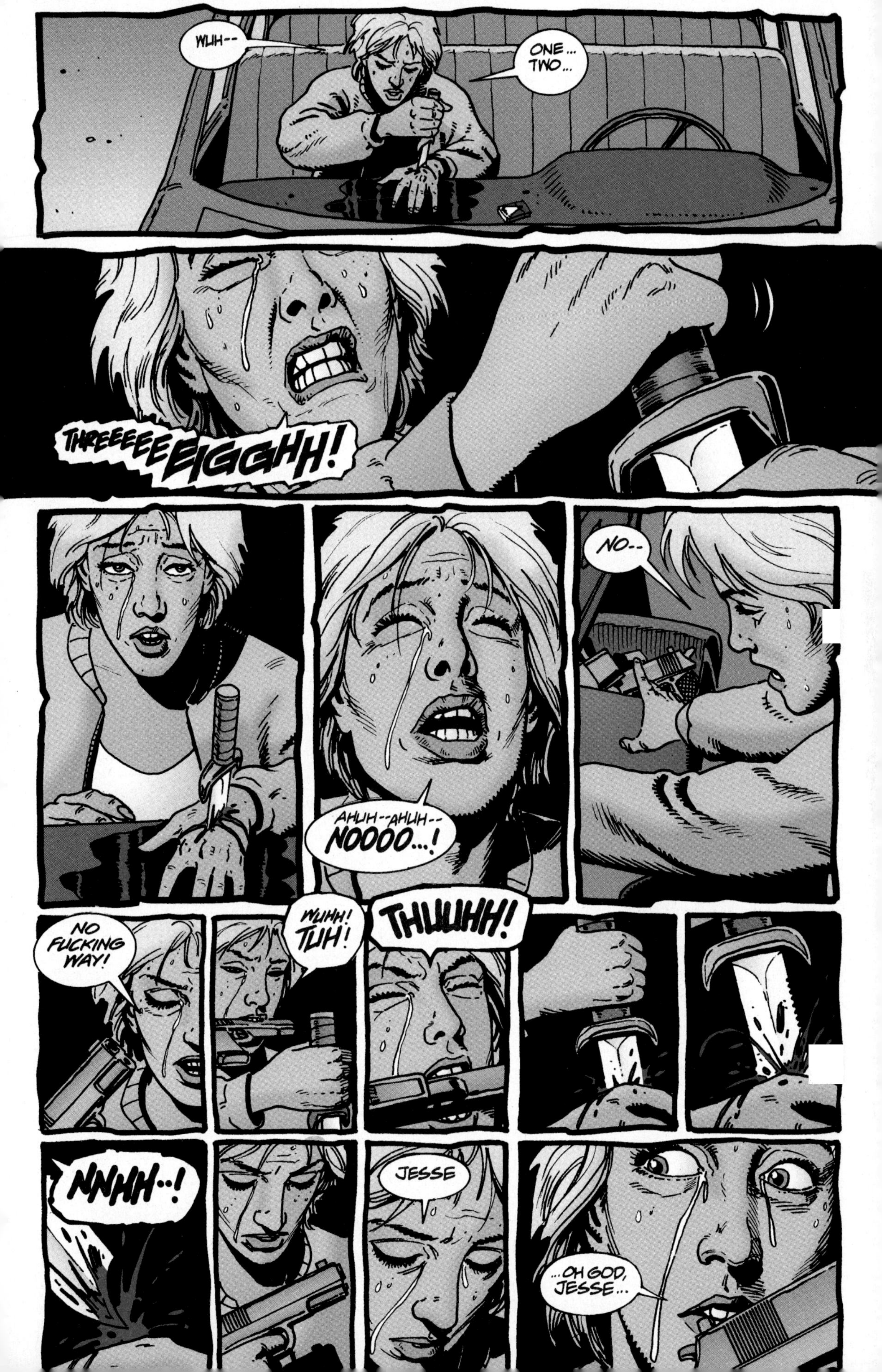
WUH--
ONE... TWO...
THREEEEEEEIGGHH!
AHUH--AHUH-- NOOOO...!
NO--
NO FUCKING WAY!
WUHH! TUH!
THUUHH!
NNHH--!
JESSE
...OH GOD, JESSE...

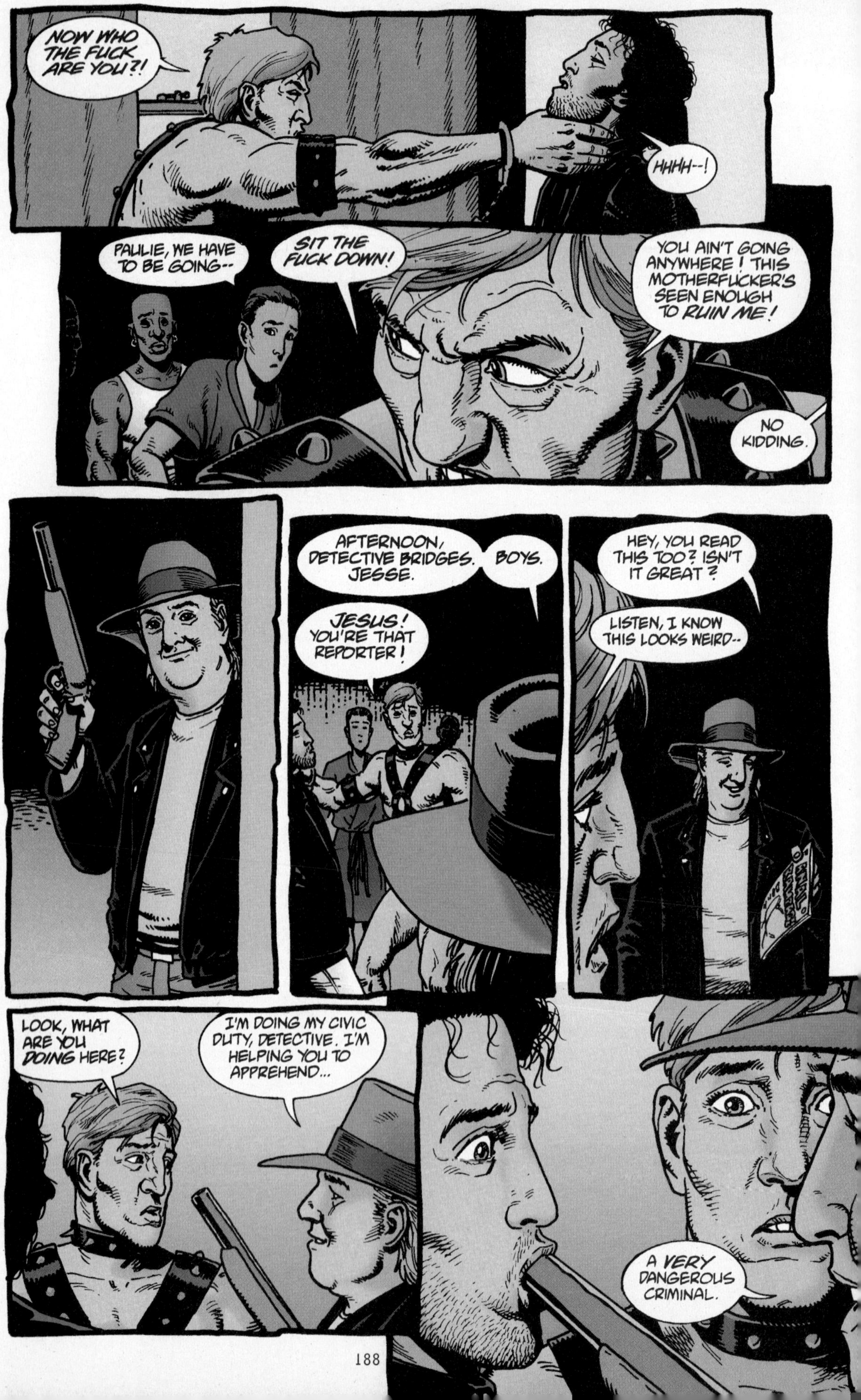
NOW WHO THE FUCK ARE YOU?!
HHHH--!
PAULIE, WE HAVE TO BE GOING--
SIT THE FUCK DOWN!
YOU AIN'T GOING ANYWHERE! THIS MOTHERFUCKER'S SEEN ENOUGH TO RUIN ME!
NO KIDDING.
AFTERNOON, DETECTIVE BRIDGES. JESSE.
BOYS.
JESUS! YOU'RE THAT REPORTER!
HEY, YOU READ THIS TOO? ISN'T IT GREAT?
LISTEN, I KNOW THIS LOOKS WEIRD--
LOOK, WHAT ARE YOU DOING HERE?
I'M DOING MY CIVIC DUTY, DETECTIVE. I'M HELPING YOU TO APPREHEND...
A VERY DANGEROUS CRIMINAL.

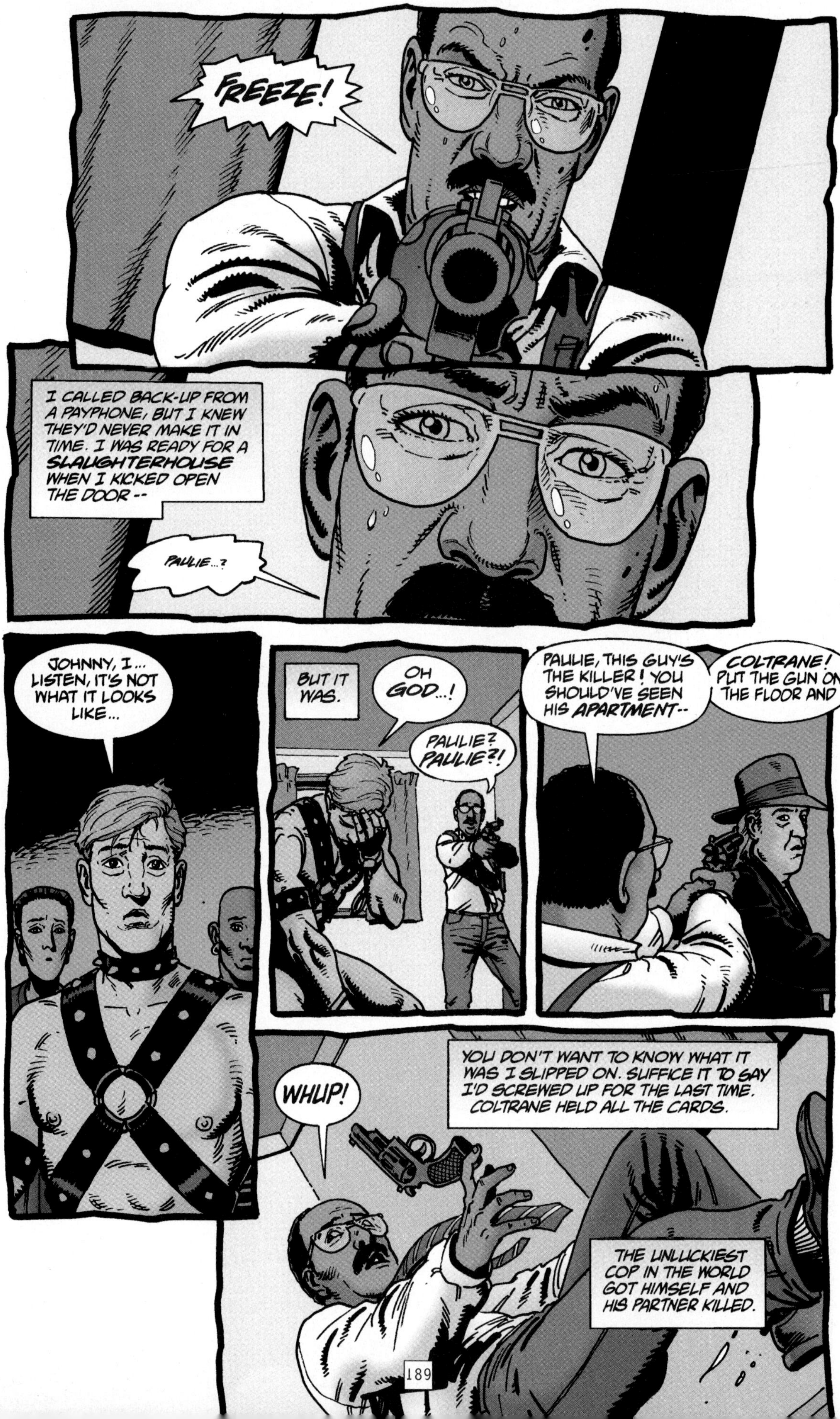
FREEZE!
I CALLED BACK-UP FROM A PAYPHONE, BUT I KNEW THEY'D NEVER MAKE IT IN TIME. I WAS READY FOR A SLAUGHTERHOUSE WHEN I KICKED OPEN THE DOOR --
PAULIE...?
JOHNNY, I... LISTEN, IT'S NOT WHAT IT LOOKS LIKE...
BUT IT WAS.
OH GOD...!
PAULIE? PAULIE?!
PAULIE, THIS GUY'S THE KILLER! YOU SHOULD'VE SEEN HIS APARTMENT--
COLTRANE! PUT THE GUN ON THE FLOOR AND
WHUP!
YOU DON'T WANT TO KNOW WHAT IT WAS I SLIPPED ON. SUFFICE IT TO SAY I'D SCREWED UP FOR THE LAST TIME. COLTRANE HELD ALL THE CARDS.
THE UNLUCKIEST COP IN THE WORLD GOT HIMSELF AND HIS PARTNER KILLED.

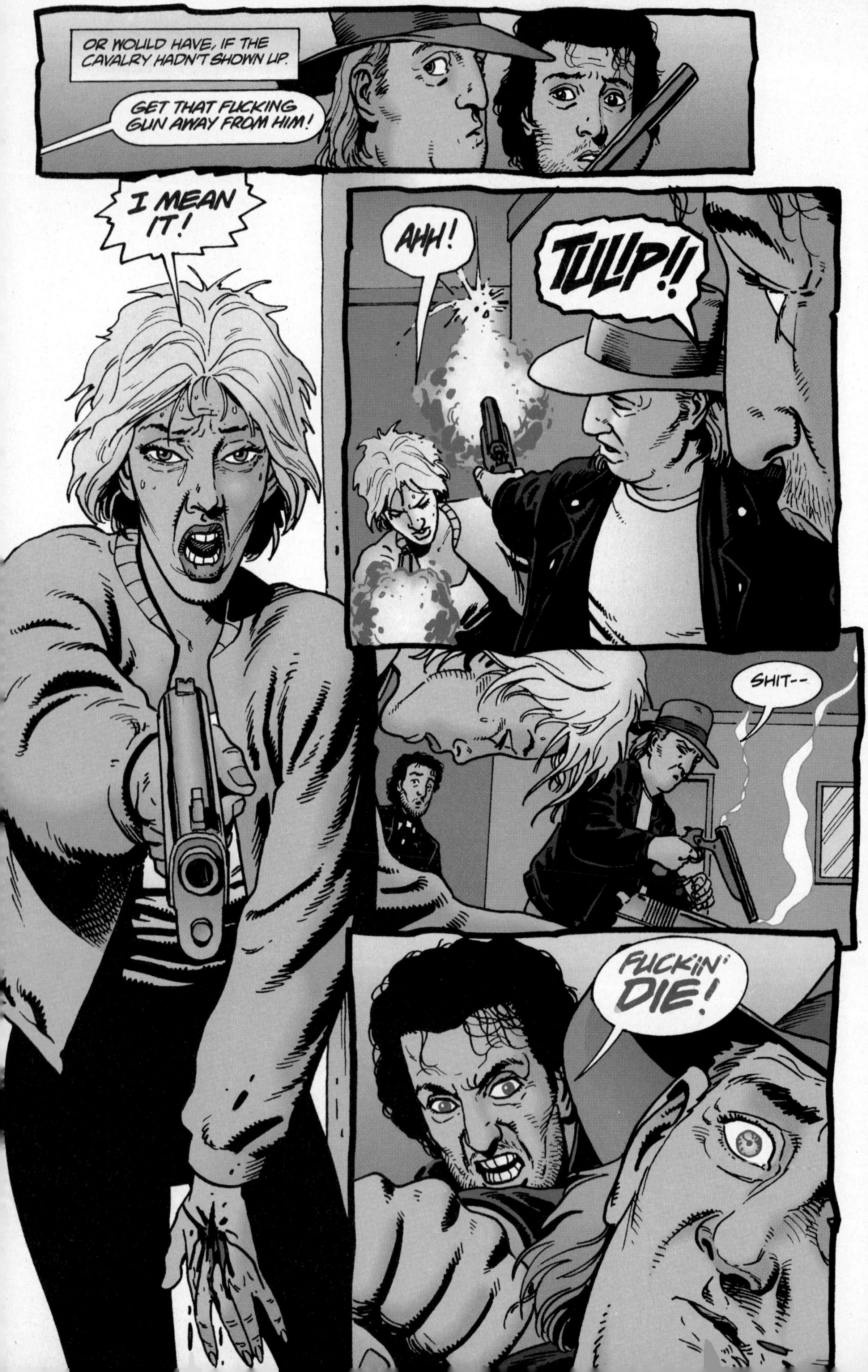
OR WOULD HAVE, IF THE CAVALRY HADN'T SHOWN UP.
GET THAT FUCKING GUN AWAY FROM HIM!
I MEAN IT!
AHH!
TULIP!!
SHIT--
FUCKIN' DIE!

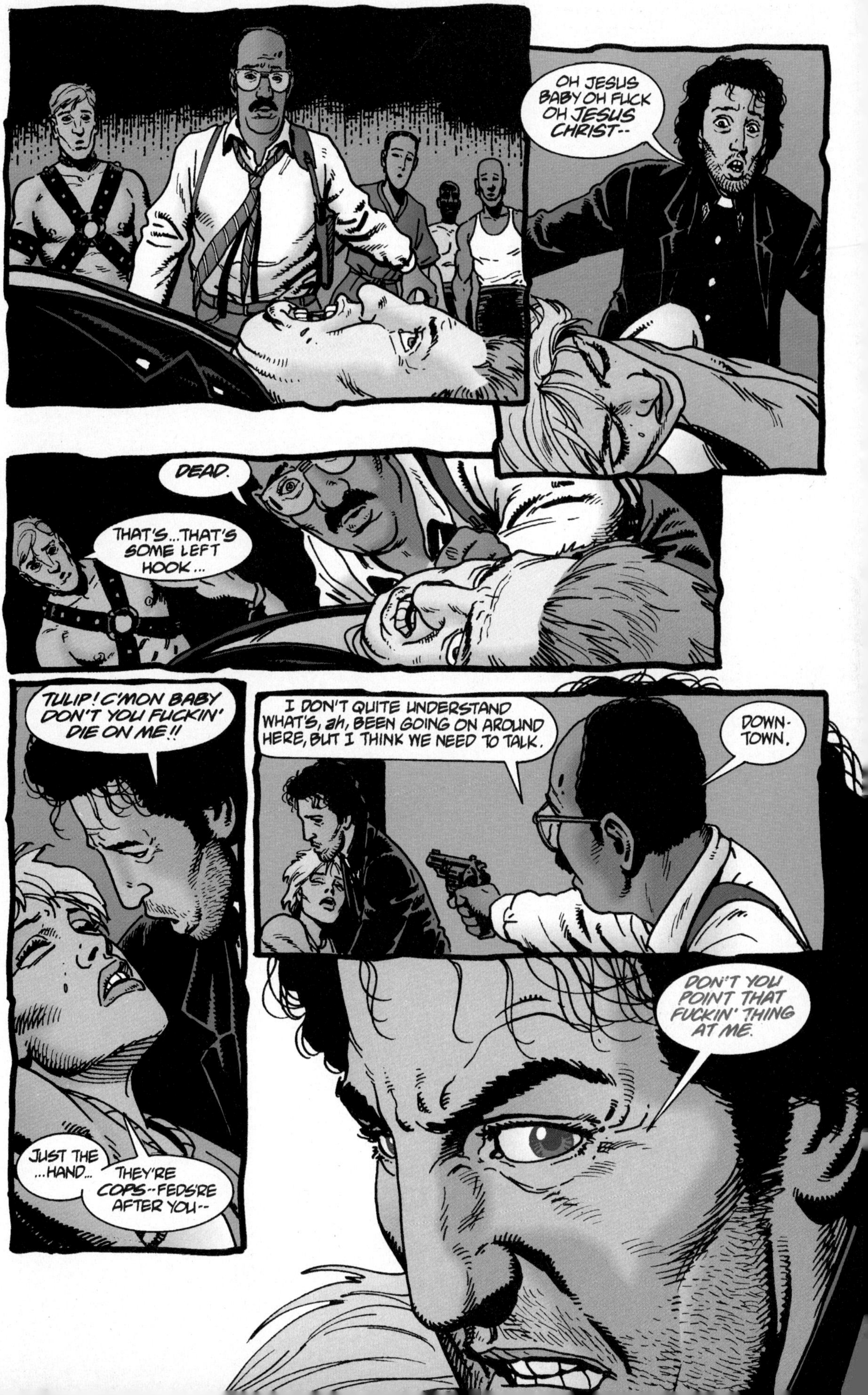
OH JESUS BABY OH FUCK OH JESUS CHRIST--
DEAD.
THAT'S...THAT'S SOME LEFT HOOK...
TULIP! C'MON BABY DON'T YOU FUCKIN' DIE ON ME!!
I DON'T QUITE UNDERSTAND WHAT'S, ah, BEEN GOING ON AROUND HERE, BUT I THINK WE NEED TO TALK.
DOWN-TOWN.
JUST THE ...HAND...
THEY'RE COPS--FEDS'RE AFTER YOU--
DON'T YOU POINT THAT FUCKIN' THING AT ME.

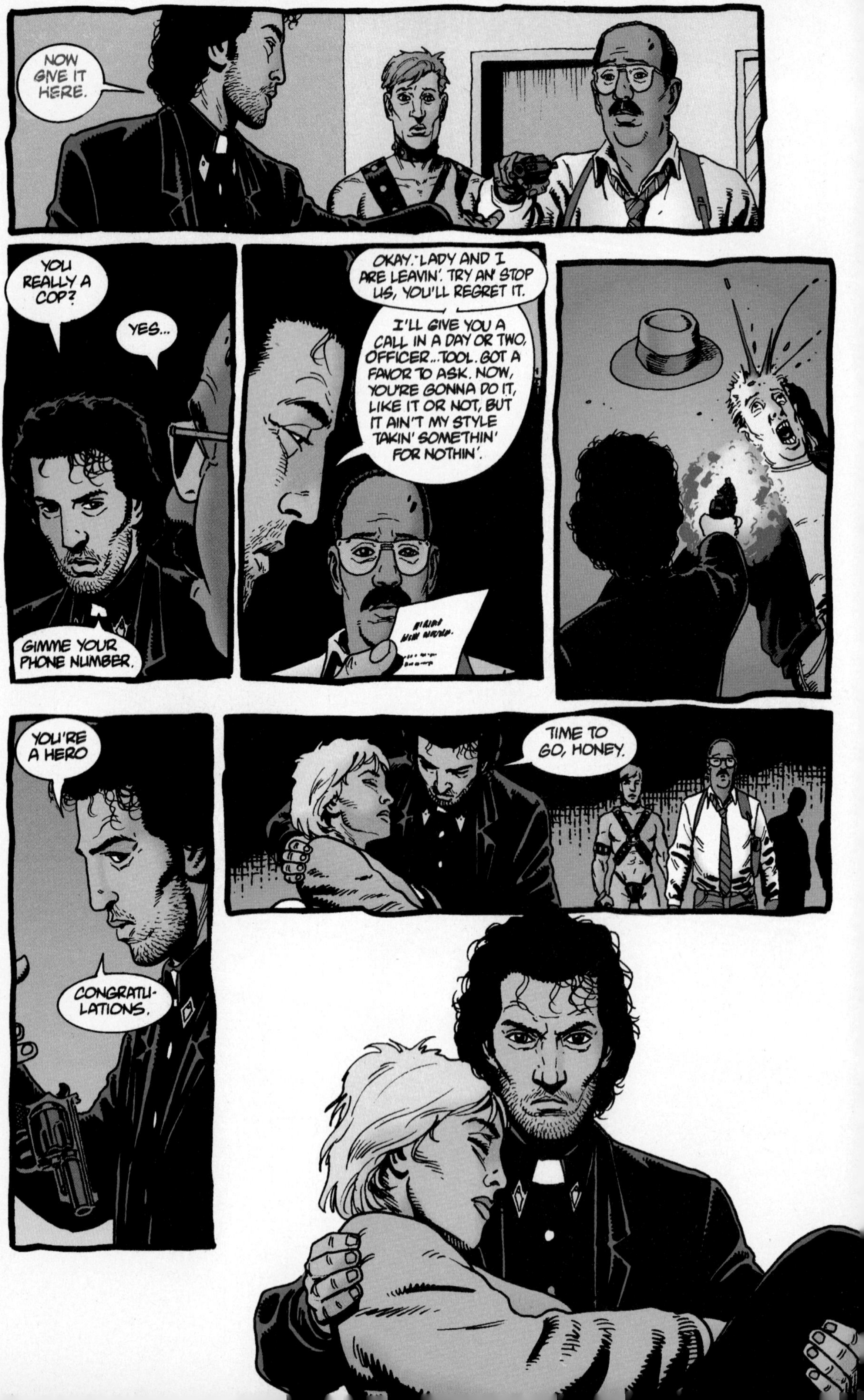
NOW GIVE IT HERE.
YOU REALLY A COP?
YES...
GIMME YOUR PHONE NUMBER.
OKAY. LADY AND I ARE LEAVIN'. TRY AN' STOP US, YOU'LL REGRET IT.
I'LL GIVE YOU A CALL IN A DAY OR TWO, OFFICER...TOOL. GOT A FAVOR TO ASK. NOW, YOU'RE GONNA DO IT, LIKE IT OR NOT, BUT IT AIN'T MY STYLE TAKIN' SOMETHIN' FOR NOTHIN'.
YOU'RE A HERO
CONGRATULATIONS.
TIME TO GO, HONEY.

WE REALLY *DO* HAVE TO GO NOW, PAULIE...

AND, *uh*, IF YOU'RE THROWING ANOTHER OF THESE LITTLE PARTIES--DON'T CALL US, OKAY?

PAULIE, *uh*... CORRECT ME IF I'M WRONG, BUT ...DON'T YOU HATE GAY PEOPLE?

I DO, JOHNNY, I DO, I DO!

BUT FUCK, I WAS JUST--I MEAN, WE'RE OUT THERE ON THE STREETS TAKING DOWN ALL THE FUCKOS AND SCUM-BAGS *AND I HATE THEM SO MUCH*, AND SUDDENLY IT WASN'T ENOUGH TO BE *TOUGH*, OR *MACHO*--I WANTED TO BE EVEN MORE--

SO I TRIED TO TAKE IT OUT ON THE *SCUM* BUT I REALIZED WHAT I WANTED WAS TO *TAKE* PAIN, NOT JUST HAND IT OUT...AND... ONE NIGHT, I SAW THOSE THREE GUYS AND I WANTED--

OH JESUS, JOHNNY!

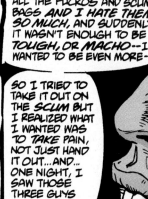

I THINK I'M GAY!

ARE YOU SURE YOU'RE NOT JUST FUCKED IN THE HEAD?

THAT WAS THE FIRST TIME IN MY LIFE I USED PROFANITY.

BUT IT'S NOT EASY, BEING A COP.

DOC BENDER'S ON HER WAY DOWN, LIEUTENANT.

I CAN'T STAY. LOOK, THE CLOTHES ARE EVIDENCE, OKAY? BE SURE TO BAG 'EM.

YOU GOT IT.

OKAY, EVERY-ONE. SAY HI TO THE NEW GUY.

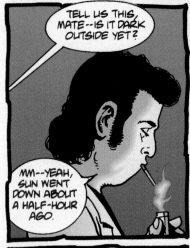

TELL US THIS, MATE--IS IT DARK OUTSIDE YET?

MM--YEAH, SUN WENT DOWN ABOUT A HALF-HOUR AGO.

AW LISTEN, I'VE GOTTA GO NOW BUT I'M DYIN' FOR A CIGARETTE. YOU COULDN'T, uh...

NICE ONE, MATE.

CHEERS.

SEE YA.

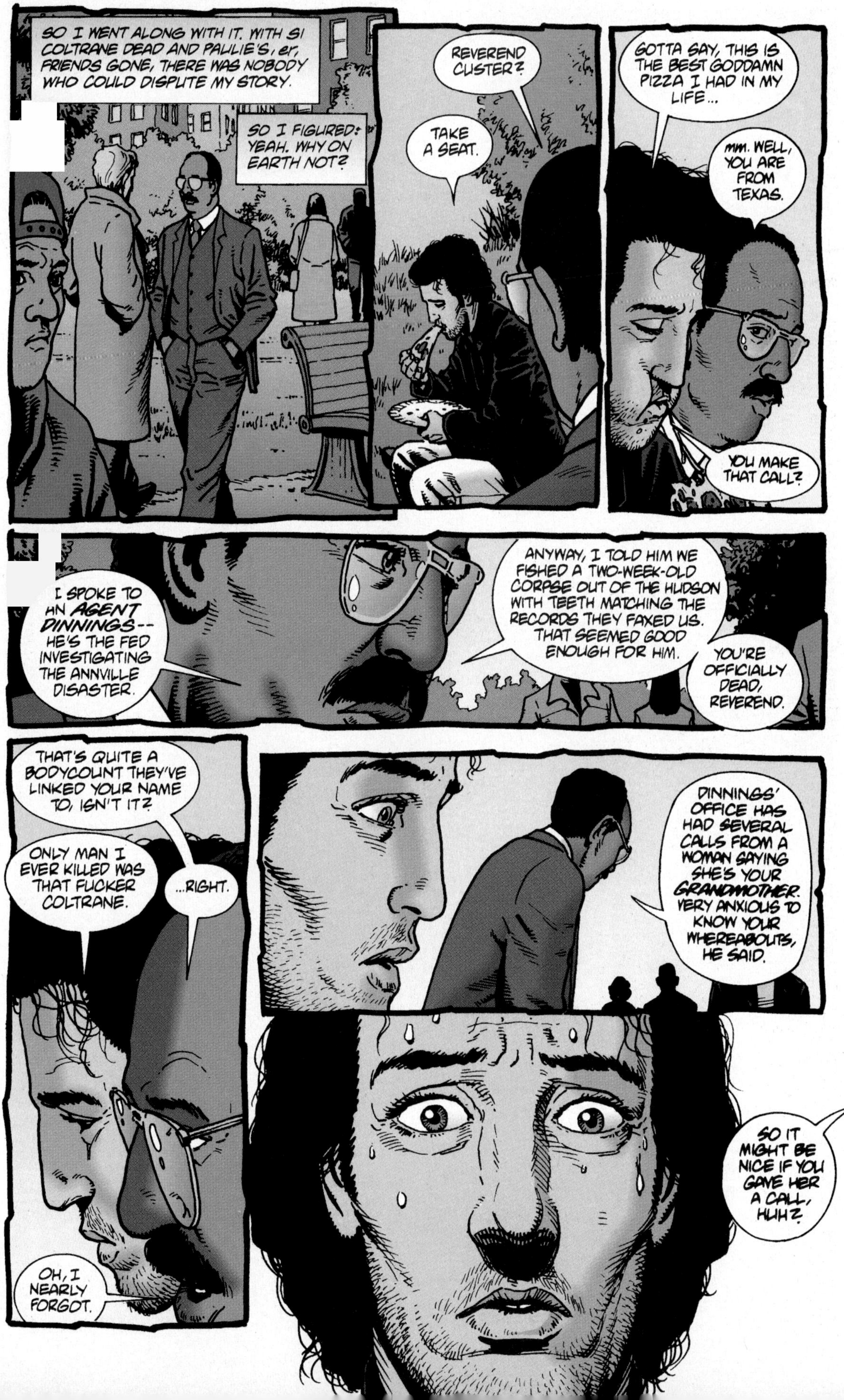
SO I WENT ALONG WITH IT. WITH SI COLTRANE DEAD AND PAULIE'S, er, FRIENDS GONE, THERE WAS NOBODY WHO COULD DISPUTE MY STORY.
SO I FIGURED: YEAH. WHY ON EARTH NOT?
REVEREND CUSTER?
TAKE A SEAT.
GOTTA SAY, THIS IS THE BEST GODDAMN PIZZA I HAD IN MY LIFE...
MM. WELL, YOU ARE FROM TEXAS.
YOU MAKE THAT CALL?
I SPOKE TO AN AGENT DINNINGS-- HE'S THE FED INVESTIGATING THE ANNVILLE DISASTER.
ANYWAY, I TOLD HIM WE FISHED A TWO-WEEK-OLD CORPSE OUT OF THE HUDSON WITH TEETH MATCHING THE RECORDS THEY FAXED US. THAT SEEMED GOOD ENOUGH FOR HIM.
YOU'RE OFFICIALLY DEAD, REVEREND.
THAT'S QUITE A BODYCOUNT THEY'VE LINKED YOUR NAME TO, ISN'T IT?
ONLY MAN I EVER KILLED WAS THAT FUCKER COLTRANE.
...RIGHT.
OH, I NEARLY FORGOT.
DINNINGS' OFFICE HAS HAD SEVERAL CALLS FROM A WOMAN SAYING SHE'S YOUR GRANDMOTHER. VERY ANXIOUS TO KNOW YOUR WHEREABOUTS, HE SAID.
SO IT MIGHT BE NICE IF YOU GAVE HER A CALL, HUH?

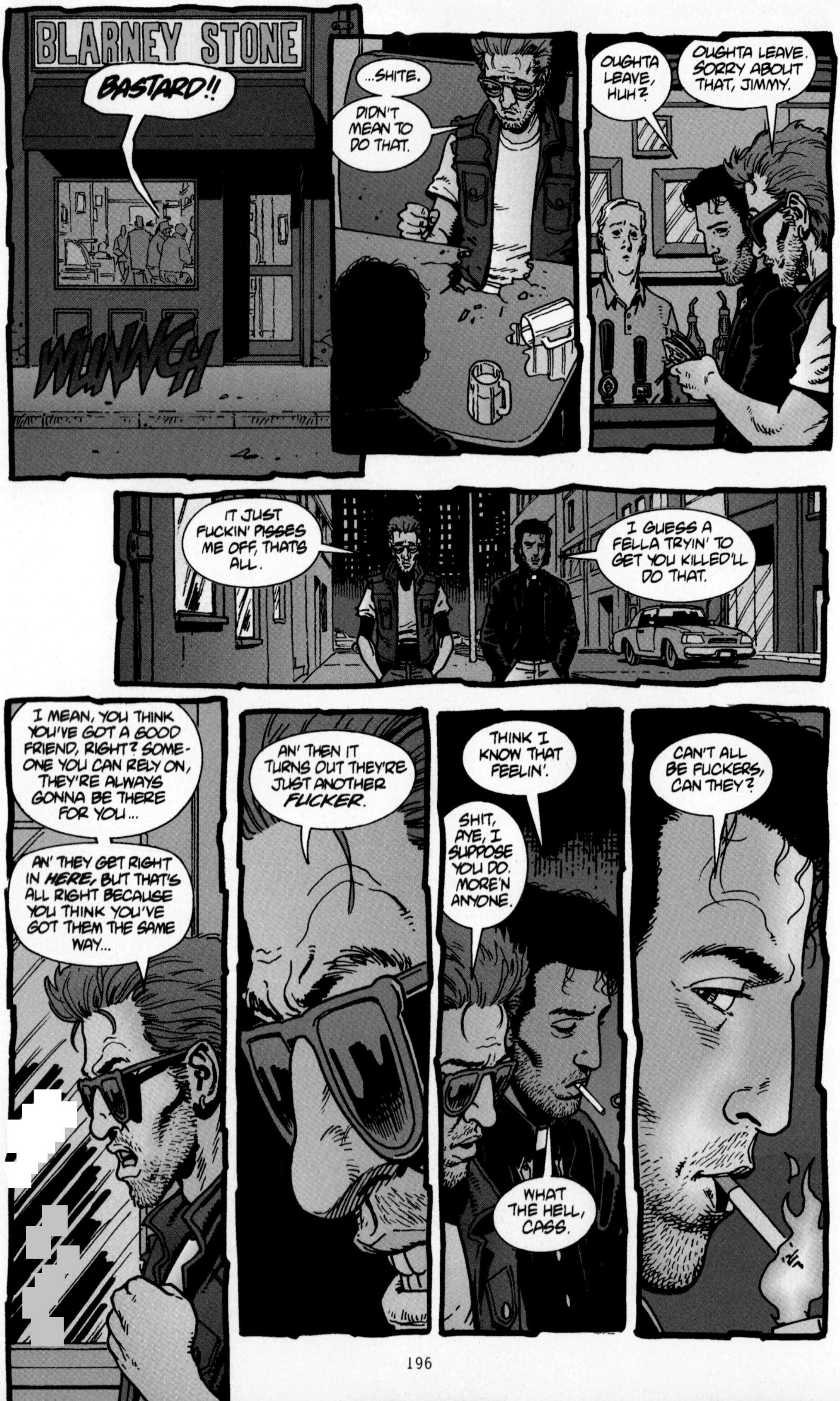
BLARNEY STONE
BASTARD!!
WUNNCH
...SHITE.
DIDN'T MEAN TO DO THAT.
OUGHTA LEAVE, HUH?
OUGHTA LEAVE. SORRY ABOUT THAT, JIMMY.
IT JUST FUCKIN' PISSES ME OFF, THAT'S ALL.
I GUESS A FELLA TRYIN' TO GET YOU KILLED'LL DO THAT.
I MEAN, YOU THINK YOU'VE GOT A GOOD FRIEND, RIGHT? SOME-ONE YOU CAN RELY ON, THEY'RE ALWAYS GONNA BE THERE FOR YOU...
AN' THEY GET RIGHT IN HERE, BUT THAT'S ALL RIGHT BECAUSE YOU THINK YOU'VE GOT THEM THE SAME WAY...
AN' THEN IT TURNS OUT THEY'RE JUST ANOTHER FUCKER.
THINK I KNOW THAT FEELIN'.
SHIT, AYE, I SUPPOSE YOU DO. MORE'N ANYONE.
WHAT THE HELL, CASS.
CAN'T ALL BE FUCKERS, CAN THEY?

S'POSE NOT.

HOW'S TULIP DOIN'?

ONE MORE NIGHT IN THE HOSPITAL. LOST A LOT'VE BLOOD.

REAL GOOD'VE YOU TO PAY HER BILL...

NO PROBS, MATE. THAT'S THE THING THAT WINDS ME UP THE MOST, Y'KNOW? BAD ENOUGH HE NEARLY DOES FOR ME, BUT TRYIN' TO KILL THE PAIR'VE YOU WHILE HE'S AT IT...

AN' I'M THE ARSE-HOLE INTRODUCED HIM TO YOU.

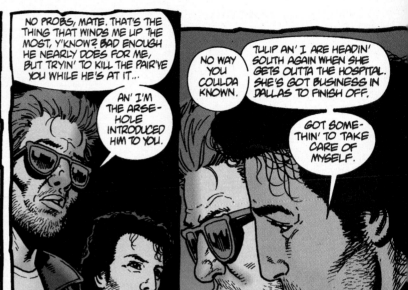

NO WAY YOU COULDA KNOWN.

TULIP AN' I ARE HEADIN' SOUTH AGAIN WHEN SHE GETS OUTTA THE HOSPITAL. SHE'S GOT BUSINESS IN DALLAS TO FINISH OFF.

GOT SOME-THIN' TO TAKE CARE OF MYSELF.

I WON'T, UH, I WON'T BE GOIN' WITH YOU, MATE. THINK I'M GONNA TAKE IT EASY FOR A WHILE.

LISTEN, HERE'S THE NUMBER I'LL BE AT IF YOU NEED TO GET IN TOUCH...

FOUR-ONE-FIVE ...SAN FRANCISCO, RIGHT?

AYE.

TAKE CARE'VE YERSELF, PREACHER MAN.

YOU TOO. YOU INSANE SON OF A BITCH.

NAH.

CAN'T ALL BE FUCKERS.

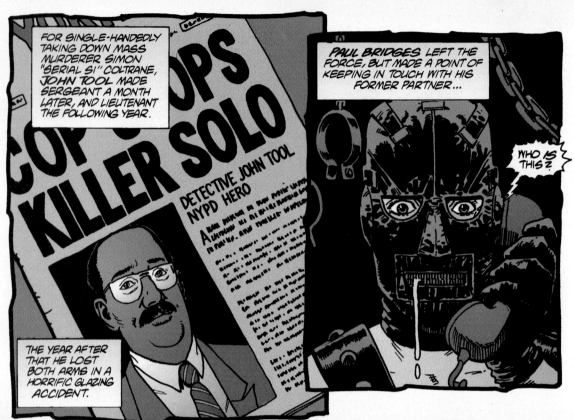

FOR SINGLE-HANDEDLY TAKING DOWN MASS MURDERER SIMON "SERIAL SI" COLTRANE, JOHN TOOL MADE SERGEANT A MONTH LATER, AND LIEUTENANT THE FOLLOWING YEAR.

THE YEAR AFTER THAT HE LOST BOTH ARMS IN A HORRIFIC GLAZING ACCIDENT.

COP STOPS KILLER SOLO

DETECTIVE JOHN TOOL NYPD HERO

PAUL BRIDGES LEFT THE FORCE, BUT MADE A POINT OF KEEPING IN TOUCH WITH HIS FORMER PARTNER...

WHO IS THIS?

CASSIDY WENT WEST, BUT NOT BEFORE STOPPING FOR A SNACK IN HIS FAVORITE BROOKLYN NEIGHBORHOOD--

WHO YOU CALLIN' GUINEA, YOU MOTHER-FUCKIN' MICK?

OF THE REVEREND JESSE CUSTER AND MS. TULIP O'HARE, THERE HAS SO FAR BEEN NO NEWS.

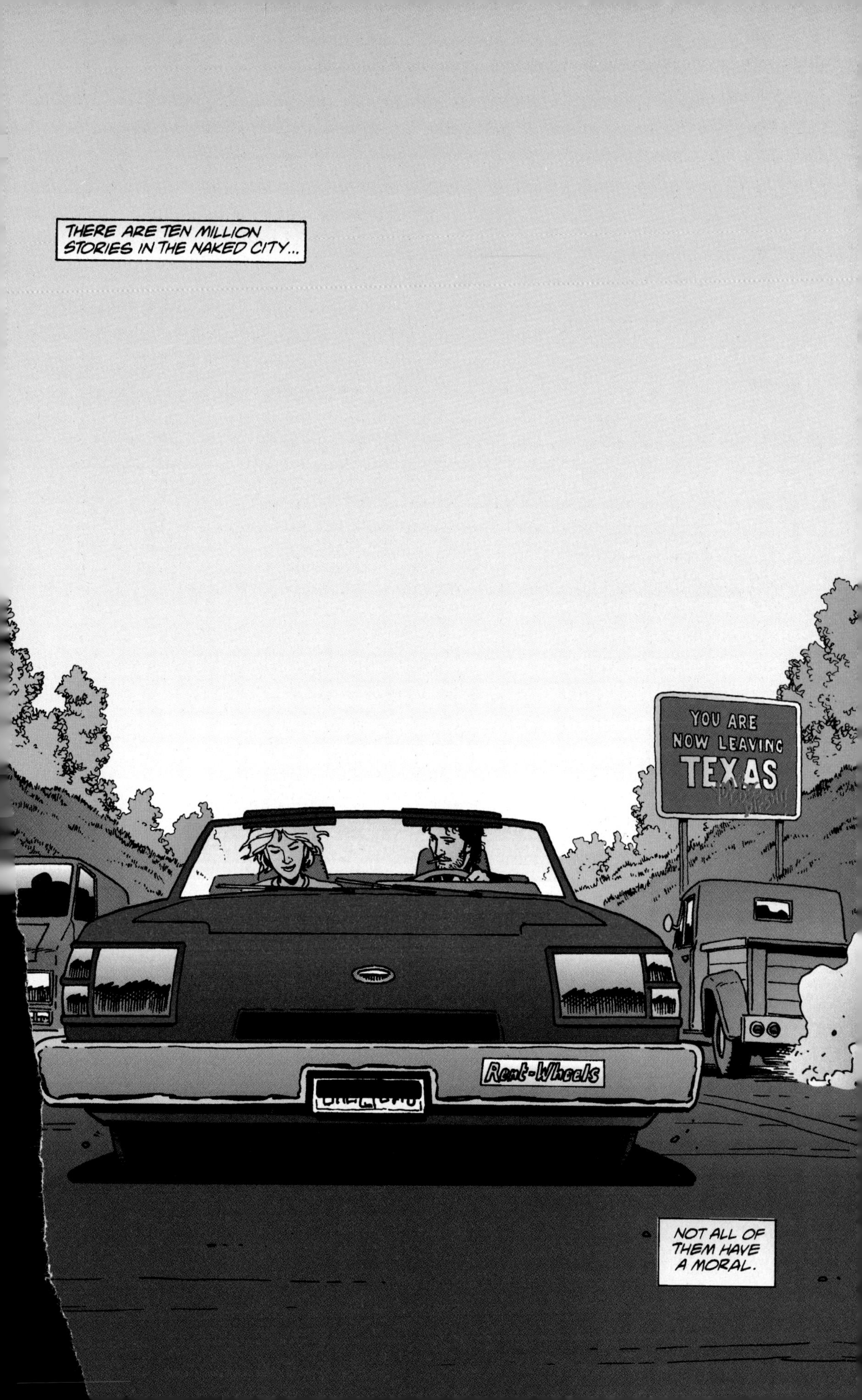
THERE ARE TEN MILLION STORIES IN THE NAKED CITY...
YOU ARE NOW LEAVING TEXAS
Rent-Wheels
NOT ALL OF THEM HAVE A MORAL.

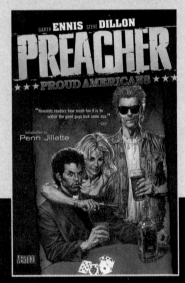 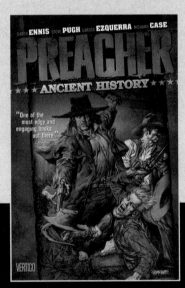